RESEARCH METHODS IN EDUCATION

RESEARCH METHODS IN EDUCATION

SECOND EDITION

LOUIS COHEN AND LAWRENCE MANION

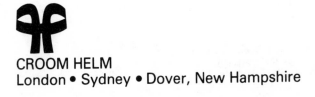

CROOM HELM
London • Sydney • Dover, New Hampshire

© 1980 Louis Cohen and Lawrence Manion
Reprinted 1981, 1982 and 1984
Second edition © 1985 Louis Cohen and Lawrence Manion

Croom Helm Ltd, Provident House, Burrell Row,
Beckenham, Kent BR3 1AT

Croom Helm Australia Pty Ltd, First Floor,
139 King Street, Sydney, NSW 2001, Australia

British Library Cataloguing in Publication Data

Cohen, Louis
    Research methods in education. — 2nd ed.
    1. Educational research
    I. Title   II. Manion, Lawrence
    370'.78   LB1028
ISBN 0-7099-3438-6

Croom Helm, 51 Washington Street, Dover, New Hampshire 03820, USA

Library of Congress Cataloging in Publication Data

Cohen, Louis, 1928-
    Research methods in education.
    Bibliography: p. 361.
    Includes index.
    1. Education — Research. 2. Education — Research —
Great Britain. I. Manion, Lawrence. II. Title.
LB1028.C572   1985   370'.7'8   85-362
ISBN 0-7099-3428-6 (pbk.)

Typeset by Leaper & Gard Limited, Bristol, England
Printed and bound in Great Britain by
Biddles Limited, Guildford and King's Lynn

CONTENTS

List of Boxes and Figures
List of Journals Abbreviated in Text
Acknowledgements
Foreword: Professor Marten Shipman

1.   Introduction: the Nature of Inquiry   1

The Search for Truth
Two Conceptions of Social Reality
Positivism
The Assumptions and Nature of Science
The Tools of Science
The Scientific Method
Criticisms of Positivism and the Scientific Method
Alternatives to Positivistic Social Science
Phenomenology, Ethnomethodology and Symbolic
    Interactionism
Criticisms of the Newer Perspectives
A Problem of Terminology: the Normative and
    Interpretive Paradigms
Methods and Methodology
Conclusion: the Role of Research in Education

2.   Historical Research   47

Introduction
Choice of Subject
Data Collection
Evaluation
Writing the Research Report
The Use of Quantitative Methods
An Example of Historical Research in Education

3.   Developmental Research   68

Introduction
The Terminology of Developmental Research
Strengths and Weaknesses of Cohort and
    Cross-sectional Studies

Strategies in Developmental Research
Examples of Developmental Research
    Example 1: A Large-scale Cohort Study
    Example 2: A Small-scale Cohort Study
    Example 3: A Cross-sectional Study
    Example 4: A Cohort/Cross-sectional Design
    Example 5: A Trend or Prediction Study

4. Surveys   94

Introduction
Some Preliminary Considerations
Survey Sampling
Sample Size: an Overview
Sampling Error
Designing the Self-completion Questionnaire
Postal Questionnaires
Processing Survey Data
Survey Research in Education: an Example

5. Case Studies   120

Introduction
The Case Study
Why Participant Observation?
Recording Observations
Educational Case Study Examples
    Cell 1: Wolcott — The Man in the Principal's Office
    Cell 2: Lambert *et al.* — The Chance of a Lifetime?
    Cell 3: King — All Things Bright and Beautiful?
    Cell 4: Adams and Biddle — Realities of Teaching
    Cell 5: Shields — A Cure of Delinquents
    Cell 6: Weinreich — Cross-ethnic Identification and
        Self-rejection in a Black Adolescent
Conclusion

6. Correlational Research   149

Introduction
Characteristics
Occasions When Appropriate
Advantages and Disadvantages
Interpreting the Correlation Coefficient
Two Examples of Correlational Research

7. Ex Post Facto Research 170

Introduction
Characteristics of *Ex Post Facto* Research
Occasions When Appropriate
Advantages and Disadvantages
Designing an *Ex Post Facto* Investigation
Procedures in *Ex Post Facto* Research
Examples of *Ex Post Facto* Research

8. Experiments, Quasi-experiments and Single-case Research 187

Introduction
Designs in Educational Experimentation
A Pre-experimental Design: the One Group
    Pretest-Post-test
A 'True' Experimental Design: the Pretest-Post-test
    Control Group Design
A Quasi-experimental Design: the Non-equivalent
    Control Group Design
The Validity of Experiments
Threats to Internal Validity
Threats of External Validity
Procedures in Conducting Experimental Research
Examples From Educational Research
    Example 1: A Pre-experimental Design
    Example 2: A Quasi-experimental Design
    Example 3: A 'True' Experimental Design
Single-case Research: ABAB Design

9. Action Research 208

Introduction
Characteristics
Occasions when Action Research as a Method is
    Appropriate
Some Issues
Procedures
Conclusion: Examples of Action Research in School
    Contexts

10. Accounts 228

Introduction

The Ethogenic Approach
Characteristics of Accounts and Episodes
Procedure in Eliciting, Analysing and Authenticating
    Accounts: an Example
Qualitative Analysis of Accounts of Social Episodes:
    Further Examples
Network Analyses of Qualitative Data
What Makes a Good Network?
Quantitative Analysis of Judgemental Ratings of Social
    Episodes
Account Gathering in Educational Research: Two
    Examples
Problems in Gathering and Analysing Accounts
Strengths of the Ethogenic Approach

11.   **Triangulation**   254

Introduction
Types of Triangulation and Their Characteristics
Occasions When Triangulation is Particularly
    Appropriate
Some Issues and Problems
Procedures
Examples of the Use of Triangular Techniques in
    Educational Research

12.   **Role-playing**   271

Introduction
Role-playing Versus Deception: the Argument
Role-playing Versus Deception: the Evidence
Role-playing in Educational Settings
The Uses of Role-playing
Strengths and Weaknesses of Role-playing and Other
    Simulation Exercises
Role-playing in an Educational Setting: an Example
Organising the Simulation Game
Evaluating Role-playing and Other Simulation
    Exercises

13.   **The Interview**   291

Introduction
Conceptions of the Interview

Some Features of the Research Interview
Some Problems Surrounding the Use of the Interview
    in Research
Procedures
The Non-directive Interview and the Focused Interview
Conclusion: Examples of the Use of Interviewing in
    Research

14.   **Personal Constructs**   315

Introduction
Characteristics of the Method
'Elicited' Versus 'Provided' Constructs
Allotting Elements To Constructs
Laddering
Grid Administration and Analysis
Procedures in Grid Administration
Procedures in Grid Analysis
Strengths of Repertory Grid Technique
Difficulties in the Use of Repertory Grid Technique
Some Examples of The Use of Repertory Grid in
    Educational Research
Recent Applications of Repertory Grid to Teaching
    and Learning
Grid Technique and Audio/Video Lesson Recording

15.   **Multidimensional Measurement**   338

Introduction
Elementary Linkage Analysis: an Example
Steps in Elementary Linkage Analysis
Cluster Analysis: an Example
Factor Analysis: an Example
Multidimensional Tables
Multidimensional Data: Some Words on Notation
Using the Chi Square Test in a Three-way
    Classification Table
Degrees of Freedom

Bibliography   361
Index   374

LIST OF BOXES AND FIGURES

Boxes

1.1	The Subjective-Objective Dimension	10
1.2	Alternative Bases for Interpreting Social Reality	11
1.3	The Functions of Science	15
1.4	The Hypothesis	20
1.5	Stages in the Development of a Science	21
1.6	Does Watching Aggression on TV Cause Kids to Become Aggressive	23
1.7	A Classroom Episode	30
1.8	An Account in Episode Analysis	30
1.9	Disrupting Social Order	35
1.10	Differing Approaches to the Study of Behaviour	41
2.1	Specific Competencies to be Developed through Instruction in the History of Education	50
2.2	Some Historical Interrelations Between Men, Movements and Institutions	50
2.3	An Example of a Historical Study in Education	53
2.4	A Brief Checklist of Some Dimensions of 'Bias'	58
2.5	Criteria for Evaluating Historical Research	61
2.6	The Purposes of Content Analysis	62
2.7	Jan Kukielka, in America, to his Wife in Poland, December 30th, 1913	63
2.8	N'ach Levels in English Literature 1550-1800 Compared with Coal Imports into London Fifty Years Later	64
2.9	Silver Street Academy	66
3.1	Types of Developmental Research	72
3.2	Advantages of Cohort over Cross-sectional Designs	73
3.3	Attrition in Sample over the 8-year Period of the Study	79
3.4	Attainment and Adjustment in Disadvantaged and Control Group Children at Ages 11+ and 15+ Years	80

3.5	In-group, Out-group Actual Friendship Choices by Age and Ethnic Group	82
3.6	In-group, Out-group Desired Friendship Choices by Age and Ethnic Origin	83
3.7	Mean Scores on Each Attitude Scale by Age and by Ethnic Group	84
3.8	Class Composition of Interviewed Sample Compared with Expected Composition of Unstratified Sample	87
3.9	Losses and Additions at Each Stage of the Study from 1 Year Through to 16 Years of Age	88
3.10	Previous and Projected Figures of Pupil Numbers in England and Wales	89
3.11	The Decline in Numbers of Pupils Aged 5 and Over in Maintained Primary and Secondary Schools, 1976 to 1986: England and Wales	91
3.12	Projected Percentage Declines in the Number of Pupils in Maintained Primary and Secondary Schools, 1976 to 1986: England and Wales	92
4.1	Stages in the Planning of a Survey	95
4.2	Distribution of Sample Means Showing the Spread of a Selection of Sample Means Around the Population Mean	102
4.3	A Flow Chart Technique for Question Planning	104
4.4	A Guide for Questionnaire Construction	106
4.5	A Flow Chart for the Planning of a Postal Survey	112
4.6	Truancy	116
4.7	Truants' Accounts of School	117
4.8	Perceived Help from Teachers	118
5.1	A Typology of Observation Studies	121
5.2	Steps in Participant Observation	126
5.3	Field Notes in Observation Studies	127
5.4	A Structured Observation Schedule for the Classroom	128
5.5	The Case Study and Problems of Selection	130
5.6	The School as a Social System	134
5.7	The Effects of Boarding on Emotional and Sexual Life	136
5.8	Lesson Profiles in Primary Classrooms	141
5.9	Lesson Profiles in Secondary Classrooms	143

5.10 Case Study Extract on Chris, a Severely Disturbed
     Adolescent   144
5.11 Changes Between John's Past and Current
     Identifications with West Indian and English People   145
5.12 Possible Advantages of Case Study   146

6.1 Common Measures of Relationship   150
6.2 Correlation Scatter Diagrams   154
6.3 Visualisation of Correlation of 0.65 Between
    Reading Grade and Arithmetic Grade   163
6.4 The Correlations Between a Preference for Violent
    Television and Peer-rated Aggression for 211 Boys
    over a 10-year Lag   168

7.1 Factors Associated with Failure at University   172
7.2 Some Procedures for Introducing Measures of
    Control into *Ex Post Facto* Reseach Designs   182
7.3 Relationship Between Mean A-Level Attainment
    and Number of Timetable Hours' Instruction in
    Twelve Subject Matter Areas   184

8.1 The Effects of Randomisation   191
8.2 The ABAB Design   205
8.3 An ABAB Design in an Educational Setting   206

9.1 Humanities Curriculum Project — Aim and
    Premisses   211
9.2 Action Research in Classroom and School   214
9.3 The Ideal Teacher for an Integrated Studies Project   215
9.4 Metaphors Reflecting Teachers' Perceptions of a
    Curriculum Project   217
9.5 The Objectives of the Evaluation Unit in the
    Humanities Curriculum Project   222
9.6 Research Action Group in English   225

10.1 Accounts of a Social Episode: House Purchase   231
10.2 Account Gathering   232
10.3 Experience Sampling Method   234
10.4 'Competence' in the Comprehensive Classroom   236
10.5 Network Analysis: Pupils' Views of their Teachers   237
10.6 Students' Perceptions of Social Episodes   240

10.7	Perception of Social Episodes	244
10.8	Person Concept Coding System	245
10.9	'Ain't nobody can talk about things being about theirselves'	247
10.10	Parents and Teachers: Divergent Viewpoints on Children's Communicative Competence	248
10.11	An Ethnographic Account of a School Carnival	249
10.12	Justification of Objective Systematic Observation in Classroom Settings	250

11.1	A Teacher's Attitude to his Role	256
11.2	The Principal Types of Triangulation Used in Research	257
11.3	A Multimethod Approach to the Study of Two Top-junior Classes	261
11.4	Kinds of Information Sought and Methods for Obtaining Them	264
11.5	Extract from the Researcher's Interview with Pupils	268

12.1	Dimensions of Role-play Methods	272
12.2	Developing Empathising Skills	273
12.3	The Stanford Prison Experiment	273
12.4	Obedience to Authority: an Explanation	276
12.5	Milgram's Experiment: an Alternative Explanation	277
12.6	A Flow Chart for Using Role-play	282
12.7	Critical Factors in a Role-play: Smoking and Young People	284

13.1	Summary of Relative Merits of Interviewing Versus Questionnaire	292
13.2	The Selection of Response Mode	307
13.3	Reasons for Subject Choice	313
13.4	Sample Questions Used in an Ethnographic Study in an Australian State High School	313

14.1	Eliciting Constructs and Constructing a Repertory Grid	317
14.2	Allotting Elements to Constructs: Three Methods	320
14.3	Laddering	322
14.4	Hierarchical Linkage Analysis Applied to Grid Data	331

14.5   Mrs C's Model of the Manner in which Children Learn   334

15.1   Rank Ordering of Ten Children on Seven Constructs   340
15.2   Intercorrelations Between Seven Personal Constructs   341
15.3   The Structuring of Relationships Among the Seven Personal Constructs   342
15.4   Central Profiles at 12-cluster Levels   344
15.5   The Deputy Head Role Definition Instrument   348
15.6   Deputy Head Role Definition Instrument Loadings on Ten Promax Factors   349
15.7   Matrix of Correlations Among Ten First Order Factors   350
15.8   Item Loadings on Second Order Factors   351
15.9   Sex, Voting Preference and Social Class: a Three-way Classification Table   353
15.10   Sex, Voting Preference and Social Class: a Three-way Notational Classification   354
15.11   Expected Frequencies in Sex, Voting Preference and Social Class   356
15.12   Expected Frequencies Assuming that Sex is Independent of Social Class and Voting Preference   359
15.13   Sex and Voting Preference: a Two-way Classification Table   359

Figures

14.1   Elements   324
14.2   Difference Score for Constructs   325
14.3   Grid Matrix   325

LIST OF JOURNALS ABBREVIATED IN TEXT

American Educational Research Journal
American Journal of Psychology
American Journal of Sociology
American Psychologist
Behaviour Research and Therapy
British Educational Research Journal
British Journal of Educational Psychology
British Journal of Medical Psychology
British Journal of Psychiatry
British Journal of Psychology
British Journal of Social and Clinical Psychology
Cambridge Journal of Education
Durham Research Review
Education
Education and Psychological Measurement
Educational Research
Educational Studies
Human Development
International Journal of Criminology and Penology
Journal of Child Psychology and Psychiatry
Journal of Educational Psychology
Journal of Educational Sociology
Journal of Experimental Education
Journal of Experimental Social Psychology
Journal of Personality and Social Psychology
Journal for the Theory of Social Behaviour
Perceptual and Motor Skills
Psychological Bulletin
Research in Education
Sagset Journal
Sociological Review
Sociology
Trends in Education

AUTHORS' NOTE TO THE SECOND EDITION

We are aware that even in the short time since *Research Methods in Education* was first published there have been developments in methodology and major researches that have been published that ought to be brought to the attention of the wide range of interests for which this introductory text has been designed.

Consequently, the second edition now includes an expansion and major rewrite of Chapter 1 *The Nature of Enquiry*; several updatings and changes in Chapter 2 *Historical Research* and Chapter 3 *Developmental Research*; the addition to Chapter 8, *Experiments and Quasi-Experiments* of a new section to do with single-case research designs; the expansion of Chapter 10, *Accounts*, to include a description and examples of network analysis; the addition to Chapter 14, *Personal Constructs*, of the application of grid techniques to audio/video lesson recording, and a rewrite of a major section of the final chapter, *Multidimensional Measurement*, to illustrate a recently-reported method of analysis of multidimensional data. In addition, in every chapter we have taken the opportunity to update examples by the inclusion of materials from British research reported since 1980.

Louis Cohen
Lawrence Manion

ACKNOWLEDGEMENTS

We should like to record our sincere thanks to colleagues at Loughborough University of Technology for their comments on initial drafts of several chapters and for their suggestions on a variety of materials for inclusion in the text. We are particularly grateful to Derek Blease, Keith Hodgkinson, Mike Holliday, Jim Hough, Morry van Ments, John Mundy, Alan Radley, Cyril Simmons, Don Smedley and Zena Stansbie. We should also like to thank Holt, Rinehart and Winston for permission to draw on Chapter One of *Perspectives on Classrooms and Schools* by the present authors.

Our special thanks go to Dora Durbidge for the indefatigable way in which she located sources of crucial information that otherwise would have escaped our notice.

Any omissions or mistakes we readily attribute to each other.

Our thanks are due to the following publishers and authors for permission to include materials in the text:

Wadsworth Publishing Co. Inc., Belmont, Calif. Notes in **Box 5.3** p. 127 from Lofland, J., *Analysing Social Settings* (1971)

American Psychological Association, Washington D.C. **Box 6.4** p. 168 from Eron, L.D. *et al.*, *American Psychologist* (April 1972) 253-63

Box 10.7 p. 244 from Forgas, J.P., *Journ. Pers. and Soc. Psychol.*, 34, 2 (1976) 199-209

Box 10.8 p. 245 from Peevers, B.H. and Secord, P.F., *Journ. Pers. and Soc. Psychol.*, 27, 1 (1973) 120-8

Open Books, London **Box 15.4** p. 344 from Bennett, N., *Teaching Styles and Pupil Progress* (1975)

Box 5.4 pp. 128 and 129 from Rutter M. *et al.*, *Fifteen Thousand Hours* (1979)

Box 2.1 p. 50 from Good, C.V., *Essentials of Educational Research* (1963)

Academic Press, New York, N.Y. **Box 10.7** p. 244 from Forgas, J.P., *Journ. Exp. Social Psychol.*, 14, (1978) 434-48

Associated Book Publishers Ltd., London **Box 14.3** p. 322 from Fransella, F., *Need to Change?* (1975)

Box 12.4 p. 276 from Brown, R. and Herrnstein, R.J., *Psychology* (1975)

Addison-Wesley Publishing Co., Reading, Mass. **Box 2.6** p. 62 from Holsti, O.R. in *The Handbook of Social Psychology, Vol. 2 Research Methods* (1968) 604

Routledge and Kegan Paul Ltd., London Words, pp. 79-85 and **Box 3.8** p. 87 from J. and E. Newson, in M.D. Shipman, *The Organisation and Impact of Social Research* (1976)

Dr. R. W. Shields, **Box 5.11** p. 145

Harcourt Brace Jovanovich, Inc., New York, N.Y. **Box 6.2** p. 154 and **Box 13.1** p. 292 from Tuckman, B.W., *Conducting Educational Research* (1969)

C.B.S. International Publishing, New York, N.Y.

Box 5.8 p. 114 and **Box 5.9** p. 143 from Adams, R.S. and Biddle, B.J., *Realities of Teaching* (1970)

Box 4.4 p. 106 from Selltiz, C. *et al., Research Methods in Social Relations* (1976)

Pergamon Press Ltd., Oxford **Box 14.4** p. 331 from Ravenette, A.T., *Journ. Child Psychol. and Psychiat.,* 16 (1975) 79-83

Weidenfeld Publishers Ltd., London **Box 5.6** p. 134, **Box 5.7** p. 136 and part of questionnaire pp. 134-5 from Lambert, R. *et al., The Chance of Lifetime?* (1975) and Lambert, R. *et al., A Manual to the Sociology of the School* (1970)

Harper and Row Publishers, London **Box 15.1** p. 340, **Box 15.2** p. 341, **Box 15.3** p. 342

National Foundation For Educational Research, Windsor **Box 3.5** p. 82, **Box 3.6** p. 83 from Jelinek, M.M. and Brittan, E.M., *Educational Research,* 18, 1 (1975) 44-53, and *Educational Research,* 19, 2 (1977) 129-41

Box 10.12 p. 250 from McAleese, R. and Hamilton, D., *Understanding Classroom Life* (1978)

Methuen & Co., London Words from Shipman, M.D., *Inside a Curriculum Project* (1974)

Scottish Academic Press Ltd., Edinburgh **Box 15.5** p. 348, **Box 15.6** p. 349, **Box 15.7** p. 350, **Box 15.8** p. 351 from Coulson, A.A., *British Journ. Educat. Psychol.*, 46 (1976) 244-52

Manchester University Press, Manchester **Box 7.3** p. 184 from Christie, T. and Oliver, R.A.C., *Research in Education*, 2 (1969) 13-31

The Open University, Milton Keynes Words from Pilliner, A., *Experiment in Educational Research*, E 341, Block 5 (1973)

Academic Press Inc. London **Box 14.2** p. 320 from Bannister, D. and Mair, J.M.M., *The Evaluation of Personal Constructs (1968)*

Hodder and Stoughton Educational, Sevenoaks **Box 9.1** p. 211, **Box 9.5** p. 222 from Butcher, H.J. and Pont, H.B., *Educational Research in Britain 3* (1973)

Her Majesty's Stationery Office, London **Box 3.10** p. 89 from *Annexe I: D.E.S. A Study of School Buildings* (1977)

Countryside Commission, Cheltenham **Box 4.1** p. 95 from Davidson, J., *Outdoor Recreation Surveys: The Design and Use of Questionnaires for Site Surveys* (1970)

Heinemann Educational Books Ltd. London p. 108-11 and **Box 4.5** p. 112 from Hoinville, G. and Jowell, R., *Survey Research Practice* (1978)

.

FOREWORD

There are three common types of books on research methods. The first leads the reader through the stages of research as if there was a mechanical sequence that, if followed, arrives invariably at reliable and valid evidence. The second type supports one approach in opposition to others. Here the reader is made aware that there are a variety of approaches and that there is disagreement over their relative virtues. But there is still an attempt to sell one of many possible ways of collecting evidence. The third type of book introduces the reader to the variety of research methods without taking sides. In all three types of book, the intended audience is the minority who undertake research.

There are a few books of a fourth type which can introduce research methods not only to those who will become researchers, but to the majority who will use the evidence produced.

Louis Cohen and Lawrence Manion have added to the small number of books that can serve both researchers and consumers of research evidence. A wide range of methods used in education are presented and these include both traditional and more recent approaches. The book is striking for its breadth, wealth of examples and balanced content. This balance is obtained by describing the method, providing examples and commenting on strengths and weaknesses. It is written in an engagingly straightforward style. Above all, it should provide an excellent introduction to the rich variety on the research menu!

Marten Shipman
Professor of Education
University of Warwick

1 INTRODUCTION: THE NATURE OF INQUIRY*

The Search for Truth

Man has long been concerned to come to grips with his environment and to understand the nature of the phenomena it presents to his senses. The means by which he sets out to achieve these ends may be classified into three broad categories: *experience, reasoning* and *research.*[1] Far from being independent and mutually exclusive, however, these categories must be seen as complementary and overlapping, features most readily in evidence where solutions to complex modern problems are sought.

The first of these categories, *experience,* does itself subsume a number of sources of information that may be called upon in a problem-solving situation. The one most immediately at hand for all people, both children and adults, is personal experience: a person may thus draw upon his own individually accumulated body of knowledge and skills derived from encounters and acquaintance with facts and events in his environment — a child repairs a puncture in a bicycle inner tube speedily and efficiently because he has done it several times previously; and an adult anticipates the problems and difficulties of buying a house because he has gone through the procedures before. Where solutions to problems clearly lie beyond this corpus of personal knowledge, a person may make use of the wider or different experience of other, often older, people in his immediate circle — a child turns to a parent or teacher; an adult consults a friend or colleague; a local manager rings up the regional supervisor. Alternatively, where these sources fail, a person may search out sources beyond his immediate circle, ones we may designate as *authoritative.* Rooted in the past or very much part of the present, these may include recognised experts in particular fields — a Dr Spock on child-rearing, for instance; a figurehead or leader, as in a religious community; or an authority source hallowed by tradition and custom — the Bible, for example.

*Parts of this chapter are taken from *Perspectives on Classrooms and Schools* by the present authors with permission from Holt, Rinehart and Winston.

In our endeavours to come to terms with the problems of day-to-day living, we are heavily dependent upon experience and authority and their value in this context should not be under-estimated. Nor should their respective roles be overlooked in the specialist sphere of research where they provide richly fertile sources of hypotheses and questions about the world, though, of course, it must be remembered that as tools for uncovering ulti-mate truth they have decided limitations. The limitations of personal experience in the form of 'common-sense knowing', for instance, can quickly be exposed when compared with features of the scientific approach to problem-solving. Consider, for example, the striking differences in the way in which theories are used. The layman bases them on haphazard events and uses them in a loose and uncritical manner. When he is required to test them, he does so in a selective fashion, often choosing only that evidence that is consistent with his hunches and ignoring that which is counter to them. The scientist, by contrast, constructs his theories carefully and systematically. Whatever hypotheses he formulates have to be tested empirically so that his explanations have a firm basis in fact. And there is the concept of 'control' distinguishing the layman's and the scientist's attitude to experience. The layman generally makes no attempt to control any extraneous sources of influence when trying to explain an occurrence. The scientist, on the other hand, only too conscious of the multiplicity of causes for a given occurrence, resorts to definite techniques and procedures to isolate and test the effect of one or more of the alleged causes. Finally, there is the difference of attitude to the relationships among phe-nomena. The layman's concern with such relationships is loose, unsystematic and uncontrolled. The chance occurrence of two events in close proximity is sufficient for him to predicate a causal link between them. The scientist, however, displays a much more serious professional concern with relationships and only as a result of rigorous experimentation will he postulate a relationship between two phenomena.

Similar warnings have been made against the unconditional acceptance of pronouncements of authorities:

Experts are essential, particularly in a complex culture such as ours, where knowledge is expanding so rapidly that no one can be an expert at everything. And obviously certain individuals have such wide experience and deep insight that their advice can be of immense benefit. Yet, it must be remembered that no one is infallible, and even the best and most competent are not exclusive possessors of 'the truth, the whole truth, and nothing but the truth'. It would be highly desirable that an 'authority' be still living; as new evidence accumulates, authorities have been known to change their mind. Thorndike reversed himself concerning the negative components of the law of effect, and Spock has changed his views concerning permissive upbringing. Ancient authorities, confronted with today's greater enlightenment, would very probably want to change their position. In fact, in many instances, their views are of greater *historical* than *substantive* interest.[1]

The second category by means of which man attempts to comprehend the world around him, namely, *reasoning*, consists of three types: deductive reasoning, inductive reasoning, and the combined inductive-deductive approach. Deductive reasoning is based on the syllogism which was Aristotle's great contribution to formal logic. In its simplest form the syllogism consists of a major premiss based on an *a priori* or self-evident proposition, a minor premiss providing a particular instance, and a conclusion. Thus:

All planets orbit the sun;
The earth is a planet;
Therefore the earth orbits the sun.

The assumption underlying the syllogism is that through a sequence of formal steps of logic, from the general to the particular, a valid conclusion can be deduced from a valid premiss. Its chief limitation is that it can handle only certain kinds of statement. The syllogism formed the basis of systematic reasoning from the time of its inception until the Renaissance. Thereafter its effectiveness was diminished because it was no longer related to observation and experience and became merely a mental exercise. One of the consequences of this was that empirical evidence as the basis of proof was superseded by authority and the more authorities one could quote, the stronger one's position. Naturally, with such abuse of its principal tool, science became sterile.

The history of reasoning was to undergo a dramatic change in the 1600s when Francis Bacon began to lay increasing stress on the observational basis of science. Being critical of the model of deductive reasoning on the grounds that its major premisses were often preconceived notions which inevitably bias the conclusions, he proposed in its place the method of inductive reasoning by means of which the study of a number of individual cases would lead to an hypothesis and eventually to a generalisation. Mouly[1] explains it like this: 'His basic premiss was that if one collected enough data without any preconceived notion about their significance and orientation — thus maintaining complete objectivity — inherent relationships pertaining to the general case would emerge to be seen by the alert observer.' Bacon's major contribution to science was thus that he was able to rescue it from the death-grip of the deductive method whose abuse had brought scientific progress to a standstill. He thus directed the attention of scientists to nature for solutions to man's problems, demanding empirical evidence for verification. Logic and authority in themselves were no longer regarded as conclusive means of proof and instead became sources of hypotheses about the world and its phenomena.

Bacon's inductive method was eventually followed by the inductive-deductive approach which combines Aristotelian deduction with Baconian induction. In Mouly's words, this consisted of:

a back-and-forth movement in which the investigator first operates inductively from observations to hypotheses, and then deductively from these hypotheses to their implications, in order to check their validity from the standpoint of compatibility with accepted knowledge. After revision, where necessary, these hypotheses are submitted to further test through the collection of data specifically designed to test their validity at the empirical level. This dual approach is the essence of the modern scientific method and marks the last stage of man's progress toward empirical science, a path that took him through folklore and mysticism, dogma and tradition, casual observation, and finally to systematic observation.

Although both deduction and induction have their weaknesses, their contributions to the development of science are enormous and fall into three categories: (1) the suggestion of hypotheses; (2) the logical development of these hypotheses; and (3) the clarification and interpretation of scientific findings and their synthesis into a conceptual framework.

The third means by which man sets out to discover truth is

research. This has been defined by Kerlinger[2] as the systematic, controlled, empirical and critical investigation of hypothetical propositions about the presumed relations among natural phenomena. Research has three characteristics in particular which distinguish it from the first means of problem-solving identified earlier, namely, experience. First, whereas experience deals with events occurring in a haphazard manner, research is systematic and controlled, basing its operations on the inductive-deductive model outlined above. Second, research is empirical. The scientist turns to experience for validation. As Kerlinger puts it, 'subjective belief ... must be checked against objective reality. The scientist must always subject his notions to the court of empirical inquiry and test.' And third, research is self-correcting. Not only does the scientific method have built-in mechanisms to protect the scientist from error as far as is humanly possible, his procedures and results are open to public scrutiny by fellow professionals. As Mouly says, 'This self-corrective function is the most important single aspect of science, guaranteeing that incorrect results will in time be found to be incorrect and duly revised or discarded.' Research is a combination of both experience and reasoning and must be regarded as the most successful approach to the discovery of truth, particularly as far as the natural sciences are concerned.

A characteristic of education in the western world has been its fitful and uneven progress. This has been attributed in the main to too great a dependence on the first of the categories identified above, namely experience, as a means of advancement and a corresponding reluctance to apply the principles of research, our third category, to educational issues. Borg[3] has succinctly highlighted the difficulty:

> Perhaps a major reason for the slow and unsure progress in education has been the inefficient and unscientific methods used by educators in acquiring knowledge and solving their problems. An uncritical acceptance of authority opinion that is not supported by objective evidence and an overdependence upon personal experience have been characteristic of the educator's problem-solving techniques.

This rather gloomy but none the less accurate assessment of the position as it obtained generally for many years and which still characterises some areas of education has now, fortunately, to be tempered by the knowledge that in the past few years modest advances have been made as a result of the application of the methods of social science to the study of education and its problems. Interestingly, this development has itself resulted in controversy and debate for, in adopting a social scientific orientation, educational research has at the same time absorbed two competing views of the social sciences — the established, traditional view and a more recently emerging radical view. The former holds that the social sciences are essentially the same as the natural sciences and are therefore concerned with discovering natural and universal laws regulating and determining individual and social behaviour; the latter view, however, while sharing the rigour of the natural sciences and the same concern of traditional social science to describe and explain human behaviour, emphasises how people differ from inanimate natural phenomena and, indeed, from each other. These contending views — and also their corresponding reflections in educational research — stem in the first instance from different conceptions of social reality and of individual and social behaviour. It will help our understanding of the issues to be developed subsequently if we examine these in a little more detail.

Two Conceptions of Social Reality

The two views of social science that we have just identified represent strikingly different ways of looking at social reality and are constructed on correspondingly different ways of interpreting it. We can perhaps most profitably approach these two conceptions of the social world by examining the explicit and implicit assumptions underpinning them. Our analysis is based on the work of Burrell and Morgan[4] who identified four sets of such assumptions.

First, there are assumptions of an *ontological* kind — assumptions which concern the very nature or essence of the social phenomena being investigated. Thus, the authors ask, is social reality *external* to the individual — imposing itself on his consciousness from without — or is it the product of individual consciousness? Is reality of an objective nature, or the result of individual cognition? Is it a given 'out there' in the world, or is it created by one's own mind? These questions spring directly from what is known in philosophy as the nominalist-realist debate. The former view holds that objects of thought are merely words and that there is no

can be con-
much more
ccupies the
tor of his
lled, the
e views
viron-
ween
ism
to

...tituting the meaning of a word.
...ds that objects have an inde-
...ent for it on the knower.

...dentified by Burrell and Morgan
.. These concern the very bases of
...d forms, how it can be acquired, and
...other human beings. The authors ask
... to identify and communicate the nature of
...g hard, real and capable of being transmitted in
...r whether "knowledge" is of a softer, more subjec-
...d or even transcendental kind, based on experience
...t of a unique and essentially personal nature. The epis-
...gical assumptions in these instances determine extreme
...tions on the issues of whether knowledge is something which
...an be acquired on the one hand, or is something which has to be
personally experienced on the other.'[4] How one aligns oneself in
this particular debate profoundly affects how one will go about
uncovering knowledge of social behaviour. The view that knowledge is hard, objective and tangible will demand of the researcher
an *observer* role, together with an allegiance to the methods of
natural science; to see knowledge as personal, subjective
and unique, however, imposes on the researcher an *involvement*
with his subjects and a rejection of the ways of the natural scientist.
To subscribe to the former is to be positivist; to the latter, anti-
positivist.

The third set of assumptions concern *human nature* and, in
particular, *the relationship between human beings and their environment*. Since the human being is both its subject and object of
study, the consequences for social science of assumptions of this
kind are indeed far-reaching. Two images of the human being
emerge from such assumptions — the one portrays him as responding mechanically to his environment; the other, as the initiator of
his own actions. Burrell and Morgan write lucidly on the distinction:

Thus, we can identify perspectives in social science which entail
a view of human beings responding in a mechanistic or even
deterministic fashion to the situations encountered in their
external world. This view tends to be one in which human
beings and their experiences are regarded as products of the
environment; one in which humans are conditioned by their

external circumstances. This extreme perspective
trasted with one which attributes to human beings
creative role: with a perspective where 'free will'
centre of the stage; where man is regarded as the cre
environment, the controller as opposed to the contro
master rather than the marionette. In these two extrem
of the relationship between human beings and their en
ment, we are identifying a great philosophical debate be
the advocates of *determinism* on the one hand and *volunta*
on the other. Whilst there are social theories which adhere
each of these extremes, the assumptions of many social scie
tists are pitched somewhere in the range between.

It would follow from what we have said so far that the three sets of
assumptions identified above have direct implications for the *methodological* concerns of the researcher since the contrasting
ontologies, epistemologies and models of man will in turn demand
different research methods. Investigators adopting an objectivist
(or positivist) approach to the social world and who treat it like the
world of natural phenomena as being hard, real and external to the
individual will choose from a range of traditional options — surveys, experiments, and the like. Others favouring the more subjec-
tivist (or anti-positivist) approach and who view the social world as
being of a much softer, personal and man-created kind will select
from a comparable range of recent and emerging techniques —
accounts, participant observation and personal constructs, for
example.

Where one subscribes to the view which treats the social world
like the natural world — as if it were a hard, external and objective
reality — then scientific investigation will be directed at analysing
the relationships and regularities between selected factors in that
world. It will be predominantly *quantitative*. 'The concern,' say
Burrell and Morgan, 'is with the identification and definition of
these elements and with the discovery of ways in which these
relationships can be expressed. The methodological issues of
importance are thus the concepts themselves, their measurement
and the identification of underlying themes. This perspective
expresses itself most forcefully in a search for universal laws which
explain and govern the reality which is being observed.'[4] An
approach characterised by procedures and methods designed to

discover general laws may be referred to as *nomothetic.*

However, if one favours the alternative view of social reality which stresses the importance of the subjective experience of individuals in the creation of the social world, then the search for understanding focuses upon different issues and approaches them in different ways. The principal concern is with an understanding of the way in which the individual creates, modifies and interprets the world in which he or she finds himself or herself. The approach now takes on a *qualitative* as well as *quantitative* aspect. As Burrell and Morgan observe, 'The emphasis in extreme cases tends to be placed upon the explanation and understanding of what is unique and particular to the individual rather than of what is general and universal. This approach questions whether there exists an external reality worthy of study. In methodological terms it is an approach which emphasizes the relativistic nature of the social world ...'[4] In its emphasis on the particular and individual this approach to understanding individual behaviour may be termed *idiographic.*

In this review of Burrell and Morgan's analysis of the ontological, epistemological, human and methodological assumptions underlying two ways of conceiving social reality, we have laid the foundations for a more extended study of the two contrasting perspectives evident in the practices of researchers investigating human behaviour and, by adoption, educational problems. Box 1.1 summarises these assumptions in graphic form along a subjective/ objective dimension. It identifies the four sets of assumptions by using terms we have adopted in the text and by which they are known in the literature of social philosophy.

Each of the two perspectives on the study of human behaviour outlined above has profound implications for research in classrooms and schools. The choice of problem, the formulation of questions to be answered, the characterisation of pupils and teachers, methodological concerns, the kinds of data sought and their mode of treatment — all will be influenced or determined by the viewpoint held. Some idea of the considerable practical implications of the contrasting views can be gained by examining Box 1.2 which compares them with respect to a number of critical issues within a broadly societal and organisational framework. Implications of the two perspectives for research into classrooms and schools will unfold in the course of the text.

Because of its significance to the epistemological basis of social

Box 1.1: The Subjective–Objective Dimension

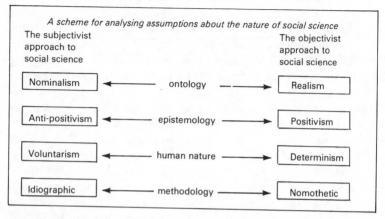

A scheme for analysing assumptions about the nature of social science

Source: Burrell and Morgan.[4]

science and its consequences for educational research, we devote much of the remainder of this chapter to the positivist and anti-positivist debate.

Positivism

Although *positivism* has been a recurrent theme in the history of western thought from the Ancient Greeks to the present day, it is historically associated with the nineteenth-century French philosopher, Auguste Comte, who was the first thinker to use the word for a philosophical position.[5] His positivism can be explained in terms of his *Law of Three Stages* according to which the human mind progresses from a theological stage through a metaphysical stage to a final positive stage.[6] At the theological stage, the most primitive, attempts are made to explain behaviour in terms of spiritual or supernatural entities. The metaphysical stage is only a modified version of the earlier stage and sets out to explain behaviour in terms of abstractions, essences or forces which Comte regarded as depersonalised beings of the earlier, theological stage. The final, positive stage dispenses with theological and metaphysical concepts and turns to observation and reason as means of understanding behaviour. More simply, explanation now proceeds by way of scientific description.

Box 1.2: Alternative Bases for Interpreting Social Reality

Dimensions of comparison:	Conceptions of social reality	
	Objectivist	*Subjectivist*
Philosophical basis	Realism: the world exists and is knowable as it really is. Organisations are real entities with a life of their own.	Idealism: the world exists but different people construe it in very different ways. Organisations are invented social reality.
The role of social science	Discovering the universal laws of society and human conduct within it.	Discovering how different people interpret the world in which they live.
Basic units of social reality	The collectivity: society or organisations.	Individuals acting singly or together.
Methods of understanding	Identifying conditions or relationships which permit the collectivity to exist. Conceiving what these conditions and relationships are.	Interpretation of the subjective meanings which individuals place upon their action. Discovering the subjective rules for such action.
Theory	A rational edifice built by scientists to explain human behaviour.	Sets of meanings which people use to make sense of their world and behaviour within it.
Research	Experimental or quasi-experimental validation of theory.	The search for meaningful relationships and the discovery of their consequences for action.
Methodology	Abstraction of reality, especially through mathematical models and quantitative analysis.	The representation of reality for purposes of comparison. Analysis of language and meaning.
Society	Ordered. Governed by a uniform set of values and made possible only by those values.	Conflicted. Governed by the values of people with access to power.
Organisations	Goal oriented. Independent of people. Instruments of order in society serving both society and the individual.	Dependent upon people and their goals. Instruments of power which some people control and can use to attain ends which seem good to them.
Organisational pathologies	Organisations get out of kilter with social values and individual needs.	Given diverse human ends, there is always conflict among people acting to pursue them.
Prescription for change	Change the structure of the organisation to meet social values and individual needs.	Find out what values are embodied in organisational action and whose they are. Change the people or change their values if you can.

Source: adapted from Barr Greenfield.[7]

Comte's position was to lead to a general doctrine of positivism which held that all genuine knowledge is based on sense experience and can only be advanced by means of observation and experiment. Following in the empiricist tradition, it limited enquiry and belief to what can be firmly established and in thus abandoning metaphysical and speculative attempts to gain knowledge by reason alone, the movement developed what has been described as a 'tough-minded orientation to facts and natural phenomena'.[5]

Since Comte, the term *positivism* has been used in such different ways by philosophers and social scientists that it is difficult to assign it a precise and consistent meaning. Moreover, the term has also been applied to the doctrine of a school of philosophy known as 'logical positivism'.[8] The central belief of the logical positivists is that the meaning of a statement is, or is given by, the method of its verification.[8] It follows from this that unverifiable statements are held to be meaningless, the utterances of traditional metaphysics and theology being included in this class.

However the term *positivism* is used by philosphers and social scientists, a residual meaning is always present and this derives from an acceptance of natural science as the paradigm of human knowledge.[9] This includes the following connected suppositions which have been identified by Giddens:[10] (1) that the *methodological* procedures of natural science may be directly applied to the social sciences. Positivism here implies a particular stance concerning the social scientist as an *observer* of social reality; and (2) that the end-product of investigations by the social scientist can be formulated in terms parallel to those of natural science. This means that his analysis must be expressed in 'laws' or 'law-like' generalisations of the same kind that have been established in relation to natural phenomena. Positivism here involves a definite view of the social scientist as *analyst* or *interpreter* of his subject matter.[10]

Positivism may be characterised by its claim that science provides man with the clearest possible ideal of knowledge. As one writer has said, 'Positivism gets much of its strength from the contrast between the continuous and agreed progress which has been achieved in the natural sciences since the time of Galileo, and the situation of deadlock and disagreement that has at all times obtained in metaphysical philosophy. This seems to suggest that in the special sciences a fruitful method has been employed, whereas metaphysical philosophers have got lost in an intellectual impasse.'[6] Where positivism is less successful, however, is in its application to the study of human behaviour where the immense complexity of human nature and the elusive and intangible quality of social phenomena contrast strikingly with the order and regularity of the natural world. This point is nowhere more apparent than in the contexts of classroom and school where the problems of teaching, learning and human interaction present the positivistic researcher with a mammoth challenge.

We now look more closely at some of the features of this 'fruitful method'.

The Assumptions and Nature of Science

Since a number of the research methods we describe in this book draw heavily on the scientific method either implicitly or explicitly and can only be fully understood within the total framework of its principles and assumptions, we will here examine some of the characteristics of science a little more closely.

We begin with an examination of the tenets of scientific faith: the kinds of assumptions held by scientists, often implicitly, as they go about their daily work. First, there is the assumption of *determinism*. This means simply that events have causes, that events are determined by other circumstances; and science proceeds on the belief that these causal links can eventually be uncovered and understood, that the events are explicable in terms of their antecedents. Moreover, not only are events in the natural world determined by other circumstances, but there is regularity about the way they are determined: the universe does not behave capriciously. It is the ultimate aim of the scientist to formulate laws to account for the happenings in the world around him, thus giving him a firm basis for prediction and control.

The second assumption is that of *empiricism*. We have already touched upon this viewpoint, which holds that certain kinds of reliable knowledge can only originate in experience. In practice, therefore, this means scientifically that the tenability of a theory or hypothesis depends on the nature of the empirical evidence for its support. 'Empirical' here means that which is verifiable by observation; and 'evidence', data yielding proof or strong confirmation, in probability terms, of a theory or hypothesis in a research setting. The viewpoint has been summed up by Barratt[11] who writes, 'The decision for empiricism as an act of scientific faith signifies that the best way to acquire reliable knowledge is the way of evidence obtained by direct experience'.

Mouly[1] has identified five steps in the process of empirical science: (a) *experience* — the starting point of scientific endeavour at the most elementary level; (b) *classification* — the formal systemisation of otherwise incomprehensible masses of data; (c) *quantification* — a more sophisticated stage where precision of measurement allows more adequate analysis of phenomena by mathematical means; (d) *discovery of relationships* — the identification and classification of functional relationships among phenomena; and (e) *approximation to the truth* — science proceeds by gradual approximations to the truth.

The third assumption underlying the work of the scientist is the *principle of parsimony*. The basic idea is that phenomena should be explained in the most economical way possible. The first historical statement of the principle was by William of Occam when he said that explanatory principles (entities) should not be needlessly multiplied. It may, of course, be interpreted in various ways: that it is preferable to account for a phenomenon by two concepts rather than three; that a simple theory is to be preferred to a complex one; or as Lloyd Morgan did as a guide to the study of animal behaviour — 'In no case may we interpret an action as the outcome of the exercise of a higher psychical faculty, if it can be interpreted as the outcome of the exercise of one which stands lower in the psychological scale.'

The final assumption, that of *generality*, played an important part in both the deductive and inductive methods of reasoning. Indeed, historically speaking, it was the problematic relationship between the concrete particular and the abstract general that was to result in two competing theories of knowledge — the rational and the empirical. Beginning with observations of the particular, the scientist sets out to generalise his findings to the world at large. This is so because he is concerned ultimately with explanation. Of course, the concept of generality presents much less of a problem to the natural scientist working chiefly with inanimate matter than to the human scientist who, of necessity having to deal with samples of larger human populations, has to exercise great caution when generalising his findings to the particular parent populations.

Having identified the basic assumptions of science, we come now to the core question: What is science? Kerlinger[2] points out that in the scientific world itself two broad views of science may be

found: the *static* and the *dynamic.* The static view, which incidentally has particular appeal for laymen, is that science is an activity
that contributes systematised information to the world. The work
of the scientist is to uncover new facts and add them to the existing
corpus of knowledge. Science is thus seen as an accumulated body
of findings, the emphasis being chiefly on the 'present state of
knowledge and adding to it'. The dynamic view, by contrast, con-
ceives science more as an activity, as something that scientists *do.*
According to this conception it is important to have an accumulated body of knowledge of course, but what really matter most are
the discoveries that scientists make. The emphasis here, then, is
more on the heuristic nature of science.

Contrasting views exist on the *functions* of science. We give a
composite summary of these in Box 1.3. For the professional
scientist, however, science is seen as a way of comprehending the
world; as a means of explanation and understanding, of prediction
and control. For him the ultimate aim of science is *theory.*

Theory has been defined by Kerlinger as 'a set of interrelated
constructs [concepts], definitions, and propositions that presents a
systematic view of phenomena by specifying relations among
variables, with the purpose of explaining and predicting the phenomena'. In a sense, theory gathers together all the isolated bits of
empirical data into a coherent conceptual framework of wider
applicability. Mouly expresses it thus: 'If nothing else, a theory is a
convenience — a necessity, really — organising a whole slough of

Box 1.3: The Functions of Science

1.	Its problem-seeking, question-asking, hunch-encouraging, hypotheses-producing function.
2.	Its testing, checking, certifying function; its trying out and testing of hypotheses; its repetition and checking of experiments; its piling up of facts.
3.	Its organising, theorising, structuring, function; its search for larger and larger generalisations.
4.	Its history-collecting, scholarly function.
5.	Its technological side; instruments, methods, techniques.
6.	Its administrative, executive, and organisational side.
7.	Its publicising and educational functions.
8.	Its applications to human use.
9.	Its appreciation, enjoyment, celebration, and glorification.

Source: Maslow.[12]

unassorted facts, laws, concepts, constructs, principles, into a meaningful and manageable form. It constitutes an attempt to make sense out of what we know concerning a given pheno-menon.' More than this, however, theory is itself a potential source of further information and discoveries. It is in this way a source of new hypotheses and hitherto unasked questions; it identifies criti-cal areas for further investigation; it discloses gaps in our know-ledge; and enables a researcher to postulate the existence of previously unknown phenomena.

The status of theory varies quite considerably according to the discipline or area of knowledge in question. Some theories, as in the natural sciences, are characterised by a high degree of elegance and sophistication; others, like educational theory, are only at the early stages of formulation and are thus characterised by great unevenness. Mouly[1] identifies the following characteristics of a good theory which may serve as suitable criteria:

1.　A theoretical system must permit deductions that can be tested empirically; that is, it must provide the means for its conform-ation or rejection. One can test the validity of a theory only through the validity of the propositions (hypotheses) that can be derived from it. If repeated attempts to disconfirm its various hypotheses fail, then greater confidence can be placed in its validity. This can go on indefinitely, until possibly some hypothesis proves untenable. This would constitute indirect evidence of the inadequacy of the theory and could lead to its rejection (or more commonly to its replacement by a more adequate theory that can incorporate the exception).

2.　Theory must be compatible with both observation and previ-ously validated theories. It must be grounded in empirical data that have been verified and must rest on sound postulates and hypotheses. The better the theory, the more adequately it can explain the phenomena under consideration, and the more facts it can incorporate into a meaningful structure of ever-greater generalisability.

3.　Theories must be stated in simple terms; that theory is best that explains the most in the simplest way. This is the law of parsimony. A theory must explain the data more adequately and yet must not be so comprehensive as to be unwieldy. On the other hand, it must not overlook variables simply because they are difficult to explain.

Sometimes the word *model* is used instead of, or interchangeably with, *theory*. Both may be seen as explanatory devices or schemes having a broadly conceptual framework, though models are often characterised by the use of analogies to give a more graphic or visual representation of a particular phenomenon. Providing they are accurate and do not misrepresent the facts, models can be of great help in achieving clarity and focusing on key issues in the nature of phenomena.

Scientific theories must, by their very nature, be provisional. A theory can never be complete in the sense that it encompasses all that can be known or understood about a given phenomenon. As Mouly says, 'Invariably, scientific theories are replaced by more sophisticated theories embodying more of the advanced state of the question so that science widens its horizons to include more and more of the facts as they accumulate. No doubt, many of the things about which there is agreement today will be found inadequate by future standards. But we must begin where we are.' We have already implied that the quality of a theory is determined by the state of development of the particular discipline. The early stages of a science must be dominated by empirical work, that is, the accumulation and classification of data. This is why, as we shall see, much of educational research is descriptive. Only as a discipline matures can an adequate body of theory be developed. Too premature a formulation of theory before the necessary empirical spadework has been done can lead to a slowing down of progress. Mouly optimistically suggests that some day a single theoretical system, unknown to us at the present time, will be used to explain the behaviour of molecules, animals and people.

In referring to *theory* and *models*, we have begun to touch upon the *tools* used by the scientist in his work. We look now in more detail at two such tools which play a crucial role in science — the *concept* and the *hypothesis*.

The Tools of Science

Concepts express generalisations from particulars — *anger, achievement, alienation, man, velocity, intelligence, democracy.* Examining these examples more closely, we see that each is a word representing an idea: more accurately, a concept is the relationship between the word (or symbol) and an idea or conception. Whoever we are and whatever we do, we all make use of concepts. Naturally, some are shared and used by all groups of people within the same culture — *child, love, justice,* for example; others, however, have a restricted currency and are used only by certain groups, specialists, or members of professions — *idioglossia, retroactive inhibition, anticipatory socialisation.*

Concepts enable us to impose some sort of meaning on the world: through them reality is given sense, order and coherence. They are the means by which we are able to come to terms with our experience. How we perceive the world, then, is highly dependent on the repertoire of concepts we can command. The more we have, the more sense data we can pick up and the surer will be our perceptual (and cognitive) grasp of whatever is 'out there'. If our perceptions of the world are determined by the concepts available to us, it follows that people with differing sets of concepts will tend to view the 'same' objective reality differently — a doctor diagnosing an illness will draw upon a vastly different range of concepts from, say, the restricted and simplistic notions of the layman in that context; and a visitor to civilisation from a distant primitive culture would be as confused by the frenetic bustle of urban life as would the mythical Martian.

So, you may ask, where is all this leading? Simply to this: that the social scientist has likewise developed, or appropriated by giving precise meaning to, a set of concepts which enable him to shape his perceptions of the world in a particular way, to represent that slice of reality which is his special study. And collectively, these concepts form part of his wider meaning system which permits him to give accounts of that reality, accounts which are rooted and validated in the direct experience of everyday life. These points may be exemplified by the concept of *social class.* Hughes says[13] that it offers 'a rule, a grid, even though vague at times, to use in talking about certain sorts of experience that have to do with economic position, life-style, life-chances, and so on. It serves to identify aspects of experience, and by relating the concept to other concepts we are able to construct theories about experience in a particular order or sphere.'

There are two important points to stress when considering scientific concepts. The first is that they do not exist independently of man: they are indeed man-made inventions enabling him to acquire some understanding at least of the apparent chaos of nature. The second is that they are limited in number and in this way contrast with the infinite number of phenomena they are required to explain.

A second tool of great importance to the scientist is *the hypothesis*. It is from this that much research proceeds, especially where cause-and-effect or concomitant relationships are being investigated. The hypothesis has been defined by Kerlinger[2] as a conjectural statement of the relations between two or more variables. More simply, it has been termed 'an educated guess', though unlike an educated guess in that it is often the result of considerable study, reflective thinking and observation. Medawar[14] writes incomparably of the hypothesis and its function in the following way:

All advances of scientific understanding, at every level, begin with a speculative adventure, an imaginative preconception *of what might be true* — a preconception which always, and necessarily, goes a little way (sometimes a long way) beyond anything which we have logical or factual authority to believe in. It is the invention of a possible world, or of a tiny fraction of that world. The conjecture is then exposed to criticism to find out whether or not that imagined world is anything like the real one. Scientific reasoning is therefore at all levels an interaction between two episodes of thought — a dialogue between two voices, the one imaginative and the other critical; a dialogue, if you like, between the possible and the actual, between proposal and disposal, conjecture and criticism, between what might be true and what is in fact the case.

Kerlinger has identified two criteria for 'good' hypotheses.[2] The first is that hypotheses are statements about the relations between variables; and second, that hypotheses carry clear implications for testing the stated relations. To these he adds two ancillary criteria: that hypotheses disclose compatibility with current knowledge; and that they are expressed as economically as possible. Thus if we conjecture that social class background determines academic achievement, we have a relationship between one variable, social class, and another, academic achievement. And since both can be measured, the primary criteria specified by Kerlinger can be met. Neither do they violate the ancillary criteria proposed by Kerlinger (see also Box 1.4).

He further identifies four reasons for the importance of hypo-

Box 1.4: The Hypothesis

Once he has a hypothesis to work on, the scientist is in business; the hypothesis will guide him to make some observations rather than others and will suggest experiments that might not otherwise have been performed. Scientists soon pick up by experience the characteristics that make a good hypothesis; ... almost all laws and hypotheses can be read in such a way as to *prohibit* the occurrence of certain phenomena ... Clearly, a hypothesis so permissive as to accommodate *any* phenomenon tells us precisely nothing; the more phenomena it prohibits, the more informative it is.

Again, a good hypothesis must also have the character of *logical immediacy*, by which I mean that it must be rather specially an explanation of whatever it is that needs to be explained and not an explanation of a great many other phenomena besides ... The great virtue of logical immediacy in a hypothesis is that it can be tested by comparatively direct and practicable means — that is, without the foundation of a new research institute or by making a journey into outer space. A large part of the *art of the soluble* is the art of devising hypotheses that can be tested by practicable experiments.

Source: Medawar.[15]

theses as tools of research. First, they organise the efforts of the researcher. The relationship expressed in the hypothesis indicates what he should do. They enable him to understand the problem with greater clarity and provide him with a framework for collecting, analysing and interpreting his data. Second, they are, in Kerlinger's words, the working instruments of theory. They can be deduced from theory or from other hypotheses. Third, they can be tested, empirically or experimentally, thus resulting in confirmation or rejection. And there is always the possibility that a hypothesis, once confirmed and established, may become a law. And fourth, hypotheses are powerful tools for the advancement of knowledge because, as Kerlinger explains, they enable man to get outside himself.

Hypotheses and concepts play a crucial part in the scientific method and it is to this that we now turn our attention.

The Scientific Method

If the most distinctive feature of science is its *empirical* nature, the next most important characteristic is its set of procedures which show not only how findings have been arrived at, but are sufficiently clear for fellow-scientists to repeat them, i.e. to check them out with the same or other materials and thereby test the results.

As Cuff and his colleagues[16] say: 'A scientific approach necessarily involves standards and procedures for demonstrating the "empirical warrant" of its findings, showing the match or fit between its statements and what is happening or has happened in the world.' These standards and procedures we will call for convenience *the scientific method*, though this can be somewhat misleading for the following reason: the combination of the definite article, adjective and singular noun conjures up in the minds of some people a single invariant approach to problem-solving, an approach frequently involving atoms or rats, and taking place within the confines of a laboratory peopled with stereotypical scientists wearing white coats and given to eccentric bouts of behaviour. Yet there is much more to it than this. The term in fact cloaks a number of methods which vary in their degree of sophistication depending on their function and the particular stage of development a science has reached. We refer you at this point to Box 1.5 which sets out the sequence of stages through which a science normally passes in its development or, perhaps more realistically, that are constantly present in its progress and on which a scientist may draw depending on the kind of information he seeks or the kind of problem confronting him. This latter point would seem to be particularly relevant in the case of an emerging science, such as the scientific study of educational problems, where many workers in different parts of the world are engaged in studying a wide range of problems in an essentially complicated area. Of particular interest to us in our efforts to

Box 1.5: Stages in the Development of a Science

1.	Definition of the science and identification of the phenomena that are to be subsumed under it.
2.	Observational stage at which the relevant factors, variables or items are identified and labelled; and at which categories and taxonomies are developed.
3.	Correlational research in which variables and parameters are related to one another and information is systematically integrated as theories begin to develop.
4.	The systematic and controlled manipulation of variables to see if experiments will produce expected results, thus moving from correlation to causality.
5.	The firm establishment of a body of theory as the outcomes of the earlier stages are accumulated. Depending on the nature of the phenomena under scrutiny, laws may be formulated and systematised.
6.	The use of the established body of theory in the resolution of problems or as a source of further hypotheses.

elucidate the term *scientific method* are stages 2, 3 and 4. Stage 2 is a relatively uncomplicated point at which the researcher is content to observe and record facts and possibly arrive at some system of classification. Much research in the field of education, especially at classroom and school level, is conducted in this way, e.g. surveys and case studies. Stage 3 introduces a note of added sophistication as attempts are made to establish relationships between variables within a loose framework of inchoate theory. Stage 4 is the most sophisticated stage and often the one that many people equate exclusively with the scientific method. In order to arrive at causality, as distinct from mere measures of association, the researcher here designs an experimental situation in which variables are manipulated to test his chosen hypothesis. Here is how one noted researcher describes the later stages:[2]

First, there is a doubt, a barrier, an indeterminate situation crying out, so to speak, to be made determinate. The scientist experiences vague doubts, emotional disturbances, inchoate ideas. He struggles to formulate the problem, even if inadequately. He studies the literature, scans his own experience and the experience of others. Often he simply has to wait for an inventive leap of mind. Maybe it will occur; maybe not. With the problem formulated, with the basic question or questions properly asked, the rest is much easier. Then the hypothesis is constructed, after which its implications are deduced, mainly along experimental lines. In this process the original problem, and of course the original hypothesis, may be changed. It may be broadened or narrowed. It may even be abandoned. Lastly, but not finally, the relation expressed by the hypothesis is tested by observation and experimentation. On the basis of the research evidence, the hypothesis is accepted or rejected. This information is then fed back to the original problem and it is kept or altered as dictated by the evidence. Dewey finally pointed out that one phase of the process may be expanded and be of great importance, another may be skimped, and there may be fewer or more steps involved. These things are not important. What is important is the overall fundamental idea of scientific research as a controlled rational process of reflective enquiry, the interdependent nature of the parts of the process, and the paramount importance of the problem and its statement.

With stages 3 and 4 of Box 1.5 in mind, we may say that the scientific method begins consciously and deliberately by selecting from the total number of elements in a given situation. The elements the researcher fastens on to will naturally be suitable for scientific formulation; this means simply that they will possess *quantitative* aspects. His principal working tool will be the hypothesis which, as we have seen, is a statement indicating a relationship (or its absence) between two or more of the chosen elements and stated in such a way as to carry clear implications for testing. The researcher then chooses the most appropriate method and puts his hypothesis to the test. Box 1.6 exemplifies these points. It is a study concerned to answer the question: Does watching aggression on television cause children to become aggressive? The elements selected for investigation were (1) the amount of time a child spends watching violence on television; and (2) his tendency to choose aggressive solutions to his problems. The hypothesis, that there is a relationship between these two factors, was tested in a simple experimental situation using a control group and an experimental group and was found to be upheld. The example is a good illustration of the positivistic approach to the study of social phenomena.

Box 1.6: Does Watching Aggression on TV Cause Kids to Become Aggressive?

A correlation exists between the amount of time a child spends watching violence on TV and his tendency to choose aggressive solutions to his problems. Does this mean that watching aggression on TV causes kids to become aggressive? Not necessarily. It might. But it might also mean that aggressive kids simply like to watch aggression, and that these kids would be just as aggressive if they watched 'Captain Kangaroo' all day long. But then some experimenters came along and proved that watching violence increases violence. How? By randomly assigning some kids to a situation in which they watched an episode of 'The Untouchables' — a TV series in which people beat, kill, rape, bite, and slug each other for fifty minutes per episode. As a control, they randomly assigned some other kids to a situation in which they watched an athletic event for some length of time. The crucial point: each kid stood an *equal chance* of being selected to watch 'The Untouchables'; therefore, any differences in character structure among the kids were neutralised across the two experimental conditions. Thus, when the investigators found that the kids who watched 'The Untouchables' showed more aggressiveness afterwards than those who watched the athletic event, it does suggest quite strongly that watching violence can lead to violence.

Source: Aronson.[17]

Criticisms of Positivism and the Scientific Method

We have spoken at some length about positivism, the nature of science and the scientific method, yet in spite of the scientific enterprise's proven success — especially in the field of natural science — its ontological and epistemological bases have been the focus of sustained and sometimes vehement criticism from some quarters. Beginning in the second half of last century, the revolt against positivism occurred on a broad front, attracting some of the best intellectuals in Europe — philosophers, scientists, social critics and creative artists; and even today opponents of positivism are made up of a similar cross-section, including some from within the ranks of social scientists themselves. Essentially, it has been a reaction against the world picture projected by science which, it is contended, denigrates life and mind. The precise target of the anti-positivists' attack has been science's mechanistic and reductionist view of nature which, by definition, excludes notions of choice, freedom, individuality, and moral responsibility. One of the earliest and most sustained attacks in the modern age came from Søren Kierkegaard, the Danish philosopher from whose work was to originate the movement that became known as Existentialism. Kierkegaard was concerned with the individual and his need to fulfil himself to the highest level of development. This realisation of a person's potential was for him the meaning of existence which he saw as 'concrete and individual, unique and irreducible, not amenable to conceputalization.'[5] Characteristic features of the age in which we live — democracy's trust in the crowd mentality, the ascendancy of reason, scientific and technological progress — all militate against the achievement of this end and contribute to the dehumanisation of the individual. In his desire to free people from their illusions, the illusion Kierkegaard was most concerned about was that of *objectivity*. By this he meant the imposition of rules of behaviour and thought, and the making of a person into an observer set on discovering general laws governing human behaviour. The capacity for *subjectivity*, he argued, should be regained. This he regarded as the ability to consider one's own relationship to whatever constitutes the focus of enquiry. The contrast he made between *objectivity* and *subjectivity* is brought out in the following passage:[18]

When the question of truth is raised in an objective manner, reflection is directed objectively to the truth as an object to which the knower is related. Reflection is not focused on the relationship, however, but upon the question of whether it is the truth to which the knower is related. If only the object to which he is related is the truth, the subject is accounted to be in the truth. When the question of truth is raised subjectively, reflection is directed subjectively to the nature of the individual's relationship; if only the mode of this relationship is in the truth, the individual is in the truth, even if he should happen to be thus related to what is not true.

For Kierkegaard, 'subjectivity and concreteness of truth are together the light. Anyone who is committed to science, or to rule-governed morality, is benighted, and needs to be rescued from his state of darkness.'[19]

Also concerned with the dehumanising effects of the social sciences is Ions.[20] While acknowledging that they can take much credit for throwing light in dark corners, he expresses serious concern at the way in which quantification and computation, assisted by statistical theory and method, are used. On this point, he writes:

The argument begins when we quantify the process and interpret the human act. In this respect, behavioural science represents a form of collectivism which runs parallel to other developments this century. However high-minded the intention, the result is depersonalization, the effects of which can be felt at the level of the individual human being, not simply at the level of culture.

His objection is not directed at quantification *per se*, but at quantification when it becomes an end in itself — 'a branch of mathematics rather than a humane study seeking to explore and elucidate the gritty circumstances of the human condition.'

Another forceful critic of the objective consciousness has been Roszak.[21] Writing of its alienating effect in contemporary life, he says:

While the art and literature of our time tell us with ever more desperation that the disease from which our age is dying is that of alienation, the sciences, in their relentless pursuit of objectivity, raise alienation to its apotheosis as our *only* means of achieving a valid relationship to reality. Objective consciousness *is* alienated life promoted to its most honorific status as the scientific method. Under its auspices we subordinate nature to our command only by estranging ourselves from more and more of what we experience, until the reality about which objectivity tells us so much finally becomes a universe of congealed alienation.

The justification for any intellectual activity lies in the effect it has on increasing our awareness and degree of consciousness. This increase, some claim, has been retarded in our time by the excessive influence the positivist paradigm has been allowed to exert on areas of our intellectual life. Holbrook, for example, affording consciousness a central position in human existence and deeply concerned with what happens to it, has written:[22]

> (O)ur approaches today to the study of man have yielded little, and are essentially dead, because they cling to positivism — that is, to an approach which demands that nothing must be regarded as real which cannot be found by empirical science and rational methods, by 'objectivity'. Since the whole problem ... belongs to 'psychic reality', to man's 'inner world', to his moral being, and to the subjective life, there can be no debate unless we are prepared to recognize the bankruptcy of positivism, and the failure of 'objectivity' to give an adequate account of existence, and are prepared to find new modes of enquiry.

Other writers question the perspective adopted by positivist social science because it presents a misleading picture of the human being. Hampden-Turner,[23] for example, concludes that the social science view of man is biased in that it is conservative and must inevitably lead to the social scientist taking an equally conservative view of the human being and having to ignore other important qualities. This restricted image of man, he contends, comes about because the social scientist concentrates on the repetitive, predictable and invariant aspects of the person; on 'visible externalities' to the exclusion of the subjective world; and — at least as far as psychology is concerned — on the parts of the person in his endeavours to understand the whole.

Two other criticisms are commonly levelled at positivistic social science from within its own ranks. The first is that it fails to take account of man's unique ability to interpret his experiences and represent them to himself. Man can, and does, construct theories about himself and his world; moreover, he acts on these theories. In failing to recognise this, positivistic social science is said to ignore the profound differences between itself and the natural sciences. Social science, unlike natural science, 'stands in a subject–subject relation to its field of study, not a subject–object relation; it deals with a pre-interpreted world in which the meanings developed by active subjects actually enter the actual constitution or production of the world'.[24]

Second, the findings of positivistic social science are often said to be so banal and trivial that they are of little consequence to those for whom they are intended, namely, teachers, social workers, counsellors, personnel managers, and the like. The more effort, it seems, that the researcher puts into his scientific experimentation in the laboratory by restricting, simplifying and controlling variables, the more likely he is to end up with a 'pruned, synthetic version of the whole, a constructed play of puppets in a restricted environment.'[25]

These are formidable criticisms; but what alternatives are proposed by the detractors of positivistic social science?

Alternatives to Positivistic Social Science

Although the opponents of positivism within social science itself subscribe to a variety of schools of thought each with its own subtly different epistemological viewpoint, they are united by their common rejection of the belief that human behaviour is governed by general laws and characterised by underlying regularities. Moreover, they would agree that the social world can only be understood from the standpoint of the individuals who are part of the ongoing action being investigated; and that their model of man is an autonomous one, not the plastic version favoured by positivist researchers. In rejecting the viewpoint of the detached, objective observer — a mandatory feature of traditional research — anti-positivists would argue that an individual's behaviour can only be understood by the researcher sharing his frame of reference: understanding of the individual's interpretations of the world around him has to come from the inside, not the outside. Social science is thus seen as a subjective rather than an objective undertaking, as a means of dealing with the direct experience of people in specific contexts. The following extract nicely captures the spirit in which the anti-positivist social scientist would work:[7]

> (T)he purpose of social science is to understand social reality as different people see it and to demonstrate how their views shape the action which they take within that reality. Since the social sciences cannot penetrate to what lies behind social reality, they must work directly with man's definitions of reality and with the rules he devises for coping with it. While the social sciences do not reveal ultimate truth, they do help us to make sense of our world. What the social sciences offer is explanation, clarification and demystification of the social forms which man has created around himself.

The anti-positivist movement has so influenced those constituent areas of social science of most concern to us, namely, psychology, social psychology and sociology, that in each case a movement reflecting its mood has developed collaterally with mainstream trends. Whether this development is seen in competitive or complementary terms depends to some extent on one's personal viewpoint. It cannot be denied, however, that in some quarters proponents of the contrasting viewpoints have been prepared to lock horns on some of the more contentious issues.

In the case of psychology, for instance, a school of humanistic psychology has emerged alongside the co-existing behaviouristic and psychoanalytic schools. Arising as a response to the challenge to combat the growing feelings of dehumanisation which characterise much of the social and cultural milieu of the twentieth century, it sets out to study and understand the person *as a whole*.[26] The humanistic psychologist presents a model of man that is positive, active and purposive, and at the same time stresses his own involvement with the life experience itself. He does not stand apart, introspective, hypothesising. His interest is directed at the *intentional* and *creative* aspects of the human being. The perspective adopted by humanistic psychologists is naturally reflected in their methodology. They are dedicated to studying the individual in preference to the group, and consequently prefer idiographic approaches to nomothetic ones. The implications of the movement's philosophy for the education of the human being have been drawn by Carl Rogers.[27]

Comparable developments within social psychology may be perceived in the emerging 'science of persons' movement. Its proponents contend that because of man's self-awareness and powers of language, he must be seen as a system of a different order of complexity from any other existing system whether natural, like an animal, or artificial — a computer, for instance. Because of this, no other system is capable of providing a sufficiently powerful model to advance our understanding of him. It is argued, therefore, that we must use *ourselves* as a key to our understanding of others and conversely, our understanding of others as a way of finding out about ourselves. What is called for is an *anthropomorphic model of man.* Since anthropomorphism means, literally, the attribution of human form and personality, the implied criticism is that social psychology as traditionally conceived has singularly failed, so far, to model man as he really is. As one wry commentator has pleaded. 'For scientific purposes, treat people as if they were human beings.'[28]

This approach would entail working from a model of man that takes account of the following uniquely human attributes:[28]

> Man is an entity who is capable of monitoring his own performance. Further, because he is aware of this self-monitoring and has the power of speech, man is able to provide commentaries on those performances and to plan ahead of them as well. Such an entity, it is held, is much inclined to using rules, to devising plans, to developing strategies in getting things done the way he wants them doing.

Social psychology's task is to understand man in the light of this anthropomorphic model. But what specifically would this involve? Proponents of this 'science of persons' approach place great store on the systematic and painstaking analysis of *social episodes.* In Box 1.7 we give an example of such an episode taken from a classroom study. Note how the particular incident would appear on an interaction analysis coding sheet of a researcher employing a positivistic approach. Note, too, how this slice of classroom life can only be understood by knowledge of the specific organisational background in which it is embedded.

The approach to analysing social episodes which we show in Box 1.8 is known as the *ethogenic method.*[30] Unlike positivistic social psychology which ignores or presumes its subjects'

Box 1.7: A Classroom Episode

Walker and Adelman describe an incident in the following manner:

One lesson the teacher was listening to the boys read through short essays that they had written for homework on the subject of 'Prisons'. After one boy, Wilson, had finished reading out his rather obviously skimped piece of work the teacher sighed and said, rather crossly:

T: Wilson, we'll have to put you away if you don't change your ways, and do your homework. Is that all you've done?
P: Strawberries, strawberries. (Laughter)

Now at first glance this is meaningless. An observer coding with Flanders Interaction Analysis Categories (FIAC) would write down:

'7' (teacher criticises) followed by a,
'4' (teacher asks question) followed by a,
'9' (pupil irritation) and finally a,
'10' (silence or confusion) to describe the laughter

Such a string of codings, however reliable and valid, would not help anyone to *understand* why such an interruption was funny. Human curiosity makes us want to know *why* everyone laughs — and so, I would argue, the social scientist needs to know too. Walker and Adelman asked subsequently why 'strawberries' was a stimulus to laughter and were told that the teacher frequently said the pupils' work was 'like strawberries — good as far as it goes, but it doesn't last nearly long enough'. Here a casual comment made in the past has become an integral part of the shared meaning system of the class. It can only be comprehended by seeing the relationship as developing over time.

Source: adapted from Delamont.[29]

Box 1.8: An Account in Episode Analysis

Observation:
A boy is seen walking down the road and swiftly using his leg to touch another boy's leg.

Boy's account of the episode:
'He called me names so I kicked him.'
'He is not a good friend.'
'No one was watching.'

Observer elicits boy's detailed definitions of 'names', 'friend', and 'no one' to extrapolate from his account the following understanding of the rules governing the particular episode.

When peers who are not good friends call me names and no salient adults are present, I will (ought, should, am entitled to) 'get even' — physical punishment being one behaviour subsumed under that act.

Source: adapted from Levine.[31]

interpretations of situations, ethogenic social psychology concentrates upon the ways in which a person construes his social world. By probing at his accounts of his actions, it endeavours to come up with an understanding of what that person was doing in the particular episode. The example is purposely simplified and intended only to illustrate the approach rather than the substance in analysing a social episode.

The anti-positivist movement in sociology is represented by three schools of thought — phenomenology, ethnomethodology and symbolic interactionism. A common thread running through the three schools is a concern with *phenomena*, that is, the things we directly apprehend through our senses as we go about our daily lives, together with a consequent emphasis on qualitative as opposed to quantitative methodology. The differences between them and the significant role each plays in contemporary research in classrooms and schools are such as to warrant a more extended consideration of them in the section which follows.

Phenomenology, Ethnomethodology and Symbolic Interactionism

In its broadest meaning, phenomenology is a theoretical point of view that advocates the study of direct experience taken at face value; and one which sees behaviour as determined by the phenomena of experience rather than by external, objective and physically described reality.[32] Although phenomenologists differ among themselves on particular issues, there is fairly general agreement on the following points identified by Curtis[33] which can be taken as distinguishing features of their philosophical viewpoint:

1. A belief in the importance, and in a sense the primacy, of *subjective consciousness*;
2. An understanding of consciousness as active, as *meaning bestowing*; and
3. A claim that there are certain *essential structures* to consciousness of which we gain direct knowledge by a certain kind of reflection. Exactly what these structures are is a point about which phenomenologists have differed.

Various strands of development may be traced in the

phenomenological movement: we shall briefly examine two of them
— the *transcendental phenomenology* of Husserl; and *existential
phenomenology*, of which Schutz is perhaps the most characteristic
representative.

Husserl, regarded by many as the founder of phenomenology,
was concerned with investigating the source of the foundation of
science and with questioning the commonsense, 'taken-for-
granted' assumptions of everyday life.[4] To do this, he set about
opening up a new direction in the analysis of consciousness. His
catchphrase was 'back to the things!' which for him meant finding
out how things appear directly to us rather than through the media
of cultural and symbolic structures. In other words, we are asked to
look beyond the details of everyday life to the essences underlying
them. To do this, Husserl exhorts us to 'put the world in brackets'
or free ourselves from our usual ways of perceiving the world.
What is left over from this reduction is our consciousness of which
there are three elements — the 'I' who thinks, the mental acts of
this thinking subject, and the intentional objects of these mental
acts.[19] The aim, then, of this method of *epoché*, as Husserl called it,
is the dismembering of the constitution of objects in such a way as
to free us from all preconceptions about the world.[19]

Schutz was concerned with relating Husserl's ideas to the issues
of sociology and to the scientific study of social behaviour. Of central concern to him was the problem of understanding the meaning
structure of the world of everyday life. The origins of meaning he
thus sought in the 'stream of consciousness' — basically an un-
broken stream of lived experiences which have no meaning in
themselves. One can only impute meaning to them retrospectively,
by the process of turning back on oneself and looking at what has
been going on.[4] In other words, meaning can be accounted for in
this way by the concept of *reflexivity*. For Schutz, the attribution of
meaning reflexively is dependent on the person's identifying the
purpose or goal he seeks.[4]

According to Schutz, the way we understand the behaviour of
others is dependent on a process of *typification* by means of which
the observer makes use of concepts resembling 'ideal types' to
make sense of what people do. These concepts are derived from
our experience of everyday life and it is through them, claims
Schutz, that we classify and organise our everyday world.[4] As Burrell and Morgan observe, 'The typifications are learned through
our biographical situation. They are handed to us according to our

social context. Knowledge of everyday life is thus socially ordered. The notion of typification is thus ... an inherent feature of our everyday world.'4

The fund of everyday knowledge by means of which we are able to typify other people's behaviour and come to terms with social reality varies from situation to situation. We thus live in a world of *multiple realities* — 'The social actor shifts between these provinces of meaning in the course of his everyday life. As he shifts from the world of work to that of home and leisure or to the world of religious experience, different ground rules are brought into play. While it is within the normal competence of the acting individual to shift from one sphere to another, to do so calls for a "leap of consciousness" to overcome the differences between the different worlds.'4

Like phenomenology, ethnomethodology is concerned with the world of everyday life. In the words of its proponent, Harold Garfinkel, it sets out 'to treat practical activities, practical circumstances, and practical sociological reasonings as topics of empirical study, and by paying to the most commonplace activities of daily life the attention usually accorded extraordinary events, seeks to learn about them as phenomena in their own right.'34 He maintains that students of the social world must doubt the reality of that world; and that in failing to view human behaviour more sceptically, sociologists have created an ordered social reality that bears little relationship to the real thing. He thereby challenges the basic sociological concept of order.

Ethnomethodology, then, is concerned with how people make sense of their everyday world. More especially, it is directed at the mechanisms by which participants achieve and sustain interaction in a social encounter — the assumptions they make, the conventions they utilise, and the practices they adopt. Ethnomethodology thus seeks to understand social accomplishments in their own terms; it is concerned to understand them *from within.*4

In identifying the 'taken-for-granted' assumptions characterising any social situation and the ways in which the people involved make their activities rationally accountable, ethnomethodologists use notions like *indexicality* and *reflexivity*. Indexicality refers to the ways in which actions and statements are related to the social contexts producing them; and to the way their meanings are shared by the participants but not necessarily stated explicitly. Indexical expressions are thus the designations imputed to a particular social occasion by the participants in order to locate the event in the sphere of reality. Reflexivity, on the other hand, refers to the way in which all accounts of social settings — descriptions, analyses, criticisms, etc. — and the social settings occasioning them are mutually interdependent.

It is convenient to distinguish between two types of ethno-methodologists: *linguistic* and *situational.* The linguistic ethno-methodologists focus upon the use of language and the ways in which conversations in everyday life are structured. Their analyses make much use of the unstated 'taken-for-granted' meanings, the use of indexical expressions and the way in which conversations convey much more than is actually said. The situational ethno-methodologists cast their view over a wider range of social activity and seek to understand the ways in which people negotiate the social contexts in which they find themselves. They are concerned to understand how people make sense of and order their environ-ment. As part of their empirical method, ethnomethodologists may consciously and deliberately disrupt or question the ordered, 'taken-for-granted' elements in everyday situations in order to reveal the underlying processes at work. An example of such a dis-ruption of the social order from Garfinkel's own work is given in Box 1.9.

The substance of ethnomethodology thus largely comprises a set of specific techniques and approaches to be used in the study of what Garfinkel has described as the 'awesome indexicality' of everyday life. It is geared to empirical study, and the stress which its practitioners place upon the uniqueness of the situation encoun-tered projects its essentially relativist standpoint. A commitment to the development of methodology and field-work has occupied first place in the interests of its adherents, so that related issues of ontology, epistemology and the nature of man have received less attention than perhaps they deserve.

Essentially, the notion of *symbolic interactionism* derives from the work of G.H. Mead.[35] Although subsequently to be associated with such noted researchers as Blumer, Hughes, Becker and Goff-man, the term does not represent a unified perspective in that it does not embrace a common set of assumptions and concepts accepted by all who subscribe to the approach. For our purposes, however, it is possible to identify three basic postulates. These have been set out by Woods as follows:[36] (1) human beings act towards things on the basis of the *meanings* they have for them.

Box 1.9: Disrupting Social Order

In order to demonstrate that the 'seen but unnoticed' order of everyday life is an accomplishment, Garfinkel asked some of his students to experiment with disrupting its taken-for-granted routine and familiar nature. The students were asked to see themselves as 'strangers' in their own society, and thereby to suspend their taken-for-granted commonsense understandings. Here is a short extract illustrating the technique:

S. Hi, Ray. How is your girl friend feeling?
E. What do you mean, 'How is she feeling?' Do you mean physical or mental?
S. I mean how is she feeling? What's the matter with you? (He looked peeved).
E. Nothing. Just explain a little clearer what do you mean?
S. Skip it. How are your Med School applications coming?
E. What do you mean? 'How are they?'
S. You know what I mean.

Experiments of this nature, Garfinkel suggests, demonstrate that in their everyday lives members expect others to know what they are really talking about. They also show the moral nature of the familiar social world: upsetting the order, not displaying one's competence, can bring moral sanctions from other members who have been 'troubled'.

Source: Garfinkel.[34]

Man inhabits two different worlds: the 'natural' world wherein he is an organism of drives and instincts and where the external world exists independently of him, and the social world where the existence of symbols, like language, enables him to give meaning to objects. This attribution of meanings, this interpreting, is what makes him distinctively human and social. Interactionists therefore focus on the world of subjective meanings and the symbols by which they are produced and represented. This means not making any prior assumptions about what is going on in an institution, and taking seriously, indeed giving priority to, inmates' own accounts. Thus, if pupils appear preoccupied for too much of the time 'being bored', 'mucking about', 'having a laugh', etc. the interactionist is keen to explore the properties and dimensions of these processes; (2) this attribution of meaning to objects through symbols is a continuous *process*. Action is not simply a consequence of psychological attributes such as drives, attitudes, or personalities, or determined by external social facts such as social structure or roles, but results from a continuous process of meaning attribution which is always emerging in a state of flux and subject to change. The individual constructs, modifies, pieces together, weighs up the pros and cons and bargains; and (3) this process takes place in a *social* context. Each individual aligns his action to that of others. He does this by 'taking the role of the other', by making indications to his 'self' about the 'other's' likely response. He constructs how others wish or might act in certain circumstances, and how he himself might act. He might try to 'manage' the impressions others have of him, put on a 'performance', try to influence the other's 'definition of the situation'.

Instead of focusing on the individual, then, and his or her personality characteristics, or on how the social structure or social situation causes individual behaviour, symbolic interactionists direct their attention at the *nature of interaction*, the dynamic activities taking place between persons. In focusing on the interaction itself as a unit of study, the symbolic interactionist creates a more active image of the human being and rejects the image of the passive, determined organism. Individuals interact; societies are made up of interacting individuals. People are constantly undergoing change in interaction and society is changing through interaction. Interaction implies human beings acting in relation to each other, taking each other into account, acting, perceiving, interpreting, acting again. Hence, a more dynamic and active human being emerges, rather than an actor merely responding to others.

A characteristic common to the phenomenological, ethnomethodological and symbolic interactionist perspectives — and one which makes them singularly attractive to the would-be educational researcher — is the way in which they 'fit' naturally to the kind of concentrated action found in classrooms and schools, an action characterised by 'pupils and teachers ... continually adjusting, reckoning, evaluating, bargaining, acting and changing.'[36] Yet another shared characteristic is the manner in which they are able to preserve the 'integrity' of the situation where they are employed. This is to say that the influence of the researcher in structuring, analysing and interpreting the situation is present to a much less degree than would be the case with a more traditionally-oriented research approach.

Criticisms of the Newer Perspectives

Critics have wasted little time in pointing out what they regard as weaknesses in these newer qualitative perspectives. They argue that while it is undeniable that our understanding of the actions of our fellow-men necessarily requires knowledge of their intentions, this, surely, cannot be said to comprise *the* purpose of a social science. As Rex has observed:[37]

> Whilst patterns of social reactions and institutions may be the product of the actors' definitions of the situations there is also the possibility that those actors might be falsely conscious and that sociologists have an obligation to seek an objective perspective which is not necessarily that of any of the participating actors at all ... We need not be confined purely and simply to that ... social reality which is made available to us by participant actors themselves.

Giddens[24] similarly argues, 'No specific person can possess detailed knowledge of anything more than the particular sector of society in which he participates, so that there still remains the task of making into an explicit and comprehensive body of knowledge that which is only known in a partial way by lay actors themselves.'

While these more recent perspectives have presented a model of man that is more in keeping with common experience, their methodologies are by no means above reproof. Some argue that advocates of an anti-positivist stance have gone too far in abandoning scientific procedures of verification and in giving up hope of discovering useful generalisations about behaviour.[38] Are there not dangers, it is suggested, in rejecting the approach of physics in favour of methods more akin to literature, biography and journalism? Some specific criticisms of the methodologies used are well directed:[38]

> ... If the carefully controlled interviews used in social surveys are inaccurate, how about the uncontrolled interviews favoured by the (newer perspectives)? If sophisticated ethological studies of behaviour are not good enough, are participant observation studies any better?

> ... And what of the insistence of interpretive methodologies on the use of verbal accounts to get at the meaning of events, rules and intentions? Are there not dangers? Subjective reports are sometimes incomplete and they are sometimes misleading?

Bernstein's criticism[39] is directed at the overriding concern of phenomenologists and ethnomethodologists with the *meanings of situations* and the ways in which these meanings are 'negotiated' by the actors involved. What is overlooked about such negotiated meanings, observes Bernstein, is that they 'presuppose a structure *of* meanings (and their history) wider than the area of negotiation. Situated activities presuppose a situation; they presuppose relationships between situations; they presuppose sets of situations.'

Bernstein's point is that the very process whereby one interprets and defines a situation is itself a product of the circumstances in which one is placed. One important factor in such circumstances that must be considered is the *power* of others to impose *their* definitions of situations upon participants. Doctors' consulting rooms and headmasters' studies are locations in which inequalities in power are regularly imposed upon 'unequal' participants. The ability of certain individuals, groups, classes, and authorities to persuade others to accept their definitions of situations demonstrates that while — as ethnomethodologists insist — social structure is a consequence of the ways in which we perceive social relations, it is clearly more than this. Conceiving of social structure as *external* to ourselves helps us take its self-evident effects upon our daily lives into our understanding of the social behaviour going on about us.

The task of social science, it is held, is to develop sets of concepts such as *norms, expectations, positions* and *roles* in order to formulate a 'generalising science of behaviour'. Only in this way is it possible to 'move from the interpretation of one specific action or event ... to a theoretical explanation of behaviour.'[40]

A Problem of Terminology: the Normative and Interpretive Paradigms

We are drawing to the close of this chapter and so far have introduced and used a variety of terms to describe the numerous branches and schools of thought embraced by the positivist and anti-positivist viewpoints. As a matter of convenience and as an aid to communication, we introduce at this point two generic terms conventionally used to describe these two perspectives and the categories subsumed under each, particularly as they refer to social psychology and sociology. The terms in question are *normative* and *interpretive.* The normative paradigm (or model) contains two major orienting ideas:[41] first, that human behaviour is essentially *rule-governed*; and second, that it should be investigated by the *methods of natural science*. The interpretive paradigm, in contrast to its normative counterpart, is characterised by a *concern for the individual*. Whereas normative studies are positivist, all theories constructed within the context of the interpretive paradigm tend to be anti-positivist.* As we have seen, the central endeavour in the context of the interpretive paradigm is to understand the subjective world of human experience. To retain the integrity of the phenomena being investigated, efforts are made to get inside the person and to understand from within. The imposition of external form and structure is resisted, since this reflects the viewpoint of the observer as opposed to that of the actor directly involved.

Two further differences between the two paradigms may be identified at this stage: the first concerns the concepts of *behaviour* and *action*; the second, the different conceptions of *theory*. A key concept within the normative paradigm, *behaviour* refers to responses either to external environmental stimuli (another person, or the demands of society, for instance) or to internal stimuli (hunger, or the need to achieve, for example). In either case, the cause of the behaviour lies in the past. Interpretive approaches, on the other hand, focus on *action*. This may be thought of as behaviour-with-meaning; it is intentional behaviour and as such, future oriented. Actions are only meaningful to us in so far as we are able to ascertain the intentions of the actor, to share his experience. A great deal of our everyday interactions with one another relies on such shared experiences. A child, for example, raises his arm and keeps it above his head. Should he do this at home while watching television, his parents are likely to find his bodily movements curious ('What's the matter with him?' i.e. what immediate, past event caused him to behave like that?). In the setting of the classroom, however, the action is perfectly understandable to all ('What does Billy want now?' i.e. what does he intend? or, alternatively, Billy is letting me know that he is ready to answer my question when I ask him, i.e. future-oriented intentional behaviour).

---

*It may seem paradoxical to some readers that, although we have just described interpretive theories as anti-positivist, they are nevertheless conventionally regarded as 'scientific' (and hence part of 'social science') in that they are concerned ultimately with describing and explaining human behaviour by means of methods that are in their own way every bit as rigorous as the ones used in positivist research (see, for example, Accounts of Episodes in Chapter 10).

As regards *theory*, the normative researcher tries to devise general theories of human behaviour and to validate them through the use of increasingly complex research methodologies which, some believe, push him further and further from the experience and understanding of the everyday world and into a world of abstraction. For him, the basic reality is the collectivity; it is external to the actor and manifest in society, its institutions and its organisations. The role of theory is to say how reality hangs together in these forms or how it might be changed so as to be more effective. The researcher's ultimate aim is to establish a comprehensive 'rational edifice', a universal theory, to account for human and social behaviour.

But what of the interpretive researcher? He begins with *the individual* and sets out to understand *his* interpretations of the world around him. Theory is emergent and must arise from particular situations; it should be 'grounded' on data generated by the research act.[42] Theory should not precede research but follow it. The investigator works directly with experience and understanding to build his theory on them. The data thus yielded will be glossed with the meanings and purposes of those people who are their source. Further, the theory so generated must make sense *to those to whom it applies*. The aim of scientific investigation for the interpretive researcher is to understand how this glossing of reality goes on at one time and in one place and compare it with what goes on in different times and places. Thus theory becomes sets of meanings which yield insight and understanding of people's behaviour. These theories are likely to be as diverse as the sets of human meanings and understandings which they are to explain. From an interpretive perspective the hope of a universal theory which characterises the normative outlook gives way to multifaceted images of human behaviour as varied as the situations and contexts supporting them.

We illustrate the distinction between interpretive and normative approaches with reference to two studies of classrooms. During months of observation in schools and in the course of detailed interviews with teachers, Hargreaves and his co-workers[43] gathered information about 'what was going on' and 'what teachers actually meant' in their interactions with pupils. In actually getting at the realities of the situation, they provide an insightful account of routine deviance in classroom settings — one, incidentally, that will be immediately recognised by experienced teachers. Essentially, these researchers were concerned to understand teachers' actions towards their pupils. Their approach was *interpretive*.

Using videotape equipment, Adams and Biddle[44] recorded teachers' interactions with pupils. Aspects of teacher behaviour were then identified by the researchers who used a coding system to quantify and classify such things as 'teacher talk', 'pupil talk' and 'teacher movement about the room'. The purpose of this study was to obtain accurate objective 'facts' about classroom inter-action. The approach was *normative*.

The application of interpretive perspectives to more substantive educational matters characterises the work of Young and his associates.[45] They see the primary purpose of a 'new sociology of education' as being to question much that is taken for granted in the day-to-day life of schools. Why, for example, are certain subjects included in the curriculum and not others? And who says what constitutes a subject? Who defines what its knowledge base should consist of? In pointing to such issues, Young 'raises questions about relations between the power structure and curricula; the access to knowledge and the opportunities to legitimate is as "superior" as the relation between knowledge and its function in different kinds of society.' The application of Young's critical perspectives can be illustrated in two recent studies. In the teaching of English, the Rosens[46] have challenged the common emphasis on the study of great literature, arguing that the hidden purpose of this approach is to impose an alien middle-class culture upon working-class pupils, in effect denying them their sense of identity.

Box 1.10: Differing Approaches to the Study of Behaviour

Normative	Interpretive
Society and the social system	The individual
Impersonal, anonymous forces regulating behaviour	Human actions continuously recreating social life
'Objectivity'	'Subjectivity'
Generalising from the specific	Interpreting the specific
Explaining behaviour	Understanding actions
Assuming the taken-for-granted	Investigating the taken-for-granted
Macro-concepts: society, institutions, norms, positions, roles, expectations	Micro-concepts: individual perspective, personal constructs, negotiated meanings, definitions of situations
Structuralists	Phenomenologists, ethnomethodologists, symbolic interactionists

A study by Sharp and Green[47] shows how subtle influences of social control intrude upon the child-centred teaching in three infant classrooms to produce similar effects to those readily observable in more formal teacher-centred classes. Studies such as these challenge the assumptions underlying much that takes place in educational practice and they bring new insights into the complexity of the teaching–learning process.

We shall review some other distinctions between the normative and interpretive paradigms at the beginning of the next chapter. For the moment, we refer you to Box 1.10 which summarises some of the broad differences between the two approaches that we have made so far.

Methods and Methodology

We return to our principal concern, methods and methodology in educational research. By *methods*, we mean that range of approaches used in educational research to gather data which are to be used as a basis for inference and interpretation, for explanation and prediction. Traditionally, the word refers to those techniques associated with the positivistic model — eliciting responses to predetermined questions, recording measurements, describing phenomena and performing experiments. For our purposes, we will extend the meaning to include not only the methods of normative research but also those associated with the interpretive paradigm — participant observation, role-playing, non-directive interviewing, episodes and accounts. Although methods may also be taken to include the more specific features of the scientific enterprise such as forming concepts and hypotheses, building models and theories, and sampling procedures, we will limit ourselves principally to the more general techniques which researchers use.

If methods refer to techniques and procedures used in the process of data-gathering, the aim of *methodology* then is, in Kaplan's[48] words

> to describe and analyse these methods, throwing light on their limitations and resources, clarifying their presuppositions and consequences, relating their potentialities to the twilight zone at the frontiers of knowledge. It is to venture generalizations from the success of particular techniques, suggesting new applications, and to unfold the specific bearings of logical and

metaphysical principles on concrete problems, suggesting new formulations.

In summary, he suggests, the aim of methodology is to help us to understand, in the broadest possible terms, not the products of scientific enquiry but the process itself.

Our review will begin by examining those techniques associated with normative studies (with the exception of historical research) and will proceed to those used by interpretive researchers. We, for our part, will attempt to present the two perspectives in complementary light and will try to lessen the tension that is sometimes generated between them. Merton and Kendall[49] express the same sentiment when they say, 'Social scientists have come to abandon the spurious choice between qualitative and quantitative data; they are concerned rather with that combination of both which makes use of the most valuable features of each. The problem becomes one of determining *at which points* they should adopt the one, and at which the other, approach.'

Conclusion: the Role of Research in Education

Our earlier remarks on the *nature of research* may best be summarised by quoting Mouly's definitive statement on the subject. He writes, 'Research is best conceived as the process of arriving at dependable solutions to problems through the planned and systematic collection, analysis, and interpretation of data. It is a most important tool for advancing knowledge, for promoting progress, and for enabling man to relate more effectively to his environment, to accomplish his purposes, and to resolve his conflicts.'[50]

The term *research* itself may take on a range of meanings and thereby be legitimately applied to a variety of contexts from, say, an investigation into the techniques of Dutch painters of the seventeenth century to the problem of finding more efficient means of improving traffic flow in major city centres. For our purposes, however, we will restrict its usages to those activities and undertakings aimed at developing *a science of behaviour*, the word 'science' itself implying both normative and interpretive perspectives. Accordingly, when we speak of social research, we have in mind the systematic and scholarly application of the principles of a science of behaviour to the problems of man within his social context; and when we use the term educational research, we likewise have in mind the application of these selfsame principles to the problems of teaching and learning within the formal educational framework and to the clarification of issues having direct or indirect bearing on these concepts.

The particular value of scientific research in education is that it will enable educators to develop the kind of sound knowledge base that characterises other professions and disciplines; and one that will ensure education a maturity and sense of progression it at present lacks.

References

1. Mouly, G.J., *Educational Research: the Art and Science of Investigation* (Allyn and Bacon, Boston, 1978).
2. Kerlinger, F.N., *Foundations of Behavioral Research* (Holt, Rinehart and Winston, New York, 1970).
3. Borg, W.R., *Educational Research: An Introduction* (Longman, London, 1963). We are not here recommending, nor would we wish to encourage, exclusive dependence on rationally derived and scientifically provable knowledge for the conduct of education — even if this were possible. There is a rich fund of traditional and cultural wisdom in teaching (as in other spheres of life) which we would ignore to our detriment. What we are suggesting, however, is that total dependence on the latter has tended in the past to lead to an impasse: and that for further development and greater understanding to be achieved education must needs resort to the methods of science.
4. Burrell, G. and Morgan, G., *Sociological Paradigms and Organizational Analysis* (Heinemann Educational Books, London, 1979).
5. Beck, R.N., *Handbook in Social Philosophy* (Macmillan, New York, 1979).
6. Acton, H.B., 'Positivism' in J.O. Urmson (ed.), *The Concise Encyclopedia of Western Philosophy* (Hutchinson, London, 1975).
7. Barr Greenfield, T., 'Theory about organisations: a new perspective and its implications for schools' in M.G. Hughes (ed.), *Administering Education: International Challenge* (Athlone Press, London, 1975).
8. Note: Primarily associated with the *Vienna* Circle of the 1920s whose most famous members included Schlick, Carnap, Neurath and Waisman.
9. Duncan Mitchell, G., *A Dictionary of Sociology* (Routledge and Kegan Paul, London, 1968).
10. Giddens, A. (ed.) *Positivism and Sociology* (Heinemann Educational Books, London, 1975).
11. Barratt, P.E.H., *Bases of Psychological Methods* (Wiley and Sons, Australasia Pty. Ltd., Queensland, Australia, 1971).
12. Maslow, A.H., *Motivation and Personality* (Harper and Row, New York, 1954).
13. Hughes, J.A., *Sociological Analysis: Methods of Discovery* (Nelson and Sons Ltd., Sunbury-on-Thames, 1978).
14. Medawar, P.B., *The Hope of Progress* (Methuen, London, 1972).
15. Medawar, P.B., *Advice to a Young Scientist* (Pan Books, London, 1981).
16. Cuff, E.C. and Payne, G.C.F. (eds), *Perspectives in Sociology* (George Allen and Unwin, London, 1979).
17. Aronson, E., *The Social Animal* (Freeman, San Francisco, 1976).

18. Kierkegaard, S., *Concluding Unscientific Postscript* (Princeton University Press, Princeton, 1974).
19. Warnock, M., *Existentialism* (Oxford University Press, London, 1970).
20. Ions, E., *Against Behaviouralism: A Critique of Behavioural Science* (Basil Blackwell, Oxford, 1977).
21. Roszak, T., *The Making of a Counter Culture* (Faber and Faber, London, 1970).
22. Holbrook, D., *Education, Nihilism and Survival* (Darton, Longman and Todd, London, 1977).
23. Hampden-Turner, C., *Radical Man* (Schenkman, Cambridge, Mass., 1970).
24. Giddens, A., *New Rules of Sociological Method: A Positive Critique of Interpretive Sociologies* (Hutchinson, London, 1976).
25. Shipman, M.D., *The Limitations of Social Research* (Longman, London, 1972).
26. Buhler, C. and Allen, M., *Introduction to Humanistic Psychology* (Brooks/Cole, Monterey, California, 1972).
27. Note: see, for example, Rogers, C.R., *Freedom to Learn* (Merrill Pub. Co., Columbus, Ohio, 1969); and also Rogers, C.R. and Stevens, B., *Person to Person: The Problem of Being Human* (Souvenir Press, London, 1967).
28. Harré, R. and Secord, P., *The Explanation of Social Behaviour* (Basil Blackwell, Oxford, 1972).
29. Delamont, S., *Interaction in the Classroom* (Methuen, London, 1976).
30. Note: investigating *Social Episodes* involves analysing the accounts of what is happening from the points of view of the actors and the participant spectator(s)/investigator(s). This is said to yield three main kinds of interlocking material: images of the self and others, definitions of situations, and rules for the proper development of the action. See Harré, R., 'The constructive role of models' in Collins, L. (ed.), *The Use of Models in the Social Sciences* (Tavistock Publications, London, 1976).
31. Levine, R.H., 'Why the ethogenic method and the dramaturgical perspective are incompatible', *Journal of the Theory of Social Behaviour*, 7, 2 (1977)
32. English, H.B. and English, A.C., *A Comprehensive Dictionary of Psychological and Psychoanalytic Terms* (Longman, London, 1958).
33. Curtis, B., Introduction to Curtis, B. and Mays, W. (eds), *Phenomenology and Education* (Methuen, London, 1978).
34. Garfinkel, H., *Studies in Ethnomethodology* (Prentice-Hall, Englewood Cliffs, N.J., 1968).
35. See Mead, G.H. (ed. Charles Morris), *Mind, Self and Society* (University of Chicago Press, Chicago, 1934).
36. Woods, P., *The Divided School* (Routledge and Kegan Paul, London, 1979).
37. Rex, J. (ed.), *Approaches to Sociology: An Introduction to Major Trends in British Sociology* (Routledge and Kegan Paul, London, 1974).
38. Argyle, M., 'Discussion chapter: an appraisal of the new approach to the study of social behaviour', in M. Brenner, P. Marsh and M. Brenner (eds), *The Social Contexts of Method* (Croom Helm, London, 1978).
39. Bernstein, B., 'Sociology and the sociology of education: a brief account', In J. Rex (ed.), *Approaches to Sociology: An Introduction to Major Trends in British Sociology* (Routledge and Kegan Paul, London, 1974).
40. Dixon, K., *Sociological Theory: Pretence and Possibility* (Routledge and Kegan Paul, London, 1973).
41. Douglas, J.D., *Understanding Everyday Life* (Routledge and Kegan Paul, London, 1973).
42. Glaser, B.G. and Strauss, A.L., *The Discovery of Grounded Theory* (Aldine, Chicago, 1967).
43. Hargreaves, D.H., Hester, S.K. and Mellor, F.J., *Deviance in Classrooms*

(Routledge and Kegan Paul, London, 1975).

44. Adams, R.S. and Biddle, B.J., *Realities of Teaching: Explorations with Videotape* (Holt, Rinehart and Winston, New York, 1970).

45. Young, M.F.D. (ed.), *Knowledge and Control: New Directions for the Sociology of Education* (Collier-Macmillan, London, 1971).

46. Rosen, C. and Rosen, H., *The Language of Primary School Children* (Penguin, London, 1973).

47. Sharp, R. and Green, A. (assisted by Lewis, J.), *Education and Social Control: A Study in Progressive Primary Education* (Routledge and Kegan Paul, London, 1975).

48. Kaplan, A., *The Conduct of Inquiry* (Intertext Books, Aylesbury, 1973).

49. Merton, R.K. and Kendall, P.L., 'The focused interview', *American Journal of Sociology* 51 (1946) 541-57.

50. See also Verma, G.K. and Beard, R.M., *What is Educational Research?* (Gower, Aldershot, 1981) for further information on the nature of educational research and also a historical perspective on the subject.

2 HISTORICAL RESEARCH

Introduction

It must seem strange, on the face of it, that among an assemblage of research methods based on the normative and interpretive paradigms we should include, and even begin with, *historical research.* A chapter devoted to a method apparently so fundamentally different from methods having a scientific or 'science of persons' basis must at first glance seem out of place. This notwithstanding, we feel it is essential to include it and base our justifications partly on reasons advanced by Travers[1] and partly on our own views. First, a considerable number of education students do pursue historical research into their subject and so the method does have topical relevance. Second, the review of the literature which an empirical researcher is required to undertake is in itself a kind of historical study because he is reconstructing what was done in the past in a particular respect; so the principles of historical research have some bearing on part of his work at least. Third, recent years have witnessed a *rapprochement* between historical research and research into other areas such as sociology and psychology, although until now historians have tended to borrow data and methods from these disciplines and to use them to enhance historical knowledge rather than radically to change its nature. And fourth, historical research does have some features in common with both normative and interpretive approaches to research. In the case of the former, it shares the quest for objectivity and the desire to minimise bias and distortion; and with the latter, it likewise sets out to describe *all* aspects of the particular situation under study, or as many as are accessible, in its search for the *whole* truth. In summary, then, we may agree with Mouly[2] who says that while historical research cannot meet some of the tests of the scientific method interpreted in the specific sense of its use in the physical sciences (it cannot depend, for instance, on direct observation or experimentation, but must make use of reports that cannot be repeated), it qualifies as a scientific endeavour from the standpoint of its subscription to the same principles and the same

47

general scholarship that characterise all scientific research.*

Historical research has been defined as the systematic and objective location, evaluation and synthesis of evidence in order to establish facts and draw conclusions about past events.[3] It is an act of reconstruction undertaken in a spirit of critical enquiry designed to achieve a faithful representation of a previous age. In seeking data from the personal experiences and observations of others, from documents and records, the researcher has often to contend with inadequate information so that his reconstruction tends to be a sketch rather than a portrait. Indeed, the difficulty of obtaining adequate data makes historical research one of the most taxing kinds of enquiry to conduct satisfactorily.[†] Reconstruction implies a holistic perspective in that the method of enquiry characterising historical research attempts to 'encompass and then explain the whole realm of man's past in a perspective that greatly accents his social, cultural, economic, and intellectual development'.[5] Ultimately, historical research is concerned with a broad view of the conditions and not necessarily the specifics which bring them about, although such a synthesis is rarely achieved without intense debate or controversy, especially on matters of detail. The act of historical research involves the identification and limitation of a problem or an area of study; sometimes the formulation of an hypothesis (or set of questions); the collection, organisation, verification, validation, analysis and selection of data; testing the hypothesis (or answering the questions) where appropriate; and writing a research report. This sequence leads to a new understanding of the past and its relevance to the present and future.

The values of historical research have been categorised by Hill and Kerber[5] as follows: (a) it enables solutions to contemporary problems to be sought in the past; (b) it throws light on present and future trends; (c) it stresses the relative importance and the effects of the various interactions that are to be found within all cultures; and (d) it allows for the revaluation of data in relation to selected hypotheses, theories and generalisations that are presently

---

*See also the opening chapters in *The Nature of Historical Explanation* by Gardiner.[4]

[†]By contrast, the historian of the modern period, i.e. the nineteenth and twentieth centuries, is more often faced in the initial stages with the problem of selecting from too much material, both at the stage of analysis and writing. Here the two most common criteria for such selection are (1) the degree of significance to be attached to data, and (2) the extent to which a specific detail may be considered typical of the whole.

held about the past. As the writers point out, the ability of history to employ the past to predict the future, and to use the present to explain the past, gives it a dual and unique quality which makes it especially useful for all sorts of scholarly study and research.*

The particular value of historical research in the field of education is unquestioned. Although one of the most difficult areas in which to undertake research, the outcomes of enquiry into this domain can bring great benefit to educationalists and the community at large. It can, for example, yield insights into some educational problems that could not be achieved by any other means. Further, the historical study of an educational idea or institution can do much to help us understand how our present educational system has come about; and this kind of understanding can in turn help to establish a sound basis for further progress. Historical research in education can also show how and why educational theories and practices developed. It enables educationalists to use former practices to evaluate newer, emerging ones. Recurrent trends can be more easily identified and assessed from an historical standpoint — witness, for example, the various guises in which progressivism in education appears. And it can contribute to a fuller understanding of the relationship between politics and education, between school and society, between local and central government, and between teacher and pupil.† Specific individual competencies that can be developed through instruction in the history of education have been listed in Box 2.1.

Historical research in education may concern itself with an individual, a group, a movement, an idea or an institution. As Best[7] points out, however, no one of these objects of historical interest and observation can be considered in isolation. No one person can be subjected to historical investigation without some consideration of his contribution to the ideas, movements or institutions of a particular time or place. These elements are always interrelated. The focus merely determines the point of emphasis towards which the historical researcher directs his attention. Box 2.2 illustrates some

---

*However, historians themselves usually reject such a direct application of their work and rarely indulge in it on the grounds that no two events or contexual circumstances, separated geographically and temporally, can possibly be equated. As the popular sayings go, 'History never repeats itself' and so 'the only thing we can learn from History is that we can learn nothing from History'.

†The present status of the history of education as an academic discipline is well summarised and illustrated in Sutherland.[8]

of these relationships from the history of education. For example, no matter whether the historian chooses for study the Jesuit order, religious teaching orders, the Counter-Reformation or Ignatius Loyola, each of the other elements appears as a prominent influence or result, and an indispensable part of the narrative.

Box 2.1: Specific Competencies to be Developed through Instruction in the History of Education

1. Understanding the dynamics of educational change.
2. Increased understanding of the relationship between education and the culture in which it operates.
3. Increased understanding of contemporary educational problems.
4. Understanding the functions and limitations of historical evidence in analysing educational problems.
5. Development of elementary ability in locating, analysing and appraising historical evidence.
6. Development of a sense of the dignity and responsibility of the teaching profession.

Source: Good.[6]

Box 2.2: Some Historical Interrelations Between Men, Movements and Institutions

Men	Movements	Institutions	
		Type	Specific
Ignatius Loyola	Counter-Reformation	Religious teaching order	Society of Jesus, 1534
Benjamin Franklin	Scientific movement; Education for Life	Academy	Philadelphia Academy, 1751
John Dewey	Experimentalism Progressive education	Experimental School	University of Chicago Elementary School, 1896

Source: adapted from Best.[7]

Choice of Subject

As with other methods we shall be considering in this book, historical research may be structured by a flexible sequence of stages, beginning with the selection and evaluation of a problem or area of study. Then follows the definition of the problem (or area of study) in more precise terms, the selection of suitable sources of data, the collection of data, the classification and processing of the data, and finally, the evaluation and synthesis of the data into a balanced and objective account of the subject under investigation. There are, however, some important differences between the method of historical research and other research methods used in education. The principal difference has been highlighted by Borg[3]:

> In historical research, it is especially important that the student carefully defines his problem and appraises its appropriateness before committing himself too fully. Many problems are not adaptable to historical research methods and cannot be adequately treated using this approach. Other problems have little or no chance of producing significant results either because of the lack of pertinent data or because the problem is a trivial one.

One can see from Borg's observations that the choice of a problem can sometimes be a daunting business for the potential researcher. Once a topic has been selected, however, and its potential and significance for historical research evaluated, the next stage is to define it more precisely, or, perhaps more pertinently, delimit it so that a more potent analysis will result. Too broad or too vague a statement can result in the final report lacking direction or impact. Best expresses it like this: 'The experienced historian realises that research must be a penetrating analysis of a limited problem, rather than the superficial examination of a broad area. The weapon of research is the rifle not the shotgun.' Various prescriptions exist for helping to define historical topics. Such a one has been suggested by Gottschalk[9] who recommends that four questions should be asked in identifying a topic:

1. Where do the events take place?
2. Who are the persons involved?
3. When do the events occur?
4. What kinds of human activity are involved?

As Travers[1] suggests, the scope of a topic can be modified by adjusting the focus of any one of the four categories: the geographical area involved can be increased or decreased; more or fewer persons can be included in the topic; the time span involved can be increased or decreased; and the human activity category can be broadened or narrowed. It sometimes happens that a piece of historical research can only begin with a rough idea of what the topic involves; and that delimitation of it can only take place after the pertinent material has been assembled.

In hand with the careful specification of the problem goes the need, where this is appropriate, for an equally specific and testable hypothesis (sometimes a sequence of questions may be substituted). As in empirical research, the hypothesis gives direction and focus to data collection and analysis. It imposes a selection, a structure on what would otherwise be an overwhelming mass of information. As Borg[3] observes:

Without hypotheses, historical research often becomes little more than an aimless gathering of facts. In searching the materials that make up the sources of historical research data, unless the student's attention is aimed at information relating to specific questions or concerned with specific hypotheses, he has little chance of extracting a body of data from the available documents that can be synthesized to provide new knowledge or new understanding of the topic studied. Even after specific hypotheses have been established, the student must exercise strict self-control in his study of historical documents or he will find himself collecting much information that is interesting but is not related to his area of inquiry. If the student's hypotheses are not sufficiently delimited or specific, it is an easy matter for him to become distracted and led astray by information that is not really related to his field of investigation.

Hill and Kerber[5] have pointed out that the evaluation and formulation of a problem associated with historical research often involve the personality of the researcher to a greater extent than do other basic types of research. They suggest that personal factors of the investigator such as interest, motivation, historical curiosity, and educational background for the interpretation of historical facts tend to influence the selection of the problem to a great extent.

Although it has been overshadowed to some extent in the past decade by a growing interest in empirical research, historical research has still a significant role to play in education, a role that will enable us to use the past to understand and explain the present more satisfactorily and also enable us to make predictions about educational trends, practices and outcomes with greater confidence. One of the commonest forms of historical research in education is the biography: a study of the life, teachings and subsequent influence of one or other of the great educators. Yet if there are priorities in this area, as determined by current needs, more fruitful problem areas exist. One of these concerns the study of

Box 2.3: An Example of a Historical Study in Education

Loughborough: From College to University. A History of Higher Education at Loughborough 1909–66

This study provides a fine example of research into an educational institution or, rather, a complex of institutions. Yet it is more than this, for in providing a case study of the pre-war development of the relationship between a local college, a local education authority, and central government and the subsequent emergence of the college as a higher technological institute, the research captures the full flavour of the struggles and achievements of individuals caught in the sweep of history during one of the most expansionist periods in the history of British Higher Education.

Here is a brief extract summarising what had been achieved by the year 1939:

'By the outbreak of war in 1939, Loughborough College had become a remarkable educational establishment. In the preceding twenty years, Schofield had enlarged it very considerably and put together a uniquely idiosyncratic institution which, thanks partly to its own very considerable merits and partly to his superb flair for gathering favourable publicity, had acquired an international reputation. An odd amalgam of red-brick buildings and huts in the centre of Loughborough, imposing collegiate-looking residences and splendid sporting facilities on the playing field site, country houses and dignified mansions in Loughborough and the surrounding district, and an aerodrome on the edge of the town, it had, like Topsy, 'just growed'. Thanks to Schofield's entrepreneurial genius and willingness to try his hand at anything, he had grafted onto its engineering staple, such apparently odd bed-fellows as teacher-training and physical education. The previous twenty years had been a period of unparalleled growth so that by 1939 Schofield could boast that his College consisted of Departments of Mechanical and Civil, Electrical, Automobile, and Aeronautical Engineering; the East Midlands Teachers' Training College; a School of Athletics, Games, and Physical Training; Departments of Industrial and Fine Art, Extra-Mural Education, and Continuative Education; and, last but not least, Loughborough College School.'

Source: Cantor and Matthews.[10]

present-day practices in education and how these developed. Studies of this kind often show that current practices were developed in the first place to meet needs that no longer exist. A cognate area is the realm of educational thought and ideas and the way in which they have influenced educational practices. Travers[1] observes, 'So often education has moved through cycles of ideas only to return, ultimately, to the starting point. A better understanding of the history of ideas in education would prevent much activity that has been called "rediscovering the wheel". So often a great new educational program is little more than one that had been in vogue thirty years previously.' An investigation, for example, of the factors contributing to the demise of progressive education in the United States some years ago would have striking relevance to the future of current informal and open movements in Great Britain and the United States.

Data Collection

One of the principal differences between historical research and other forms of research is that historical research must deal with data that already exist. Hockett[11] expresses it thus:

> History is not a science of *direct* observation, like chemistry and physics. The historian like the geologist interprets past events by the traces they have left; he deals with the evidence of man's past acts and thoughts. But the historian, no less than the scientist, must utilize evidence resting on reliable observation. The difference in procedure is due to the fact that the historian usually does not make his own observations, and that those upon whose observations he must depend are, or were, often if not usually untrained observers. Historical method is, strictly speaking, a process *supplementary* to observations, a process by which the historian attempts to test the truthfulness of the reports of observations made by others. Like the scientist, he examines his data and formulates hypotheses, i.e. tentative conclusions. These conjectures he must test by seeking fresh evidence or re-examining the old, and this process he must continue until, in the light of all available evidence, the hypotheses are abandoned as untenable or modified until they are brought into conformity with the available evidence.

Sources of data in historical research may be classified into two main groups: *primary sources*, which are the life-blood of historical research; and *secondary sources*, which may be used in the absence of, or to supplement, primary data.

Primary sources of data have been described as those items that are original to the problem under study and may be thought of as being in two categories, thus:

1. The remains or relics of a given period. Although such remains and artefacts as skeletons, fossils, weapons, tools, utensils, buildings, pictures, furniture, coins and *objets d'art* were not meant to transmit information to subsequent eras, nevertheless they may be useful sources providing sound evidence about the past.

2. Those items that have had a direct physical relationship with the events being reconstructed. This category would include not only the written and oral testimony provided by actual participants in, or witnesses of, an event, but also the participants themselves. Documents considered as primary sources include manuscripts, charters, laws; archives of official minutes or records, files, letters, memoranda, memoirs, biography, offical publications, wills, newspapers and magazines, maps, diagrams, catalogues, films, paintings, inscriptions, recordings, transcriptions, log books and research reports. All these are, intentionally or unintentionally, capable of transmitting a first-hand account of an event and are therefore considered as sources of primary data. Historical research in education draws chiefly on the kind of sources identified in this second category.

Secondary sources are those that do not bear a direct physical relationship to the event being studied. They are made up of data that cannot be described as original. A secondary source would thus be one in which the person describing the event was not actually present but who obtained his descriptions from another person or source. These may or may not have been primary sources. Other instances of secondary sources used in historical research include: quoted material, textbooks, encyclopedias, other reproductions of material or information, prints of paintings or replicas of art objects. Best[7] points out that secondary sources of data are usually of limited worth because of the errors that result when information is passed on from one person to another.

Various commentators stress the importance of using primary sources of data where possible. Hill and Kerber[5] say in this connection for instance:

> In the process of conducting historical research the investigator should never be satisfied with copies of documents that can be obtained in original form ... Relatively insignificant errors in reproduction processes may, through additive or multiplicative effects, produce a resultant error of comparatively great magnitude in the final form of the data. This condition is particularly well illustrated in reporting census data in various forms and indexes, where these final forms are derived through the operations of addition, subtraction, multiplication, and/or division.

The value, too, of secondary sources should not be minimised. There are numerous occasions where a secondary source can contribute significantly to more valid and reliable historical research than would otherwise be the case.

One further point: the review of the literature in other forms of educational research is regarded as a preparatory stage to gathering data and serves to acquaint the researcher with previous research on the topic he himself is studying. It thus enables him to continue in a tradition, to place his work in context, and to learn from earlier endeavours. The function of the review of the literature in historical research, however, is different in that it provides the data for research; the researcher's acceptance or otherwise of his hypothesis will depend on his selection of information from the review and the interpretation he puts on it. Borg[3] has identified other differences: one is that the historical researcher will have to peruse longer documents than the empirical researcher who normally studies articles very much more succinct and precise. Further, documents required in historical research often date back much further than those in empirical research. And one final point: documents in education often consist of unpublished material and are therefore less accessible than reports of empirical studies in professional journals.

For a detailed consideration of the specific problems of documentary research, the reader is referred to the articles by Platt[12] where she considers those of authenticity, availability of documents, sampling problems, inference and interpretation.

Evaluation

Because a worker in the field of historical research gathers much of his data and information from records and documents, they must be carefully evaluated so as to attest their worth for the purposes of the particular study. Evaluation of historical data and information is often referred to as historical criticism and the reliable data yielded by the process are known as historical evidence. Historical evidence has thus been described as that body of validated facts and information which can be accepted as trustworthy, as a valid basis for the testing and interpretation of hypotheses. Historical criticism is usually undertaken in two stages: first, the *authenticity* of the source is appraised; and second, the *accuracy* or *worth* of the data is evaluated. The two processes are known as *external* and *internal* criticism respectively, and since they each present problems of evaluation they merit further inspection.

External Criticism

External criticism is concerned with establishing the authenticity or genuineness of data. It is therefore aimed at the document (or other source) itself rather than the statements it contains; with analytic forms of the data rather than the interpretation or meaning of them in relation to the study. It therefore sets out to uncover frauds, forgeries, hoaxes, inventions or distortions. To this end, the tasks of establishing the age or authorship of a document may involve tests of factors such as signatures, handwriting, script, type, style, spelling and place-names. Further, was the knowledge it purports to transmit available at the time and is it consistent with what is known about the author or period from another source? Increasingly sophisticated analyses of physical factors can also yield clues establishing authenticity or otherwise: physical and chemical tests of ink, paper, parchment, cloth and other materials, for example. Investigations in the field of educational history are less likely to encounter deliberate forgeries than in, say, political or social history, though it is possible to find that official documents, correspondence and autobiographies have been 'ghosted', that is, prepared by a person other than the alleged author or signer.

Internal Criticism

Having established the authenticity of the document, the researcher's next task is to evaluate the accuracy and worth of the data contained therein. While they may be genuine, they may not necessarily disclose the most faithful picture. In his concern to establish the meaning and reliability of data, the investigator is confronted with a more difficult problem than external criticism because he has to establish the credibility of the author of the document. Travers[1] has listed those characteristics commonly considered in making evaluations of writers, thus: was he a trained or untrained observer of the event? In other words, how competent was he? What was his relationship to the event? To what extent was he under pressure, from fear or vanity, say, to distort or omit facts? What was the intent of the writer of the document? To what extent was he an expert at recording the particular event? Were the habits of the author such that they might interfere with the accuracy of recording? Was he too antagonistic or too sympathetic to give a true picture? How long after the event did he record his testimony? And was he able to remember accurately? Finally, is he in agreement with other independent witnesses?

Box 2.4: A Brief Checklist of Some Dimensions of 'Bias'

Source One: The Life History Informant
   Is misinformation (unintended) given?
   Has there been evasion?
   Is there evidence of direct lying and deception?
   Is a 'front' being presented?
   What may the informant 'take for granted' and hence not reveal?
   How far is the informant 'pleasing you'?
   How much has been forgotten?
   How much may be self-deception?

Source Two: The Social Scientist Researcher
   Could any of the following be shaping the outcome?
      (a) Attitudes of researcher: age, gender, class, race, etc.
      (b) Demeanour of researcher: dress, speech, body language, etc.
      (c) Personality of researcher: anxiety, need for approval, hostility, warmth, etc.
      (d) Attitudes of researcher: religion, politics, tolerance, general assumptions.
      (e) Scientific role of researcher: theory held, etc. (researcher expectancy).

Source Three: The Interaction
   The joint act needs to be examined. Is bias coming from
      (a) The physical setting — 'social space'?
      (b) The prior interaction?
      (c) Non-verbal communication?
      (d) Vocal behaviour?

Source: Plummer.[13]

Many documents in the history of education tend to be neutral in character, though it is possible that some may be in error because of these kinds of observer-characteristics.

A particular problem arising from the questions posed by Travers is that of *bias*. This can be particularly acute where life histories are being studied. The chief concern here, as Plummer[13] reminds us, resides in examining possible sources of bias which prevent the researcher from finding out what is wanted and using techniques to minimise the possible sources of bias.

Researchers generally recognise *three sources of bias*: those arising from the subject being interviewed, those arising from the researcher himself, and those arising from the subject-researcher interaction.[13] Box 2.4 gives Plummer's summary of possible sources of bias under these three headings.

Writing the Research Report

Once the data have been gathered and subjected to external criticism for authenticity and to internal criticism for accuracy, the researcher is next confronted with the task of piecing together an account of the events embraced by the research problem. This stage is known as the *process of synthesis*. It is probably the most difficult phase in the project and calls for considerable imagination and resourcefulness. The resulting pattern is then applied to the testing of the hypothesis.

The writing of the final report is equally demanding and calls for creativity and high standards of objective and systematic analysis.

Best[7] has listed the kinds of problems occurring in the various types of historical research projects submitted by students. These include:

1. Problem too broadly stated.
2. Tendency to use easy-to-find secondary sources of data rather than sufficient primary sources which are harder to locate but usually more trustworthy.
3. Inadequate historical criticism of data, due to failure to establish authenticity of sources and trustworthiness of data. For example, there is often a tendency to accept a statement as necessarily true when several observers agree. It is possible

that one may have influenced the others, or that all were influenced by the same inaccurate source of information.

4. Poor logical analysis resulting from:

   (a) Oversimplication — failure to recognise the fact that causes of events are more often multiple and complex than single and simple.

   (b) Overgeneralisation on the basis of insufficient evidence, and false reasoning by analogy, basing conclusions upon superficial similarities of situations.

   (c) Failure to interpret words and expression in the light of their accepted meaning in an earlier period.

   (d) Failure to distinguish between significant facts in a situation and those that are irrelevant or unimportant.

5. Expression of personal bias, as revealed by statements lifted out of context for purposes of persuasion, assuming too generous or uncritical an attitude towards a person or idea (or being too unfriendly or critical), excessive admiration for the past (sometimes known as the 'old oaken bucket' delusion), or an equally unrealistic admiration for the new or contemporary, assuming that all change represents progress.

6. Poor reporting in a style that is dull and colourless, too flowery or flippant, too persuasive or of the 'soap-box' type, or lacking in proper usage.

In addition to these, Sutherland[8] has brilliantly illustrated two further common errors among historians of education. These are: (a) projecting current battles backwards onto an historical background which leads to distortion; and (b) 'description in a vacuum' which fails to illustrate the relationship of the educational system to the structure of society.

To conclude on a more positive note, we refer you to Box 2.5 which itemises five basic criteria for evaluating historical research.

The Use of Quantitative Methods

By far the greater part of research in historical studies is qualitative in nature. This is so because the proper subject-matter of historical research consists to a great extent of verbal and other symbolic material emanating from a society's or a culture's past. The basic skills required of the researcher to analyse this kind of qualitative

Box 2.5: Criteria for Evaluating Historical Research

<table>
<tr><td>1.</td><td>Problem: Has the problem been clearly defined? It is difficult enough to conduct historical research adequately without adding to the confusion by starting out with a nebulous problem. Is the problem capable of solution? Is it within the competence of the investigator?</td></tr>
<tr><td>2.</td><td>Data: Are data of a primary nature available in sufficient completeness to provide a solution, or has there been an overdependence on secondary or unverifiable sources?</td></tr>
<tr><td>3.</td><td>Analysis: Has the dependability of the data been adequately established? Has the relevance of the data been adequately explored?</td></tr>
<tr><td>4.</td><td>Interpretation: Does the author display adequate mastery of his data and insight into their relative significance? Does he display adequate historical perspective? Does he maintain his objectivity or does he allow personal bias to distort the evidence? Are his hypotheses plausible? Have they been adequately tested? Does he take a sufficiently broad view of the total situation? Does he see the relationship between his data and other 'historical facts'?</td></tr>
<tr><td>5.</td><td>Presentation: Does the style of writing attract as well as inform? Does the report make a contribution on the basis of newly discovered data or new interpretation, or is it simply 'uninspired hack-work'? Does it reflect scholarliness?</td></tr>
</table>

Source: from Mouly.[2]

or symbolic material involve collecting, classifying, ordering, synthesising, evaluating and interpreting. At the basis of all these acts lies sound personal judgement. In the comparatively recent past, however, attempts have been made to apply the quantitative methods of the scientist to the solution of historical problems[14]. Of these methods, the one having greatest relevance to historical research is that of *content analysis,* the basic goal of which is to take a verbal, non-quantitative document and transform it into quantitative data.[15]

Content analysis itself has been defined as 'a multipurpose research method developed specifically for investigating a broad spectrum of problems in which the content of communication serves as a basis of inference.'[16] The use of content analysis as a technique in social research dates from the early years of this century and since then the method has gone through a number of phases. The earliest attempts at using content analysis involve word counts. As Travers[1] explains, 'Writers typically use particular words at their own frequency rates. A word that has a high usage rate by one writer may have a low usage rate by another. The usage rates of different words can be studied to throw light on the authenticity of the source of a document. Word-usage rates can also be used as a basis for inferring inner emotional states, such as anxiety.' More sophisticated approaches to content analysis are careful to identify appropriate *categories* and *units of analysis*, both of which will reflect the nature of the document being analysed and the purpose of the research. *Categories* are normally determined after initial inspection of the document and will cover the main areas of content (categories identifying trends in newspaper content, for example, may include (1) domestic news; (2) foreign affairs; (3) business and financial news; (4) sport; (5) art criticism; (6) television and radio; (7) children's items; and (8) cartoons). *Units of analysis* may include (1) the single word; (2) a theme; (3) a character (of a play or novel); (4) a sentence; and (5) a paragraph.

We can readily see how the technique of content analysis may be applied to selected aspects of historical research in education. It could be used, for instance, in the analysis of educational documents. In addition to elucidating the content of the document, the method may throw additional light on the source of the communication, its author, and on its intended recipients, those to whom the message is directed. Further, an analysis of this kind would tell us more about the social context and the kinds of factors stressed or ignored, and of the influence of political factors, for instance. It follows from this that content analysis may form the basis of comparative or cross-cultural studies. Another usage that comes readily to mind would be an examination of the content of textbooks at different points in recent history as a means of indicating, say, cultural differences, cultural censorship or cultural change. Box 2.6 itemises the seven purposes of content analysis identified by Holsti.[16]

Two very different examples of the use of content analysis in

Box 2.6: The Purposes of Content Analysis

1.	To describe trends in communication content.
2.	To relate known characteristics of sources to messages they produce.
3.	To audit communication content against standards.
4.	To analyse techniques of persuasion.
5.	To analyse style.
6.	To relate known attributes of the audience to messages produced for them.
7.	To describe patterns of communication.

Source: from Holsti.[16]

historical contexts are provided by Thomas and Znaniecki[17] and Bradburn and Berlew.[18]

In a classical study, Thomas and Znaniecki employ content analysis to study 'the role of human attitudes' in the social life of Polish families living 'under strain' at the beginning of the present century as a result of the emigration of family members to the United States of America. Their data consist of exchange letters between the Old and the New World, letters which reflect the changing relationships within peasant primary groups as communities and families are disrupted by the long absence of an important member as well as by the changing social organisation of one rural segment of Western Europe.[19] Thomas and Znaniecki introduce each particular volume of letters with interpretations that clarify words or phrases, and explain the attitudes and actions described in the letters. Their introduction to Volume I, for example, runs to some two hundred pages. The amount and the depth of the analyses vary from one series of letters to another. Riley[19] describes them as generally rather 'loose and intuitive'. Often, she observes, the researchers have obtained only one side of the epistolary exchange and, in consequence, are able to cover only part of the interaction. Where however the exchanges represent the entire communication process (that is to say, the letters *are* the

Box 2.7: Jan Kukielka, in America, to his Wife in Poland, December 30th, 1913

... And now, dear wife and daughters, write to me, when do you think it best for me to return home? On Easter or at some other time? And now I greet you, dear wife and daughters, and I greet my dear sisters Katarzyna, Rozalia, Maryanna, with their husbands and children. And now I greet the whole household of father-in-law, father and mother and brothers-in-law. And now, dear wife I inform you [send you this] through the Mrozys [who are returning], and I send you 4 roubles for your expenses. Buy for yourself, Rózia, a white waist and for Nastusia and Jagusia shawls that you may have them for summer when I come home. And now dear wife, tell my sister Rozalia Figlisz not to allow her daughter Marysia to marry Bzdziuch, because no good will come of it. As the father, so is the son, as the tree, so is the wedge. And then it is a near family, and therefore God will not bless such a marriage, because there are enough people in the world. If she does not believe my words let her be persuaded by the example of those who married their relatives. As a good brother, I admonish Sister Rozalia, let her not do it, what she intends to do. [More greetings for the whole family.]

Your husband
Jan Kukielka

Source: adapted from Thomas and Znaniecki.[17]

Box 2.8: N'ach Levels in English Literature 1550–1800 Compared with Coal Imports into London Fifty Years Later

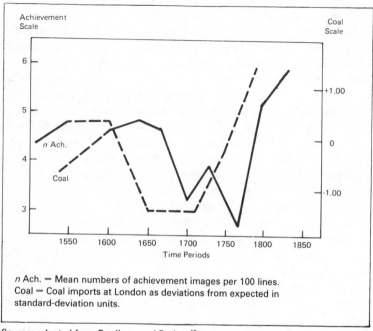

n Ach. = Mean numbers of achievement images per 100 lines.
Coal = Coal imports at London as deviations from expected in standard-deviation units.

Source: adapted from Bradburn and Berlew.[18]

interaction), then they provide data that are free from the potential errors that so often beset the observer or the questioner insofar as the preconceptions of the investigator cannot affect what the group members actually write to one another nor is there any opportunity for selective reporting by a researcher. Box 2.7 shows one of the exchange letters that constitute the Thomas and Znaniecki data.

The second example of content analysis in historical settings has to do with McClelland's[20] study of the relationship between the need to achieve (n'ach, for short) among members of a society and the economic growth of the particular society in question. McClelland and his associates develop a measure which they call 'achievement imagery' and seek to relate the frequency of this factor in the popular literature of a specific period in history to economic indicators of growth and development in the society under investigation. Box 2.8 shows some of McClelland's findings as they relate to the close association between achievement imagery data and the scale of imports of coal into the port of London over a three hundred year period, after the researchers had allowed for a time lag of some fifty years between their two sets of figures.

Finally, for a more detailed and technical consideration of the use of quantitative methods in historical research, a study which looks at the classifying and arranging of historical data and reviews basic descriptive statistics, we refer the reader to Floud.[21]

An Example of Historical Research in Education

We conclude this chapter with a short review of a piece of historical research in education. In their study of private schools in Leicester and the county, 1780–1840, Crook and Simon[22] show how, for various reasons, local educational needs in both the town and county were almost wholly met by a variety of private schools. Some idea of the nature of these private schools, most of which had left no records, was gained by the researchers from the study of local memoirs and from advertisements in the main local newspaper of the time, the *Leicester Journal.*

The study begins with an examination of Leicestershire at the end of the eighteenth century with particular reference to topographical, industrial and demographic features, as well as educational. The roles of the church and prominent citizens are also considered.

The study then looks at the way the children of local worthies were educated, the somewhat unsystematic nature of the process being readily apparent, and how various kinds of private schools arose to provide for the different sections of the community. Brief sketches of some of these reveal interesting differences in terms of personnel, aims, curriculum and fees. See Box 2.9 for a description of one of the main boys' school at the time. After 1801, the growth in the number of such schools in Leicester reflected the growth in the population.

In the county there were private schools around the main towns, most of which took boarders, and some in more rural areas. The proliferation of such schools in Hinckley is examined, as are their varying curricula and fees. Establishments ranged from a commercial academy of some standing in Leicester itself to village schools; or from the classical school kept by a non-resident cleric in the county town to the handful of younger boys prepared by country incumbents for entry to the endowed grammar schools. Addi-

Box 2.9: Silver Street Academy

The main boys' school in Leicester in the later eighteenth century was evidently the Silver Street academy, under Henry Carrick; advertisements continue up to 1809 when another master took over. Though this is described as a boarding school, with fees of £12 a year in 1799, day pupils were also taken. Offering practical subjects 'for those destined for a commercial life', it also had an eye to the more fashionable world for special masters taught French, Italian, music, dancing and drawing. Masters of these last subjects, it may be noted, sometimes set up their own account in the town — for instance, Monsieur Samson, who first advertised French classes in 1796, announced two years later that he was employing an assistant to teach in the evening and also offered Italian.

Source: adapted from Crook and Simon.[22]

tionally, the larger private schools run by lay masters provided 'a clear alternative to the grammar school, in terms of a practical, commercially biased programme supplemented by some instruction in Latin, if required'.

The researchers then go on to consider in some detail the establishment and nature of two important institutions in Leicester in the 1830s — the Leicester and Leicestershire Collegiate School and the Proprietary School for Leicester and Leicestershire, the general aim of the latter being to provide 'a sound classical education with those studies which more especially qualify for the pursuits of an active and commercial life.' Interestingly, also in the case of the Proprietary School, the headmaster in 1840 ascribed good behaviour to the practice of sending parents a monthly report which gave 'the inestimable privilege of parental supervision and control'.

As the authors observe in their conclusion, the need on the part of Leicestershire's middle classes for a useful, commercially biased education played an important part in the establishment of private school provision in the county during the period in question.

References

1. Travers, R.M.W., *An Introduction to Educational Research* (Collier-Macmillan, London, 1969).
2. Mouly, G.J., *Educational Research: The Art and Science of Investigation* (Allyn and Bacon, Boston, 1978).
3. Borg, W.R., *Educational Research: An Introduction* (Longman, London, 1963).
4. Gardiner, P., *The Nature of Historical Explanation* (Oxford University Press,

Oxford, 1961, reprinted 1978).

5. Hill, J.E. and Kerber, A., *Models, Methods and Analytical Procedures in Educational Research* (Wayne State University Press, Detroit, 1967).

6. Good, C.V., *Essentials of Educational Research* (Appleton-Century-Crofts, New York, 1963).

7. Best, J.W., *Research in Education* (Prentice-Hall, Englewood Cliffs, New Jersey, 1970).

8. Sutherland, G., 'The study of the history of education', *History*, 54, no. 180, February, 1969.

9. Gottschalk, L., *Understanding History* (Alfred A. Knopf, New York, 1951).

10. Cantor, L.M. and Matthews, G.F., *Loughborough: From College to University. A History of Higher Education at Loughborough 1909–1966* (Loughborough University of Technology, 1977).

11. Hockett, H.C., *The Critical Method in Historical Research and Writing* (Macmillan, London, 1955).

12. Platt, J., 'Evidence and proof in documentary research. 1. Some specific problems of documentary research; and 2. Some shared problems of documentary research.' *Sociol. Rev.*, 29, 1 (1981) 31–52, 53–66.

13. Plummer, K., *Documents of Life: An Introduction to the Problems and Literature of a Humanistic Method* (George Allen and Unwin, London, 1983).

14. Travers.[1] See also the Social Science Research Council's *Research in Economic and Social History* (Heinemann, London, 1971), Chapters 2 and 3.

15. Bailey, K.D., *Methods of Social Research* (Collier-Macmillan, London, 1978).

16. Holsti, O.R., 'Content Analysis', in G. Lindzey and E. Aronson (eds), *The Handbook of Social Psychology. Volume 2: Research Methods* (Addison-Wesley, Reading, Mass. 1968). For a recent detailed account of the methods and problems involved in establishing the reliability of the content analysis of written data, see: Everett, M., 'The Scottish Comprehensive School: Its function and the roles of its teachers with special reference to the opinions of pupils and student teachers.' Unpublished Ph.D. dissertation, School of Education, University of Durham, 1984.

17. Thomas, W.I. and Znaniecki, F., *The Polish Peasant in Europe and America* (University of Chicago Press, Chicago, 1918). For a fuller discussion of the monumental work of Thomas and Znaniecki, the reader is referred to Plummer, K., *Documents of Life: An Introduction to the Problems and Literature of a Humanistic Method* (George Allen and Unwin, London 1983), especially Chapter 3, 'The Making of a Method', and to Madge, J., *The Origin of Scientific Sociology* (Tavistock, London, 1963).

18. Bradburn, N.M. and Berlew, D.E., *Economic Development and Cultural Change* (University of Chicago Press, Chicago, 1961).

19. Riley, M.W. *Sociological Research I: A Case Approach* (Harcourt, Brace and World, Inc. New York, 1963).

20. McClelland, D.C., Atkinson, J.W., Clark, R.A. and Lowell, E.L., *The Achievement Motive* (Appleton-Century-Crofts, New York, 1953).

21. Floud, R., *An Introduction to Quantitative Methods for Historians*, 2nd edn (Methuen, London, 1979).

22. Crook, Z. and Simon, B., 'Private schools in Leicester and the County 1780–1840', in B. Simon (ed.), *Education in Leicestershire 1540–1940* (Leicester University Press, Leicester, 1968).

3 DEVELOPMENTAL RESEARCH

Introduction

Most educational research methods are descriptive; that is, they set out to describe and to interpret *what is.*[1] Descriptive research, according to Best, is concerned with

> conditions or relationships that exist; practices that prevail; beliefs, points of view, or attitudes that are held; processes that are going on; effects that are being felt; or trends that are developing. At times, descriptive research is concerned with how *what is* or *what exists* is related to some preceding event that has influenced or affected a present condition or event.

The previous and the present chapter and, indeed, most of the chapters that follow deal with descriptive research. Chapter 8, 'Experiments, Quasi-experiments and Single-case Research', is a clear exception, descriptive research being fundamentally different from experimental research in that in the former, the researcher accounts for what has already occurred; in the latter, he arranges for events to happen.[1] This overall balance in the text reflects the fact that the majority of education studies that are reported in the literature are descriptive rather than experimental. They look at individuals, groups, institutions, methods and materials in order to describe, compare, contrast, classify, analyse and interpret the entities and the events that constitute their various fields of enquiry.

This chapter deals with three types of descriptive research which for the present we shall refer to loosely as longitudinal, cross-sectional and trend or prediction studies. Collectively they are termed *developmental research* because they are concerned both to describe what the present relationships are among variables in a given situation and to account for changes occurring in those relationships as a function of time. The term 'developmental' is primarily biological, having to do with the organisation and the life processes of living things. The concept has been appropriated and applied to diverse educational, historical, sociological and psychological phenomena.[2] In education, developmental studies often retain the original biological orientation of the term, having to do with the acquisition of motor and perceptual skills in young children. However, the designation 'developmental' has wider application in education, for example, in connection with Piaget's studies of qualitative changes occurring in children's thinking, and Kohlberg's work on moral development.

Because education is primarily concerned with the individual's physical, social, intellectual and emotional growth, developmental studies continue to occupy a central place in the methodologies used by the educational researcher.

The Terminology of Developmental Research

The term *longitudinal* is used to describe a variety of studies that are conducted over a period of time. Often, as we have seen, the word *developmental* is employed in connection with longitudinal studies that deal specifically with aspects of human growth.

A clear distinction is drawn between *longitudinal* and *cross-sectional* studies. The longitudinal study gathers data over an extended period of time; a short-term investigation may take several weeks or months; a long-term study can extend over many years. Where successive measures are taken at different points in time from the *same* respondents, the term *follow-up study* or *cohort study* is used in the British literature, the equivalent term in the United States being the *panel study*. Where *different* respondents are studied at different points in time, the study is called *cross-sectional*. Where a few selected factors are studied continuously over time, the term *trend study* is employed.

Cohort studies and trend studies are *prospective* longitudinal methods in that they are ongoing in their collection of information about individuals or their monitoring of specific events. *Retrospective* longitudinal studies, on the other hand, focus upon individuals who have reached some defined end-point or state.[3] For example, a group of young people may be the researcher's particular interest (intending social workers, convicted drug offenders or university dropouts, for example), and the questions to which he will address himself are likely to include ones such as: is there anything about the previous experience of these individuals that can account for their present situation?[3]

A cross-sectional study is one that produces a 'snapshot' of a population at a particular point in time. The epitome of the cross-sectional study is a national census in which a representative sample of the population consisting of individuals of different ages, different occupations, different educational and income levels, and residing in different parts of the country, is interviewed on the same day.[4] More typically in education, cross-sectional studies involve indirect measures of the nature and rate of changes in the physical and intellectual development of samples of children drawn from representative age levels. The single 'snapshot' of the cross-sectional study provides the researcher with data for either a retrospective or a prospective enquiry.

Trend or *prediction studies* have an obvious importance to the educational administrator or planner. Like cohort studies, they may be of relatively short or long duration. Essentially, the trend study examines recorded data to establish patterns of change that have already occurred in order to predict what will be likely to occur in the future. A major difficulty the researcher faces in conducting trend analyses is the intrusion of unpredictable factors that invalidate forecasts formulated on past data. For this reason, short-term trend studies tend to be more accurate than long-term analyses. The distinctions we have drawn between the various terms used in developmental research are illustrated in Box 3.1.

Strengths and Weaknesses of Cohort and Cross-sectional Studies

Longitudinal studies of the cohort analysis type have an important place in the research armoury of the educational investigator. Cohort studies of human growth and development conducted on representative samples of populations are uniquely able to identify typical patterns of development and to reveal factors operating on those samples which elude other research designs. They permit the researcher to examine individual variations in characteristics or traits, and to produce individual growth curves. Cohort studies, too, are particularly appropriate when the investigator attempts to establish causal relationships, for this task involves identifying changes in certain characteristics that result in changes in others. Cross-sectional designs are inappropriate in causal research. Cohort analysis is especially useful in sociological research because it can show how changing properties of individuals fit together into changing properties of social systems as a whole.[5] For example, the study of staff morale and its association with the emerging organisational climate of a newly-opened school would lend itself to this type of developmental research. A further strength of cohort studies in schools is that they provide longitudinal records whose value derives in part from the known fallibility of any single test or assessment.[3] Finally, *time*, always a limiting factor in experimental and interview settings, is generally more readily available in cohort studies, allowing the researcher greater opportunity to observe trends and to distinguish 'real' changes from chance occurrences.[4]

Longitudinal studies suffer several disadvantages, though the gravity of these weaknesses is challenged by supporters of cohort analysis (see Box 3.2). First, they are time-consuming and expensive because the researcher is obliged to wait for growth data to accumulate. Second, there is the difficulty of *sample mortality*. Inevitably during the course of a long-term cohort study, subjects drop out, are lost or refuse further co-operation. Such attrition makes it unlikely that those who remain in the study are as representative of the population as the sample that was originally drawn. Sometimes attempts are made to lessen the effects of sample mortality by introducing aspects of cross-sectional study design, that is, 'topping up' the original cohort sample size at each time of re-testing with the same number of respondents drawn from the same population. The problem here is that differences arising in the data from one survey to the next may then be accounted for by differences in the persons surveyed rather than by genuine changes or trends. A third difficulty has been termed *control effect* (sometimes referred to as *measurement effect*). Often, repeated interviewing results in an undesired and confusing effect on the actions or attitudes under study, influencing the behaviour of subjects, sensitising them to matters that have hitherto passed unnoticed, or stimulating them to communication with others on unwanted topics.[5] Finally, cohort studies in education pose considerable problems of organisation due to the continuous changes that occur in pupils, staff, teaching methods and the like. Such changes make it highly unlikely that a study will be completed in the way that it was originally planned.

Cohort studies, as we have seen, are particularly appropriate in research on human growth and development. Why then are so many studies in this area cross-sectional in design? The reason is

Box 3.1: Types of Developmental Research

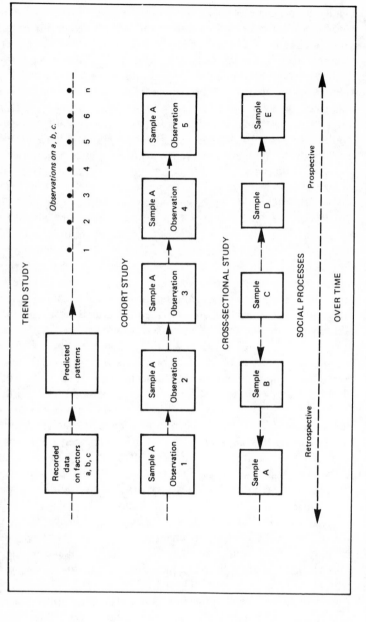

that they have a number of advantages over cohort studies: they are less expensive than cohort analyses; they produce findings more quickly; they are less likely to suffer from control effects; and they are more likely to secure the co-operation of respondents on a 'one-off' basis. Generally, cross-sectional designs are able to include more subjects than are cohort designs.

The strengths of cohort analysis are the weaknesses of the cross-sectional design. The cross-sectional study is a less effective method for the researcher who is concerned to identify individual variations in growth or to establish causal relationships between variables. Sampling in the cross-sectional study is complicated because different subjects are involved at each age level and may not be comparable. Further problems arising out of selection effects and the obscuring of irregularities in growth weaken the cross-sectional study so much that one observer[6] dismisses the

Box 3.2: Advantages of Cohort over Cross-sectional Designs

1. Some types of information, for example, on attitudes or assessment of potential ability, are only meaningful if collected contemporaneously. Other types are more complete or more accurate if collected during the course of a longitudinal survey, though they are likely to have some value even if collected retrospectively, for example, length of schooling, job history, geographical movement.

2. In cohort studies, no duplication of information occurs, whereas in cross-sectional studies the same type of backgroup information has to be collected on each occasion. This increases the interviewing costs.

3. The omission of even a single variable, later found to be important, from a cross-sectional study is a disaster, whereas it is usually possible in a cohort study to fill the gap, even if only partially, in a subsequent interview.

4. A cohort study allows the accumulation of a much larger number of variables, extending over a much wider area of knowledge than would be possible in a cross-sectional study. This is of course because the collection can be spread over many interviews. Moreover, information may be obtained at the most appropriate time, for example, information on job entry may be obtained when it occurs even if this varies from one member of the sample to another.

5. Starting with a birth cohort removes later problems of sampling and allows the extensive use of subsamples. It also eases problems of estimating bias and reliability.

6. Longitudinal studies are free of one of the major obstacles to causal analysis, namely, the re-interpretation of remembered information so that it conforms with conventional views on causation. It also provides the means to assess the direction of effect.

Source: adapted from Douglas.[7]

method as a highly unsatisfactory way of obtaining developmental data except for the crudest purposes.

Douglas,[7] who pioneered the first national cohort study to be undertaken in any country, makes a spirited defence of the method against the common criticisms that are levelled against it — that it is expensive and time-consuming. We summarise his account of the advantages of cohort analysis over cross-sectional designs in Box 3.2.

Strategies in Developmental Research

Having identified some strengths and weaknesses in cohort and cross-sectional analyses, we now look at actual decisions made by researchers in planning their studies in light of the phenomena with which they have to deal and the support upon which they can draw. In this section, we examine a number of developmental studies in education to see the constraints under which they have been conducted, the techniques that have been employed, and the retrospective views of the researchers themselves about their design decisions.

Examples of Developmental Research

Example 1: A Large-scale Cohort Study: Douglas[7] — the 1946 National Cohort Study

For more than a quarter of a century, Douglas was concerned with a longitudinal study for the Medical Research Council involving over 5,000 children born in the year 1946. Among the numerous books and research reports[9] that have arisen out of the study of this cohort, *The Home and the School* (1964) is perhaps the most widely known by educationalists.

At its inception in 1946, Douglas's study had the support of the Royal Commission on Population and the financial backing of the Nuffield Foundation and the National Birthday Trust Fund. The research followed a national cohort of children from birth, through adolescence and into adulthood. At each stage, the study involved a lengthy questionnaire enquiry beginning in 1946 with detailed descriptions of maternity care and child-rearing practices, and extended as the children grew older with information on physical, intellectual and social characteristics gathered from school records and teachers' assessments. In 1961 when the sample reached statutory school-leaving age, 62 per cent who left for employment were followed up by youth employment officers, contact with those remaining at school being maintained through headteachers and their staffs. In 1972, approximately 100 professional interviewers were recruited to make contact with the total sample in one-and-a-quarter-hour interviews, and to obtain data on family and household affairs, employment histories, religious beliefs and membership of clubs and other organisations.

Over the 26 years of the study, contact was maintained with between 80 per cent and 90 per cent of the original sample and a mass of data were accumulated from earliest infant experiences to adult employment and family affairs. Complete longitudinal data exist for 70 per cent of the sample with an additional 10 per cent of information on respondents marred only by occasional loss of contact. Detailed accounts of the main survey findings and of subsidiary investigations are reported in Douglas.[9] For present purposes, Douglas[7] discusses a number of problems in the design and execution of the 1946 National Cohort Study which we now relate to our previous account of the strengths and weaknesses of cohort analysis.

Sampling Decisions. Douglas's decision to select a single week's births in Great Britain (some 15,000 in number) in the week beginning 3 March 1946 was governed primarily by questions of finance and the availability of coding help. Spreading the sample throughout the year by selecting six separate days would have made it more representative but would have proved more costly than funds permitted. Because the only source of coders of questionnaire data were students available only in the summer vacation, Douglas 'worked backwards' from the early summer, and allowing time for the administration of interviews and the initial processing of questionnaire data, arrived at the most propitious week, 3–9 March.

In 1947, financial constraints led to the decision to cut the original 15,000 sample to approximately 5,000. The interests of the research team in *equality of opportunity* led to the retention of the total number of children in the non-manual working-class group and the group designated agricultural workers. All in all, some 5,362 children constituted the cohort in 1947 of whom approximately half had parents who were non-manual workers. Retrospectively, Douglas[7] says of his original sampling decisions:

> If I were to repeat the 1946 study I would take a six-day sample spread throughout the year. For the whole sample I would get minimal birth information and for the follow-up would divide each day's births into two random groups. One would be used largely as a control, the other would be followed up in detail. This would give a main sample of about 7,000 and an equal number of controls. The controls would show up any biases introduced by the exposure of the main longitudinal sample to repeated interviews, examinations, and tests. They could also provide additional information, at widely spaced intervals, on major and checkable events such as accidents, hospital admissions and school achievement. By spreading the sample over the year the dangers of seasonal bias would be avoided. Moreover, the load of examinations and interviewing would be spread evenly and this would make it reasonable to ask for yearly contacts.

In addition to financial constraints then, the specific interests of the research team and the seasonal availability of assistance governed the sampling decisions taken by Douglas and his associates.

Sampling Mortality. The very low sample mortality reported by Douglas stemmed in part from the fact that in a national cohort study internal migration is more a problem of contact than of outright losses and renewed contact was made easier because the intervals between interviews was never more than two years.[7] Comparisons of the characteristics of those who were lost with those of the remaining sample revealed that the resulting bias was not large enough to cause concern.

Control Effects. Douglas's check for bias introduced as a result of control effects involved taking one quarter of the manual working-class children in the 1946 sample (that is, some 5,000 of those in the original 15,000 sample) and using them as a control group. Eleven years later, using data collected from interviews and from school medical records, Douglas found no evidence of bias apart from a greater incidence of treatment for minor speech and eye defects in the longitudinal sample.

Interviewers — Professional or Amateur? The dangers arising out of the use of health visitors, nurses, employment officers and school teachers rather than trained professional interviewers as data collectors are discussed at length by Douglas. On balance, he concluded that the lack of medical, industrial and educational knowledge in the trained group outweighed any advantages that might have accrued as a result of their professional interviewing skills.

In conclusion, the National Cohort Study of Douglas and his associates serves as an excellent example of what can be achieved by the long-term cohort analysis, based upon a large representative sample and backed by adequate funding agencies. Those aspects of the study that are of particular interest to educationalists are to do with the wastage of ability among working-class children during their primary and secondary schooling. The cohort design enabled Douglas to establish causal relationships between variables. Thus, he was able to show the extent to which adverse effects of local educational provision were cumulative as his sample of children grew older. Other analyses were able to relate early illnesses and adverse home conditions to indices of health and behaviour in early adulthood. By using a large sampling frame, Douglas was able to introduce controls when examining relationships between independent and dependent variables (see Chapter 8 for the meaning of dependent and independent variables). Thus, geographical variation in the provision of selective school places, he found, accounted for approximately half of the social inequalities in secondary education after controlling for ability. Douglas makes a strong case for the retention of cohort studies:

> My contention is that cohort studies provide the most efficient and also the cheapest opportunities to assess the effectiveness of new services and new policies ... If we need to know what benefits accrue, for example, from spending £X million on pre-school education and which sections of the population are receiving the greatest benefits from this provision, comparisons between cohorts will provide the best answers.

Example 2: A Small-scale Cohort Study: Cox[10] — *Culturally Disadvantaged Children*

As part of the Schools Council Research and Development Project in Compensatory Education (1967–72) an intensive study of a subsample of children in infant schools in 'deprived areas' was undertaken with the major aim of examining the effects of material and cultural disadvantage in the home on the development and adjustment of children in school.

Fifty-two children from 'disadvantaged' homes (as judged by a structured parental interview in the home) were matched* by age, sex, non-verbal I.Q. and school with a control group consisting of fifty-two children from more advantaged backgrounds, both groups, incidentally, drawn from predominantly working-class backgrounds.

The Disadvantaged Group (DG) and the Control Group (CG) were tested on a wide range of linguistic, achievement, and personality measures and were rated by their teachers on their adjustment to school on three separate occasions: at 7 years of age, at 11+, and at 15+ years. Box 3.3 shows the small attrition in numbers in the DG and CG groups during the eight years of the study.

Cox found that the two groups of children were most sharply differentiated in favour of the Control Group (i.e. those from 'advantaged homes') on measures of scholastic attainment and, to a lesser degree, on measures of oral language skills, self-concepts of ability and attitudes towards school. On the basis of parents' and teachers' judgements, disadvantaged children were less well-adjusted to school both socially and emotionally. Moreover, there was a widening gap between the two groups in the period between 11 and 15 years of age as the graphs of performance and personal adjustment in Box 3.4 reveal.

Cox sees the size of the sample as one of the main strengths of his study. It was small enough to allow an intensive study of the children and their homes but large enough to sustain the use of a variety of statistical techniques including multivariate analysis of variance. Because the prime purpose of the study was to highlight the influence of disadvantageous home factors upon children's progress and adjustment in their schooling, Cox adopted a simple research design based upon contrasted groups rather than one involving a large sample representing a wider cross-section of the social class spectrum for which correlational analysis would have

*35 per cent of the sample, that is to say 16 pairs of children, were 'matched' at all three stages of the cohort study — at input, junior and secondary schools. A further 46 per cent, i.e. 21 pairs of children, were matched over two stages of schooling (infant and junior or secondary, or junior and secondary). In all 80 per cent of the children in the sample were matched for school in at least two of the three stages of their schooling.

Box 3.3: Attrition in Sample over the 8-year Period of the Study

Age	DG (n)	CG (n)
7+	52	52
11+	47	50
15+	48	46

been appropriate. One particularly interesting question that Cox's study threw up concerned those children from disadvantaged homes who apparently flourished educationally and conversely, those from more supportive homes who did poorly in school. Case-studies, he suggests, might be the more appropriate methodology for teasing out the complex interactions between home, school and other environmental variables on the one hand and 'within-child' factors such as cognition, motivation and temperament.

Example 3: A Cross-sectional Study: Jelinek and Brittan[11] Multiracial Education

One of the first large-scale attempts to explore pupils' attitudes towards multiracial education is chosen as an example of cross-sectional research. A national sample of boys and girls in multiracial schools in England answered questions about their actual and their desired friendship choices and completed a 20-item questionnaire about their attitudes towards (a) the atmosphere of the multiracial school; (b) their school work; and (c) the school in general.

Inter-ethnic Friendship Patterns. Three questions to do with friendships in a sample consisting of 677 eight year olds, 611 ten year olds, 1,507 twelve year olds, and 1,505 fourteen year olds, who were further differentiated by sex and by ethnic group (British, Indian, Pakistani, West Indian, Kenyan, Asian, Cypriot, Italian, Others).

The Criswell Index of Self-preference was used to obtain indices of in-group and out-group friendship choices. Basically, the Criswell Index is a ratio of two ratios, one giving the relative strengths of observed in-group and out-group choices, the other giving the relative strengths which could be expected on the basis of chance alone. In the present study, out-group was defined as all other

Box 3.4: Attainment and Adjustment in Disadvantaged and Control Group Children at Ages 11+ and 15+ Years

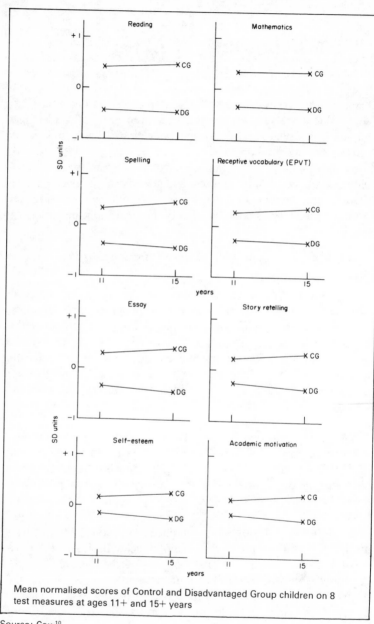

Mean normalised scores of Control and Disadvantaged Group children on 8 test measures at ages 11+ and 15+ years

Source: Cox.[10]

ethnic groups in the particular school other than that of the chooser. The Criswell Index allows for variability in the size of the groups and variability in the number of friendship choices that are made.

Where the Criswell Index is equal to 1.0 it indicates that a completely balanced pattern of choice between in-group and out-group choices has been made. Values *less than 1.0* indicate a tendency towards *out-group* friendship choices; and values *greater than 1.0* indicate a tendency towards *in-group* friendship choices. Boxes 3.5 and 3.6 show the Criswell Indices for each of the age-based samples in respect of *actual* and *desired* friendship choices.

The most striking feature of the data in Boxes 3.5 and 3.6 is the high incidence of own-group preferences and the noticeable increase in own-group preferences that occurs in the older age groups. One important finding of the study is the relatively early age (8+) at which ethnicity features in friendship choices in the context of British schools. Another is the greater incidence of balanced indices in respect of desired friendship choices (Box 3.6) as compared with actual friendship choices (Box 3.5) implying that barriers exist to inter-ethnic friendships.

These data raise tantalising questions, the answers to which are beyond the scope of a cross-sectional enquiry. Why, for example, are there such striking differences in the sizes of the indices between schools with roughly the same ethnic mixes? And to what extent does the Criswell Index's lumping together of all other ethnic groups from that of the chooser disguise complex differences which might reveal a very different state of affairs from that shown in Boxes 3.5 and 3.6?

Pupil's Attitudes. A glance at the analysis of pupils' attitudes shown in Box 3.7 reveals the strengths and the weaknesses of the cross-sectional design. In this part of the study, the researchers were able to contact a large sample of children (n = 3,551), gather attitudinal data which were then subdivided by age and ethnic origin, and compute mean scores for each subsample. Analysis of variance and t-tests were then used to test for significance. With such large numbers in the various subsamples, very small mean score differences reach statistical significance. Thus:[10]

Relative to the others, Asian pupils held favourable attitudes to the multiracial school but were also much more concerned

Box 3.5: In-group, Out-group Actual Friendship Choices by Age and Ethnic Group

Junior School No.	Age 8+ (N = 677)								Age 10+ (N = 611)							
	B	I	P	K	AS	WI	C	IT	B	I	P	K	AS	WI	C	IT
1	1		7		10	6			3	2			4	2		
2	2	.7	3		3	3			2	2	4		2	4		
4	3	.2	0		2	2			.7	1		4	2	7		
5	2	2			2	5			2	3			4	1		
6	2	4	0		3	2			3	1	5	10	3	6		
7	2					1			2					1		
8	2					8	1		2					.3	2	
10	1					2	3		2					1	2	
11	3	13			13				11							
13	3	3			3	.6		6	3	3		4	3	2		3

Secondary School No.	Age 12+ (N = 1507)								Age 14+ (N = 1505)							
	B	I	P	K	AS	WI	C	IT	B	I	P	K	AS	WI	C	IT
14 (1)	2	6	12	42	10	7			4	3	7		7	6		
15 (2)	5	4		13	6	6			5	6	4	1	12	6		
16 (4)	4	5	4	3	2	31			9	4	0	4	8	13		
17 (4)	8	2	10	4	4	9			13	.6	4	3	2	15		
18 (6)	3	4	3		6	6			2	23	39	4	31	4		
19 (7)	2				5	3			2				3	7		
20 (8)	4				3	7	8		4				7	9	4	
21 (10)	2				.9	4	4		3				3	6	4	
22 (11)	5	14		5	15				4	12		7	13			
23 (11)	2	5		3	4				7	6		3	5			
24 (13)	4	17			16			8	3	17			9	7		4
25 (13)	4	9		3	16	20		10	2	17		33	27	3		20

Note:
1. The numbers in brackets refer to the junior school situated in the same locality as each secondary school: 3 infant schools are excluded from the list as having no pupils in the age-group involved in this aspect of the study.
2. The indices for 'Asians' are derived from the combined data of Indian, Pakistani and Kenyan Asian pupils.
3. Key to Ethnic Groups:
   B — British   I — Indian   P — Pakistani   K — Kenyan Asian
   AS — Asian   WI — West Indian   C — Cypriot   IT — Italian

Source: from Jelinek and Brittan.[11]

Box 3.6: In-group, Out-Group Desired Friendship Choices by Age and Ethnic Group

Junior School No.	Age 8+ (N = 677)								Age 10+ (N = 611)							
	B	I	P	K	AS	WI	C	IT	B	I	P	K	AS	WI	C	IT
1	.5		1		1	2			3		.2		.1	2		
2	1	2			1	4			2	2	4		2	2		
4	1	.9	3		9	2			.7	.9		3	2	3		
5	2	0			.2	2			2	1			1	1		
6	3	2			2	1			3	1	1	0	2	3		
7	2					1			.9					2		
8	2				2	.6			1					3	1	
10	1				.6	2			2					2	1	
11	5	2			2				8							
13	2	.7			.7	1		2	3	.9			2	.8	.9	2

Secondary School No.	Age 12+ (N = 1507)								Age 14+ (N = 1505)							
	B	I	P	K	AS	WI	C	IT	B	I	P	K	AS	WI	C	IT
14 (1)	2	0	5	19	4	5			7	0	9		7	1		
15 (2)	4	5			3	4			3	4	2	3	7	5		
16 (4)	3	1	4	2	3	8			10	6		3	4	8		
17 (4)	4	1	3	4	3	9			8	5		2	3	35		
18 (6)	2	5	2	4	3	3			1	45	36		35	6		
19 (7)	2				4	2			1				0	2		
20 (8)	2				4	4	2		2				3	14	5	
21 (10)	1				0	2	2		1				0	4	4	
22 (11)	7	2		.8	1				5	5			4	8		
23 (11)	4	4			2				12	3			3	5		
24 (13)	3	4			4			6	4	14			12	4	2	
25 (13)	2	0		13	4	7		2	2	3			4	4	8	7

Note:
1. The numbers in brackets refer to the junior school situated in the same locality as each secondary school: 3 infant schools are excluded from the list as having no pupils in the age-group involved in this aspect of the study.
2. The indices for 'Asians' are derived from the combined data of Indian, Pakistani and Kenyan Asian pupils.
3. Key to Ethnic Groups:
   B — British   I — Indian   P — Pakistani   K — Kenyan Asian
   AS — Asian   WI — West Indian   C — Cypriot   IT — Italian

Source: from Jelinek and Brittan.[11]

Box 3.7: Mean Scores on Each Attitude Scale by Age and by Ethnic Group

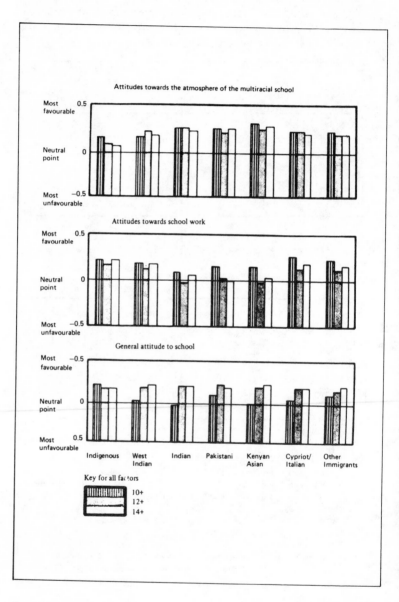

Source: from Jelinek and Brittan.[11]

about their work ... The European pupils, like the indigenous pupils, were generally less anxious than those from other ethnic backgrounds. West Indian pupils held distinctly different views (from other groups) about the multiracial school. Their attitude was less favourable than others at 10+, most favourable at 12+, and average at 14+.

Par excellence, the cross-sectional design is able to show the pattern of differences that exist between the various age/ethnic subsamples. The problem arises when an interpretation of the differences is attempted. The researchers are justly cautious:

The attitude of pupils from minority ethnic groups toward school was less favourable in the lowest age group but was found to have improved among older children. On the other hand, this might reflect how they became gradually used to the existing norms as they came to know the whole system better, or they acquired a better knowledge of English and perhaps some English friends.

In an ideal solution, the cohorts of pupils would be followed throughout their school career to allow for thorough observation of the development of their attitudes within the school situation. This was however a cross-sectional study ... so any conclusions about trends in the development of the pupils' attitudes to school can only be assumptions ... The observed differences could have originated in three different ways: from differences between cohorts, from different perceptions of the core items, or from the influence of items added for the two older groups. A more precise explanation can only be supplied by further studies.[11]

Example 4: A Cohort/Cross-sectional Design: the Newsons' Child Development Research Unit Study[12]

The long-term research into child upbringing undertaken by the Newsons at the Child Development Research Unit at Nottingham University is of major importance as a developmental study and, for our purposes, a useful illustration of a combination of cohort and cross-sectional designs.

Each publication[12] that has arisen out of this ongoing investigation has an immediate appeal in the way that the researchers have captured the richness and variety of life in contemporary urban society. At one, four and seven years of age (and more studies are promised) the reader is presented with descriptive accounts of the social and material contexts of the lives of some 700 Nottingham children. The Newsons' objective is to obtain detailed pictures of these children at successive stages of their development from baby-hood, through adolescence and into adulthood — pictures, they say, built up from the children's behaviour in the natural habitats of the homes, backyards and neighbourhoods that constitute the 'Kaleidoscope of their everyday environment'. Our particular interest is in the design decisions governing the research itself and with the constraints under which those decisions were taken.

At the beginning of the study the sample target aimed at by the Newsons was 700 completed interviews with mothers about a variety of infant-rearing practices. To obtain 700 completed schedules, 773 interviews were attempted altogether.

At the initial and subsequent stages in the ongoing study the researchers worked with a class-stratified randon sample. To begin with, a fully random sample was drawn from the birth records of the City of Nottingham Health Department. Because the study is primarily concerned with normal children in ordinary family situa-tions, illegitimate children and those known to have gross disabi-lities were excluded from the outset. So too were children not in the care of their mothers and children whose parents were recent immigrants to Britain. This allowed the Newsons to establish the social class composition of the sample. In this way, 500 completed interviews were obtained. At the second stage of the initial survey, the researchers began by drawing random samples which were then interviewed by health visitors who forwarded details of the social class composition of these groups to the investigators. With this information, the researchers were able to adjust their sample numbers to increase the overall representation of groups that were not numerically well-represented by simple random sampling procedures. Stage two, then, involved stratified random sampling on the basis of social class data. This sampling practice has been carried out at each successive stage, the strategy being to include at least 100 cases in each of the numerically smaller social class groups. In Box 3.8, which shows the sample interviewed at the seven-year-old stage of the study, the numbers in brackets identify the expected composition of the groups had simple random

Box 3.8: Class Composition of Interviewed Sample Compared with (bracketed) Expected Composition of Unstratified Sample

	social class						summary		
	I&II	*IIIwc*	*III man*	*IV*	*V*		*I&II, IIIwc*	*IIIman, IV, V*	*Total*
	N	N	N	N	N		N	N	N
boys	69	58	105	81	57		127	243	370
	(49)	(45)	(175)	(52)	(27)		(94)	(254)	(348)
girls	65	49	99	75	39		114	213	327
	(49)	(45)	(175)	(52)	(27)		(94)	(254)	(348)
both	134	107	204	156	96		241	456	697
	(98)	(90)	(350)	(104)	(54)		(188)	(508)	(696)
	14%	13%	50%	15%	8%		27%	73%	100%

Source: from J. and E. Newson.[12]

sampling rather than stratified random sampling been adopted. It will be seen that the total group for Social Class V just fails to meet the 100-cases criterion that the Newsons aimed for.

Losses from the Study. Out of 708 children whose mothers were interviewed when their children were one year old, 274 matched follow-up cases were made at the four-year-old stage, making possible cohort-type analyses of the sort undertaken by Douglas and his associates in the previously reported study. There were 426 new cases whose mothers were seen for the first time when their children were four years old. Box 3.9 (from a personal communication, Dr J. Newson, 9 March 1979) shows losses and additions at each stage of the study to date (1979).

Cohort analyses are being undertaken in respect of a variety of longitudinal data. With successive losses from the original cohort at each stage of the enquiry and the 'topping up' of the sample to around 700, it seems that the cross-sectional nature of the data must take on increasing importance, restricting the ability of the researchers to speculate about causal relationships.

The retrospective account of the early years of this research study stands in stark contrast to that of Douglas.[9] 'How do you get a good idea off the ground if you have no money, no resources, no academic patron, and no one has ever heard of you?' The Newsons go on to say how — and leave the reader full of admiration for their tenacity, single-mindedness and diligence. Without

Box 3.9: Losses and Additions at Each Stage of the Study from 1 Year Through to 16 Years of Age

the resources of the national cohort-type study, they opted for a sophisticated use of the interview as a research tool, a decision which they freely admit was influenced by factors of practical expediency rather than an original commitment to the interview as a research instrument. None the less, their detailed account of the use of the interview technique bears close reading. In contrast to Douglas's faith in the interview data collected by his health visitor teams, it was the disparity which the Newsons found between their own focused interviews and those conducted by health visitors which led them to develop the tape-recorded interview as a research instrument.[8]

Example 5: A Trend or Prediction Study — Department of Education and Science, A Study of School Buildings[13]

As an example of a trend or prediction study, we present an outline of the work involved in estimating the overall number of school children in 1986 who will need to be catered for in school buildings, and the consequent scale of work involved in 'basic need' and 'improvement' building programmes. The phase of the Department of Education and Science study that we describe only partly follows the lines of the trend study set out in Box 3.1 in so far as its primary concern is with predicting future demands.

Box 3.10: Previous and Projected Figures of Pupil Numbers in England and Wales

Pupils of Primary age (5 and over) in maintained primary and secondary schools in England and Wales: 1965 to 1976 and projections to 1996

(1) 1975 projection
(2) 1976 projection
(3) "Continuing low" variant of 1975 projection

Pupils of Secondary age in maintained primary and secondary schools in England and Wales 1965 to 1976 and projections to 1996

(1) 1975 projection
(2) 1976 projection
(3) "Continuing low" variant of 1975 projection

Source: HMSO.[13]

First, past and projected numbers of births are used to arrive at a projection of the overall school population in 1986. (In practice, a series of projections is made based upon different assumptions about birth trends. The graphs in Box 3.10 show three such projections.) This overall population is then differentiated by regions of England and Wales. Estimates are then made of the number of pupils who will be in school places provided between now (1976) and 1986 under basic need building programmes. Finally, the number of pupils who will need to be catered for in 1986 in the then existing buildings is arrived at: 3,069,000 primary and 2,871,000 secondary school pupils.

Box 3.10 shows the run of previous figures and projected figures of the number of pupils of primary and secondary age in maintained schools in England and Wales up to the year 1996. The graphs for primary and secondary projections are similar in shape, though differently sequenced chronologically, each showing an upturn towards the 1990s. The upturns are based on a number of assumptions:

> one of the reasons for the low numbers of births in the last few years is that many women have postponed, rather than abandoned, starting or adding to their families. The annual number of births is therefore projected to recover quite soon as these women 'catch up'.
>
> The projection also incorporates the assumption that the average completed family size in the medium-term future will be about 2.1 children.

What these projections mean in the actual scale of the decline in school numbers between the years 1976 and 1986 is shown in Box 3.11.

Box 3.11 shows a 28 per cent decline in the primary school population by the year 1986, the corresponding decline in the secondary school age being some 9 per cent. The researchers then go on to estimate the percentage declines in the various regions of England and Wales. These data are shown in Box 3.12. Estimates are then made of the number of places that will be made available through the basic need building programme between 1976 and 1986. Finally, projected needs and estimated availability are brought together to arrive at 'hard' data on which policy decisions can be made for regional planning and expenditure forecasting.

Box 3.11: The Decline in the Numbers of Pupils Aged 5 and Over in Maintained Primary and Secondary Schools, 1976 to 1986: England and Wales

	School population ('000)		Projected decline 1976 to 1986	
	1976	1986 (projected)	Thousands	As a percentage of the 1976 population
Pupils of primary age	4,763	3,429	1,334	28.0%
Pupils of secondary age	3,900	3,545	335	9.1%

Source: HMSO.[13]

Problems in Trend or Prediction Studies. We referred earlier to the intrusion of unpredictable factors in trend analyses that make long-term forecasting hazardous. In the present study the researchers identify a number of uncertainties in connection with their predictions.

First, projections of the number of pupils aged under five in 1986 are subject to uncertainty, the number depending upon the number of three and four year olds in the population, the amount of available space, the various admission policies for this age group and the amount of money available. Projections about this age group are therefore excluded from the calculations. As a matter of interest, there were 380,000 under-fives in schools in 1976 and 32,000 in nursery classes. Clearly, these groups must figure in long-term estimates of school building needs. Second, the definition of basic need school building is somewhat ambiguous. Conventionally, say the researchers, school building in a given year comprises basic need building plus improvement building. The basic need part covers places that are built to cater for local increases in the school population. In the past, the demand for basic need building has been thought of as comprising two elements — an overall growth in the school population, and an allowance for pupils shifting from one area of the country to another. In times of growth in pupil numbers the shift allowance hardly figures in estimates when compared with the overall growth aspect. With the decline in school population, the basic need school building becomes simply an estimate of the shift element, a factor that is open to a variety of unknown influences over the projected period

Box 3.12: Projected Percentage Declines in the Number of Pupils in Maintained Primary and Secondary Schools, 1976 to 1986: England and Wales

Area	Pupils of primary age	Pupils of secondary age
Non-Metropolitan Counties	%	%
North	30	15
Yorkshire & Humberside	26	9
North West	24	6
East Midlands	23	6
West Midlands	21	4
East Anglia	18	4
South East	28	5
South West	25	9
Metropolian Counties		
North	37	22
Yorkshire & Humberside	28	12
North West	33	15
West Midlands	27	5
Greater London	34	14
Wales	27	9
England and Wales	28	9

Source: HMSO.[13]

of the study.

Third, the estimate of basic need building between 1976 and 1986 is based upon projects actually started, on local authority bids for work from 1976 onwards, and on expectations that the shift-based demand during the 1980s will fall faster than the school population, it being assumed that migration will be proportional to the school population but that more empty places will be available to accommodate the migrants.[13]

It can be seen how difficult the task of the school building planner is in having to work not only with uncertainties but with imprecise criteria in respect of the very trends that he is trying to predict.

References

1. Best, J.W., *Research in Education* (Prentice-Hall, Englewood Cliffs, New Jersey, 1970).
2. Good, C.V., *Introduction to Educational Research* (Appleton-Century-Crofts, New York, 1963).
3. Davie, R., 'The longitudinal approach', *Trends in Education*, 28 (1972) 8–13.
4. Bailey, K.D., *Methods of Social Research* (Collier-Macmillan, London, 1978).

5. Riley, M.W., *Sociological Research I: A Case Approach* (Harcourt, Brace and World, New York, 1963).

6. Travers, R.M.W., *An Introduction to Educational Research* (Collier-Macmillan, London, 1969).

7. Douglas, J.W.B., 'The use and abuse of national cohorts', in M.D. Shipman, *The Organization and Impact of Social Research* (Routledge and Kegan Paul, London, 1976).
   For the most recent account of the National Child Development Study of a cohort of 15,000 children (now adults), see Fogelman, K. (ed.), *Growing Up in Great Britain: Papers from the National Child Development Study*, Macmillan, London, 1983).

8. The discussion draws upon several papers in Shipman, M.D. (ed.), *The Organization and Impact of Social Research* (Routledge and Kegan Paul, London, 1976).

9. See also: Douglas, J.W.B. and Blomfield, J.M., *Maternity in Great Britain* (Oxford University Press, London, 1948); Douglas, J.W.B. and Blomfield, J.M., *Children Under Five* (Allen and Unwin, London, 1958); Douglas, J.W.B., Ross, J.M. and Simpson, H.R., *All Our Future* (P. Davies, London, 1968).

10. Cox, T., 'Children's adjustment to school over six years, *Journal of Child Psychology and Psychiatry*, 19 (1978) 363–72.
    Cox, T., 'A follow-up study of reading attainment in a sample of eleven year old disadvantaged children', *Educational Studies*, 5, 1 (1979) 53–60.
    Cox, T., 'Disadvantaged fifteen year olds: initial findings from a longitudinal study'. *Eductional Studies*, 8, 1 (1982) 1–13.

11. Jelinek, M.M. and Brittan, E.M., 'Multiracial education 1. Inter-ethnic friendship patterns', *Educational Research*, 18, 1 (1975) 44–53;
    Jelinek, M.M., 'Multiracial education 3. Pupils' attitudes to the multiracial school', *Educational Research*, 19, 2 (1977) 129–41.

12. J. and E. Newson, *Infant Care in an Urban Community* (Allen and Unwin, London, 1963); *Four Years Old in an Urban Community* (Allen and Unwin, London, 1968); *Seven Years Old in an Urban Community* (Allen and Unwin, London, 1976); *Perspectives on School at Seven Years Old* (Allen and Unwin, London, 1977).

13. Annex 1: Department of Education and Science, *A Study of School Buildings* (London, HMSO, 1977).

4 SURVEYS

Introduction

In this chapter we discuss what is perhaps the most commonly used descriptive method in educational research — *the survey*. Typically, surveys gather data at a particular point in time with the intention of (a) describing the nature of existing conditions, or (b) identifying standards against which existing conditions can be compared, or (c) determining the relationships that exist between specific events. Thus, surveys may vary in their levels of complexity from those which provide simple frequency counts to those which present relational analysis.

Surveys may be further differentiated in terms of their scope. A study of contemporary developments in post-secondary education, for example, might encompass the whole of Western Europe; a study of subject choice, on the other hand, might be confined to one secondary school. The complexity and scope of surveys in education can be illustrated by reference to familiar examples. The surveys undertaken for the Plowden Committee on primary school children[1] collected a wealth of information on children, teachers and parents and used sophisticated analytical techniques to predict pupil attainment. By contrast, the small-scale survey of Jackson and Marsden[2] involved a detailed study of the backgrounds and values of 88 working-class adults who had achieved success through selective secondary education.

Whether the survey is large-scale and undertaken by some governmental bureau or small-scale and carried out by the lone researcher, the collection of information typically involves one or more of the following data-gathering techniques: structured or semi-structured interviews, self-completion or postal questionnaires, standardised tests of attainment or performance, and attitude scales. Typically, too, surveys proceed through well-defined stages, though not every stage that we outline in Box 4.1 is required for the successful completion of a survey.

We begin with a consideration of some necessary preliminaries to survey planning before going on to outline a variety of sampling strategies that are used in survey research. We then discuss the

Box 4.1: Stages in the Planning of a Survey

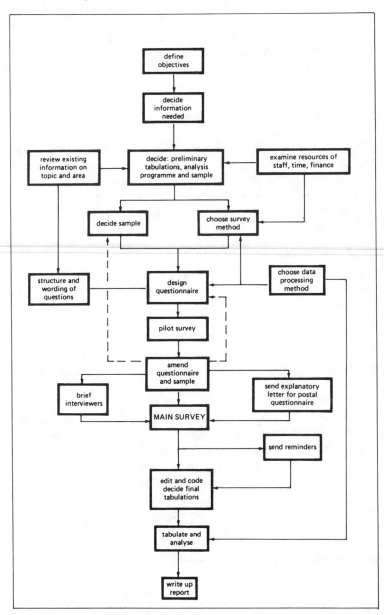

Source: adapted from Davidson.[4]

construction and sequencing of questions in both interviews and questionnaires prior to a detailed examination of the postal questionnaire as a survey technique. Finally, we identify some of the procedures involved in processing and analysing the results of survey research. Our discussion follows the sequential stages in survey design set out in Box 4.1.

Some Preliminary Considerations

Three prerequisites to the design of any survey are the specification of (1) the exact purpose of the enquiry; (2) the population on which it is to focus; and (3) the resources that are available. Hoinville and Jowell's[3] consideration of each of these key factors in survey planning can be illustrated in relation to the design of an educational enquiry.

The Purpose of the Enquiry

First, a survey's general purpose must be translated into a specific central aim. Thus, 'to explore teachers' views about in-service work' is somewhat nebulous, whereas 'to obtain a detailed description of primary and secondary teachers' priorities in the provision of in-service education courses' is reasonably specific. Having decided upon and specified the primary objective of the survey, the second phase of the planning involves the identification and itemising of subsidiary topics that relate to its central purpose. In our example, subsidiary issues might well include: (1) the types of courses required; (2) the content of courses; (3) the location of courses; (4) the timing of courses; (5) the design of courses; and (6) the financing of courses.

The third phase follows the identification and itemisation of subsidiary topics and involves formulating specific information requirements relating to each of these issues. For example, with respect to *the type of courses required*, detailed information would be needed about the *duration* of courses (one meeting, several meetings, a week, a month, a term or a year), the status of courses (non-award bearing, award bearing, with certificate, diploma, degree granted by college, polytechnic or university), the *orientation* of courses (theoretically oriented involving lectures, readings, etc., or practically oriented involving workshops and the production of curriculum materials).

As these details unfold, note Hoinville and Jowell, consideration would have to be given to the most appropriate ways of
collecting items of information (interviews with selected teachers,
postal questionnaires to selected schools, etc.).

The Population upon which the Survey is Focused

The second prerequisite to survey design, the specification of the
population to which the enquiry is addressed, affects decisions that
the researcher must make both about sampling and resources. In
our hypothetical survey of in-service requirements, for example,
we might specify the population as 'those primary and secondary
teachers employed in schools within a thirty-mile radius of Loughborough University of Technology'. In this case, the population is
readily identifiable and, given sufficient resources to contact every
member of the designated group, sampling decisions do not arise.
Things are rarely so straightforward, however. Often the criteria by
which populations are specified ('severely handicapped', 'under-
achievers', 'intending teachers' or 'highly anxious') are difficult to
operationalise. Populations, moreover, vary considerably in their
accessibility; pupils and student teachers are relatively easy to
survey, gypsy children and headteachers are more elusive. More
importantly, in a large survey the researcher usually draws a
sample from the population to be studied; rarely does he attempt
to contact every member. We deal with the question of sampling
shortly.

The Resources Available

The third important factor in designing and planning a survey is
the financial cost. Sample surveys are labour-intensive,[4] the largest
single expenditure being the fieldwork where costs arise out of the
interviewing time, travel time and transport claims of the interviewers themselves. There are additional demands on the survey
budget. Training and supervising the panel of interviewers can
often be as expensive as the costs incurred during the time that
they actually spend in the field. Questionnaire construction, piloting, printing, posting, coding, together with card punching, card
correction, computer programming — all eat into financial
resources.

Proposals from intending education researchers seeking governmental or private funding are often weakest in the amount of time
and thought devoted to a detailed planning of the financial

implications of the projected enquiries. (In this chapter we confine ourselves from this point to a discussion of surveys based on *self-completion questionnaires*. A full account of the interview as a research technique is given in Chapter 13.)

Survey Sampling

Because questions to do with sampling arise directly from the second of our preliminary considerations, that is, defining the population upon which the survey is to focus, the researcher must take sampling decisions early in the overall planning of a survey (see Box 4.1). We have already seen that due to factors of expense, time and accessibility, it is not always possible or practical to obtain measures from a population. The researcher endeavours therefore to collect information from a smaller group or subset of the population in such a way that the knowledge gained is representative of the total population under study. This smaller group or subset is a *sample*. Notice how the competent researcher starts with the total population and works down to the sample. By contrast, the novice works from the bottom up, that is, he determines the minimum number of respondents needed to conduct a successful survey[5]. However, unless he identifies the total population in advance, it is virtually impossible for him to assess how representative the sample is that he has drawn. There are two methods of sampling. One yields *probability samples* in which, as the term implies, the probability of selection of each respondent is known. The other yields *non-probability samples* in which the probability of selection is unknown. We deal first with various methods of probability sampling[6].

Simple Random Sampling

In simple random sampling, each member of the population under study has an equal chance of being selected. The method involves selecting at random from a list of the population (a sampling frame) the required number of subjects for the sample. Because of probability and chance, the sample should contain subjects with characteristics similar to the population as a whole, i.e. some old, some young, some tall, some short, some fit, some unfit, some rich, some poor, etc. One problem associated with this particular sampling method is that a complete list of the population is needed and this is not always readily available.

Systematic Sampling

This method is a modified form of simple random sampling. It involves selecting subjects from a population list in a systematic rather than a random fashion. For example, if from a population of, say, 2,000, a sample of 100 is required, then every twentieth person can be selected. The starting point for the selection is chosen at random.

Stratified Sampling

Stratified sampling involves dividing the population into homogeneous groups, each group containing subjects with similar characteristics. For example, group A might contain males and group B, females. In order to obtain a sample representative of the whole population in terms of sex, a random selection of subjects from group A and group B must be taken. If needed, the exact proportion of males to females in the whole population can be reflected in the sample.

Cluster Sampling

When the population is large and widely dispersed, gathering a simple random sample poses administrative problems. Suppose we want to survey children's fitness levels in a particularly large community. It would be quite impractical randomly to select children and spend an inordinate amount of time travelling about in order to test them. By cluster sampling, we can randomly select a specific number of schools and test all the children in those selected schools.

Stage Sampling

Stage sampling is an extension of cluster sampling. It involves selecting the sample in stages, that is, taking samples from samples. Using the large community example referred to earlier, one type of stage sampling might be to select a number of schools at random, and from within each of these schools select a number of classes at random, and from within these classes select a number of pupils.

Small-scale surveys often resort to the use of non-probability samples because, despite the disadvantages that arise from their non-representativeness, they are far less complicated to set up, they are considerably less expensive, and can prove perfectly adequate where the researcher does not intend to generalise his findings beyond the sample in question or where he is simply piloting a survey questionnaire as a prelude to his main study. The chief kinds of non-probability sampling are as follows:

Convenience Sampling

Convenience sampling — or as it is sometimes called, accidental sampling — involves choosing the nearest individuals to serve as respondents and continuing that process until the required sample size has been obtained. Captive audiences such as pupils or student teachers often serve as respondents in surveys based upon convenience sampling.

Quota Sampling

Quota sampling has been described[5] as the non-probability equivalent of stratified sampling. It attempts to obtain representatives of the various elements of the total population in the proportions in which they occur there. Thus, a researcher interested in race relations in a particular community might set a quota for each ethnic group that is proportionate to its representation in the total population in the area under survey.

Purposive Sampling

In purposive sampling, the researcher handpicks the cases to be included in his sample on the basis of his judgement of their typicality. In this way, he builds up a sample that is satisfactory to his specific needs.

Dimensional Sampling

Dimensional sampling is simply a further refinement of quota sampling. It involves identifying various factors of interest in a population and obtaining at least one respondent for every combination of those factors. Thus, in the study of race relations to which we referred earlier, within each ethnic group the researcher may wish to distinguish between the attitudes of recent immigrants, those who have been in the country for some period of time, and those members of the ethnic group who were born in Great Britain. His sampling plan might take the form of a multidimensional table with *ethnic group* across the top and *length of stay* down the side.

Snowball Sampling

In snowball sampling, the researcher identifies a small number of individuals who have the characteristics that he requires. These people are then used as informants to identify others who qualify for inclusion and these, in turn, identify yet others — hence the term snowball sampling.

Sample Size: an Overview

A question that often plagues the novice researcher is just how large his sample should be in order to conduct an adequate survey. There is, of course, no clear-cut answer, for the correct sample size depends upon the purpose of the study and the nature of the population under scrutiny. However, it is possible to give some advice on this matter. Thus, a sample size of 30 is held by many to be the minimum number of cases if the researcher plans to use some form of statistical analysis on his data, though techniques are available for the analysis of samples below 30. Of more import to the researcher is the need to think out *in advance* of any data collection the sorts of relationships that he wishes to explore within subgroups of his eventual sample. The number of variables the researcher sets out to control in his analysis and the types of statistical tests he wishes to make must inform his decision about sample size prior to the actual research undertaking.

Sample Size: Some Statistical Considerations

As well as the requirement of a minimum number of cases in order to examine relationships within subgroups, the researcher must obtain the minimum sample size that will accurately represent the population under survey. Where simple random sampling is used, the sample size needed to reflect the population value of a particular variable depends both upon the size of the population and the amount of heterogeneity of the variable in the population.[5] Generally, for populations of equal heterogeneity, the larger the population, the larger the sample that must be drawn. For populations of equal size, the greater the heterogeneity on a particular variable, the larger the sample that is needed. To the extent that a sample fails to represent accurately the population under survey, there is *sampling error*.

Sampling Error[6]

If many samples are taken from the same population, it is unlikely that they will all have characteristics identical either with each other or with the population. In brief, there will be sampling error. Sampling error is not necessarily the result of mistakes made in sampling procedures. Rather, variations may occur due to the chance selection of different individuals. For example, if we take a large number of samples from the population and measure the mean value of each sample, then the sample means will not be identical. Some will be relatively high, some relatively low, and many will cluster around an average or mean value of the samples. Why should this occur? We can explain the phenomenon by reference to the *Central Limit Theorem* which is derived from the laws of probability. This states that if random, large samples of equal size are repeatedly drawn from any population, then the means of those samples will be approximately normally distributed. Moreover, the average or mean of the sample means will be approximately the same as the population mean. We show this diagrammatically in Box 4.2.

Box 4.2: Distribution of Sample Means Showing the Spread of a Selection of Sample Means Around the Population Mean

Source: Cohen and Holliday.[6]

By drawing a large number of samples of equal size from a population, we create a sampling distribution. We can calculate the error involved in such sampling. The standard deviation of the theoretical distribution of sample means is a measure of sampling error and is called the *standard error of the mean* (SE_M). Thus,

$$SE_M = \frac{SD_s}{N}$$

where SD_s = the standard deviation of the sample and
N = the number in the sample

Strictly speaking, the formula for the standard error of the mean is:

$$SE_M = \frac{SD_{pop}}{N}$$

where SD_{pop} = the standard deviation of the population

However, as we are usually unable to ascertain the SD of the total population, the standard deviation of the sample is used instead. The standard error of the mean provides the best estimate of the sampling error. Clearly, the sampling error depends upon the variability (i.e. the heterogeneity) in the population as measured by SD_{pop} as well as the sample size (N). The smaller the SD_{pop}, the smaller the sampling error; the larger the N, the smaller the sampling error. Where the SD_{pop} is very large, then N needs to be very large to counteract it. Where SD_{pop} is very small, then N, too, can be small and still give a reasonably small sampling error.

Designing the Self-completion Questionnaire

An ideal questionnaire possesses the same properties as a good law:

It is clear, unambiguous and uniformly workable. Its design must minimize potential errors from respondents ... and coders. And since people's participation in surveys is voluntary, a questionnaire has to help in engaging their interest, encouraging their co-operation, and eliciting answers as close as possible to the truth.[4]

With these qualities in mind, we turn to the problem of designing a self-completion questionnaire. Having identified subsidiary topics of interest in his survey and itemised specific information requirements relating to them, the researcher's task now involves the structure of the questionnaire itself.

At this preliminary stage of design, it can sometimes be helpful to use a flow chart technique to plan the sequencing of questions. In this way, the researcher is able to anticipate the type and range

Box 4.3: A Flow Chart Technique for Question Planning

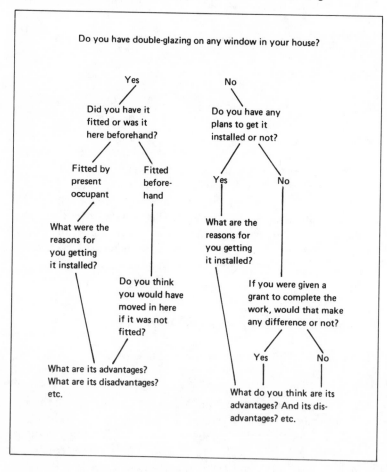

Source: Social and Community Planning Research.[7]

of responses that his questions are likely to elicit. In Box 4.3, we illustrate a flow chart employed in a commercial survey based upon an interview schedule, though the application of the method to a self-completion questionnaire is self-evident.

Using a flow chart in questionnaire design brings home to the researcher the paramount importance of the *question* in any form of survey work. Whole books have been written on the art of questioning. The brief space we are able to allot to this vital topic in no way reflects the priority that should be given to the framing and testing of questions before any survey is undertaken. We discuss various forms of questions (structured, unstructured and the funnel varieties) in Chapter 13 and illustrate some ways in which respondents may record their answers. For the present, we identify some pitfalls in question construction.

'Avoid' Questions

1. Avoid *leading* questions, that is, questions which are worded (or their response categories presented) in such a way as to suggest to respondents that there is only one acceptable answer. For example:

> Do you prefer abstract, academic-type courses, or down-to-earth, practical courses that have some pay-off in your day-to-day teaching?

2. Avoid *highbrow* questions even with sophisticated respondents. For example:

> What particular aspects of the current positivistic/interpretive debate would you like to see reflected in a course of developmental psychology aimed at a teacher audience?

Where the sample being surveyed is representative of the whole adult population, misunderstandings of what the researcher takes to be clear, unambiguous language are commonplace.

3. Avoid *complex* questions. For example:

> Would you prefer a short, non-award bearing course (3, 4 or 5 sessions) with part-day release (e.g. Wednesday afternoons) and one evening per week attendance with financial reimbursement

Box 4.4: A Guide for Questionnaire Construction

A. *Decisions about question content*
1. Is the question necessary? Just how will it be useful?
2. Are several questions needed on the subject matter of this question?
3. Do respondents have the information necessary to answer the question?
4. Does the question need to be more concrete, specific and closely related to the respondent's personal experience?
5. Is the question content sufficiently general and free from spurious concreteness and specificity?
6. Do the replies express general attitudes and only seem to be as specific as they sound?
7. Is the question content biased or loaded in one direction, without accompanying questions to balance the emphasis?
8. Will the respondents give the information that is asked for?

B. *Decisions about question wording*
1. Can the question be misunderstood? Does it contain difficult or unclear phraseology?
2. Does the question adequately express the alternative with respect to the point?
3. Is the question misleading because of unstated assumptions or unseen implications?
4. Is the wording biased? Is it emotionally loaded or slanted towards a particular kind of answer?
5. Is the question wording likely to be objectionable to the respondent in any way?
6. Would a more personalised wording of the question produce better results?
7. Can the question be better asked in a more direct or a more indirect form?

C. *Decisions about form of response to the question*
1. Can the question best be asked in a form calling for check answer (or short answer of a word or two, or a number), free answer or check answer with follow-up answer?
2. If a check answer is used, which is the best type for this question — dichotomous, multiple-choice ('cafeteria' question), or scale?
3. If a checklist is used, does it cover adequately all the significant alternatives without overlapping and in a defensible order? Is it of reasonable length? Is the wording of items impartial and balanced?
4. Is the form of response easy, definite, uniform and adequate for the purpose?

D. *Decisions about the place of the question in the sequence*
1. Is the answer to the question likely to be influenced by the content of preceding questions?
2. Is the question led up to in a natural way? Is it in correct psychological order?
3. Does the question come too early or too late from the point of view of arousing interest and receiving sufficient attention, avoiding resistance, and so on?

Source: from Selltiz, Wrightsman and Cook.[8]

for travel, or a longer, non-award bearing course (6, 7 or 8 sessions) with full-day release, or the whole course designed on part-day release without evening attendance?

4. Avoid *irritating* questions or instructions. For example:

Have you ever attended an in-service course of any kind during your entire teaching career?
   If you are over 40, and have never attended an in-service course, put one tick in the box marked *NEVER* and another in the box marked *OLD*.

5. Avoid questions that use negatives. For example:

How strongly do you feel that no teacher should enrol on the in-service, award-bearing course who has not completed at least two years full-time teaching?

6. Avoid *open-ended* questions on self-completion questionnaires. Because self-completion questionnaires cannot probe the respondent to find out just what he means by a particular response, the open-ended question is a less satisfactory way of eliciting information. (This caution does not hold in the interview situation, however.) Open-ended questions, moreover, are too demanding of most respondents' time. Nothing can be more off-putting that the following format:

Use pages 5, 6 and 7 respectively to respond to each of the questions about your attitudes to in-service courses in general and your beliefs about their value in the professional life of the serving teacher.

On a more positive note, Selltiz and her associates[8] have provided a fairly exhaustive guide to the researcher in constructing his questionnaire which we summarise in Box 4.4.

Postal Questionnaires

Frequently, the postal questionnaire is the best form of survey in carrying out an educational enquiry. Take, for example, the researcher. In Box 13.1 (p. 292), we summarise the relative merits new curriculum series in secondary schools in England and Wales. An interview survey based upon some sampling of the population of schools would be both expensive and time-consuming. A postal questionnaire, on the other hand, would have several distinct advantages. Moreover, given the usual constraints over finance and resources, it might well prove the only viable way of carrying through such an enquiry.

What evidence we have about the advantages and disadvantages of postal survey derives from settings other than educational. Many of the findings, however, have relevance to the educational researcher. In Box 13.1 (p. 292), we summarise the relative merits of self-completion questionnaires as compared with interview procedures. Here, we focus upon some of the ways in which the educational researcher can maximise the response level that he obtains when using a postal survey.

Research shows[3] that a number of myths about postal questionnaires are not borne out by the evidence. Response levels to postal surveys are not invariably less than those obtained by interview procedures; frequently they equal, and in some cases surpass, those achieved in interviews. Nor does the questionnaire necessarily have to be short in order to obtain a satisfactory response level. With sophisticated respondents, for example, a short questionnaire might appear to trivialise complex issues with which they are familiar. Hoinville and Jowell[3] identify a number of factors in securing a good response rate to a postal questionnaire:

1. The appearance of the questionnaire is vitally important. It must look easy and attractive. A compressed layout is uninviting; a larger questionnaire with plenty of space for questions and answers is more encouraging to respondents.
2. Clarity of wording and simplicity of design are essential. Clear instructions should guide the respondent — 'Put a tick', for example, invites participation, whereas complicated instructions and complex procedures intimidate respondents.
3. Arrange the contents of the questionnaire in such a way as to maximise co-operation. For example, include questions that are likely to be of general interest. Make sure that questions which appear early in the format do not suggest to respondents that the enquiry is not intended for them. Intersperse attitude questions throughout the schedule to allow respondents to air

their views rather than merely describe their behaviour. Such questions relieve boredom and frustration as well as providing valuable information in the process.

At a more detailed level, several aspects of design and layout have been shown to produce high levels of response to postal questionnaires. Thus:

4. Coloured pages can help to clarify the overall structure of the questionnaire and the use of different colours for instructions can assist the respondent.
5. Putting ticks in boxes by way of answering a questionnaire is familiar to most respondents whereas requests to circle precoded numbers at the right-hand side of the questionnaire can be a source of confusion and error.
6. The practice of sublettering questions (e.g. Q9 (a) (b) (c) ...) is a useful technique for grouping together questions to do with a specific issue. It is also a way of making the questionnaire look smaller than it actually is!
7. Repeating instructions as often as necessary is good practice in a postal questionnaire. Since everything hinges on the respondent knowing exactly what is required of him, clear, unambiguous instructions, boldly and attractively displayed, are essential.
8. Completing a questionnaire can be seen as a learning process in which the respondent becomes more at home with the task as he proceeds. Initial questions should therefore be simple, have high interest value, and encourage participation. The middle section of the questionnaire should contain the difficult questions; the last few questions should be of high interest in order to encourage the respondents to return the completed schedule.
9. It bears repeating that the wording of the self-completion questionnaire is of paramount importance and that pretesting is crucial to its success.
10. Finally, a brief note at the very end of the questionnaire can: (a) ask the respondent to check that no answer has been inadvertently missed out; (b) solicit an early return of the completed schedule; (c) thank the respondent for his participation; and (d) offer to send a short abstract of the major findings when the analysis is completed.

Apart from the design of the questionnaire, Hoinville and Jowell[3] consider the effects of four other factors in maximising the response rate of postal questionnaires. These are: the initial mailing, the covering letter, follow-up letters and incentives.

The following practices are to be recommended in *initial mailing*:

(a) use good-quality envelopes, typed and addressed to a named person wherever possible;

(b) use first-class postage, stamped rather than franked wherever possible;

(c) enclose a first-class stamped envelope for the respondent's reply;

(d) in surveys of the general population, Thursday is the best day for mailing out; in surveys of organisations, Monday or Tuesday are recommended; and

(e) avoid at all costs a December survey.

The purpose of the *covering letter* is to indicate the aim of the survey, to convey to the respondent its importance, to assure him of confidentiality, and to encourage his reply. With these intentions in mind, the following practices are to be recommended:

(a) the appeal in the covering letter must be tailored to suit the particular audience. Thus, a survey of teachers might stress the importance of the study to the profession as a whole;

(b) neither the use of prestigious signatories, nor appeals to altruism, nor the addition of handwritten postscripts affect response levels to postal questionnaires;

(c) the name of the sponsor or the organisation conducting the survey should appear on the letterhead as well as in the body of the covering letter;

(d) a direct reference should be made to the confidentiality of the respondent's answers and the purposes of any serial numbers and codings should be explained;

(e) a presurvey letter advising respondents of the forthcoming questionnaire has been shown to have substantial effect on response rates; and

(f) a short covering letter is most effective; aim at no more than one page.

Of the four factors that Hoinville and Jowell[3] discuss in connection with maximising response levels, the *follow-up letter* has been shown to be the most productive. The following points should be borne in mind in preparing reminder letters:

(a) all of the rules that apply to the covering letter apply even more strongly to the follow-up letter;
(b) the follow-up should re-emphasise the importance of the study and the value of the respondent's participation;
(c) the use of the second person singular, the conveying of an air of disappointment at non-response and some surprise at non-cooperation have been shown to be effective ploys;
(d) nowhere should the follow-up give the impression that non-response is normal or that numerous non-responses have occurred in the particular study; and
(e) the follow-up letter must be accompanied by a further copy of the questionnaire together with a stamped addressed envelope for its return.

Second and third reminder letters suffer from the law of diminishing returns, so how many follow-ups are recommended and what success rates do they achieve? It is difficult to generalise, but the following points are worth bearing in mind. A well-planned postal survey should obtain at least a 40 per cent response rate and with the judicious use of reminders, a 70 per cent to 80 per cent response level should be possible. A preliminary pilot survey is invaluable in that it can indicate the general level of response to be expected. The main survey should generally achieve at least as high as and normally a higher level of return than the pilot enquiry. The Government Social Survey (now the Office of Population Censuses and Surveys) recommends the use of three reminders which, they say, can increase the original return by as much as 30 per cent in surveys of the general public. A typical pattern of responses to the three follow-ups is as follows:

Original despatch	40 %
1st follow-up	+20 %
2nd follow-up	+10 %
3rd follow-up	+ 5 %
Total	75 %

The fourth and final factor in maximising response rates is the *use of incentives*. Although the use of incentives is comparatively rare in British surveys, it can substantially reduce non-response rates particularly when the chosen incentives accompany the initial mailing rather than being mailed subsequently as rewards for the return of completed schedules. The explanation of the effective-

Box 4.5: A Flow Chart for the Planning of a Postal Survey

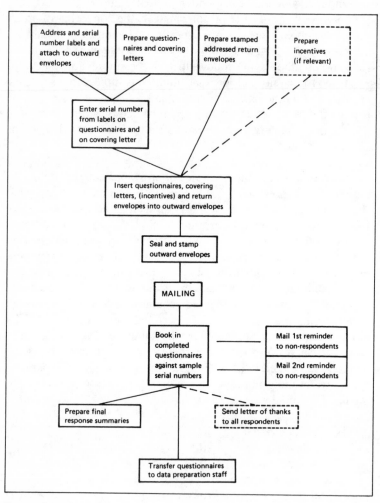

Source: Hoinville and Jowell.[3]

ness of this particular ploy appears to lie in the sense of obligation that is created in the recipient. Care is needed in selecting the most appropriate type of incentive. It should clearly be seen as a token rather than a payment for the respondent's efforts and, according to Hoinville and Jowell, should be as neutral as possible. In this respect, they suggest that books of postage stamps or ballpoint pens are cheap, easily packaged in the questionnaire envelopes, and appropriate to the task required of the respondent.

In conclusion, the preparation of a flow chart can help the researcher to plan the timing and the sequencing of the various parts of a postal survey. One such flow chart suggested by Hoinville and Jowell is shown in Box 4.5. The researcher might wish to add a chronological chart alongside it to help plan the exact timing of the events shown here.

Processing Survey Data

Let us assume that the researcher has followed the advice we have given about the planning of postal questionnaires and has secured a high response rate to his survey. His task is now to reduce the mass of data he has obtained to a form suitable for analysis. *Data reduction*, as the process is called, generally consists of coding data in preparation for analysis — by hand in the case of small surveys; by computers when numbers are larger. First, however, prior to coding, the questionnaires have to be checked. This task is referred to as *editing*.

Editing

Editing interview schedules or self-completion questionnaires is intended to identify and eliminate errors made by interviewers or respondents. (In addition to the clerical editing that we discuss in this section, editing checks are also performed by the computer. For an account of computer-run *structure* checks and *valid coding range* checks, see Hoinville and Jowell[3] pp. 150–5.) Moser and Kalton[9] point to three central tasks in editing: (1) *completeness*: a check is made that there is an answer to every question. In most surveys, interviewers are required to record an answer to every question (a 'not applicable' category always being available). Missing answers can sometimes be cross-checked from other sections of the survey. At worst, the respondent can be contacted again to supply the missing information. (2) *accuracy*: as far as is possible a check is made that all questions are answered accurately. Inaccuracies arise out of carelessness on the part of either the interviewer or the respondent. Sometimes a deliberate attempt is made to mislead. A tick in the wrong box, a ring round the wrong code, an error in simple arithmetic — all can reduce the validity of the data unless they are picked up in the editing process. (3) *uniformity*: a check is made that interviewers have interpreted instructions and questions uniformly. Sometimes the failure to give explicit instructions over the interpretation of respondents' replies leads to interviewers recording the same answer in a variety of answer codes instead of one. A check on uniformity can help eradicate this source of error.

Coding

The primary task of data reduction is coding, that is, assigning a code number to each answer to a survey question. Of course, not all answers to survey questions can be reduced to code numbers. Many open-ended questions, for example, are not reducible in this way for computer analysis. Coding can be built into the construction of the questionnaire itself. In this case, we talk of *precoded* answers. Where coding is developed after the questionnaire has been administered and answered by respondents, we refer to *post-coded* answers. Precoding is appropriate for closed-ended questions — male 1, female 0, for example; or single 0, married 1, separated 2, divorced 3. For questions such as those whose *answer categories* are known in advance, a *coding frame* is generally developed before the interviewing commences so that it can be printed into the questionnaire itself. For open-ended questions (Why did you choose this particular in-service course rather than XYZ?), a coding frame has to be devised after the completion of the questionnaire. This is best done by taking a random sample of the questionnaires (10 per cent or more, time permitting) and generating a frequency tally of the range of responses as a preliminary to coding classification. Having devised the coding frame, the researcher can make a further check on its validity by using it to code up a further sample of the questionnaires. It is vital to get coding frames right from the outset — extending them or making alterations at a later point in the study is both expensive and wearisome.

Survey Research in Education: an Example

Gray, McPherson and Raffe[10] report a large-scale survey conducted in Scotland in 1977. The study involved some 20,000 young people who had left school in the previous academic session (1975–6). It sampled former pupils from nearly all of Scotland's secondary schools. Various groupings of young people in the sample were sent questionnaires (some sixteen pages in length, some twelve, others six). The questionnaires asked about several aspects of their secondary schooling, including their performance in school and public examinations, their experience of corporal punishment and truancy, their relationships with teachers and their current opinions on the value of their school years.

The researchers achieved an overall response rate of 82%, remarkable at first sight, when one considers that the sample included those who left school without any formal qualifications. However, reading the researchers' report of their preparatory work for the survey, it appears that they designed and pilot-tested a number of questionnaires specifically aimed at unqualified school leavers and found considerable interest among this group of young people in the questions that were asked.

In order to increase the range of topics covered in the study, Gray and his associates administered twenty-one overlapping versions of the survey questionnaire to random sub-sets of the sample. Certain key questions, however, appeared in all twenty-one versions. By way of illustrating some of the findings that are reported, we focus attention on the researchers' explanation of *truancy*.

From an analysis of data such as that shown in Box 4.6 Gray and his co-workers argue that the phenomenon of truancy cannot be explained solely in terms of the pathology of individual pupils and their family circumstances. So widespread is the incidence of truancy that the researchers look for additional ways of accounting for the problem.

By defining 'truancy' so that it refers to a very small minority, by assuming that school experiences are common to all pupils, and by discounting the reports of one group of participants (the pupils), such explanations easily lead to the conclusion that disadvantage associated with 'family circumstances' is the single major cause of truancy.

Box 4.6: Truancy

'Did you ever play truant during your fourth year at school?' By social class, sex and SCE attainment respectively: percentage of leavers

	Never	A lesson here and there	A day here and there	Several days at a time	Weeks at a time	Total	Unweighted n
(a) All leavers	37	26	24	7	6	100	(15,682)
(b) I Professional	49	32	15	3	2	101	(812)
II Intermediate	42	32	20	4	2	100	(2,406)
IIIN Skilled non-manual	44	29	19	5	3	100	(1,258)
IIIM Skilled manual	35	25	26	8	6	100	(6,449)
IV Partly skilled	36	24	24	9	7	100	(2,497)
V Unskilled	33	22	24	11	10	100	(557)
Unclassified	32	22	26	10	10	100	(1,703)
(c) Boys	32	25	27	8	7	99	(7,678)
Girls	42	26	21	6	5	100	(8,004)
(d) Any Highers passes	50	36	13	1	< 0.5	100	(5,039)
4 or more O-grades (A–C)	41	32	24	3	1	101	(1,779)
1–3 O-grades (A–C)	37	27	27	6	3	100	(3,590)
D or E awards only	35	24	30	8	3	100	(1,302)
No awards	28	17	28	13	14	100	(3,972)

Source: adopted from Gray, McPherson and Raffe.[10]

Gray's survey shows not a deviant minority who truant, but a substantial majority (63 per cent) who admit to some truancy in their fourth year of secondary schooling!

The data in Box 4.6 suggest that truancy may be associated with the different effects of the school system on different pupils. Specifically they reveal that those who truanted most frequently tended to be those who were excluded from work that was award-bearing. In a word, the pupils who were rejected tended, in turn, to reject school. The researchers argue that it is dangerous and misleading to discount the *role of the school system itself in the promotion of truancy*. They support their case by a systematic content analysis of 750 accounts written by non-certificate pupils (i.e. those in classes which did not lead to the award of any certificate of academic attainment).

The researchers then relate the extent of self-reported truancy among the non-certificate school leavers to the amount of help that these young people say they received from their teachers and to various learning experiences that the youngsters report during their last year in school. The data are summarised in Box 4.8.

To have been a non-certificate pupil in a Scottish secondary school, the researchers conclude, was almost certainly a different and, in many ways, a more negative experience than to have been a certificate pupil. Moreover, among the non-certificate respondents, those who truanted more extensively reported more negative

Box 4.7: Truants' Accounts of School

> The reason I played truant so much was because I hated the teachers, for the simple reason that I wasn't too bright at school, and if I didn't catch something the teacher said, or couldn't do something right, I was scared to ask the teacher because eight out of ten (he) would just tell me I should have been listening or to just get a copy off a friend so when it came to exams I just didn't have a clue what to do.
>
> All I can say about my self is I am shy and nervous and do my fare share of work and I never go out at night. I was hardly ever at school the last year cause I never liked it as I never had anybody to go about with and when I had to answer a question my face went all red because the people in my class started to look at me and I would get all mixed up and the teacher would make it worse for me as they made me sit at the front of the class and I was scared to answer in case I was wrong and they would all laugh at me. I don't really know if he could have made the time more useful. I'm sure it was up to myself to make the time more useful.

Source: adapted from Gray, McPherson and Raffe.[10]

Box 4.8: Perceived Help from Teachers, various experiences and attitudes, by extent of self-reported truancy: percentage of non-certificate leavers only

	Never	A lesson here and there	A day here and there	Several days at a time	Weeks at a time
Percentage reporting a lot of help from teachers with:					
1 lessons	66	62	48	35	31
2 learning things useful for jobs	44	36	33	19	13
3 learning about jobs	44	37	34	33	17
4 learning useful things	51	46	34	39	26
5 becoming independent	45	34	32	27	23
6 spare-time activities	29	22	22	22	13
7 getting on with others	36	35	27	23	23
8 personal problems	23	18	19	18	15
9 Percentage treated too much as a child	12	19	17	21	29
10 Percentage belted often or quite often	21	39	50	60	64
11 Percentage enjoying last year	66	63	42	26	21
12 Percentage saying last year worthwhile	30	29	21	16	8
13 Percentage saying last year very or quite useful	53	42	31	22	12
14 Percentage finding reading easy or quite easy	56	55	63	68	70
15 Percentage finding writing easy or quite easy	61	60	56	63	62
16 Percentage finding sums easy or quite easy	29	29	30	29	36
17 Percentage with part-time job while at school	33	33	39	40	39

Source: adapted from Gray, McPherson and Raffe.[10]

attitudes and experiences than those who truanted less or not at all. Finally, whilst Gray and his colleagues concede that pupils' accounts cannot be considered adequate by themselves any more than can official or other explanations, they would be surprised, they say, if additional research did not allow considerable validity to leavers' reports of their school experiences.

In conclusion, we suggest that this chapter be studied alongside Chapter 13 which deals with interviews and interviewing.

References

1. Central Advisory Council for Education, *Children and their Primary Schools* (HMSO, London, 1967).
2. Jackson, B. and Marsden, D., *Education and the Working Class* (Routledge and Kegan Paul, London, 1962).
3. Hoinville, G. and Jowell, R., *Survey Research Practice* (Heinemann Educational Books, London, 1978).
4. Davidson, J., *Outdoor Recreation Surveys: The Design and Use of Questionnaires for Site Surveys* (Countryside Commission, London, 1970).
5. Bailey, K.D., *Methods of Social Research* (Collier-Macmillan, London, 1978).
6. Cohen, L. and Holliday, M., *Statistics for Education and Physical Education* (Harper and Row, London, 1979).
7. Social and Community Planning Research, *Questionnaire Design Manual, No. 5* (London: 16 Duncan Terrace, N1 8BZ, 1972).
8. Selltiz, C., Wrightsman, L.S. and Cook, S.W., *Reseach Methods in Social Relations* (Holt, Rinehart and Winston, New York, 1976).
9. Moser, C.A. and Kalton, G., *Survey Methods in Social Investigation* (Heinemann Educational Books, London, 1977).
10. Gray, J., McPherson, A.F. and Raffe, D., *Reconstructions of Secondary Education — Theory, Myth and Practice Since the War* (Routledge and Kegan Paul, London, 1983).

5   CASE STUDIES

Introduction

How can knowledge of the ways in which children learn and the means by which schools achieve their goals be verified, built upon and extended? This is a central question for educational research. The problem of verification and cumulation of educational knowledge is implicit in our discussion of the nature of educational enquiry in the opening chapter of the book. There, we outline two broad approaches to educational research. The first, based on the *scientific* paradigm, rests upon the creation of theoretical frameworks that can be tested by experimentation, replication and refinement. We illustrate this approach in Chapter 8. Against this scientific, experimental paradigm, we posit an alternative perspective which we describe as *interpretive* and *subjective*, a focus we hasten to add that should be seen as complementing rather than competing with the experimental stance.

In the present chapter, although our presentation emphasises the interpretive, subjective dimensions of educational phenomena that are best explored by case study methods, we balance this with examples of quantitative case study research. Our broad treatment of case study techniques follows directly from a *typology of observation studies* that we develop shortly. We begin with a brief description of the case study itself.

The Case Study

Unlike the experimenter who manipulates variables to determine their causal significance or the surveyor who asks standardised questions of large, representative samples of individuals, the case study researcher typically *observes* the characteristics of an individual unit — a child, a clique, a class, a school or a community. The purpose of such observation is to probe deeply and to analyse intensively the multifarious phenomena that constitute the life cycle of the unit with a view to establishing generalisations about the wider population to which that unit belongs.

Box 5.1: A Typology of Observation Studies

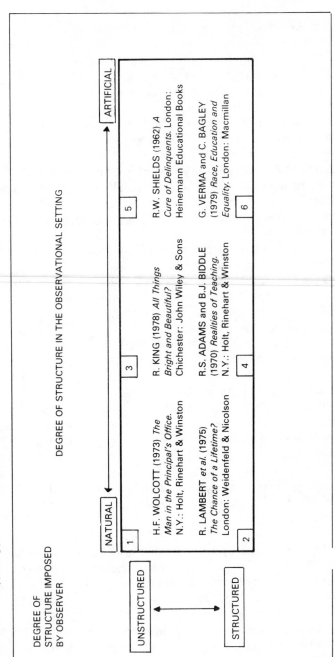

DEGREE OF
STRUCTURE IMPOSED
BY OBSERVER

DEGREE OF STRUCTURE IN THE OBSERVATIONAL SETTING

NATURAL — ARTIFICIAL

UNSTRUCTURED ↔ STRUCTURED

1
H.F. WOLCOTT (1973) *The Man in the Principal's Office.* N.Y.: Holt, Rinehart & Winston

3
R. KING (1978) *All Things Bright and Beautiful?* Chichester: John Wiley & Sons

5
R.W. SHIELDS (1962) *A Cure of Delinquents.* London: Heinemann Educational Books

2
R. LAMBERT *et al.* (1975) *The Chance of a Lifetime?* London: Weidenfeld & Nicolson

4
R.S. ADAMS and B.J. BIDDLE (1970) *Realities of Teaching.* N.Y.: Holt, Rinehart & Winston

6
G. VERMA and C. BAGLEY (1979) *Race, Education and Equality.* London: Macmillan

Source: adapted from Bailey.[6]

Present antipathy towards the statistical-experimental paradigm has created something of a boom industry in case study research. Delinquents,[1] dropouts[2] and drug-users[3] to say nothing of studies of all types of schools,[4] attest to the wide use of the case study in contemporary social science and educational research. Such wide use is marked by an equally diverse range of techniques employed in the collection and analysis of both qualitative and quantitative data. Whatever the problem or the approach, at the heart of every case study lies a *method of observation.*

In this chapter, we discuss six educational case studies. They are chosen to illustrate the use of a particular *style* of observation within a particular observational *setting.* In Box 5.1, we set out a typology of observation studies on the basis of which our six examples are selected.

There are two principal types of observation — *participant observation* and *non-participant observation.* In the former, the observer engages in the very activities he sets out to observe. Often, his 'cover' is so incomplete that as far as the other participants are concerned, he is simply one of the group. In the case of Patrick[1] for example, born and bred in Glasgow, his researcher role remained hidden from the members of the Glasgow gang in whose activities he participated for a period of four months. Such complete anonymity is not always possible, however. Thus in Parker's[2] study of downtown Liverpool adolescents, it was generally known that the researcher was waiting to take up a post at the university. In the meantime, 'knocking around' during the day with the lads and frequenting their pub at night rapidly established that he was 'OK'.

> I was a drinker, a hanger-arounder, and had been tested in illegal 'business' matters and could be relied on to say nothing since I 'knew the score'.

Cover is not necessarily a prerequisite of participant observation. In an intensive study of a small group of working-class boys during their last two years at school and their first months in employment, Willis[5] attended all the different subject classes at school — 'not as a teacher, but as a member of the class' — and worked alongside each boy in industry for a short period.

A non-participant observer, on the other hand, stands aloof from the group activities he is investigating and eschews group membership — no great difficulty for King,[4] an adult observer in infant classrooms. Listen to him recounting how he firmly established his *non-participant* status* with young children:

> I rapidly learnt that children in infants' classrooms define any adult as another teacher or teacher surrogate. To avoid being engaged in conversation, being asked to spell words or admire pictures, I evolved the following technique.
>
> To begin with, I kept standing so that physical height created social distance ... Next, I did not show immediate interest in what the children were doing, or talk to them. When I was talked to I smiled politely and if necessary I referred the child asking a question to the teacher. Most importantly, I avoided eye contact; if you do not look you will not be seen.

The best illustration of the non-participant observer role is perhaps the case of the researcher sitting at the back of a classroom coding up every three seconds the verbal exchanges between teacher and pupils by means of a structured set of observational categories.

It is frequently the case that the *type of observation* undertaken by the reseacher is associated with the *type of setting* in which the research takes place. In Box 5.1 we identify a continuum of settings ranging from the artificial environments of the therapist's clinic (Cell 5) and the social psychological laboratory (Cell 6) to the natural environments of the community in which the professional life of a headteacher is embedded (Cell 1) and the academic, social and religious life associated with boarding school education (Cell 2). Because our continuum is crude and arbitrary, we are at liberty to locate a study of infant schools (Cell 3) somewhere between the artificial and natural poles.

Although in theory each of the six examples of case studies in Box 5.1 could have been undertaken either as a participant or as a non-participant observation study, a number of factors intrude to make one or other of the observational strategies the dominant mode of enquiry in a particular type of setting. Bailey[6] explains as follows:

> In a natural setting it is difficult for the researcher who wishes to

---

* King's study as a whole is based upon *unstructured* observations in infant classrooms. It is different in its approach from other studies by him.

be covert not to act as a participant. If the researcher does not participate, there is little to explain his presence, as he is very obvious to the actual participants ... Most studies in a natural setting are unstructured participant observation studies ... Much the opposite is true in an artificial environment. Since there is no natural setting, in a sense none of the persons being studied are really participants of long standing, and thus may accept a non-participant observer more readily ... Laboratory settings also enable a non-participant observer to use sophisticated equipment such as videotape and tape recordings ... Thus most studies in an artificial laboratory setting will be structured and will be non-participant studies.

What we are saying is simply this: that the unstructured, ethnographic account of the headteacher (Cell 1) is the most typical method of observation in the natural surroundings of school, home, church and community in which that study was conducted. Similarly, the structured questions and the quantitative techniques employed in the study of the black adolescent (Cell 6) reflect a common approach in the artificial setting of a social psychological laboratory.

Why Participant Observation?

The current vogue enjoyed by the case study conducted on participant observation lines is not difficult to account for. This form of research is eminently suitable to many of the problems that the educational investigator faces.

The natural scientist, Schutz[7] points out, explores a field that means nothing to the molecules, atoms and electrons therein. By contrast, the subject matter of the world in which the educational researcher is interested is composed of people and is essentially meaningful. That world is subjectively structured, possessing particular meanings for its inhabitants. The task of the educational investigator is very often to explain the means by which an orderly social world is established and maintained in terms of its shared meanings. How do participant observation techniques assist the researcher in this task? Bailey[6] identifies some inherent advantages in the participant observation approach:

1. Observation studies are superior to experiments and surveys

when data are being collected on non-verbal behaviour.

2. In the observation study, the investigator is able to discern ongoing behaviour as it occurs and is able to make appropriate notes about its salient features.

3. Because case study observations take place over an extended period of time, the researcher can develop a more intimate and informal relationship with those he is observing, generally in more natural environments than those in which experiments and surveys are conducted.

4. Case study observations are less reactive than other types of data-gathering methods. For example, in laboratory-based experiments and in surveys that depend upon verbal responses to structured questions, bias can be introduced in the very data that the researcher is attempting to study.

On the other hand, participant observation studies are not without their critics. The accounts that typically emerge from participant observations are often decried as subjective, biased, impressionistic, idiosyncratic and lacking in the precise quantifiable measures that are the hallmark of survey research and experimentation. Whilst it is probably true that nothing can give better insight into the life of a gang of juvenile delinquents than going to live with them for an extended period of time, the critic of participant observation studies will point to the dangers of 'going native' as a result of playing a role within such a group. How do we know that the observer does not lose his perspective and become blind to the peculiarities that he is supposed to be investigating?

These criticisms raise questions about two types of validity in observation-based research. In effect, comments about the subjective and idiosyncratic nature of the participant observation study are to do with its *external validity*. How do we know that the results of this one piece of research are applicable to other situations? Fears that the observer's judgement will be affected by his close involvement in the group relate to the *internal validity* of the method. How do we know that the results of this one piece of research represent the real thing, the genuine product? In our outline of one of the educational case study examples we refer to a number of techniques (quota sampling, snowball sampling, the search for exceptions) that researchers employ as a way of checking on the representativeness of the events that they observe and of cross-checking their interpretations of the meanings of those events

Box 5.2: Steps in Participant Observation

---

1. A rough definition of the phenomenon is formulated.
2. A hypothetical explanation of that phenomenon is formulated.
3. One case is studied in the light of the hypothesis, with the object of determining whether or not the hypothesis fits the facts in that case.
4. If the hypothesis does not fit the facts, either the hypothesis is reformulated or the phenomenon to be explained is redefined so that the case is excluded.
5. Practical certainty may be attained after a small number of cases has been examined, but the discovery of negative cases disproves the explanation and requires a reformulation.
6. This procedure of examining cases, redefining the phenomenon, and reformulating the hypothesis is continued until a universal relationship is established, each negative case calling for a redefinition of a reformulation.

Source: Denzin.[8]

(see also our discussion in Chapter 10, 'Accounts'). We can best illustrate the concern of the participant observer for the validity of his data by the following brief outline of a typical strategy in participant observation research. Denzin[8] uses the term 'analytical induction' to describe a broad strategy of participant observation which we set out in Box 5.2.

Recording Observations

> I filled thirty-two notebooks with about half a million words of notes made during nearly six hundred hours [of observation] (King).[4]

The recording of observations is a frequent source of concern to the inexperienced case study researcher. How much ought to be recorded? In what form should the recordings be made? What does one do with the mass of recorded data? Lofland[9] gives a number of useful suggestions about collecting field notes which we summarise in Box 5.3.

The sort of note-taking recommended by Lofland[9] and actually undertaken by King[4] and Wolcott[10] in their ethnographic accounts grows out of the nature of the unstructured observation study. Note-taking, confessed Wolcott, helped him fight the acute boredom that he sometimes felt when observing the interminable meetings that are the daily lot of the school principal. Occasionally, however, a series of events would occur so quickly that Wolcott

Box 5.3: Field Notes in Observation Studies

1.	Record the notes as quickly as possible after observation, since the quantity of information forgotten is very slight over a short period of time but accelerates quickly as more time passes.
2.	Discipline yourself to write notes quickly and reconcile yourself to the fact that although it may seem ironic, recording of field notes can be expected to take as long as is spent in actual observation.
3.	Dictating rather than writing is acceptable if one can afford it, but writing has the advantage of stimulating thought.
4.	Typing field notes is vastly preferable to handwriting because it is faster and easier to read, especially when making multiple copies.
5.	It is advisable to make at least two copies of field notes and preferable to type on a master for reproduction. One original copy is retained for reference and other copies can be used as rough draught to be cut up, reorganised and rewritten.
6.	The notes ought to be full enough adequately to summon up for one again, months later, a reasonably vivid picture of any described event. This probably means that one ought to be writing up, at the very minimum, at least a couple of single space typed pages for every hour of observation.

Source: Lofland.[9]

had time only to make cursory notes which he supplemented later with fuller accounts. One useful tip from this experienced ethnographer is worth noting: never resume your observations until the notes from the preceding observation are complete. There is nothing to be gained merely by your presence as an observer. Until your observations and impressions from one visit are a matter of record, there is little point in returning to the classroom or school and reducing the impact of one set of events by superimposing another and more recent set. Indeed, when to record one's data is but one of a number of practical problems identified by Walker[11] which we have listed in Box 5.5.

Recording observations in structured settings calls for quite different techniques as the observation schedule in Box 5.4 clearly shows. Because Rutter and his colleagues[12] were aiming to collect fairly simple descriptive data about lessons and classrooms, the observation schedules that we show in Box 5.4 were entirely adequate for their purposes.

Educational Case Study Examples

We turn now to a brief exposition of each of the case study examples identified in our observation typology in Box 5.1.

Box 5.4: A Structured Observation Schedule for the Classroom

1. Number   Late
2. Pencils
3. Uniform
4. Overcoats
5. Chairs
6. Windows
7. Condition   Clean
                    Tidy
                    Plants
                    Posters
                    Pictures
   Total
8. Work on walls   0   1   2   3   4
9. Graffiti   0   1   2   3   4

Classroom observation schedule — definitions

This observation schedule was used during the series of classroom obervations of the third year and during the administration of the pupil questionnaire.

1. The number of pupils in the class and the number who arrived after the start of the lesson.
2. The number of pencils borrowed from the researchers during the administration of the questionnaire.
3. The number of children not in correct school uniform (as defined by the school).
4. The number of children in outdoor coats or anoraks.
5. The number of broken chairs in the classroom.
6. The number of broken or cracked windows.
7. The decorative condition of the room. One point was given for each of the five items and a total score assigned to each room.
8. The amount of children's work on the walls, coded from 0 to 4.0 — none, 1 — one quarter of available wall space, 2 — one half of available wall space, 3 — three quarters of available wall space, 4 — all available wall space.
9. The amount of graffiti, coded as item 8.

Source: Rutter *et al*.[12]

Checklist for beginning and ending of lessons

TO LESSON

33	Start/after break/N.K.		0
	Same room/Double		1
	V. slow		2

34	Lost	0	1
35	Fight	0	1
36	750 yards	0	1

START

37	Outside:	Mill	0
		Enter room	1
		Line up	2
	Inside:	Muddle	0
		Sit	1
		Stand	2
39	Off-task chat to T		0	1
40	Silence		0	1
41	Greeting		0	1
42	Register		0	1
43	Ritual		0	1
44	Seating:	Chosen by children	0
		T directs some	1
		T directs all	2
		N/K	9
45	Resources:	Brought by children	0
		On desk	1
		Distrib. by T	2
		Distrib. by monitors	3
		Collected by children	4

46–7 Time to start of work:

48   No. Late:

END

49	Timing:	Long	0
		Good	1
		Short	2
		Dismiss before bell	3
50	Stand behind chairs	0	1
51	Silence	0	1
52	Farewell	0	1
53	Line-up	0	1
54	Off-task chat to T	0	1
55	Tidy room	0	1
56	Dismiss by row/group/sex	0	1
57	Reports:	Individual	0	1
58		Class	0	1
59	Resources:	
	Collected by T	0
	Collected by monitor	1
	Replaced by children	2
	Kept by children	3

CHECKLIST

60	Homework set	0	1
61	Homework returned	0	1

Outings/trips

Formal punishments:

Formal rewards:

Jobs of e.g. monitors

Box 5.5: The Case Study and Problems of Selection

> Among the issues confronting the researcher at the outset of his case study are the problems of selection. The following questions indicate some of the obstacles in this respect:
>
> 1.   How do you get from the initial idea to the working design (from the idea to a specification, to usable data)?
> 2.   What do you lose in the process?
> 3.   What unwanted concerns do you take on board as a result?
> 4.   How do you find a site which provides the best location for the design?
> 5.   How do you locate, identify and approach key informants?
> 6.   How they see you creates a context within which you see them. How can you handle such social complexities?
> 7.   How do you record evidence? When? How much?
> 8.   How do you file and categorise it?
> 9.   How much time do you give to thinking and reflecting about what you are doing?
> 10.   At what points do you show your subject what you are doing?
> 11.   At what points do you give them control over who sees what?
> 12.   Who sees the reports first?

Source: adapted from Walker.[11]

Cell 1: Wolcott[10] — The Man in the Principal's Office

Participant observation has been described as a 'process of waiting to be impressed by recurrent themes that reappear in various contexts'. Wolcott's account[10] of the career of an elementary school principal well illustrates the 'waiting role' of the participant observer. Wolcott shadowed Ed Bell, the school principal, for a period of two years, spending several days every week with him in school, at home, at church meetings, accompanying him on school business away from the school building and even going to the local store with him to purchase household requirements. During all of these events, Wolcott maintained a constant written record of the behaviour he saw and the conversations he heard between the school principal and staff, children, family and friends. With the principal's permission, the researcher sifted through his notes, files and personal records. Extensive tape recordings were made of interviews with members of the school staff. The principal himself was persuaded to keep an account of recurring school problems for a period of several weeks. A further observational device used by Wolcott involved noting the activity and the social interaction patterns of the school principal every minute for periods of two hours at a time. This procedure included recording the person with whom the principal interacted, who initiated the interaction, where and when, who was talking, and how many people were involved. Over a period of several weeks Wolcott generated a set of categories for tabulating these interactions. By a careful sampling of the data from these two-hour recordings over ten consecutive school days, the researcher built up a detailed picture of the multifarious demands made upon the school principal in his day-to-day life.

To what end? The objective of this particularly intensive form of participant observation has been cogently put by Diesing[13] as follows:

> The ... method involves taking data as they come, and they usually come in scattered, disconnected fragments. Unlike the experimentalist, who can demand evidence on a specific question from his subject matter, the participant observer must adapt his thinking to what his subject happens to be doing. He has to observe each casual interchange as it happens, participate in the ceremony of the day since it may not occur again for two years, talk to the informants who are available, and get involved in whatever problems and controversies are prominent at the moment. At the end of the day he comes home with a wealth of information on a variety of points, but nothing conclusive on any one point. Over the weeks and months his evidence on a given point gradually accumulates and the various points start to fit together into a tentative pattern.

Wolcott's painstaking and detailed observing and recording led to the gradual identification and piecing together of several important strands in the professional life of the school principal. The researcher reveals the complex demands that are made of a school leader and the degree to which Ed Bell succeeds both in his own estimation and in the judgements of those who have to work with him. We illustrate the point with an example.

One particularly difficult task that American school principals face each year is staff evaluation. Because permanence of tenure and financial advancement hang upon a satisfactory evaluation from the principal, the exercise is charged with tension and anxiety on the part of the teachers and principal alike. (The common practice in North America is that the teacher reads what the school principal has to say about her teaching ability and signs the document in his presence.) Wolcott's observation and recording of the evaluation exercise gathered information from the principal and from various teachers. His account shows how the task of teacher evaluation set the principal most clearly apart from his staff and challenged him with difficult decisions which he tackled with an indecisiveness that only added to the stress that everyone involved experienced:

> After I read the evaluation, I said to Ed, 'So you're going to try to stop me from teaching by saying such things as: I expect that ten years from now you'll be teaching the same way as you're teaching now! On what grounds can anyone say this? Why, I wasn't teaching the same way as I was a year ago, and certainly not ten years ago ...'

Ed Bell is not at all happy with one of his teachers, Mrs Alma Skirmish, and is all set to write a report that will exclude her from his school for the following session. In the end, however, he has a change of heart following evaluation meetings with her such as the one we report above.

> She really seemed to listen to the things I had to say ... She runs her classroom like a classroom now, not a Sunday school class ... She's doing a better job ... Maybe next year I'll regret it. But right now I feel I'm right.

Outside of the actual interchanges between principal and teachers, Wolcott is able to look at the staff evaluation exercise and bring to it his own assessment of the principal's leadership:

> I could never escape a personal feeling that Ed made his assessments about new staff quickly (probably on first impression), independent of performance observed in the classroom, and then subsequently accumulated whatever evidence he felt he needed to support those impressions. Although he tended to be cautious when screening candidates for his school or the district, once he decided to accept a candidate for the Taft faculty, the extent of his enthusiasm and optimism took a predictable upwards swing.

Wolcott's ethnographic study is a very readable and 'real'

account of the life of a school principal. The researcher himself is a strong advocate of this particular method of participant observation.* At the same time, he is concerned that would-be researchers are aware of the pitfalls of the approach. It is, he says, an excellent method for obtaining certain kinds of data, but it cannot by itself provide the whole picture. One always faces the problem of generalisability in pursuing an in-depth study of a single case. The participant observer approach, Wolcott adds, is a high-risk, low-yield adventure. It is high risk because unless the fieldwork is eventually translated into a significant, readable (and read) monograph, the only possible gain is that made by the researcher in terms of his own research experience. The participant observer approach is low yield because of the considerable investment of time and personal effort that has to be made in order to obtain basic and often commonplace data. Finally, Wolcott adds, the researcher contemplating ethnographic studies in educational settings faces unique problems in that he assumes the role of formal observer in an institutional framework with which he has probably been in continuous contact since the age of five. It should make any intending researcher consider the crucial nature of *himself as an instrument* in collecting data through participant observation and interviewing techniques.

Cell 2: Lambert et al.[14] — The Chance of a Lifetime?

Like Wolcott, Lambert and his associates[14] used a variety of techniques including focused, depth interviews in gathering data in their massive study of 66 boarding schools throughout England and Wales. In the *intensive* sample of seven schools with which we deal here, the bulk of the information was obtained from a lengthy questionnaire which was completed by 1,238 senior pupils under examination conditions. More importantly, the questionnaire was designed to provide statistical evidence by means of which the researchers could test a number of hypotheses arising out of their view of the school as an organisation. Lambert describes the theoretical orientation of his study as largely deriving from a *conflict* view of society although he concedes that the approach 'combines *functional* and *conflict* models and adds a third sociological approach. This is a *developmental* approach which emphasises the

---

* See also: H.F. Wolcott, 'Criteria for an ethnographic approach to research in schools', *Human Organization*, 34, 2 (1975) 111-27.

Box 5.6: The School as a Social System

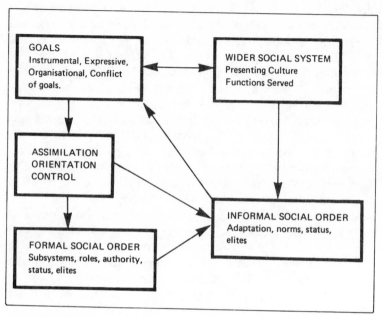

Source: Lambert *et al.*[14]

ways in which the [school as an] organisation has changed or developed over a period of time'. The model of the school that guided the research is set out in Box 5.6.

To convey to the reader the flavour of the highly structured approach used in the intensive sample study we include part of the questionnaire in which the researchers sought information on the effects of boarding school life on the emotional and sexual life of the pupils. By way of introducing the section we give details from the *Manual*[14] in which Lambert outlines the theoretical ideas which guided the choice of questions.

Questions 51, 52, 53, 54, 55, 56, 57:

Besides giving further data on peer associations both within and outside or based on the school, these questions are some of several which explore reactions to the opposite sex. They relate thus to the sections on *adaptation, patterns of association, sexual adaptations* and *school and society.* The data on the opposite sex correlates with that gained from the Thematic Apperception Test which we used and that based on Merton's paradigm (conformity, ritualism, innovation, retreatism, rebellion). It also refers to the following hypotheses:

H. 57: The age of boarding influences the boarder's affective relationships in depth.

H. 59: Boarders from single sex boarding schools find difficulty in responding to the other sex in a natural way on leaving.

H. 60: The more total the one sex institution the greater is the incidence of deviant sexual adaptations to it.

H. 61: Where the expressive stress and provision of the school is limited deviant sexual adaptations will be more dominant.

H. 62: While there is no evidence that boarding schools produce more homosexuals than day schools it is likely that those that have homosexual and heterosexual tendencies are sensitized more on the homosexual side than in a day school.

H. 74: Boarding reduces superficial strains in family relationships but inhibits communications at deeper levels.

The section of the questionnaire to which these hypotheses are directed is set out in Box 5.7

Lambert and his colleagues tested their hypotheses in percentage comparisons between boarding school boys' responses and those of control groups drawn from single-sex day schools. Thus, in respect of Hypothesis 59 they reported:

A majority of boarders (56 to 67 %) were uneasy or lacking in assurance with girls compared with a majority of day boys in the same or similar single sex schools (58 to 63 %) who claimed to be perfectly at ease in the company of the other sex.

Our reasons for classifying this study at the natural end of the observational setting continuum become clear from the details that Lambert and his associates give about the overall framework of the research programme.

Box 5.7: Effects of Boarding on Emotional and Sexual Life

Q.51   Have you any close friends of your own age and sex near here
(apart from boys actually at this school now)?
Tick:

Yes, connected with the school ....
Yes, not connected with the school ....
No ....

Q.52   Have you a girl friend near here at present (apart from one you may
have at home)?
Tick:

Yes ....
No ....

Q.53   Do you think that the senior boys at this school (tick which one)

see too much of the other sex ....
see about enough of them ....
see too little of them ....
anything else ....

Q.54   What about *you* personally:
Would you like to have more to do with girls here if it were possible?
(Tick)

Yes ....
No ....
Don't know ....

Q.55   Which of the following most nearly describes your own reaction
when in the company of a girl? (Tick)

I'm usually quite at ease ....
I look self-confident but don't feel it ....
I tend to put on a bit of a show ....
I feel a bit embarrassed ....
I feel uneasy ....
Any alternatives or additions ....

Q.56   Has being away from girls and women had any effect on your
attitudes or reactions to them?

....
....

Q.57   In your experience are there any good or bad effects produced by
living in a community all of your own sex?

(a)   the good effects ....

(b)   the bad effects ....

Source: Lambert *et al.*[14]

In the extensive sample of 59 schools, the researchers visited each school for usually two weeks or more, living and sleeping on the premises, joining in the everyday pattern of life in an endeavour to experience all aspects of the school — 'classroom, chapel, games, social services, corps, the pupil world, the staff common room, meetings and social life'. Subsequent visits were made to about a quarter of the schools and contact was maintained for several years. Interviews were conducted with approximately 1 in 4 of the housemasters, 1 in 4 of the matrons, and 1 in 7 of the school doctors. In order to explore the family life of the boarding school boy, the parents of a stratified random sample of 179 boys were interviewed for three hours in their own homes. The researchers were able to compare the boys' questionnaires (completed at school) with the data derived from the parent interviews with what they describe as 'fascinating results'.

Cell 3: King[4] — All Things Bright and Beautiful?

Unlike Lambert and his associates whose structured approach to their boarding school enquiry derived from a particular model of the school as a social system, King[4] began his study of infant schools unfettered by preplanned questionnaires and interview schedules:

> I asked the headmistress of a large infants' school ... if she would allow me to make observations in one of the classrooms. I was not able to give her any clear idea of what I was trying to do because I did not know exactly myself.

This is not to say, however, that King did not have a theoretical orientation. He had, so he says, a 'vaguely anthropological model of trying to understand life in classrooms, the key word in that sentence being *understand* '. King's orientation towards *Verstehen* (the study of meanings) reveals that like Lambert, he too had a guiding model, in his case derived from Max Weber[15] and action theory rather than Talcott Parsons[16] and Ralph Dahrendorf.[17] At the beginning of his research, King was anxious to follow some of the ideas of two American sociologists, Glaser and Strauss,[18] who argue that sociological theories should be grounded in data that are generated by the act of research. In short, theory should follow from research, not precede it. This argument has a familiar ring; it is essentially the one made by Diesing[13] which we quoted in our outline of Wolcott's study of the school principal in Cell 1. Not unexpectedly, King's research strategy is very similar to that adopted by Wolcott.

How did King set about the task of observing and making sense of the kaleidoscope of activities that typifies the busy infant classroom? Quota sampling, snowball sampling and the search for exceptions are three commonly-used procedures in participant observation. King used all three.

Quota sampling involves interviewing certain individuals from particular categories that the researcher has delineated. In King's study, one such category, *infant teacher*, is self-evident. He was interested in the fact that most of the things that happened in the classes he observed were arranged to happen or allowed to happen by the teachers. Gradually, he began to discern the structure of infant teachers' ideologies which guided their classroom behaviour. We give the following examples from King's own account:

> *Developmentalism*:
> Small boy picks up work card from tray.
> *Teacher*: You're too young to do those sums.
> *Individualism*:
> *Teacher*: If your approach doesn't suit a particular child then change it — the approach, not the child.
> *Play as learning*:
> *Teacher*: Most of what adults would regard as play is, in reality, of the deepest significance in the child's intellectual development.
> *Childhood innocence*:
> A girl complains to the teacher: 'Gary keeps flicking paint on my picture.'
> *Teacher*: I'm sure he didn't mean it.

Snowball sampling involves recording a particular incident and then looking for another example of it, then another, and another, and so on (see Box 5.2). King used this technique in looking at the various methods of social control used by infant teachers in the three schools under study. Thus, he was able to interpret five distinct *teacher voices*:

> 'Now we are going to do something exciting' voice.
> 'Slightly aggrieved, sad' voice.

'I'm being very patient with you' voice.
'Oh, nevermind, don't let's have a fuss' voice.
'Listen to me, I'm saying something important' voice.

The *search for exceptions* (see Box 5.2) is a way of falsifying working hypotheses or reformulating them. King's search for the general rules governing the behaviour of infant teachers towards pupils led him to suspect the occasional incidence of certain child-ren being permitted a special status by their teachers. His subsequent search for exceptions led him to delineate a group whom he termed, '*permitted eccentric children from professional homes*'.

One boy came to school for several days in a kilt. It was not his, he was not even Scottish.
Strange child — her father's a psychologist.

The Nature of Infant Education. King's methodology has much in common with the ethogenic approach that we outline in Chapter 10, and his final chapter is in the style of an *account of accounts* in which the researcher, having made explicit the methods he has applied in eliciting his information from informants and the processes he has employed in transforming his data, attempts to place his findings in a wider theoretical perspective. King argues as follows:

The child-centred ideologies which represent what is real about children and their learning to infants' teachers are social constructs; that is to say, there was a time when they did not exist nor are they accepted by everyone. With this in mind, it is possible to discuss and to evaluate classroom practices and ideologies independently of any claim for their being either the most appropriate or the truth.

This is what King proceeds to do, showing the consequences of teachers' insistence on 'play is learning' and 'childhood innocence' and their adherence to 'family-home background' theories of child deficiencies in learning. He concludes his analysis with the proposition that infant education can be viewed as a middle-class institution.

Cell 4: Adams and Biddle[19] — Realities of Teaching

Adams and Biddle's[19] study of 16 classrooms involved making videotape recordings of 32 lessons, half of which were in primary schools and half in secondary. The sample of lessons they recorded ranged across the curriculum — half the sessions consisted of social studies, the other half arithmetic (in primary classes) and mathematics in the secondary classes. Half of the teachers were male, and half female. Moreover, half the teachers were over 40 years of age, and half under 30. Clearly, the researchers had in mind controlling a number of variables they believed would affect the 'realities of teaching' that constituted the foci of their study. But why videotape? Adams and Biddle claim three major advantages of this method. First, it provides an extremely comprehensive record of classroom behaviour that can be preserved for subsequent analysis. Second, what they term the fidelity of the system is good, that is to say, the cameras can deal with conventional classroom settings, and microphones are able to pick up the greater proportion of the public utterances that take place. Third, the stop-rewind facility of the tape recorder permits sequences of behaviour to be viewed and reviewed at will during data-coding. Recorded data were analysed as follows. The coder identified a sought-for activity on the video screen, stopped the tape and rewound beyond the point at which the activity occurred. He then replayed the episode and on reaching the particular point, took a reading from a time counter and recorded it on coding sheets. The tape recorder was kept running until the end of the sought-for activity whereupon another reading was recorded from the time counter. In this way, two kinds of measurements were obtained: (1) an *incident* count, registering each instance when the different kinds of behaviour occurred; and (2) a *duration* count which registered the time-span of each particular incident. Computer analysis later provided data on the number of incidents and the total amount of time spent on each kind of behaviour. Thus a complete record was accumulated of all instances of particular activities in the 32 classrooms, showing the number of times that an activity occurred and how long it lasted. That record, the researchers propose, tells something of the story of *life in classrooms*, where typically a scene of rapid and frequent change is the order of the day involving some 371 activity episodes in the average lesson and some 4,500 episodes in the busiest classrooms in one school day. From this mass of data, Adams and

Box 5.8: Lesson Profiles in Primary Classrooms

Central Group
1. Role Allocation (who the emitter, target, audience, and residue members are)
2. Emitter Location (where the emitters are)
3. Target Location (where the targets are)
4. Audience Location (where the audience is)
5. Functional Code (what the educative process is about)
6. Role Structure (how many roles are operating at one time)
7. Communication Structure (what sorts of groups exist)

First Peripheral Group
8. Role Allocation (who the emitter, target, audience, and residue members are)
9. Emitter Location (where the emitters are)
10. Target Location (where the targets are)
11. Audience Location (where the audience is)
12. Functional Code (what the educative process is about)
13. Role Structure (how many roles are operating at one time

Second Peripheral Group
14. Role Allocation (who the emitter, target, audience, and residue members are)
15. Emitter Location (where the emitters are)
16. Target Location (where the targets are)
17. Audience Location (where the audience is)
18. Functional Code (what the educative process is about)
19. Role Structure (how many roles are operating at one time)

Teacher
20. Teacher Role Assignment (whether the teacher is emitter, target, or audience member)
21. Teacher Location (where the teacher is)

Source: Adams and Biddle.[19]

Biddle develop *lesson profiles*, classifying incidents according to the *roles* that teachers and pupils adopt, the *location* and the *function* of various activities in which they are engaged, and whether the participants in the interpersonal exchanges are *emitters* or *targets*. Box 5.8 shows a series of lesson profiles developed from data gathered in the classrooms of younger children.

Each 'block' in the profiles shows how many instances occurred of a particular kind of activity. For example, Block 21 at the extreme right hand side of the profiles shows the number of teacher locations. Inspection of the profiles in Box 5.8 shows that whilst classroom activities differ from room to room, there is a common pattern discernible in the lessons that have been observed and analysed. Notice how the 'ends' of the profiles in each case are higher than the 'middles'. Notice, too, the height of teacher blocks 20 and 21. The higher the block, the more frequently the teacher changed roles from emitter to target, to audience and back. The profiles in Box 5.8 suggest that teachers of younger children initiate a great deal of role switching. The extent to which they diversify their teaching activities can be judged by comparison with the profiles of their secondary school colleagues teaching social studies and mathematics in classes of older students (Box 5.9).

Realities of Teaching is a good example of the type of case study in which the individual unit of analysis is the relatively natural setting of the classroom and the observational approach is highly structured, gathering data that are objective and capable of quantification.

Cell 5: Shields[20] — *A Cure of Delinquents*

Bredinghurst was an experimental school for maladjusted boys set up by the then London County Council to provide a specialised environment for anti-social children who, over a period of time, were helped to come to grips with their own personal problems instead of compulsively seeking temporary solutions to them in anti-social behaviour. Shield's case study report[20] on Chris is an account of a three-month involvement in twice-weekly sessions with a severely disturbed adolescent. Throughout the therapy, Shields offered no structural set of categories to the boy as a way of mounting an active rescue programme. Rather, Chris was the one who structured the situations that governed the ongoing therapy sessions. In this way, the boy provided the therapist with a view of the world through the eyes of a disturbed youngster and

Box 5.9: Lesson Profiles in Secondary Classrooms

Source: Adams and Biddle.[19]

thus, an insight into the nature of his underlying problems.

To the extent that the therapy sessions occurred under clinical conditions we have classified this case study as taking place in an artificial setting. The degree to which it was unstructured by the observer can be judged from the extract from the case study reports given in Box 5.10

Cell 6: Weinreich (in Verma and Bagley, eds)[21] — Cross-ethnic Identification and Self-rejection in a Black Adolescent

Our final example of a case study was also undertaken in the artificial setting of a clinical laboratory but, as will become apparent, the account shows a considerable degree of structure in the observational techniques that were employed by the researcher. The

Box 5.10: Case Study Extract on Chris, a Severely Disturbed Adolescent

Chris reported these things to me also, saying that in his nightmares he had repeatedly dreamt that he was about to die or be killed, and he asked many questions about death ...

I arranged to see him again the next day, and he arrived in a furious mood. He stalked up and down my room swearing at me, accusing me of being a liar, an ignoramus, bad like the rest.

'I would like to kick your fire in', he said, and did in fact kick at the gas-fire. 'Why my fire?' I asked. 'All right, then', he yelled, 'I'd like to kick your f ..... g teeth in!'

His whole body was trembling as he went on to say what cruel and vicious things he would like to do to me, ending up, 'and cut out your guts and smear them all over the bleeding wall'.

He clenched his fists so that the nails cut into the flesh and he bit the back of his hand till the blood began to flow. By now he was trembling so much that he had to sit down ...

Pulling up his trouser leg he drew a long sheath knife from his stocking and leapt at me holding the knife against my chest. His face contorted with fury, he shouted, 'I've only got to push this one inch further and you're dead ...'

Facetiously I reminded him that a condemned man was allowed to smoke one last cigarette and asked if he would permit this indulgence. This infuriated him further but he agreed. Then he turned the knife against himself ... finally he flung it at the door with such force that it stuck into the wood ...

Suddenly all the fight went out of him and he slipped to the floor sobbing loudly and uncontrollably ... Towards the end of this long session lasting nearly three hours, he said, 'I've never talked to anyone like this before. It's all been terribly frightening, but I'm glad now I told you everything I felt.'

'Why aren't you afraid of me? I've never met anyone like you before. Why don't you get mad with me? I could have killed you, you know.'

Source: adapted from Shields.[20]

study[21] was concerned with the problem of cross-ethnic identification in a 16-year-old West Indian adolescent boy. *Cross-ethnic identification* was defined as the extent to which John, the boy in question, identified with the indigenous white population but knew that he himself was black, that is, he did not mis-identify himself as white. The researcher elicited personal constructs (see Chapter 14) from the transcripts of interviews carried out with John. These constructs were presented to the boy, one at a time, on rating sheets on which he systematically construed aspects of his self-image alongside significant individuals and groups from his own social world. The number of constructs entering the analyses was about 15 to 20 whilst the number of social entities was about 10 (see Box 5.11).

Box 5.11: Changes Between John's Past and Current Identifications with West Indian and English People

Social entity	Past identification	Current identification	Direction of change
West Indian people	.27	.08	less current iden.
West Indian boys	.40	.38	less current iden.
West Indian girls	.20	.15	less current iden.
Black Power	.27	.15	less current iden.
That little group of blacks	.53	.08	less current iden.
English people	.27	.46	greater current iden.
White boys	.20	.31	greater current iden.
White girls	.27	.40	greater current iden.
Friendly whites	.33	.62	greater current iden.
Me as whites see me	.33	.54	greater current iden.

Source: adapted from Verma and Bagley.[21]

The following extracts from the interview data show the degree of structure employed by the observer in his various lines of enquiry, and at the same time demonstrate his ability to make use of focused interview techniques (see Chapter 13) to get beneath John's initial bland responses to certain key issues.

Questioner: What do people respect you for?

John: I goes around with whites, 'cos not many kids do that.

Questioner: Do you think you'll get married to a white girl sometime?

John: No, I don't think so. I'd like to, but I don't think so. Wouldn't be right for the children, would it? When they grow up, you know what be said about them.

John is talking about his skin colour and his experience of prejudice:

John: I don't like my own colour. I must admit that.

Questioner: Why is that?

John: It seems to be bogging me down, fellows come up in the open ... I feel afraid.

Questioner: You feel afraid because of the reactions of white people?

John: Yes. But I prefer white to black ... I would rather be white. What they don't realize is that if they were in our position they would know what it feels like, see. They would have to take it then.

Box 5.11 shows the changes that have occurred between John's past and current identifications with West Indian and English

Box 5.12: Possible Advantages of Case Study

Case studies have a number of advantages that make them attractive to educational evaluators or researchers. Thus:

1. Case study data, paradoxically, is 'strong in reality' but difficult to organise. In contrast, other research data is often 'weak in reality' but susceptible to ready organisation. This strength in reality is because case studies are down-to-earth and attention holding, in harmony with the reader's own experience, and thus provide a 'natural' basis for generalisation.

2. Case studies allow generalisations either about an instance or from an instance to a class. Their peculiar strength lies in their attention to the subtlety and complexity of the case in its own right.

3. Case studies recognise the complexity and 'embeddedness' of social truths. By carefully attending to social situations, case studies can represent something of the discrepancies or conflicts between the viewpoints held by participants. The best case studies are capable of offering some support to alternative interpretations.

4. Case studies, considered as products, may form an archive of descriptive material sufficiently rich to admit subsequent reinterpretation. Given the variety and complexity of educational purposes and environments, there is an obvious value in having a data source for researchers and users whose purposes may be different from our own.

5. Case studies are 'a step to action'. They begin in a world of action and contribute to it. Their insights may be directly interpreted and put to use; for staff or individual self-development, for within-institutional feedback; for formative evaluation; and in educational policy making.

6. Case studies present research or evaluation data in a more publicly accessible form than other kinds of research report, although this virtue is to some extent bought at the expense of their length. The language and the form of the presentation is hopefully less esoteric and less dependent on specialised interpretation than conventional research reports. The case study is capable of serving multiple audiences. It reduces the dependence of the reader upon unstated implicit assumptions ... and makes the research process itself accessible. Case studies, therefore, may contribute towards the 'democratisation' of decision-making (and knowledge itself). At its best, they allow the reader to judge the implications of a study for himself.

Source: adapted from Adelman *et al.*[22]

people. The correlations are to be interpreted as 0.00 indicating a total absence of identification while 1.00 represents maximum identification.

Weinreich draws two specific conclusions from his analysis of John's identity structure. First, the process of identity diffusion resolution does not necessarily mean that the person becomes better adapted to his own situation as judged in mental health terms. It may even be that the terminology of mental health is inappropriate in this case. From one vantage point, Weinreich suggests, John has improved. His self-evaluation is becoming more positive and his behaviour more controlled. From a different vantage point, however, things are far from well. John dislikes his own skin colour and dissociates himself from his own ethnic group. It is the understanding of John's identity structure, the research suggests, which is an essential prerequisite to any therapeutic aid that might be undertaken by a black therapist.

To conclude, the very different strategies we have illustrated in our six examples of educational case studies suggest that *participant observation* is best thought of as a generic term that describes a methodological approach rather than one specific method. What our examples have shown is that the representativeness of a particular sample often relates to the observational strategy open to the researcher. Generally speaking, the larger the example, the more representative it is, and the more likely that the observer's role is of a participant nature.

Conclusion

The reader will now have a good idea of the nature and possibilities of case study research and of its particular value to educational researchers. To conclude this chapter, we refer to some of the advantages of this style of research as outlined by Adelman and his colleagues[22] which we have listed in Box 5.12. Indeed, we recommend the reader to peruse the whole set of readings from which this particular paper is drawn.[23]

References

1. Patrick, J., *A Glasgow Gang Observed* (Eyre Methuen, London, 1973).

2.   Parker, H.J., *View from the Boys* (David and Charles, Newton Abbot, 1974).
3.   Young, J., *The Drugtakers* (Paladin, London, 1971).
4.   King, R. *All Things Bright and Beautiful?* (John Wiley, Chichester, 1979); Sharp, R. and Green, A. *Education and Social Control* (Routledge and Kegan Paul, London, 1975); Hargreaves, D.H., *Social Relations in a Secondary School* (Routledge and Kegan Paul, London, 1967); Lacey, C., *Hightown Grammar* (Manchester University Press, Manchester, 1970); Woods, P., *The Divided School* (Routledge and Kegan Paul, London, 1979).
5.   Willis, P.E., *Learning to Labour* (Saxon House, London, 1977).
6.   Bailey, K.D., *Methods of Social Research* (Collier-Macmillan, London, 1978).
7.   Schutz, A., *Collected Papers* (Nijhoff, The Hague, 1962).
8.   Denzin, N.K., *The Research Act in Sociology: A Theoretical Introduction to Sociological Methods* (The Butterworth Group, London, 1970).
9.   Lofland, J., *Analysing Social Settings* (Wadsworth, Belmont, Calif., 1971).
10.   Wolcott, H.F., *The Man in the Principal's Office* (Holt, Rinehart and Winston, New York, 1973). For a recent British study employing ethnographic techniques and looking, *inter alia*, at the leadership of the head teacher, see: Burgess, R.G., *Experiencing Comprehensive Education* (Methuen, London, 1983). For a detailed analysis of one comprehensive school, see: Ball, S.J., *Beachside Comprehensive: A Case Study of Secondary Schooling* (Cambridge University Press, Cambridge, 1981).
11.   Walker, R., 'Making sense and losing meaning: Problems of selection in doing Case Study', in Simons, H., (ed.), *Towards a Science of the Singular* (Centre for Applied Research in Education, University of East Anglia, 1980).
12.   Rutter, M., Maughan, B., Mortimore, P. and Ouston, J., *Fifteen Thousand Hours* (Open Books, London, 1979).
13.   Diesing, P., *Patterns of Discovery in the Social Sciences* (Aldine, Chicago, 1971).
14.   Lambert, R., Bullock, R. and Millham, S., *The Chance of a Lifetime?* (Weidenfeld and Nicholson, London, 1975); Lambert, R., Millham, S. and Bullock, R., *A Manual to the Sociology of the School* (Weidenfeld and Nicholson, London, 1970).
15.   Weber, M., *Essays in Sociology* (Routledge and Kegan Paul, London, 1948); Weber, M., *The Theory of Social and Economic Organization* (Free Press, Glencoe, 1964).
16.   Parsons, T., *The Social System* (Free Press, New York, 1951).
17.   Dahrendorf, R., *Class and Class Conflict in Industrial Society* (Routledge and Kegan Paul, London, 1959).
18.   Glaser, B.G. and Strauss, A.L., *The Discovery of Grounded Theory* (Aldine, Chicago, 1967).
19.   Adams, R.S. and Biddle, B.J., *Realities of Teaching: Explorations with Videotape* (Holt, Rinehart and Winston, New York, 1970).
20.   Shields, R.W., *A Cure of Delinquents* (Heinemann Educational Books, London, 1962).
21.   Verma, G. and Bagley, C. (eds) *Race, Education and Equality* (Macmillan, London, 1979).
22.   Adelman, C., Jenkins, D. and Kemmis, S., 'Rethinking case study: Notes from the Second Cambridge Conference', in Simons.[23]
23.   Simons, H. (ed.), *Towards a Science of the Singular* (Centre for Applied Research in Education, University of East Anglia, 1980).

6 CORRELATIONAL RESEARCH

Introduction

Human behaviour at both the individual and social level is characterised by great complexity, a complexity about which we understand comparatively little, given the present state of social research. One approach to a fuller understanding of human behaviour is to begin by teasing out simple relationships between those factors and elements deemed to have some bearing on the phenomena in question. The value of correlational research is that it is able to achieve this end.

Before we attempt to describe correlational research as such, it might be useful if we begin by examining *correlation* and related terms and indicating the purposes they fulfil in statistical analysis. We saw in the introduction that one of the primary purposes of science as it is traditionally conceived is to discover relationships among phenomena with a view ultimately to predicting and, in some situations, controlling their occurrence. As we suggested above, much of social research in general, and educational research more particularly, is concerned at our present stage of development with the first step in this sequence — establishing interrelationships among variables. We may wish to know, for example, how delinquency is related to social class background; or whether an association exists between the number of years spent in full-time education and subsequent annual income; or whether there is a link between personality and achievement. Numerous techniques have been devised to provide us with numerical representations of such relationships and they are known as *measures of association*. We list the principal ones in Box 6.1.

At this point it's pertinent to say a few words about some terms used in Box 6.1 to describe the nature of variables. It enables us to draw a distinction between the concepts of *association* and *correlation*. A full treatment of that distinction is inappropriate in an introductory chapter such as this. The interested reader is referred to Cohen and Holliday,[2] a text containing worked examples of the appropriate use (and limitations) of the correlational techniques outlined in Box 6.1 together with other measures of association such

149

Box 6.1: Common Measures of Relationship

Measure	Nature of Variables	Comment
Pearson product moment *r*	Two continuous variables; interval or ratio scale	Relationship linear
Rank order or Kendall's tau	Two continuous variables; ordinal scale	
Correlation ratio, η (eta)	One variable continuous, other either continuous or discrete	Relationship nonlinear
Intraclass	One variable continuous; other discrete; interval or ratio scale	Purpose: to determine within-group similarity
Biserial, r_{bis} Point biserial, $r_{pt.bis}$	One variable continuous; other (a) continuous but dichotomised, r_{bis}, or (b) true dichotomy, $r_{pt.bis}$	Index of item discrimination (used in item analysis)
Phi coefficient, φ	Two true dichotomies; nominal or ordinal series	
Partial correlation $r_{12.3...}$	Three or more continuous variables	Purpose: to determine relationship between two variables, with effect of third held constant
Multiple correlation $r_{1.234...}$	Three or more continuous variables	Purpose: to predict one variable from a linear weighted combination of two or more independent variables
Kendall's coefficient of concordance, ω	Three or more continuous variables; ordinal series	Purpose: to determine the degree of (say, interrater) agreement

Source: Mouly.[1]

as Kruskal's *gamma*, Somer's *d*, and Guttman's *lambda*.

Look at the words used at the top of the Box to explain the nature of variables in connection with the measure called the Pearson product moment *r*. The variables, we learn, are *continuous* and at the *interval* or the *ratio* scale of measurement.

A *continuous variable* is one that, theoretically at least, can take any value between two points on a scale. *Weight,* for example, is a continuous variable; so too is *time*, so also is *height*. *Weight, time* and *height* can take on any number of possible values between nought and infinity, the feasibility of measuring them across such a range being limited only by the variability of suitable measuring instruments. A *ratio* scale includes an absolute zero and provides equal *intervals*. Using weight as our example, we can say that no mass at all is a zero measure and that 1,000 grams is 400 grams heavier than 600 grams and twice as heavy as 500. In our discussion of correlational research that follows, we refer to a relationship as a *correlation* rather than an *association* whenever that relationship can be further specified in terms of an increase or a decrease of a *certain number of units* in the one variable (I.Q. for example) producing an increase or a decrease of a *related number of units* of the other (e.g. mathematical ability).

Turning again to Box 6.1, we read in connection with the second measure shown there (Rank order or Kendall's tau) that the two continuous variables are at the *ordinal* scale of measurement. An *ordinal* scale is used to indicate rank order; that is to say, it arranges individuals or objects in a series ranging from the highest to the lowest according to the particular characteristic being measured. In contrast to the interval scale discussed earlier, ordinal numbers assigned to such a series do not indicate absolute quantities nor can one assume that the intervals between the numbers are equal. For example, in a class of children rated by a teacher on the degree of their co-operativeness and ranged from highest to lowest according to that attribute, it cannot be assumed that the difference in the degree of co-operativeness between subjects ranked one and two is the same as that obtaining between subjects nine and ten; nor can it be taken that subject one possesses ten times the quantity of co-operativeness of subject ten.

The variables involved in connection with the Phi coefficient measure of association (half-way down Box 6.1) are described as *true dichotomies* and at the *nominal* scale of measurement. *Truly dichotomous* variables (such as *sex* or *driving test result*) can take only two values (male or female; pass or fail). The *nominal* scale is the most elementary scale of measurement. It does no more than identify the categories into which individuals, objects or events may be classified. Those categories have to be *mutually exclusive* of course, and a nominal scale should also be *complete*; that is to say it should include all possible classifications of a particular type.

The classification of votes in a by-election (Conservative, Labour, Liberal, SDP, Communist, Independent, Ecology, etc.) is an example of the use of a complete nominal scale, complete, that is, in the sense that all of the political parties fighting the by-election are represented in the final count of voting preferences.

To conclude our explanation of terminology, readers should note the use of the term *discrete variable* in the description of the third correlation ratio (eta) in Box 6.1. We said earlier that a *continuous variable* can take on *any value* between two points on a scale. A *discrete* variable, however, can only take on numerals or values that are specific points on a scale. The number of players in a football team is a discrete variable. It's usually eleven; it could be less than eleven, but it could never be $7\frac{1}{4}$!

In our discussion of the principal correlational techniques shown in Box 6.1, three are of special interest to us and these form the basis of much of the rest of the chapter. They are the Pearson product moment correlation coefficient, multiple correlation, and partial correlation.

Correlational techniques are generally intended to answer three questions about two variables or two sets of data:[2] (a) is there a relationship between the two variables (or sets of data)? If the answer to this question is 'yes', then two other questions follow: (b) what is the direction of the relationship? and (c) what is the magnitude?

Relationship in this context refers to any tendency for the two variables (or sets of data) to vary consistently. Pearson's product moment coefficient of correlation, one of the best-known measures of association, is a statistical value ranging from -1.0 to $+1.0$ and expresses this relationship in quantitative form. The coefficient is represented by the symbol *r*. Where the two variables (or sets of data) fluctuate in the same direction, i.e. as one increases so does the other or as one decreases so does the other, a *positive* relationship is said to exist. Correlations reflecting this pattern are prefaced with a plus sign to indicate the positive nature of the relationship. Thus, $+1.0$ would indicate perfect positive correlation between two factors, as with the radius and diameter of a circle, and $+.80$ a high positive correlation, as between academic achievement and intelligence, for example. Where the sign has been omitted, a plus sign is assumed.

A negative correlation or relationship, on the other hand, is to be found when an increase in one variable is accompanied by a decrease in the other variable. Negative correlations are prefaced with a minus sign. Thus, -1.0 would represent perfect negative correlation, as between the number of errors children make on a spelling test and their score on the test, and -0.20 a low negative correlation, as between absenteeism and intelligence, say. There is no other meaning to the signs used; they indicate nothing more than which pattern holds for any two variables (or sets of data).

Generally speaking, researchers tend to be more interested in the magnitude or size of an obtained correlation than they are in its direction. Correlational procedures have been developed so that no relationship whatever between two variables is represented by zero (or 0.00), as between body weight and intelligence, possibly. This means that a person's performance on one variable is totally unrelated to his performance on a second variable. If he is high on one, for example, he is just as likely to be high or low on the other. Perfect correlations of $+1.00$ or -1.00 are rarely found and, as we shall see, most coefficients of correlation in social research are around $+0.50$ or less. The correlation coefficient may be seen then as an indication of the predictability of one variable given the other: it is an indication of covariation. The relationship between two variables can be examined visually by plotting the paired measurements on graph paper with each pair of observations being represented by a point. The resulting arrangement of points is known as a *scatter diagram* and enables us to assess graphically the degree of relationship between the characteristics being measured. Box 6.2 gives some examples of scatter diagrams in the field of educational research.

The coefficient of correlation, then, tells us something about the relationship between *two variables*. Other measures exist, however, which allow us to specify relationships when more than two variables are involved. These are known as measures of *multiple correlation* and *partial correlation*.

Multiple correlation measures indicate the degree of association between three or more variables simultaneously. We may want to know, for example, the degree of association between delinquency, social class background and leisure facilities. Or we may be interested in finding out the relationship between academic achievement, intelligence and neuroticism. Multiple correlation, or *regression* as it is sometimes called, indicates the degree of association between *n* variables. It is related not only to the correlations of the independent variable with the dependent variables, but also to the

Box 6.2: Correlation Scatter Diagrams

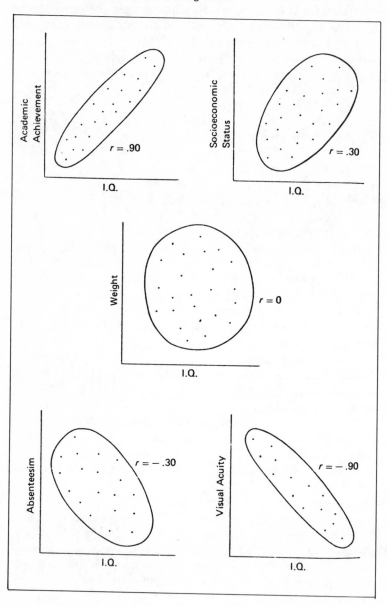

Source: Tuckman.[5]

intercorrelations between the dependent variables.

Partial correlation aims at establishing the degree of association between two variables after the influence of a third has been controlled or partialled out. Guilford and Fruchter[4] define a partial correlation between two variables as

> one that nullifies the effects of a third variable (or a number of variables) upon both the variables being correlated. The correlation between height and weight of boys in a group where age is permitted to vary would be higher than the correlation between height and weight in a group at constant age. The reason is obvious. Because certain boys are older, they are both heavier and taller. Age is a factor that enhances the strength of correspondence between height and weight. With age held constant, the correlation would still be positive and significant because at any age, taller boys tend to be heavier.

Consider, too, the relationship between success in basketball and previous experience in the game. Suppose, also, that the presence of a third factor, the height of the players, was known to have an important influence on the other two factors. The use of partial correlation techniques would enable a measure of the two primary variables to be achieved freed from the influence of the secondary variable.

It follows from what we have said so far that *correlational research* embraces those studies and projects in which attempts are made to discover or clarify relationships through the use of correlation coefficients. Relationships thus disclosed may simply indicate what goes with what in a given context, or else they may provide a basis on which to make predictions about the variables being studied. The basic design of correlational research is simple and involves collecting two or more scores on the same group of subjects and computing correlation coefficients. Many useful studies have been based on this simple design. Those involving more complex relationships, however, utilise multiple and partial correlations in order to provide a clearer picture of the relationships being investigated. One observer[6] points out, however, that the quality of correlation studies is determined not by the complexity of the design or the sophistication of the correlational techniques used but by the level of planning and the depth of the theoretical constructs going into the development of the hypotheses.

One final point: it is important to stress that correlations refer to measures of association and do not necessarily indicate causal relationships between variables. Mouly[1] puts it like this:

> The correlation simply implies concomitance; it is not synonymous with causation. It may suggest causation in the same sense that the variables involved are part of a cause and effect system, but the nature of the system and the direction in which the components operate is not specified in the correlation. The two variables are not necessarily (or perhaps even commonly) the 'cause' and 'effect' of each other. The correlation between X and Y is often nothing more than the reflection of the operation of a third factor.

Characteristics

We indicated above that correlational studies may be broadly classified as either *relational studies* or as *prediction studies*. We now look at each a little more closely.

In the case of the first of these two categories, correlational research is mainly concerned with achieving a fuller understanding of the complexity of phenomena or, in the matter of behavioural and educational research, behavioural patterns by studying the relationships between the variables which the researcher hypothesises as being related. As a method, it is particularly useful in exploratory studies into fields where little or no previous research has been undertaken. It is often a shot in the dark aimed at verifying hunches a researcher has about a presumed relationship between characteristics or variables. Take a complex notion like *teacher effectiveness*, for example. This is dependent upon a number of less complex factors operating singly or in combination. Factors such as intelligence, motivation, person perception, verbal skills and empathy come to mind as possibly having an effect on teaching outcomes. A review of the literature of research will confirm or reject these possibilities. Once an appropriate number have been identified in this way, suitable measures may then be chosen or developed to assess them. They are then given to a representative sample and the scores obtained are then correlated with a measure of the complex factor being investigated, namely, teacher effectiveness. As it is an exploratory undertaking, the analysis will consist of correlation coefficients only, though if it is designed carefully, we will begin to achieve some understanding of the particular behaviour being studied. The investigation and its outcomes may then be used as a basis for further research or as a source for additional hypotheses.

Exploratory relationship studies may also employ partial correlational techniques. Partial correlation is a particularly suitable approach when a researcher wishes to nullify the influence of one or more important factors upon behaviour in order to bring the effect of less important factors into greater prominence. If, for example, we wanted to understand more fully the determinants of academic achievement in a comprehensive school, we might begin by acknowledging the importance of the factor of intelligence and establishing a relationship between intelligence and academic achievement. The intelligence factor could then be held constant by partial correlation, thus enabling the investigator to clarify other, lesser factors such as motivation, parental encouragement or vocational aspiration. Clearly, motivation is related to academic achievement but if a pupil's motivation score is correlated with academic achievement without controlling the intelligence factor, it will be difficult to assess the true effect of motivation on achievement because the pupil with high intelligence but low motivation may possibly achieve more than pupils with lower intelligence but higher motivation. Once intelligence has been nullified, it is possible to see more clearly the relationship between motivation and achievement. The next stage might be to control the effects of both intelligence and motivation and then to seek a clearer idea of the effects of other selected factors — parental encouragement or vocational aspiration, for instance.

In contrast to exploratory relationship studies, prediction studies are usually undertaken in areas having a firmer and securer knowledge base. Prediction through the use of correlational techniques is based on the assumption that at least some of the factors that will lead to the behaviour to be predicted are present and measurable at the time the prediction is made.[6] If, for example, we wanted to predict the probable success of a group of salesmen on an intensive training course, we would start with variables that have been found in previous research to be related to later success in saleswork. These might include: enterprise, verbal ability, achievement motivation, emotional maturity, sociability and so on. The extent to which these predictors correlate with the particular behaviour we wish to predict, namely, successful salesmanship, will determine the accuracy of our prediction. Clearly, variables crucial to success cannot be predicted if they are not present at the time of making the prediction. A salesman's ability to fit in with a team of fellow salesmen cannot be predicted where these future colleagues are unknown.

In order to be valuable in prediction, the magnitude of association between two variables must be substantial; and the greater the association, the more accurate the prediction it permits. In practice, this means that anything less than perfect correlation will permit errors in predicting one variable from a knowledge of the other. As Mouly[1] explains,

> The correlation must, of course, represent a real relationship rather than simply the operation of chance. Beyond this, what constitutes an adequate correlation between two variables can be appraised only on the basis of what can logically be expected, and, of course, what accuracy of prediction is required to serve the purpose of the study. A coefficient of correlation of +0.35 between motivation and grades, for example, is perhaps all that can be expected from our presently crude measures of motivation and of grades.

Borg[6] recalls that much prediction research in the United States has been carried out in the field of scholastic success. Some studies in this connection have been aimed at short-term prediction of students' performance in specific courses of study, while other studies have been directed at long-term prediction of general academic success. Sometimes, short-term academic prediction is based upon a single predictor variable. Most efforts to predict future behaviours, however, are based upon scores on a number of predictor variables each of which is useful in predicting a specific aspect of future behaviour. In the prediction of college success, for example, a single variable such as academic achievement is less effective as a predictor than a combination of variables such as academic achievement together with, say, motivation, intelligence, study habits, etc. More complex studies of this kind, therefore, generally make use of multiple correlation and multiple regression equations.

Predicting behaviours or events likely to occur in the near future is easier and less hazardous than predicting behaviours likely to occur in the more distant future. The reason is that in short-term prediction, more of the factors leading to success in the predicted behaviour are likely to be present. In addition, short-term prediction allows less time for important predictor variables to change or for the individual to gain experience that would tend to change his likelihood of success in the predicted behaviour.

One further point: correlation, as Mouly observes, is a group concept, a generalised measure that is useful basically in predicting group performance. Whereas, for instance, it can be predicted that gifted children as a group will succeed at school, it cannot be predicted with certainty that one particular gifted child will excel. As to the relative value of the correlation coefficient he notes,

> Since most correlations between the variables of interest in the social sciences are of the order of 0.50, relatively little confidence can be placed in such prediction in the individual case. It is, therefore, necessary to raise the correlation on the basis of which predictions are made in order to increase their precision. This can be done by refining the instruments used and/or the criterion being predicted, and ... by combining a number of variables into a composite predictor of the criterion.

Occasions When Appropriate

From the preceding discussion, we may readily see that the techniques of correlational research are particularly useful in social and educational investigations. Abstracting from the main points of the arguments, then, we may say that correlational research is appropriate in the following *two* instances. *First*, it is appropriate when there is a need to *discover* or *clarify* relationships and where correlation coefficients will achieve these ends. It is especially useful in this connection in the initial stages of a project where a certain amount of basic groundwork has to be covered to get some idea of the structure of the relationships. In this way it gets at degrees of relationships rather than the all-or-nothing question posed by experimental design — is an effect present or absent? Beyond this stage, relationships may become a source of hypotheses and further research. The correlational approach is also valuable when variables are complex and do not lend themselves therefore to the experimental method and controlled manipulation. It also permits the measurement of several variables and their interrelationships simultaneously in realistic settings. Both of these later instances will be characterised by the use of multiple and partial correlations.

Second, correlational research is appropriate where the objective, or one of a set of objectives, is to achieve some degree of prediction. Correlational techniques make up one of a range of alternative approaches in this regard. We have already identified a number of characteristics of prediction studies and it is sufficient at this point to note them as being occasions when a predictive approach may be fruitful. Thus, prediction studies are appropriate where a firm basis of previous knowledge is present, the assumption being that at least some of the factors will relate to the behaviour to be predicted. There needs, too, to be a reasonable chance of achieving a high or moderately high correlation coefficient. Low coefficients will have little predictive value. Further, for confident results prediction research is more appropriate for events likely to occur in the immediate future than at some point in the distant future. Finally, prediction studies are suitable where a group as opposed to an individual is the focus of a project. Only a high correlation can be regarded as valid for individual prediction.

Advantages and Disadvantages

Correlational research possesses a number of advantages and disadvantages which we will here briefly review. As regards its advantages, correlational research is particularly useful in tackling the problems of education and the social sciences because it allows for the measurement of a number of variables and their relationships simultaneously. The experimental approach, by contrast, is characterised by the manipulation of a single variable and is thus appropriate for dealing with problems where simple causal relationships exist. In educational and behavioural research, it is invariably the case that a number of variables contribute to a particular outcome. Experimental research thus introduces a note of unreality into research, whereas correlational approaches, while less rigorous, allow for the study of behaviour in more realistic settings. Where an element of control is required, however, partial correlation achieves this without changing the context in which the study takes place.

A second advantage of correlational research we have already noted: it yields information concerning the degree of relationship between the variables being studied. It thus provides the researcher with insights into the way variables operate that cannot be gained by other means. We may itemise the remaining strengths of the method in a few words: as a basis for prediction studies, it enables researchers to make estimates of the probable accuracy of their predictions; it is especially useful for lower-level ground work where it serves as a powerful exploratory tool; and it does not require large samples.

Among its limitations, correlational research only identifies what goes with what — it only implies concomitance and therefore does not necessarily establish cause-and-effect relationships; it is less rigorous than the experimental approach because it exercises less control over the independent variables; it is prone to identify spurious relational patterns; it adopts an atomistic approach; and the correlation index is relatively imprecise, being limited by the unreliability of the measurements of the variables.

Interpreting the Correlation Coefficient

Once a correlation coefficient has been computed, there remains the problem of interpreting it. A question often asked in this connection is how large should the coefficient be for it to be meaningful. The question may be approached in three ways: (1) by examining the strength of the relationship; (2) by examining the statistical significance of the relationship; and (3) by examining the square of the correlation coefficient.

Inspection of the numerical value of a correlation coefficient will yield clear indication of the *strength* of the relationship between the variables in question. Low or near zero values indicate weak relationships, while those nearer to $+1$ or -1 suggest stronger relationships. Imagine, for instance, that a measure of a teacher's success in the classroom after five years in the profession is correlated with his final school experience grade as a student and that it was found that $r = 0.19$. Suppose now that his score on classroom success is correlated with a measure of need for professional achievement and that this yielded a correlation of 0.65. It could be concluded that there is a stronger relationship between success and professional achievement scores than between success and final student grade.

Where a correlation coefficient has been derived from a sample and one wishes to use it as a basis for inference about the parent population, the *statistical significance* of the obtained correlation must be considered. Statistical significance when applied to a correlation coefficient indicates whether or not the correlation is different from zero at a given level of confidence. A statistically significant correlation is indicative of an actual relationship rather than one due entirely to chance. The level of statistical significance of a correlation is determined to a great extent by the number of cases upon which the correlation is based. Thus, the more cases, the smaller the correlation coefficient need be to be significant at a given level of confidence.

Exploratory relationship studies are generally interpreted with reference to their statistical significance, whereas prediction studies depend for their efficacy on the strength of the correlation coefficients. These need to be considerably higher than those found in exploratory relationship studies and for this reason rarely invoke the concept of significance.

The third approach to interpreting a coefficient is provided by examining the *square* of the coefficient of correlation, r^2. This shows the proportion of variance in one variable that can be attributed to its linear relationship with the second variable. In other words, it indicates the amount the two variables have in common. If, for example, two variables A and B have a correlation of 0.50, then $(0.50)^2$ or 0.25 of the variation shown by the B scores can be attributed to the tendency of B to vary linearly with A. Box 6.3 shows graphically the common variance between reading grade and arithmetic grade having a correlation of 0.65.

There are three cautions to be borne in mind when one is interpreting a correlation coefficient. First, a coefficient is a simple number and must not be interpreted as a percentage. A correlation of 0.50, for instance, does not mean 50 per cent relationship between the variables. Further, a correlation of 0.50 does *not* indicate twice as much relationship as that shown by a correlation of 0.25. A correlation of 0.50 actually indicates more than twice the relationship shown by a correlation of 0.25. In fact, as coefficients approach +1 or −1, a difference in the absolute values of the coefficients becomes more important than the same numerical difference between lower correlations would be.

Second, a correlation does not necessarily imply a cause-and-effect relationship between two factors, as we have previously

Box 6.3: Visualisation of Correlation of 0.65 Between Reading Grade and Arithmetic Grade

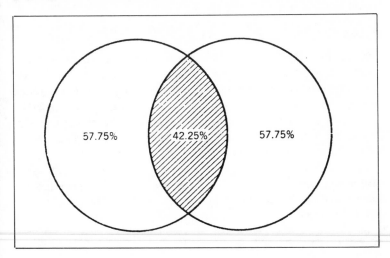

Source: Fox.[3]

indicated. It should not therefore be interpreted as meaning that one factor is causing the scores on the other to be as they are. There are invariably other factors influencing both variables under consideration. Suspected cause-and-effect relationships would have to be confirmed by subsequent experimental study.

Third, a correlation coefficient is not to be interpreted in any absolute sense. A correlational value for a given sample of a population may not necessarily be the same as that found in another sample from the same population. Many factors influence the value of a given correlation coefficient and if a researcher wishes to extrapolate to the population from which he drew his sample, he will then have to test the significance of the correlation.

We now offer some general guidelines for interpreting correlation coefficients. They are based on Borg's[6] analysis and assume that the correlations relate to a hundred or more subjects.

Correlations Ranging from 0.20 to 0.35

Correlations within this range show only very slight relationship between variables although they may be statistically significant. A correlation of 0.20 shows that only 4 per cent of the variance is common to the two measures. Whereas correlations at this level may have limited meaning in exploratory relationship research, they are of no value in either individual or group prediction studies.

Correlations Ranging from 0.35 to 0.65

Within this range, correlations are statistically significant beyond the 1 per cent level. When correlations are around 0.40, crude group prediction may be possible. As Borg notes, correlations within this range are useful, however, when combined with other correlations in a multiple regression equation. Combining several correlations in this range can in some cases yield individual predictions that are correct within an acceptable margin of error. Correlations at this level used singly are of little use for individual prediction because they yield only a few more correct predictions than could be accomplished by guessing or by using some chance selection procedure.

Correlations Ranging from 0.65 to 0.85

Correlations within this range make possible group predictions that are accurate enough for most purposes. Nearer the top of the range, group predictions can be made very accurately, usually predicting the proportion of successful candidates in selection problems within a very small margin of error. Near the top of this correlation range individual predictions can be made that are considerably more accurate than would occur if no such selection procedures were used.

Correlations Over 0.85

Correlations as high as this indicate a close relationship between the two variables correlated. A correlation of 0.85 indicates that the measure used for prediction has about 72 per cent variance in common with the performance being predicted. Prediction studies in education very rarely yield correlations this high. When correlations at this level are obtained, however, they are very useful for either individual or group prediction.

Two Examples of Correlational Research

Correlational research is one of the more popular kinds of investigation in both social and educational fields. That correlational studies in these areas are relatively easy to design and coefficients comparatively easy to compute has contributed to the popularity of the approach. To conclude this chapter we illustrate the use of correlational coefficients in examples drawn from education and social research.

The first[7] is concerned with predicting future success in graduate school from a set of entrance tests consisting of several measures of ability.

The setting is the University of New Hampshire where, typically, students who wish to pursue advanced studies beyond their bachelor degrees are required to take a series of tests called the Graduate Record Examinations Aptitude Tests (GRE) to assist admissions tutors make decisions as to who is most likely to succeed. In this study by Herbert and Holmes,[7] the records of 67 Master of Education degree candidates are examined to determine the relationship between their scores on three GRE measures (GRE-V, verbal ability; GRE-Q, numerical ability and GRE-T, total ability) at time of entry and their graduate grade point averages (GGPA*) at the end of the three-year course of advanced study. The researchers report the following results:

The correlation between the verbal ability test (GRE-V) and GGPA = 0.35 ($p < 0.005$)

The correlation between the numerical ability test (GRE-Q) and GGPA = 0.18 (n.s.)

and The correlation between the total ability test score (GRE-T) and GGPA = 0.34 ($p < .005$)

A word of explanation about these findings. In the case of the GRE−V/GGPA and the GRE−T/GGPA correlations, both are described as *statistically significant* at the 0.005 level of significance. Simply put, correlation coefficients of 0.35 and 0.34 respectively in a sample of 67 could only occur *by chance* five times in a thousand, i.e. ($p < 0.005$). In other words, nine hundred and ninety-five times in a thousand the relationships would not

---

*Grade points average (GPA) is the widely-accepted method of assessing academic performance in both undergraduate and postgraduate schools of study in North America. Thus, where D = 1, C = 2, B = 3, and A = 4, an overall GPA of 3.8 is a very creditable performance whereas a GPA of, say, 1.3 would cause dismay both to students and professors!

occur by chance; rather, they point to an association between students' 'verbal' and 'total' abilities when applying for graduate school studies and their final performances as measured by the grade point averages. Notice that in this particular institution and on this specific course of study, numerical ability (GRE–Q) does *not* predict GGPA. That is to say, a correlation coefficient of 0.18 between GRE–Q and GGPA is not statistically significant (n.s). We might surmise that had the New Hampshire graduate school of study been concerned with Mathematics rather than Education, then the correlation between GRE–Q and GGPA might well have been quite different. One final word before we move on to our second example of correlational research. It's important to distinguish between *statistical significance* and *educational significance.* What may be statistically significant may be of no educational significance whatsoever. Take, for example, the finding that the GRE–V and GGPA correlate at 0.35 (p $<$0.005). One way to estimate the 'educational' usefulness of that correlation is to square it $(0.35^2=0.1225)$ and use the square as an indication of the amount of variance that GRE–V and GGPA have in common. Put differently, only just over 12 per cent of the variance in graduate grade point average is 'explained' by the verbal ability test required on entry to graduate school. It follows therefore that almost 88 per cent of success in graduate school is 'explained' by other factors (motivation, interest, relationships with tutors, luck, etc.). Perhaps admissions tutors at the New Hampshire Graduate School of Education would do well to look for measures with considerably higher predictive validity than the GRE test battery.

Our second example of correlational research is drawn from the broad area of social psychology.

Suppose a researcher were interested in the alleged connection between watching violence on television and subsequent aggressive behaviour. After a little thought on the matter, he would probably come to the conclusion that there are four competing hypotheses accounting for the phenomenon: (1) that aggression is the independent variable and television violence the dependent variable; (2) that television violence is the independent variable and aggression the dependent variable; (3) that both aggression and television violence are independent variables; or (4) that both aggression and television violence are dependent variables and that some other, as yet unspecified, variable is their common cause.

A study by Eron, Huesman, Lefkowitz and Walder[8] has

attempted to unravel just such a situation. Concerned about the increasing prominence of violence in society, the researchers followed up earlier studies in this area in which a definite relationship between overt aggression and television habits had been demonstrated by attempting to establish a causal link between the two. Their hypothesis posited, therefore, that a young adult's aggressiveness is positively related to his preference for violent television when he was eight or nine years of age and that his preference for violent television during this critical period is one cause for his aggressiveness.

The approach adopted by the researchers was to examine the correlations across the two variables over a period of time within the framework of a longitudinal design. The cross-lagged analysis which was used in this instance examined the temporal cross correlations of the variables, thus enabling the investigators to eliminate some of the rival hypotheses. Briefly, longitudinal data were collected on 427 teenagers of an original group of 875 children who had taken part in a study of third-grade children (8–9 years old) ten years earlier in 1960. Data on the 427 teenagers were therefore collected in 1970. Of this number, 211 were boys and it is the part of the study involving these that we are particularly interested in. Two measures were taken on both occasions — measures of the boys' aggressive behaviour and measures of their preference for watching violence on television programmes. In addition, other variables which may have contributed to either interest in television violence or aggressiveness were controlled by means of partial correlations.

The correlations between a preference for violent television and aggression for the 211 boys over the ten-year period are illustrated in Box 6.4. In examining the 'outer' correlations, we notice a small but positive relationship between the preference for violent television and aggression among the third graders (0.21), but only a tiny, negative relationship between the same variables when the boys were in the thirteenth grade (19 years old) (−0.05). Further, there is little relationship between the boys' viewing habits in childhood and their television preferences as adolescents (0.05), but a higher correlation between aggression in the third grade and aggression in the thirteenth grade, which seems to suggest that the pattern of aggression persists once learnt.

If we now inspect the cross-lagged correlations, we see a negligible correlation of 0.01 between aggression in the third grade and

Box 6.4: The Correlations Between a Preference for Violent Television and Peer-rated Aggression for 211 Boys Over a 10-year Lag

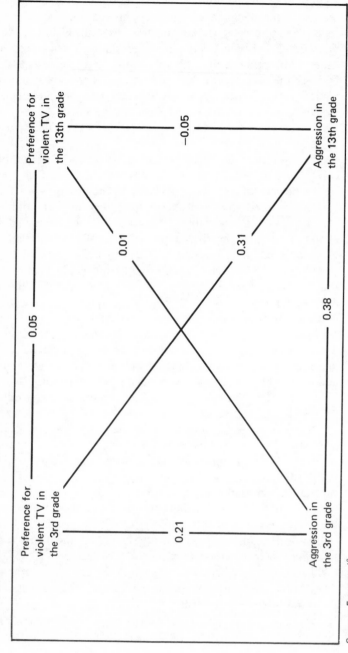

Source: Eron *et al*.[8]

a preference for violent television in the thirteenth grade and this would seem to rule out the possibility that aggression was a determinant of the boys' subsequent television habits. If we now examine the correlation between preference for television violence in the third grade and aggression in the thirteenth grade, we see a highly significant relationship. This effect was not apparent for the girls in the group. As the researchers themselves explain:

> While the correlation between third-grade preferences and thirteenth-grade peer-rated aggression explains only 10 % of the variance in aggression, 10 % is impressive when one considers the probable limitations on the size of the correlation imposed by the skewed distributions of the variables, the large number of variables affecting aggression, the comparatively small explanatory power of these other variables, and the 10-year lag between measurement times. The extremely low likelihood of achieving such a correlation by chance is a good indicator of the strength of the relation between preference for violent television at age 8 years and peer-rated aggression at age 19.

The researchers conclude by suggesting that watching violent television programmes in the early formative years has a probable causative influence on later aggression. This interesting study is an excellent example of the use of correlation in relational research and of the sophisticated ends to which it can be put.

References

1. Mouly, G.J., *Educational Research: The Art and Science of Investigation* (Allyn and Bacon, Boston, 1978).
2. Cohen, L. and Holliday, M., *Statistics for Social Scientists* (Harper and Row, London, 1982).
3. Fox, D.J., *The Research Process in Education* (Holt, Rinehart and Winston, New York, 1969).
4. Guilford, J.P. and Fruchter, B. *Fundamental Statistics in Psychology and Education* (McGraw Hill, New York, 1973).
5. Tuckman, B.W., *Conducting Educational Research* (Harcourt Brace Jovanovich, New York, 1972).
6. Borg, W.R., *Educational Research: An Introduction* (Longman, London, 1963).
7. Herbert, D.J. and Holmes, A.F., 'Graduate record examinations aptitude test scores as a predictor of graduate grade point average', *Educational and Psychological Measurement*, 39 (1979) 415–19.
8. Eron, L.D., Huesman, L.R., Lefkowitz, M.M. and Walder, L.O., 'Does television violence cause aggression?', *American Psychologist* (April 1972) 253–63.

7 *EX POST FACTO* RESEARCH

Introduction

When translated literally, *ex post facto* means 'from what is done afterwards'. In the context of social and educational research the phrase means 'after the fact' or 'retrospectively' and refers to those studies which investigate possible cause-and-effect relationships by observing an existing condition or state of affairs and searching back in time for plausible causal factors. In effect, the researcher asks himself what factors seem to be associated with certain occurrences, or conditions, or aspects of behaviour. *Ex post facto* research, then, is a method of teasing out possible antecedents of events that have happened and cannot, because of this fact, be engineered or manipulated by the investigator. The following example will illustrate the basic idea. Imagine a situation in which there has been a dramatic increase in the number of fatal road accidents in a particular locality. An expert is called in to investigate. Naturally, there is no way in which he can study the actual accidents because they have happened; nor can he turn to technology for a video replay of the incidents. What he can do, however, is attempt to reconstruct what happened by studying the statistics, examining the accident spots, and taking note of the statements given by victims and witnesses. In this way the expert will be in a position to identify possible determinants of the accidents. These may include excessive speed, poor road conditions, careless driving, frustration, inefficient vehicles, the effects of drugs or alcohol and so on. On the basis of his examination, he can formulate hypotheses as to the likely causes and submit them to the appropriate authority in the form of recommendations. These may include improving road conditions, or lowering the speed limit, or increasing police surveillance, for instance. The point of interest to us is that in identifying the causes *retrospectively*, the expert adopts an *ex post facto* perspective.

Kerlinger[1] has defined *ex post facto* research more formally as that in which the independent variable or variables have already occurred and in which the researcher starts with the observation of a dependent variable or variables. He then studies the independent variable or variables in retrospect for their possible relationship to, and effects on, the dependent variable or variables. The researcher is thus examining retrospectively the effects of a naturally occurring event on a subsequent outcome with a view to establishing a causal link between them. Interestingly, some instances of *ex post facto* designs correspond to experimental research in reverse, for instead of taking groups that are equivalent and subjecting them to different treatments so as to bring about differences in the dependent variables to be measured, an *ex post facto* experiment begins with groups that are already different in some respect and searches in retrospect for the factor that brought about the difference.

Two kinds of design may be identified in *ex post facto* research — the *co-relational study* and the *criterion group study*. The former is sometimes termed *causal research* and the latter, *causal-comparative research*. A co-relational (or causal) study is concerned with identifying the antecedents of a present condition. As its name suggests, it involves the collection of two sets of data, one of which will be retrospective, with a view to determining the relationship between them. The basic design of such an experiment may be represented thus:*

A study by Borkowsky[3] was based upon this kind of design. He attempted to show a relationship between the quality of a music teacher's undergraduate training (X) and his subsequent effectiveness as a teacher of his subject (O). Measures of the quality of a music teacher's college training can include grades in specific courses, overall grade average and self-ratings, etc. Teacher effectiveness can be assessed by indices of pupil performance, pupil knowledge, pupil attitudes and judgement of experts, etc. Correlations between all measures were obtained to determine the relationship. At most, this study could show that a relationship existed, after the fact, between the quality of teacher preparation and subsequent teacher effectiveness. Where a strong relationship is found between the independent and dependent variables, three possible interpretations are open to the researcher:

*In Chapters 7 and 8, we adopt the symbols and conventions used by Campbell and Stanley[2]. These are presented fully on p. 188.

1. that the variable X has caused O;
2. that the variable O has caused X; or
3. that some third unidentified, and therefore unmeasured, variable has caused X and O.

It is often the case that a researcher cannot tell which of these is correct.

The value of co-relational or causal studies lies chiefly in their exploratory or suggestive character for, as we have seen, while they are not always adequate in themselves for establishing causal relationships among variables, they are a useful first step in this direction in that they do yield measures of association.

In the criterion-group (or causal-comparative) approach, the investigator sets out to discover possible causes for a phenomenon being studied by comparing the subjects in which the variable is present with similar subjects in whom it is absent. The basic design in this kind of study may be represented thus:

If, for example, a researcher chose such a design to investigate factors contributing to teacher effectiveness, the criterion group

Box 7.1: Factors Associated with Failure at University

Out of 802 students who began their studies at the University of Bradford in 1966, 102 dropped out at the end of their first year. On entry to the university the whole freshman intake had provided academic and personal information about their backgrounds, their interests, their motivations and values.

In an *ex post facto* research design, comparisons were made between dropouts and non-dropouts in an attempt to discover factors associated with university failure.

In line with previous studies, university failure was found to relate (1) to inferior educational qualifications on entry; (2) to less certainty about choice of career; (3) to a greater degree of worry over abilities to pursue a university course of study; and (4) to feelings of being overwhelmed by the academic work demanded.

Source: adapted from Cohen and Child.[4]

O₁, the effective teachers, and its counterpart O₂, a group *not* showing the characteristics of the criterion group, are identified by measuring the differential effects of the groups on classes of children. The researcher may then examine X, some variable or event, i.e. the background, training, skills and personality of the groups to discover what might 'cause' only some teachers to be effective.

Criterion-group or causal-comparative studies may be seen as bridging the gap between descriptive research methods on the one hand and true experimental research on the other. In Box 7.1 we give a brief summary of an example of the use of the causal comparative design in an investigation into university failure.

Characteristics of *Ex Post Facto* Research

The most distinctive feature of both causal and causal-comparative research we have already established. That they are *ex post facto* indicates that data are collected after the presumed cause or causes have occurred. The researcher takes the effect (or dependent variable) and examines the data retrospectively to establish causes, relationships or associations, and their meanings.

Other characteristcs of *ex post facto* research become apparent when it is contrasted with true experimental research. Kerlinger describes the *modus operandi* of the experimental researcher. ('If x, then y' in Kerlinger's usage. We have substituted X for x and O for y to fit in with Campbell and Stanley's conventions throughout the chapter.) He hypothesises: if X, then O; if frustration, then aggression. Depending on circumstances and his own predilections in research design, he uses some method to manipulate X. He then observes O to see if concomitant variation, the variation expected or predicted from the variation in X, occurs. If it does, this is evidence for the validity of the proposition, X−O, meaning 'If X, then O'. Note that the scientist here predicts from a controlled X to O. To help him achieve control, he can use the principle of randomisation and active manipulation of X and can assume, other things being equal, that O is varying as a result of the manipulation of X.

In *ex post facto* designs, on the other hand, O is observed. Then a retrospective search for X ensues. An X is found that is plausible and agrees with the hypothesis. Due to lack of control of X and other possible Xs, the truth of the hypothesised relation between X and O cannot be asserted with the confidence of the experimental researcher. Basically, then, *ex post facto* investigations have, so to speak, a built-in weakness: lack of control of the independent variable or variables.

This brief comparison highlights the most important difference between the two designs — control. In the experimental situation, the investigator at least has manipulative control: he has as a minimum one active variable. If an experiment is a 'true' experiment, he can also exercise control by randomisation. He can assign subjects to groups randomly; or, at the very least, he can assign treatments to groups at random. In the *ex post facto* research situation, this control of the independent variable is not possible, and what is perhaps more important, neither is randomisation. The investigator must take things as they are and try to disentangle them, though having said this, we must point out that he can make use of selected procedures that will give him an element of control in this research. These we shall touch upon shortly.

By their very nature, *ex post facto* experiments can provide support for any number of different, perhaps even contradictory, hypotheses; they are so completely flexible that it is largely a matter of postulating hypotheses according to one's personal preference. The investigator begins with certain data and looks for an interpretation consistent with them; often, however, a number of interpretations may be at hand. Consider again the hypothetical increase in road accidents in a given town. A retrospective search for causes will disclose half a dozen plausible ones. Experimental studies, by contrast, begin with a specific interpretation and then determine whether it is congruent with externally derived data. Frequently, causal relationships seem to be established on nothing more substantial than the premise that any related event occurring prior to the phenomenon under study is assumed to be its cause — the classical *post hoc ergo propter hoc* fallacy. Overlooked is the fact that even when we do find a relationship between two variables, we must recognise the possibility that both are individual results of a common third factor rather than the first being necessarily the cause of the second. And as we have seen earlier, there is also the real possibility of reverse causation, e.g. that a heart condition promotes obesity rather than the other way around, or that they encourage each other. The point is that the evidence simply illustrates the hypothesis; it does not test it, since hypotheses cannot be tested on the same data from which they were derived. The relationship noted may actually exist, but it is not necessarily the only relationship, or perhaps the crucial one. Before we can accept that smoking is the primary cause of lung cancer, we have to rule out alternative hypotheses.

We must not conclude from what has just been said that *ex post facto* studies are of little value; many of our important investigations in education and psychology are *ex post facto* designs. There is often no choice in the matter: an investigator cannot cause one group to become failures, delinquent, suicidal, brain-damaged or dropouts. He must of necessity rely on existing groups. On the other hand, the inability of *ex post facto* designs to incorporate the basic need for control (e.g. through manipulation or randomisation) makes them vulnerable from a scientific point of view and the possibility of their being misleading should be clearly acknowledged. *Ex post facto* designs are probably better conceived more circumspectly, not as experiments with the greater certainty that these denote, but more as surveys, useful as sources of hypotheses to be tested by more conventional experimental means at a later date.

Occasions When Appropriate

It would follow from what we have said in the preceding section that *ex post facto* designs are appropriate in circumstances where the more powerful experimental method is not possible. These would arise when, for example, it is not always possible to select, control and manipulate the factors necessary to study cause-and-effect relationships directly; or when the control of all variables except a single independent variable may be unrealistic and artificial, preventing the normal interaction with other influential variables; or when laboratory controls for many research purposes would be impractical, costly or ethically undesirable.

Ex post facto research is particularly suitable in social, educational and — to a lesser extent — psychological contexts where the independent variable or variables lie outside the researcher's control. Examples of the method abound in these areas: the research on cigarette-smoking and lung cancer, for instance; or studies of teacher characteristics; or studies examining the relationship between political and religious affiliation and attitudes; or investigations into the relationship between school achievement and independent variables such as social class, race, sex and intelligence. Many of these may be divided into large- or small-scale *ex post facto* studies.

In the former category, for example, Kerlinger refers to a study by Caldwell and Courtis,[5] *Then and Now in Education*, which attempted to compare the results of twentieth-century education with nineteenth-century education. It is a classic example of *ex post facto* research. The investigators compared the achievements of Boston High School children in history, geography, arithmetic, grammar and so on in 1845 with those of high school children all over the United States in 1919. Actually, the 'selected best' of the 1845 pupils were compared with the unselected lower 40 per cent of the 1919 pupils. The same tests that were given to the 1845 pupils were administered to the 1919 pupils.

It was found, among other things, that the 1919 pupils tended to make lower scores on memory and abstract skill questions and higher scores on thought questions. The results were consistent throughout the United States. The authors concluded that the pupils today were much like those of 1845: they tended to achieve the same successes and make the same errors.

The lack of control in this study is of course obvious; and though the findings are of little scientific value, the study within its limits is an interesting one.

Kerlinger also refers to a good example of small-scale *ex post facto* research in the field of education. It is a cross-cultural study of school children's anxiety by Sarnoff and his colleagues.[6] The researchers here used the English eleven-plus examination system in which the outcomes of a group of tests determined the direction of a child's educational future. The investigators reasoned that, since the eleven-plus examination was so crucial to British children, it would probably produce *test anxiety*. They further reasoned that American children would probably not have as high test anxiety because of the difference in their educational system. The basic hypothesis, therefore, was that a difference would be found between English and American children in the degree of test anxiety and that there would be no difference between the groups in *general anxiety* if comparable English and American groups were studied.

The study skilfully used an existing independent variable, test examinations, to test a hypothesis on *presumed* existing differences between national groups. Because the researchers seemingly predicted from X to O, and because they matched their samples so carefully, some students of research might say that this is not an *ex post facto* study at all. In fact, however, it is a characteristic example because it was *not* experimental; experimental manipulation and randomisation were lacking, so that the basic approach was the same as that of the cigarette-smoking and lung cancer study. What is particularly noteworthy is that the investigators tested a 'control hypothesis' — that there would be a difference between the two groups on *test anxiety* but not on *general anxiety*.

Advantages and Disadvantages

We have already touched incidentally on some of the strengths and weaknesses of *ex post facto* research. We will now look at them more systematically. Among the advantages of the approach we may identify the following: (1) *ex post facto* research meets an important need of the researcher where the more rigorous experimental approach is not possible. In the case of the alleged relationship between smoking and lung cancer, for instance, this cannot be tested experimentally (at least as far as human beings are concerned); (2) the method yields useful information concerning the nature of phenomena — what goes with what and under what conditions. In this way, *ex post facto* research is a valuable exploratory tool; (3) improvements in statistical techniques and general methodology have made *ex post facto* designs more defensible; (4) in some ways and in certain situations the method is more useful than the experimental method, especially where the setting up of the latter would introduce a note of artificiality into research proceedings; (5) *ex post facto* research is particularly appropriate when simple cause-and-effect relationships are being explored; and (6) the method can give a sense of direction and provide a fruitful source of hypotheses that can be tested by the more rigorous experimental method subsequently.

Among the limitations and weaknesses of *ex post facto* designs the following may be mentioned: (1) there is the problem of lack of control in that the researcher is unable to manipulate the independent variable or to randomise his subjects; (2) one cannot know for certain whether the causative factor has been included or even identified; (3) it may be that no one single factor is the cause; (4) a particular outcome may result from different causes on different occasions; (5) when a relationship has been discovered, there is the problem of deciding which is the cause and which the effect: the possibility of reverse causation has to be considered; (6) that two factors are related does not establish cause and effect; (7) classifying into dichotomous groups can be problematic; (8) there is the difficulty of interpretation and the danger of the *post hoc* assumption being made, that is, believing that because X procedes O, X causes O; (9) it often bases its conclusions on too limited a sample or number of occurrences; (10) it frequently fails to single out the really signficant factor or factors, and fails to recognise that events have multiple rather than single causes; (11) as a method it is regarded by some as too flexible; and (12) it lacks nullifiability and confirmation.

Designing an *Ex Post Facto* Investigation

We earlier referred to the two basic designs embraced by *ex post facto* research — the co-relational (or causal) model and the criterion group (or causal-comparative) model. We return to them again here in order to consider designing both types of investigation. As we saw, the causal model attempts to identify the antecedent of a present condition and may be represented thus:

Independent variable   *Dependent variable*

X	O

Although one variable in an *ex post facto* study cannot be confidently said to depend upon the other as would be the case in a truly experimental investigation, it is nevertheless usual to designate one of the variables as independent (X) and the other as dependent (O). The left to right dimension indicates the temporal order, though having established this, we must not overlook the possibility of reverse causality.

In a typical investigation of this kind, then, two sets of data relating to the independent and dependent variables respectively will be gathered. As indicated earlier in the chapter, the data on the independent variable (X) will be retrospective in character and as such will be prone to the kinds of weakness, limitations and distortions to which all historical evidence is subject. Let us now translate the design into a hypothetical situation. Imagine a secondary school in which it is hypothesised that low staff morale (O) has come about as a direct result of comprehensive reorganisation some two years earlier, say. A number of key factors distinguishing the new organisation from the previous one can be readily identified. Collectively these could represent or contain the independent variable X and data on them could be accumulated retrospectively. They could include, for example, the introduction of mixed ability and team teaching, curricular innovation, loss of teacher status, decline in pupil motivation, modifications to the school catchment area, or the appointment of a new headmaster. These could then be checked against a measure of prevailing teachers' attitudes (O), thus providing the researcher with some leads at least as to possible causes of current discontent.

The second model, the causal-comparative, may be represented schematically as shown:

Group	Independent variable	Dependent variable
E	X	O_1
C		O_2

Using this model, the investigator hypothesises the independent variable and then compares two groups, as experimental group (E) which has been exposed to the presumed independent variable X and a control group (C) which has not. (The dashed line in the model shows that the comparison groups E and C are not equated by random assignment. See p. 193.) Alternatively, he may examine two groups that are different in some way or ways and then try to account for the difference or differences by investigating possible antecedents. These two examples reflect two types of approach to causal-comparative research: the 'cause-to-effect' kind and the 'effect-to-cause' kind.[7]

The basic design of causal-comparative investigations is similar to an experimentally designed study. The chief difference resides in the nature of the independent variable, X. In a truly experimental situation, this will be under control of the investigator and may therefore be described as manipulable. In the causal-comparative model (and also the causal model), however, the independent variable is beyond his control, having already occurred. It may therefore be described in this design as non-manipulable.

Two brief examples will underscore these two types of research design: the 'cause-to-effect' kind and the 'effect-to-cause' kind. A researcher may study the influence of school reorganisation on low staff morale and then compare staff attitudes with those of teachers in a comparable school, though not having undergone reorganisation. Or a researcher may investigate the problems of the college dropout by comparing personality characteristics of the dropouts with those of students who stay the course. He may thereby be able to identify the antecedents of failure to stay the course on the part of the dropouts.

Procedures in *Ex Post Facto* Research

Ex post facto research is concerned with discovering relationships among variables in one's data; and we have seen how this may be accomplished by using either a causal or causal-comparative model. We now examine the steps involved in implementing a piece of *ex post facto* research. We may begin by identifying the problem area to be investigated. This stage will be followed by a clear and precise statement of the hypothesis to be tested or questions to be answered. The next step will be to make explicit the assumptions on which the hypothesis and subsequent procedures will be based. A review of the research literature will follow. This will enable the investigator to ascertain the kinds of issues, problems, stacles and findings disclosed by previous studies in the area. There will then follow the planning of the actual investigation and this will consist of three broad stages — identification of the population and samples; the selection and construction of techniques for collecting data; and the establishment of categories for classifying the data. The final stage will involve the description, analysis and interpretation of the findings.

It was noted earlier that the principal weakness of *ex post facto* research is the absence of control over the independent variable influencing the dependent variable in the case of causal designs or affecting observed differences between dependent variables in the case of causal-comparative designs. (We take up the question of *control* in experimental research in greater detail in the next chapter.)

Although the *ex post facto* researcher is denied not only this kind of control but also the principle of randomisation, he can nevertheless utilise procedures that will give him some measure of control in his investigation. And it is to some of these that we now turn.

One of the commonest means of introducing control into this type of research is that of matching the subjects in the experimental and control groups where the design is causal-comparative. One group of writers[8] explain it thus:

> The matching is usually done on a subject-to-subject basis to form matched pairs. For example, if one were interested in the relationship between scouting experiences and delinquency, he could locate two groups of boys classified as delinquent and non-delinquent according to specified criteria. It would be wise in such a study to select pairs from these groups matched on the basis of socio-economic status, family structure, and other variables known to be related to both scouting experience and delinquency. Analysis of the data from the matched samples could be made to determine whether or not scouting characterized the non-delinquent and was absent in the background of the delinquent.

There are difficulties with this procedure, however, for it assumes that the investigator knows what the relevant factors are, that is, the factors that may be related to the dependent variable. Further, there is the possibility of losing those subjects which cannot be matched, thus reducing one's sample.

As an alternative procedure for introducing a degree of control into *ex post facto* research, Ary and his colleagues[8] suggest building the extraneous independent variables into the design and using an analysis of variance technique. They explain:

> Assume that intelligence is a relevant extraneous variable and it is not feasible to control it through matching or other means. In this case, intelligence could be added to the design as another independent variable and the subjects of the study classified in terms of intelligence levels. The dependent variable measures would then be analysed through an analysis of variance and the main and interaction effects of intelligence might be determined. Such a procedure would reveal any significant

differences among the groups on the dependent variable, but no causal relationship between intelligence and the dependent variable could be assumed. Other extraneous variables could be operating to produce both the main effect and any interaction effects.

Yet another procedure which may be adopted for introducing a measure of control into *ex post facto* designs is that of selecting samples that are as homogeneous as possible on a given variable. The writers quoted above illustrate the procedure with the following example.

> If intelligence were a relevant extraneous variable, its effects could be controlled by using subjects from only one intelligence level. This procedure serves the purpose of disentangling the independent variable in which the investigator may be interested from other variables with which it is commonly associated, so that any effects that are found can justifiably be associated with the independent variable.

Finally, control may be introduced into an *ex post facto* investigation by stating and testing any alternative hypotheses that might be plausible explanations for the empirical outcomes of the study.[8] A researcher has thus to beware of accepting the first likely explanation of relationships in an *ex post facto* study as necessarily the only or final one. A well-known recent instance is the presumed relationship between cigarette-smoking and lung cancer. Government health officials have been quick to seize on the explanation that smoking causes lung cancer. Tobacco firms, however, have put forward an alternative hypothesis — that both

Box 7.2: Some Procedures for Introducing Measures of Control into *Ex Post Facto* Research Designs

1.	Matching of the subjects in the experimental and control groups where the design of the study is causal-comparative.
2.	Building extraneous independent variables into the design and using an analysis of variance technique.
3.	Using, where possible, homogeneous samples on a given variable.
4.	The testing of rival hypotheses offering alternative explanations.

smoking and lung cancer are possibly the result of a third, as yet unspecified, factor. In other words, the possibility that both the independent and dependent variables are simply two separate results of a single common cause cannot be ignored.

And, of course, in some situations there is the possibility of reverse causality. Thus, instead of claiming that A causes B, it might be that B is the cause of A. A researcher might, for instance, hypothesise that aggressive behaviour is the result of watching violent television programmes. Reverse causality, however, would posit that some people choose to watch violent television programmes because they are aggressive in the first place. Box 7.2 summarises the procedures just reviewed.

Examples of *Ex Post Facto* Research

In a period marked by fundamental changes in the organisation of education, the question may be asked: what effects do such changes have on educational outcomes? Can a relationship be shown to exist between the way a school is organised in certain respects and pupil achievement? Such a question was posed by two British researchers, Christie and Oliver,[9] working in the 1960s, who investigated the academic performance of 18-year-olds as related to school organisation. The study is a good example of *ex post facto* research using a causal model: the dependent variable (O) was represented by pupil achievement in A-level examinations and the independent variable (X), by school organisation. The latter related particularly to the organisation of school time and staffing.

The sample consisted of 73 boys' maintained grammar schools drawn roughly from the northern half of England. Although all were local authority schools, there was considerable fluctuation in the total number of hours available for sixth-form work, the range varying from 1,525 to 1,975 hours, a difference of the order of nine 40-minute periods a week.

It was found that within this framework, time was allocated to four major purposes: (1) a quasi-statutory allocation of time to physical education, games and religious instruction; (2) time set aside to counteract the effects of specialisation (minority time); (3) the major allocation of time for A-level specialisation; and (4) time for private study. Box 7.3 indicates the relationship between mean

Box 7.3: Relationship Between Mean A-Level Attainment and Number of Timetable Hours' Instruction in Twelve Subject Matter Areas

	Number of schools	Mean A-level grade (1)		Mean O-level grade (2)		Number of hours' instruction (3)		Correlations with mean A-level grade		
								Mean O-level level grade (2)	Number of hours (3)	O-level held constant r 13.2 hours
		mean	s.d.	mean	s.d.	mean	s.d.			
Art	26	3.29	1.04	49.55	6.04	303.94	80.52	0.33	0.22	0.25
French	34	2.78	0.98	54.27	3.94	350.74	40.73	0.58**	−0.25	−0.11
German	22	2.63	1.27	56.55	6.22	343.01	40.65	0.63**	−0.34	−0.09
Latin	24	2.97	1.24	57.83	5.27	350.71	49.11	0.64**	−0.07	0.06
English	36	2.78	0.93	52.32	4.46	349.89	39.50	0.29	0.14	0.19
History	36	2.85	0.79	52.19	4.08	351.86	32.28	0.27	0.21	0.29
Geography	36	3.46	0.97	51.97	4.75	351.50	38.47	0.00	−0.16	
Economics	16	3.01	1.20	50.46	4.04	359.75	44.88	0.13	0.08	
Mathematics	38	3.00	0.79	55.43	4.04	386.11	60.78	0.41*	−0.07	−0.03
Physics	38	3.16	0.67	55.51	3.21	383.00	47.87	0.25	0.00	
Chemistry	38	3.03	0.76	55.46	3.74	382.42	43.28	0.51**	0.33	0.45**
Biology	26	2.46	0.92	54.88	4.58	365.38	55.17	0.37	−0.27	−0.30

* Significant beyond the 5 per cent level.
** Significant beyond the 1 per cent level.

Source: Christie and Oliver.[9]

A-level attainment and the number of timetabled hours' instruction in twelve subject matter areas.

An interesting conclusion arising from an analysis of A-level grades in relation to the number of hours of A-level teaching was that, beyond a certain point, about 300 hours of A-level teaching or about four hours a week on average, additional teaching time does not, with the exception of chemistry, lead to higher A-level grades. The researchers inferred that more time could be devoted to other purposes such as minority time courses or general studies without jeopardising achievement in A-level subjects.

A more recent study[10] using an *ex post facto* approach has been undertaken by researchers at Chelsea College, London, who wanted to find out how teachers can help children to stop making common errors in mathematics. Using findings from an earlier study, *Concepts in Secondary Mathematics and Science*, which disclosed 'an unexpectedly high incidence of certain wrong answers', the researchers believed there are widespread misconceptions among secondary school children which led to what they describe as 'inappropriate strategies'.

One set of problems investigated by the researchers concerned ratio. The earlier study had shown that children could handle some questions involving ratio, but chiefly because they were using a tactic that would only work in some circumstances.

The Chelsea researchers therefore tested children in five London comprehensives for the ratio study. Those who used the wrong methods were later interviewed to discuss how they arrived at their answers. Using this information, teaching modules were designed to eliminate incorrect methods and replace them with a workable strategy. One of these focused on the multiplication of fractions. It was not generally successful, but subsequent modification of the module did result in an improved performance by the children.

The study shows the use to which *ex post facto* techniques can be put in identifying problems and in introducing new strategies that make for better understanding and more effective learning.

Finally, we refer the reader to a study by Galloway[11] the principal aim of which was to investigate the psychological, social and educational characteristics of pupils suspended from Sheffield schools. One of the subsidiary aims was to obtain information on the events leading up to the suspension. Methods used included interviews with parents, teachers and pupils, as well as the collation of pertinent information from external agencies such as social workers and the police. While the researcher is careful to make clear that the evidence did not justify any statement about cause and effect, nevertheless the results suggested that pupils 'at risk' of suspension had educational and possibly constitutional problems independent of their behaviour. The researcher argues that these pupils would cause concern at any school, but that variables within their schools were critical in determining whether their behaviour resulted in suspension.

References

1. Kerlinger, F.N., *Foundations of Behavioural Research* (Holt, Rinehart and Winston, New York, 1970).
2. Campbell, D.T. and Stanley, J.C., 'Experimental and quasi-experimental designs for research on teaching', in N.L. Gage (ed.), *Handbook of Research on Teaching* (Rand McNally, Chicago, 1963).
3. Borkowsky, F.T., 'The relationship of work quality in undergraduate music curricula to effectiveness in instrumental music teaching in the public schools', *J. Exp. Educ.*, 39 (1970) 14–19.
4. Cohen, L. and Child, D., 'Some sociological and psychological factors in university failure', *Durham Research Review*, 22 (1969) 365–72.
5. Caldwell, O. and Courtis, S., *Then and Now in Education* (Harcourt, New York, 1925).
6. Sarnoff, I. *et al.*, 'A cross-cultural study of anxiety among American and English school children', *J. Educ. Psychol.*, 49 (1958) 129–36.
7. Chapin, F.S., *Experimental Designs in Sociological Research* (Harper and Row, New York, 1947).
8. Ary, D., Jacobs, L.C. and Razavieh, A., *Introduction to Research in Education* (Holt, Rinehart and Winston, New York, 1972).
9. Christie, T. and Oliver, R.A.C., 'Academic performance at age 18+ as related to school organization', *Research in Education*, 2 (November 1969) 13–31.
10. Review article, 'Why can't children do proportion sums?' *Education*, 18 May (1984) 403.
11. Galloway, D., 'A study of pupils suspended from schools', *Brit. J. Educ. Psychol.*, 52 (1982) 205–12.

8 EXPERIMENTS, QUASI-EXPERIMENTS AND SINGLE-CASE RESEARCH

Introduction

In Chapter 7, we described *ex post facto* research as experimentation in reverse in that *ex post facto* studies start with groups that are already different with regard to certain characteristics and then proceed to search, in retrospect, for the factors that brought about those differences. We then went on to cite Kerlinger's[1] description of the experimental researcher's approach:

> If x, then y; if frustration, then aggression ... the researcher uses some method to measure x and then observes y to see if concomitant variation occurs.

The essential feature of experimental research is that the investigator deliberately controls and manipulates the conditions which determine the events in which he is interested. At its simplest, an experiment involves making a change in the value of one variable — called the independent variable — and observing the effect of that change on another variable — called the dependent variable. Frequently in learning experiments in classroom settings the independent variable is a stimulus of some kind, a new method in arithmetical computation for example, and the dependent variable is a response, the time taken to do 20 sums using the new method. Most empirical studies in educational settings, however, are quasi-experimental rather than experimental. The single most important difference between the quasi-experiment and the true experiment is that in the former case, the researcher undertakes his study with groups that are *intact*, that is to say, the groups have been constituted by means other than random selection. Later in the chapter we present an example of a quasi-experimental design in an ongoing education study specifically undertaken to improve upon an earlier research project employing a pre-experimental methodology.

First however, we begin by identifying the essential features of pre-experimental, true experimental and quasi-experimental designs, our intention being to introduce the reader to the meaning and purpose of *control* in educational experimentation.

Designs in Educational Experimentation

In the outline of research designs that follows we use symbols and conventions from Campbell and Stanley:[2]

1. X represents the exposure of a group to an experimental variable or event, the effects of which are to be measured.
2. O refers to the process of observation or measurement.
3. Xs and Os in a given row are applied to the same persons.
4. Left to right order indicates temporal sequence.
5. Xs and Os vertical to one another are simultaneous.
6. R indicates random assignment to separate treatment groups.
7. Parallel rows unseparated by dashes represent comparison groups equated by randomisation while those separated by a dashed line represent groups not equated by random assignment.

A Pre-experimental Design: the One Group Pretest-Post-test

Very often, reports about the value of a new teaching method or the interest aroused by some curriculum innovation or other reveal that a researcher has measured a group on a dependent variable (O_1), for example, attitudes towards minority groups, and then introduced an experimental manipulation (X), perhaps a ten-week curriculum project designed to increase tolerance of ethnic minorities. Following the experimental treatment, the researcher has again measured group attitudes (O_2) and proceeded to account for differences between pretest and post-test scores by reference to the effects of X.

The one group pretest-post-test design can be represented as:

(Experimental) O_1 X O_2

Suppose that just such a project has been undertaken and that the researcher finds that O_2 scores indicate greater tolerance of ethnic minorities than O_1 scores. How justified is he in attributing the cause of $O_1 - O_2$ differences to the experimental treatment (X), that is, the term's project work? At first glance the assumption of causality seems reasonable enough. The situation is not that simple, however. Compare for a moment the circumstances represented in our hypothetical educational example with those which typically obtain in experiments in the physical sciences. A physicist who applies heat to a metal bar can confidently attribute the observed expansion to the rise in temperature that he has introduced because within the confines of his laboratory he has excluded (i.e. *controlled*) all other extraneous sources of variation (this example is suggested by Pilliner[4]).

The same degree of control can never be attained in educational experimentation. At this point the reader may care to reflect upon some possible influences other than the ten-week curriculum project that might account for the O_1-O_2 differences in our hypothetical educational example.

He may conclude that factors to do with the pupils, the teacher, the school, the classroom organisation, the curriculum materials and their presentation, the way that the subjects' attitudes were measured, to say nothing of the thousand and one other events that occurred in and about the school during the course of the term's work, might all have exerted some influence upon the observed differences in attitude. These kinds of extraneous variables which are outside of an experimenter's *control* in a one-group pretest-post-test design threaten to invalidate his research efforts. We later identify a number of such threats to the validity of educational experimentation.

The problems arising out of the use of pre-experimental designs are graphically illustrated in the comments of a researcher who employed a pretest-post-test design in six secondary schools in an evaluation of the use of archive materials in the teaching of history.[3]

The pretests were taken by 158 children in six schools ... not all the children who had taken the pretests either used the Unit [farming in Leicestershire] or took the post-tests, which were completed by only 72 children. Without the backing of a national body like the Schools Council, one's status and purpose are suspect and offers of assistance are not readily forthcoming ... The six schools used were the only ones to offer assistance after a request had been sent to most secondary schools in [the county]. This had two main results. In the first place, the need to work with any school classes whose teachers offered to co-operate in order to obtain a sample of adequate size meant that variables such as age, intelligence, previous learning experiences, etc. could not be controlled ... Secondly, although all classes used the same materials, it was impossible to insist on common teaching patterns, equal provision of additional resources, similar periods of time devoted to each section of the materials or the use of control groups. Drop out during the use of the materials due to natural causes such as illness or a teacher's practice of allowing unrestricted choice of work patterns also reduced the size of the sample, resulting in different sample sizes for pre- and post-tests.

A 'True' Experimental Design: the Pretest-Post-test Control Group Design

A complete exposition of experimental designs is beyond the scope of the present chapter. In the brief outline that follows, we have selected one design from the comprehensive treatment of the subject by Campbell and Stanley[2] in order to identify the essential features of what they term a 'true experimental' and what Kerlinger[1] refers to as a 'good' design. Along with its variants, the chosen design is commonly used in educational experimentation.

The pretest-post-test control group design can be represented as:

(Experimental)	RO_1	X	O_2
(Control)	RO_3		O_4

It differs from the pre-experimental design that we have just described in that it involves the use of two groups which have been constituted by *randomisation*. As Kerlinger[1] observes, *in theory*, random assignment to E and C conditions controls *all* possible independent variables. *In practice*, of course, it is only when enough subjects are included in the experiment that the principle of randomisation has a chance to operate as a powerful control.

Box 8.1: The Effects of Randomisation

Select twenty cards from a pack, ten red and ten black. Shuffle and deal into two ten-card piles. Now count the number of red cards and black cards in either pile and record the results. Repeat the whole sequence many times, recording the results each time.

You will soon convince yourself that the most likely distribution of reds and blacks in a pile is five in each; the next most likely, six red (or black) and four black (or red); and so on. You will be lucky (or unlucky for the purposes of the demonstration!) to achieve one pile of red and the other entirely of black cards. The probability of this happening is 1 in 92,378! On the other hand, the probability of obtaining a 'mix' not more than 6 of one colour and 4 of the other is about 82 in 100.

If you now imagine the red cards to stand for the 'better' ten children and the black cards for the 'poorer' ten children in a class of twenty, you will conclude that the operation of the laws of chance alone will almost probably give you close equivalent 'mixes' of 'better' and 'poorer' children in the experimental and control groups.

Source: adapted from Pilliner.[4]

However, the effects of randomisation even with a small number of subjects is well illustrated in Box 8.1.

Randomisation, then, ensures the greater likelihood of equivalence, that is, the apportioning* out between the experimental and control groups of any other factors or characteristics of the subjects which might conceivably affect the experimental variables in which the researcher is interested. It is, as Kerlinger notes, the addition of the *control group* in our present example and the random assignment of subjects to E and C groups that radically alters the situation from that which obtains in the pre-experimental design outlined earlier. For if the groups are made equivalent, then any so-called 'clouding' effects should be present in both groups.

If the mental ages of the children of the experimental group increase, so should the mental ages of the children of the control group ... If something happens to affect the experimental

Randomisation is one way of apportioning out or controlling for extraneous variables. Alternatively, the experimenter may use *matched cases*, that is, subjects are matched in pairs in terms of some other variable thought likely to affect scores on the dependent variable and pairs are then allocated randomly to E and C conditions in such a way that the means and variances of the two groups are as nearly equal as possible. Finally, *analysis of covariance* is a powerful statistical procedure which uses pretest mean scores as covariates to control for initial differences between E and C groups on a number of independent variables.

subjects between the pretest and the post-test, this something should also affect the subjects of the control groups.[1]

So strong is this simple and elegant true experimental design, that all the threats to internal validity identified below are, according to Campbell and Stanley,[2] controlled in the pretest-post-test control group design.

One problem that has been identified with this particular experimental design is the *interaction effect of testing*. Good[5] explains the interaction effect weakness in the pretest-post-test control group design as follows:

Whereas the various threats to the validity of the experiment that we have listed below can be thought of as *main effects*, manifesting themselves in mean differences independently of the presence of other variables, interaction effects, as their name implies, are *joint effects* and may occur even when no main effects are present. For example, an interaction effect may occur as a result of the pretest measure sensitising the subjects to the experimental variable. Interaction effects can be controlled for by adding to the pretest-post-test control group design two more groups that do not experience the pretest measures. The result is a *four-group design* as suggested by Solomon.[6] Later in the chapter, we describe an educational study which built into a pretest-post-test group design a further control group to take account of the possibility of pretest sensitisation.

A Quasi-experimental Design: the Non-equivalent Control Group Design

Often in educational research, it is simply not possible for investigators to undertake true experiments. At best, they may be able to employ something approaching a true experimental design in which they have control over what Campbell and Stanley[2] refer to as '*the who and to whom of measurement*' but lack control over '*the when and to whom of exposure*', *or the randomisation of* exposures — essential if true experimentation is to take place. These situations are quasi-experimental and the methodologies employed by researchers are termed quasi-experimental designs. (Kerlinger refers to quasi-experimental situations as '*compromise designs*', an apt description when applied to much educational research where the random selection or random assignment of schools and classrooms is quite impracticable.)

One of the most commonly used quasi-experimental designs in educational research can be represented as:

(Experimental)	O_1	X	O_2
(Control)	O_3		O_4

The dashed line separating the parallel rows in the diagram of the non-equivalent control group indicates that the experimental and control groups have not been equated by randomisation — hence the term 'non-equivalent'. The addition of a control group makes the present design a decided improvement over the one group pretest-post-test design, for to the degree that the experimenter can make E and C groups as equivalent as possible, he can avoid the equivocality of interpretations that plague the pre-experimental design discussed earlier. The equivalence of groups can be strengthened by matching, followed by random assignment to E and C treatments. Later in the chapter, we illustrate the use of matching on such key variables as socio-economic background of pupils, school size, organisation and teaching methods in an on-going study of reading in middle schools. Where matching is not possible, the researcher is advised[1] to use samples from the same population or samples that are as alike as possible. Where intact groups differ substantially, however, matching is unsatisfactory due to regression effects which lead to different group means on post-test measures. Campbell and Stanley[2] put it this way:

> If [in the non-equivalent control group design] the means of the groups are substantially different, then the process of matching not only fails to provide the intended equation but in addition insures the occurrence of unwanted regression effects. It becomes predictably certain that the two groups will differ on their post-test scores altogether independently of any effects of X, and that this difference will vary directly with the difference between the total populations from which the selection was made and inversely with the test-retest correlation.

The Validity of Experiments

As we have seen, the fundamental purpose of experimental design is to impose control over conditions that would otherwise cloud the true effects of the independent variables upon the dependent variables.

Clouding conditions that threaten to jeopardise the validity of experiments have been identified by Campbell and Stanley[2] and by Bracht and Glass,[7] conditions incidentally that are of greater consequence to the validity of quasi-experiments (more typical in educational research) than to true experiments in which random assignment to treatments occurs and where both treatment and measurement can be more adequately controlled by the researcher. The following summaries adapted from Campbell and Stanley[2] and Bracht and Glass[7] distinguish between *internal validity* and *external validity.*

Internal validity is concerned with the question, do the experimental treatments, in fact, make a difference in the specific experiments under scrutiny?

External validity, on the other hand, asks the question, given these demonstrable effects, to what populations or settings can they be generalised?

Threats to Internal Validity

1. History

Frequently in educational research, events other than the experimental treatments occur during the time between pretest and posttest observations. Such events produce effects that can mistakenly be attributed to differences in treatment.

2. Maturation

Between any two observations subjects change in a variety of ways. Such changes can produce differences that are independent of the experimental treatments. The problem of maturation is more acute in protracted educational studies than in brief laboratory experiments.

3. Statistical Regression

Like maturation effects, regression effects increase systematically with the time interval between pre- and post-tests. Statistical regression occurs in educational (and other) research due to the unreliability of measuring instruments and to extraneous factors unique to each experimental group. Regression means, simply, that subjects scoring highest on a pretest are likely to score relatively lower on a post-test; conversely, those scoring lowest on a pretest are likely to score relatively higher on a post-test. In a word, in pretest-post-test situations, there is regression to the mean. Regression effects can lead the educational researcher mistakenly to attribute post-test gains and losses to low scoring and high scoring respectively.

4. Testing

Pretests at the beginning of experiments can produce effects other than those due to the experimental treatments. Such effects can include sensitising subjects to the true purposes of the experiment and practice effects which produce higher scores on post-test measures.

5. Instrumentation

Unreliable tests or instruments can introduce serious errors into experiments. With human observers or judges, error can result from changes in their skills and levels of concentration over the course of the experiment.

6. Selection

Bias may be introduced as a result of differences in the selection of subjects for the comparison groups or when intact classes are employed as experimental or control groups. Selection bias, moreover, may interact with other factors (history, maturation, etc.) to cloud even further the effects of the comparative treatments.

7. Experimental Mortality

The loss of subjects through dropout often occurs in long-running experiments and may result in confounding the effects of the experimental variables, for whereas initially the groups may have been randomly selected, the residue that stays the course is likely to be different from the unbiased sample that began it.

Threats to External Validity

Threats to external validity are likely to limit the degree to which generalisations can be made from the particular experimental conditions to other populations or settings. Below, we summarise a number of factors (adapted from Campbell and Stanley[2] and Bracht and Glass[7]) that jeopardise external validity.

1. Failure to Describe Independent Variables Explicitly

Unless independent variables are adequately described by the researcher, future replications of the experimental conditions are virtually impossible.

2. Lack of Representativeness of Available and Target Populations

Whilst those participating in the experiment may be representative of an available population, they may not be representative of the population to which the experimenter seeks to generalise his findings.

3. Hawthorne Effect

Medical research has long recognised the psychological effects that arise out of mere participation in drug experiments, and placebos and double-blind designs are commonly employed to counteract the biasing effects of participation. Similarly, so-called Hawthorne effects threaten to contaminate experimental treatments in educational research when subjects realise their role as guinea pigs.

4. Inadequate Operationalising of Dependent Variables

Dependent variables that the experimenter operationalises must have validity in the non-experimental setting to which he wishes to generalise his findings. A paper and pencil questionnaire on career choice, for example, may have little validity in respect of the actual employment decisions made by undergraduates on leaving university.

5. Sensitisation to Experimental Conditions

As with threats to internal validity, pretests may cause changes in the subjects' sensitivity to the experimental variables and thus cloud the true effects of the experimental treatment.

6. Interaction Effects of Extraneous Factors and Experimental Treatments

All of the above threats to external validity represent interactions of various clouding factors with treatments. As well as these, interaction effects may also arise as a result of any or all of those factors identified under the section on Threats to Internal Validity above.

By way of summary, we have seen that an experiment can be said to be *internally* valid to the extent that *within its own confines*, its results are credible;[4] but for those results to be useful, they must be generalisable beyond the confines of the particular experiment; in a word, they must be *externally* valid also. Pilliner[4] points to a lop-sided relationship between internal and external validity. Without internal validity an experiment cannot possibly be externally valid. But the converse does not necessarily follow: an internally valid experiment may or may not have external validity. Thus, the most carefully designed experiment involving a sample of Welsh-speaking children is not necessarily generalisable to a target population which includes non-Welsh-speaking subjects.

It follows, then, that the way to good experimentation in schools and classrooms lies in maximising both internal and external validity.

Procedures in Conducting Experimental Research

In Chapter 7, we identified a sequence of steps in carrying out an *ex post facto* study. An experimental investigation must also follow a set of logical procedures. Those that we now enumerate, however, should be treated with some circumspection. It is extraordinarily difficult (and indeed, foolhardy) to lay down clear-cut rules as guides to experimental research. At best, we can identify an ideal route to be followed, knowing full well that educational research rarely proceeds in such a systematic fashion. (For a detailed discussion of the practical problems in educational experimentation, see Evans,[8] Chapter 4, 'Planning experimental work'.)

First, the researcher must identify and define the research problem as precisely as possible, always supposing that the problem is amenable to experimental methods.

Second, he must formulate hypotheses that he wishes to test. This involves making predictions about relationships between specific variables and at the same time making decisions about other variables that are to be excluded from the experiment by means of controls.

Variables, remember, must have two properties.[9] Firstly, they must be measurable. Physical fitness, for example, is not directly measurable until it has been operationally defined. Making the variable 'physical fitness' *operational* means simply defining it by letting something else that is measurable stand for it — a gymnastics test, perhaps. Secondly, the proxy variable must be a *valid indicator* of the hypothetical variable in which one is interested. That is to say, a gymnastics test probably is a reasonable proxy for physical fitness; height on the other hand most certainly is not. Excluding variables from the experiment is inevitable, given constraints of time and money. It follows therefore that one must set up priorities among the variables in which one is interested so that the most important of them can be varied experimentally whilst others are held constant.

Third, the researcher must select appropriate *levels* at which to test the independent variables. By way of example,[9] suppose an educational psychologist wishes to find out whether longer or shorter periods of reading make for reading attainment in school settings. He will hardly select 5 hour and 5 minute periods as appropriate levels; rather, he is more likely to choose 30 minute and 60 minute levels in order to compare with the usual timetabled periods of 45 minutes duration. In other words, the experimenter will vary the stimuli at such levels as are of *practical interest in the real-life situation.*[9] Pursuing the example of reading attainment somewhat further, our hypothetical experimenter will be wise to vary the stimuli in large enough intervals so as to obtain measurable results. Comparing reading periods of 44 minutes or 46 minutes with timetabled reading lessons of 45 minutes is scarcely likely to result in observable differences in attainment.

Fourth, in planning the design of the experiment, the researcher must take account of the population to which he wishes to generalise his results. This involves him in decisions over sample sizes and sampling methods. Sampling decisions are bound up with questions of funds, manpower and the amount of time available for experimentation.

Fifth, with problems of validity in mind, the researcher must select instruments, choose tests and decide upon appropriate methods of analysis.

Sixth, before embarking upon the actual experiment the researcher must pilot test the experimental procedures to identify possible snags in connection with any aspect of the investigation. This is of crucial importance as the following comment from a highly-experienced experimenter makes plain:

> Conduct a pretest and then revise your procedure in light of what you learn from the pretest. Run another pretest. Revise again. And so on until your experimental procedure is pat and airtight.[9]

Seventh, during the experiment itself, the researcher must endeavour to follow tested and agreed-on procedures to the letter. The standardisation of instructions, the exact timing of experimental sequences, the meticulous recording and checking of observations — these are the hallmark of the competent researcher.

With his data collected, the researcher faces the most important part of the whole enterprise. Processing data, analysing results and drafting reports are all extremely demanding activities both in intellectual effort and time. Often this last part of the experimental research is given too little time in the overall planning of the investigation. Experienced researchers rarely make such a mistake: card 'wrecks', programme faults, and a dozen more unanticipated disasters teach the hard lesson of leaving ample time for the analysis and interpretation of experimental findings. And on this last point, one final tip from the experienced experimenter we quoted earlier:

> This is a particularly good time to discuss your work with your fellow students and staff members. Show them a brief write up of what you are doing and your preliminary results. One of my own major shortcomings as a researcher is that I do too little of this, largely because I hesitate to ask people. I hope that you are less shy about this than I am, but you should at least recognize that someone is doing you one of the greatest favours it is possible for one person to confer on another when she gives you the benefit of her attention, experience and critical imagination.[9]

Examples From Educational Research

Example 1: A Pre-experimental Design

A pre-experimental design was employed in a study undertaken for the New Zealand Book Council. In 1973, the New Zealand Council for Educational Research began work on a research project concerned with the effects of a 'book flood' on the reading habits, tastes and abilities of school children. Two schools with an intake aged from 5 years to 11 years were involved in the study. Over half of their intake were Maori children many of whom were said to have 'limited access to books'. Suitable books were selected by a committee of teachers and librarians and introduced into the schools over a period two terms. To assess the impact of the flood of books, a series of baseline assessments of reading skills and attitudes was obtained between March and May 1976 before the books arrived and then again six months after the initial influx of books had taken place. The pretest battery included tests of reading comprehension, vocabulary and listening, and scales to assess children's interests in books, attitudes to school, to reading and to themselves. The amount of reading undertaken in a two-week period was recorded by the children themselves and teachers' ratings of interest in reading were also obtained. Case studies were made of five children in each class and information was obtained about the books the children owned and had read, their home background, parental interest, library borrowing and TV viewing. Finally, informal reading inventories were used to study the children's reading behaviour.

The effects of the book flood were analysed in terms of the amount of reading undertaken by the children during the course of the project, their reading skills, reading interests and their attitudes toward reading in general.

Using the symbols and conventions adopted earlier (p. 188) to represent research designs, we can illustrate the New Zealand study* as:

(Experimental)

$$O_1 \qquad X \qquad O_2$$

The briefest consideration reveals inadequacies in the design. Indeed, Campbell and Stanley[2] describe *the one group pretest-post-test design* as 'a "bad example" to illustrate several of the

---

*Despite the fact that two schools were employed, thus offering the possibility of replication, the New Zealand study is essentially a *one group pretest-post-test design*.

confounded extraneous variables than can jeopardize internal validity. These variables offer plausible hypotheses explaining an O_1–O_2 difference, rival to the hypothesis that caused the difference'.

Nevertheless, the New Zealand researchers confidently report that the first six months of the book flood produced significant changes in the amount of their subjects' voluntary reading, and improvements in their reading abilities, attitudes and interests. The reader may care to formulate alternative explanations of the incremental gains reported in the study after consulting the various threats to internal validity which we detailed on p. 194.

Example 2: A Quasi-experimental Design

The Bradford Book Flood Experiment[10] began in 1976 with two aims in view. First, to study the effects of a book flood on children's reading abilities and interests. Second, to improve upon the research design used in the New Zealand study within the limits imposed by funding and the requests that could be made for changes in the timetabling and day-to-day organisation of the participating schools. The design finally adopted by the Bradford research team after considerable discussion may be represented thus:

(Experimental)	O_1	X	O_2
(Control)	O_3		O_4

It is, of course, the *non-equivalent control group design* outlined earlier in the chapter in which the parallel rows separated by the dashed line represent groups that have not been equated by random assignment.

Four middle schools took part in the Bradford study, two serving as experimental and two as control schools. Two schools forming a matched pair were situated on council estates, the second matched pair being located in inner city areas. Allocation to experiment or control treatments was made on the flip of a coin.

The schools were selected by a senior educational adviser who attempted to choose schools of similar size, background, organisation, teaching methods and catering for children of a similar range of abilities. Unlike the New Zealand study, the Bradford research followed one particular year group (second year pupils) through the school.

Pretest and post-test measures of reading skills, attitudes and interests were supplemented by classroom observation and interviews with selected children, the analysis of diaries and reading record forms, and the use of teachers' assessments. In the light of the problems of *instrumentation* to which we referred earlier, particular care was taken to select reading tests that: (1) had been recently constructed or recently restandardised; (2) had British norms; (3) were reliable and valid; (4) were suitable for the age group under study; and (5) were appropriate over the two-year testing sessions. Unlike the New Zealand study, the Bradford design attempted to use both matching and random allocation (of a sort) to obtain equivalent groups at the outset of the research. Despite this, the study remains firmly quasi-experimental rather than experimental since random allocation to experimental and control groups at the level of individual pupils was clearly impossible and what random allocation did take place at the level of institutions was of little consequence because of the small number of schools involved. Although the Bradford investigators attempted to exercise control over extraneous variables, it is not difficult to criticise the study in respect of each of the threats to internal and external validity that we identified earlier. For example, the matching of schools that was undertaken was relatively crude and did not take account of the important variations in the intrasessional histories of the schools that participated. Of equal import, it does not appear that a precise, unequivocal description of the experimental treatment was ever undertaken. What exactly constitutes a book flood? One could go on raising aspects of design weakness which jeopardise the validity of the Bradford research project, but such criticisms would serve only to reinforce the point that true experimentation in education is rarely, if ever, achieved.

Example 3: A 'True' Experimental Design

We have chosen a study[11] of children's understanding of a scientific concept to illustrate a stronger design than the pretest-post-test control group design that was discussed earlier in the chapter. The experimental design adopted by the researchers owes its origins to Solomon[6] and can be represented as:

(Experimental)	RO_1	X	O_2
(1st Control)	RO_3		O_4
(2nd Control)		X	O_5

This three-group design provides all that the *pretest-post-test control group design* does by the way of control, but in addition, it enables the researcher to test whether the pretest exercises any significant influence on the performance in the post-test situation. Suppose, for example, that it is found that the average score of the experimental group (top line in the diagram) is significantly greater than that of the first control group. Can it be concluded that this effect is entirely due to the experimental treatment X or could it possibly have resulted from an increased sensitisation among the experimental subjects as a result of the pretest? The average score of the second control group (bottom line) enables us to test our suspicion. If the average score of the second control group is also significantly greater than that of the first control group, then it is safe to conclude that the pretest itself does not exercise any sensitising effect upon the experimental subjects. In the actual research study, Harvey and Cooper tested for a pretest sensitisation effect in second, third and fourth year junior school pupils randomly assigned to experimental and control groups in a *Solomon three-group design*. Their results provided conclusive proof of a lack of pretest sensitisation.

	Mean post-test scores		
	Experimental	*1st Control*	*2nd Control*
4th year groups	8.78	3.25	7.52
3rd year groups	6.65	2.38	7.56
2nd year groups	6.56	2.25	5.38

Source: adapted from Harvey and Cooper.[11]

Inter alia, the experiment provided evidence that a teaching programme to do with basic electricity, presented over a two-week period in four 30-minute lessons, could produce a significant incremental effect in the performance of children on a hierarchically structured concept-formation test. Of particular interest was the discovery that children of the youngest age group showed increased understanding of the concepts at all levels despite differences in reading ability when compared with older age groups.

Single-case Research: ABAB Design

At the beginning of Chapter 5, we described case study researchers as typically engaged in *observing* the characteristics of an individual unit, be it a child, a classroom, a school, or a whole community. We went on to contrast case study researchers with *experimenters* whom we described as typically concerned with the *manipulation* of variables in order to determine their causal significance. That distinction, as we shall see, is only partly true.

Increasingly, in recent years, single-case research as an *experimental methodology* has extended to such diverse fields as clinical psychology, medicine, education, social work, psychiatry, and counselling. Most of the single-case studies carried out in these (and other) areas share the following characteristics:[12]

(1) they involve the *continuous assessment* of some aspect of human behaviour over a period of time, requiring on the part of the researcher the administration of measures on multiple occasions within separate phases of a study.
(2) they involve what is termed *intervention effects* which are replicated in the same subject(s) over time.

Continuous assessment measures are used as a basis for drawing inferences about the effectiveness of intervention procedures.

The characteristics of single-case research studies are discussed by Kazdin[12] in terms of ABAB designs, the basic experimental format in most single-case researches. ABAB designs, Kazdin observes, consist of a family of procedures in which observations of performance are made over time for a given client or group of clients. Over the course of the investigation, changes are made in the experimental conditions to which the client is exposed. The basic rationale of the ABAB design is illustrated in Box 8.2. What

Box 8.2: The ABAB Design

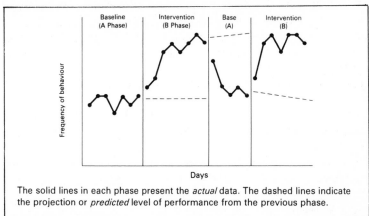

The solid lines in each phase present the *actual* data. The dashed lines indicate the projection or *predicted* level of performance from the previous phase.

Source: adapted from Kazdin.[12]

it does is this. It examines the effects of an intervention by alternating the baseline condition (the A phase), when no intervention is in effect, with the intervention condition (the B phase). The A and B phases are then repeated to complete the four phases. As Kazdin says, the effects of the intervention are clear if performance improves during the first intervention phase, reverts to or approaches original baseline levels of performance when the treatment is withdrawn, and improves again when treatment is recommenced in the second intervention phase.

An example of the application of the ABAB design in an educational setting is provided by Dietz[13] whose single-case study sought to measure the effect that a teacher could have upon the disruptive behaviour of a mentally-retarded adolescent boy in a special education class whose persistent talking disturbed his fellow classmates.

In order to decrease the unwelcomed behaviour, a reinforcement programme was devised in which the boy could earn extra time with the teacher by decreasing the number of times he called out. The boy was told that when he made three (or less) interruptions during any fifty-five minute class period the teacher would spend extra time working with him. In the technical language of behaviour modification theory, the pupil would receive reinforcing consequences when he was able to show a low rate of disruptive

Box 8.3: An ABAB Design in an Educational Setting

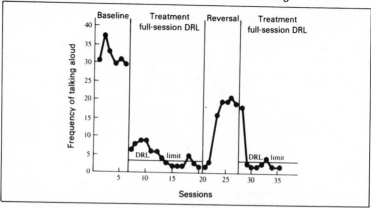

Source: Kazdin.[12]

behaviour (in Box 8.3 this is referred to as *differential reinforcement of low rates* or *DRL*).

When the retarded child was able to desist from talking aloud on fewer than three occasions during any timetabled period, he was rewarded by the teacher spending fifteen minutes with him helping him with his learning tasks. The pattern of results displayed in Box 8.3 shows the considerable changes that occurred in the boy's behaviour when the intervention procedures were carried out and the substantial increases in disruptions towards baseline levels when the teacher's rewarding strategies were withdrawn. Finally, when the intervention was reinstated, the boy's behaviour is seen to improve again.

By way of conclusion the single-case research design is uniquely able to provide an experimental technique for evaluating interventions for the individual subject. Moreover such interventions can be directed towards a particular subject or group and replicated over time or across behaviours, situations, or persons.[12] Single-case research offers an alternative strategy to the more usual methodologies based on between-group designs. There are, however, a number of problems that arise in connection with the use of single-case designs having to do with ambiguities introduced by trends and variations in baseline phase data and with the generality of results from single-case research. The interested reader is directed to Kazdin,[12] Borg[14] and Vasta.[15]

References

1. Kerlinger, F.N., *Foundations of Behavioural Research* (Holt, Rinehart and Winston, New York, 1970).
2. Campbell, D.T. and Stanley, J.C., 'Experimental and quasi-experimental designs for research on teaching', in N.L. Gage (ed.), *Handbook of Research on Teaching* (Rand McNally, Chicago, 1963).
3. Palmer, M., 'An experimental study of the use of archive materials in the secondary school history curriculum', PhD dissertation (University of Leicester, 1976).
4. Pilliner, A., *Experiment in Education Research*, E341 Block 5. (The Open University Press, Bletchley, 1973).
5. Good, C.V., *Introduction to Educational Research* (Appleton-Century-Crofts, New York, 1963).
6. Solomon, R.L., 'An extension of control group design', *Psychol. Bull.*, 46 (1949) 137–50.
7. Bracht, G.H. and Glass, G.V., 'The external validity of experiments', *Amer. Educ. Res. Journ.*, 4, 5 (1968) 437–74.
8. Evans, K.M., *Planning Small Scale Research* (NFER Publishing Co., Windsor, 1978).
9. Simon, J.L., *Basic Research Methods in Social Sciences* (Random House, New York, 1978).
10. Beard, R., Cohen, L. and Verma, G., *The Bradford Book Flood Experiment* (School of Research in Education, University of Bradford, 1978). For a full account of the research see Ingham, J., *Books and Reading Development* (Heinemann Educational Books, London, 1981).
11. Harvey, T.J. and Cooper, C.J., 'An investigation into some possible factors affecting children's understanding of the concept of an electric circuit in the age range 8–11 years old', *Educational Studies*, 4, 2 (1978) 149–55.
12. Kazdin, A.E., *Single-case Research Designs* (Oxford University Press, New York, 1982).
13. Dietz, S.M., 'An analysis of programming DRL schedules in educational settings', *Behaviour Research and Therapy*, 15 (1977) 103–11.
14. Borg, W.R., *Applying Educational Research: A Practical Guide for Teachers* (Longman, New York, 1981) 218–19.
15. Vasta, R., *Studying Children: An Introduction to Research Methods* (W.H. Freeman, San Francisco, 1979).

9 ACTION RESEARCH

Introduction

We come now to a style of research that has received rather more publicity over the years that most other methods in the social sciences. This may indeed stem from the implied tension in its name, *action research*, for *action* and *research* as separate activities in whatever context each have their own ideology and modus operandi and when conjoined in this way, lie as uneasy bedfellows. To give a comprehensive definition of the term at this stage is difficult because usage varies with time, place and setting. None the less, we may offer a conventional definition and use this as a starting point: *action research is small-scale intervention in the functioning of the real world and a close examination of the effects of such intervention.*[1] By looking at a few examples of the use of the method in the research literature, we may further identify other tangible features: action research is *situational* — it is concerned with diagnosing a problem in a specific context and attempting to solve it in that context; it is usually (though not inevitably) *collaborative* — teams of researchers and practitioners work together on a project; it is *participatory* — team members themselves take part directly or indirectly in implementing the research; and it is *self-evaluative* — modifications are continuously evaluated within the ongoing situation, the ultimate objective being to improve practice in some way or other. According to Blum,[2] the use of action research in the social sciences can be resolved into two stages: a *diagnostic stage* in which the problems are analysed and the hypotheses developed; and a *therapeutic stage* in which the hypotheses are tested by a consciously directed change experiment, preferably in a social life situation. As far as educational contexts are concerned, however, Stenhouse[3] is careful to stress that action research should contribute not only to practice but to 'a theory of education and teaching which is accessible to other teachers'.

The scope of action research as a method is impressive. Its usage may range at one extreme from a teacher trying out a novel way of teaching social studies with his class to, at another, a sophisticated study of organisational change in industry using a large research team and backed by government sponsors. Whatever the situation, however, the method's evaluative frame of reference remains the same, namely, to add to the practitioner's *functional knowledge* of the phenomena he deals with. This type of research is therefore usually considered in conjunction with social or educational aims.[4]

It will be useful here if we distinguish *action research* from *applied research*, for although they are similar in some ways, there are important differences between them which need to be made explicit, for confusion between the two does sometimes arise. Both utilise the scientific method. Since applied research is concerned mainly with establishing relationships and testing theories, it is quite rigorous in its application of the conditions of this method. To this end, therefore, it insists on: studying a large number of cases; establishing as much control as possible over variables; precise sampling techniques; and a serious concern to generalise its findings to comparable situations. It does not claim to contribute directly to the solution of problems. Action research, by contrast, interprets the scientific method much more loosely, chiefly because its focus is a specific problem in a specific setting. The emphasis is not so much on obtaining generalisable scientific knowledge as on precise knowledge for a particular situation and purpose. The conditions imposed on applied research, therefore, are normally relaxed with action research. Of course, as action research projects become more extensive in their coverage, the boundary between the two methods becomes less easy to define. A curriculum project involving 100 schools, say, or a community action programme embracing a number of major conurbations, will tend to yield rather more generalisable knowledge and information than purely localised undertakings.

Having drawn this distinction between action research and applied research, we are now free to concentrate on the former and ask ourselves the question: what kinds of intervention programme are featured in action research? The following examples, while by no means exhaustive, give some idea of the contexts in which the method may be used. They are not mutually exclusive so there may be considerable overlap between some of them. There is the kind: (1) which acts as *a spur to action*, its objective being to get something done more expeditiously than would be the case with alternative means; (2) which addresses itself to *personal functioning, human relations and morale* and is thus concerned with people's job efficiency, their motivations, relationships and general well-being; (3) which focuses on *job analysis* and aims at improving professional functioning and efficiency; (4) which is concerned with *organisational change* in so far as it results in improved functioning in business or industry; (5) which is concerned with *planning and policy-making*, generally in the field of social administration; (6) which is concerned with *innovation and change* and the ways in which these may be implemented in ongoing systems; (7) which concentrates on *problem-solving* virtually in any context in which a specific problem needs solving; and (8) which provides the opportunity to develop *theoretical knowledge*, the emphasis here being more on the research element of the method.

Equally diverse are the situations in which these different kinds of intervention may be used — almost any setting, in fact, where a problem involving people, tasks and procedures cries out for solution, or where some change of feature results in a more desirable outcome. Notable instances of the use of action research may be found in such starkly contrasting worlds as insurance, prisons, social administration, ships, hospitals, community projects, education, industry, coal-mining and business management. Examination of the work of the Tavistock Institute of Human Relations which has done so much to develop action research as a methodology will illustrate how the method may be applied in these diverse areas.[5] For our own purposes, however, we shall now restrict our discussion chiefly to the use of action research in the field of education.

Although the action research movement in education was initiated in the United States in the 1940s, the scene for its appearance began to be set in that country in the 1920s with the application of the scientific method to the study of educational problems, growing interest in group interaction and group processes, and the emerging progressive movement. Indeed, the latter is seen by some as the principal causal agent for subsequent developments in action research. One writer[6] says: 'Action research ... is a direct and logical outcome of the progressive position. After showing children how to work together to solve their problems, the next step was for teachers to adopt the methods they had been teaching their children, and learn to solve their own problems co-operatively.' Reaching its peak in the 1960s, the movement had multifarious aims of a decidedly practical nature which were often embellished with ideological, even political, counterpoints. Some, for instance, saw it as a necessary corrective to the failure of official bodies to implement traditional research findings; others, as a means of improving the quality of life. Action research in Britain has enjoyed something of a revival since the establishment of the Schools Council in 1964 under whose aegis it has been used to implement curriculum research and development. The purposes of action research in school and classroom fall broadly into five categories: (1) it is a means of remedying problems diagnosed in specific situations, or of improving in some way a given set of circumstances; (2) it is a means of in-service training, thereby equipping the teacher with new skills and methods, sharpening his analytical powers and heightening his self-awareness; (3) it is a means of injecting additional or innovatory approaches to teaching and learning into an ongoing system which normally inhibits innovation and change; (4) it is a means of improving the normally poor communications between the practising teacher and the academic researcher, and of remedying the failure of traditional research to give clear prescriptions; and (5) although lacking the rigour of true scientific research, it is a means of providing a preferable alternative to the more subjective, impressionistic approach to problem-solving in the classroom.

We close our introduction by asking: who actually undertakes action research in schools? Three possibilities present themselves.

Box 9.1: Humanities Curriculum Project — Aim and Premisses

Aim:
To develop an understanding of social situations and human acts and of the controversial value issues which they raise.

Premisses:
1. That controversial issues should be handled in the classroom.
2. That the teacher should accept the need to submit his teaching in controversial areas to the criterion of neutrality at this stage of education, i.e. that he should regard it as part of his responsibility not to promote his own view.
3. That the mode of enquiry in controversial areas should have discussion, rather than instruction, as its core.
4. That the discussion should protect divergence of view among participants, rather than attempt to achieve consensus.
5. That the teacher as chairman of the discussion should have responsibility for quality and standards of learning.

Source: Butcher and Pont.[7]

First, there is the single teacher operating on his own with his class. He will feel the need for some kind of change or improvement in teaching, learning or organisation, for example, and will be in a position to translate his ideas into action in his own classroom. He is, as it were, both practitioner and researcher in one and will integrate the practical and theoretical orientations within himself. Second, action research may be pursued by a group of teachers working co-operatively within one school, though of necessity functioning against a bigger backdrop than the teacher working solo. They may or may not be advised by an outside researcher. And third, there is the occasion — perhaps the most characteristic in recent years — where a team of teachers work alongside a team of researchers in a sustained relationship, possibly with other interested parties, like advisers, university departments and sponsors, on the periphery. This third possibility, though potentially the most promising, may also be the most problematic, at least initially, because of rival characterisations of action and research by the teachers and researchers respectively. We shall return to this point at the end of the chapter. Advocates of action research believe that little can be achieved if only one person is involved in changing his ideas and practices. For this reason, co-operative research tends to be emphasised and encouraged. One commentator[8] notes:

> Action research functions best when it is co-operative action research. This method of research incorporates the ideas and expectations of all persons involved in the situation. Co-operative action research has the concomitants of beneficial effects for workers, and the improvement of the services, conditions, and functions of the situation. In education this activity translates into more practice in research and problem-solving by teachers, administrators, pupils, and certain community personnel, while the quality of teaching and learning is in the process of being improved.

We refer the reader at this point to Nixon's[9] book which sets out to offer teachers guidelines to help them develop an action research style of their own. The first part presents a number of research reports serving as examples of ways of doing research by a teacher in his or her own classroom. The second part places action research in its social context with four studies exploring some of the problems of implementing school-based research. Ways of overcoming problems of organisational constraint are suggested. The final part of the book is concerned with help from outside agencies. Box 9.2 offers a digest of the rationale behind Nixon's compilation of the classroom and school-based studies used.

Characteristics

The principal characteristics of action research which we hereupon describe are more or less present in all instances of its usage (those having an experimental slant need to be considered in a somewhat different category). We have already referred to its prime feature — that it is essentially an on-the-spot procedure designed to deal with a concrete problem located in an immediate situation. This means that the step-by-step process is constantly monitored (ideally, that is) over varying periods of time and by a variety of mechanisms (questionnaires, diaries, interviews and case studies, for example) so that the ensuing feedback may be translated into modifications, adjustments, directional changes, re-definitions, as necessary, so as to bring about lasting benefit to the ongoing process itself rather than to some future occasion, as is the purpose of more traditionally oriented research. Unlike other methods, no attempt is made to identify one particular factor and study it in isolation, divorced from the context giving it meaning. That the findings are applied immediately, then, or in the short term is another important characteristic, although having made this point we need to qualify it to the extent that members of research teams — especially in curriculum projects — frequently have a more long-term perspective. The following extract from Stenhouse's[10] account of the Humanities Curriculum Project illustrates how some of the points we have just made appear 'in the field':

> During the session 1968–9 the schools worked on collections on war, education, and the family. Feedback on materials was by questionnaire supported by interviews with the schools officer or other team members when they visited schools. Information was sought on coverage of the collection, accessibility of the material to the students (readability and sophistication of ideas), and the extent to which materials provoked or supported discussion. Most schools used only a small proportion of materials (as was intended) so that feedback on any one piece was not

Box 9.2: Action Research in Classroom and School

1. All teachers possess certain skills which can contribute to the research task. The important thing is to clarify and define one's own particular set of skills. Some teachers, for example, are able to collect and interpret statistical data; others to record in retrospective accounts the key moments of a lesson. One teacher may know something about questionnaire design; another have a natural flair for interviewing. It is essential that teachers work from their own particular strengths when developing the research.

2. The situations within which teachers work impose different kinds of constraints. Some schools, for example, are equipped with the most up-to-date audio-visual equipment, others cannot even boast a cassette tape-recorder. Some have spare rooms in which interviews could be carried out, others hardly have enough space to implement the existing time-table. Action research must be designed in such a way as to be easily implemented within the pattern of constraints existing within the school.

3. Any initial definition of the research problem will almost certainly be modified as the research proceeds. Nevertheless, this definition is important because it helps to set limits to the enquiry. If, for example, a teacher sets out to explore through action research the problem of how to start a lesson effectively, the research will tend to focus upon the first few minutes of the lesson. The question of what data to collect is very largely answered by a clear definition of the research problem.

Source: Nixon.[9]

extensive. It was also frequently contradictory, particularly as to readability. Collections were radically re-edited as a result of experience in schools; often only half the trial pack survived.

The principal justification for the use of action research in the context of the school is improvement of practice. This can be achieved only if teachers are able to change their attitudes and behaviour. One of the best means of bringing about these kind of changes is pressure from the group with which one works. As we have seen, because the problems of teachers are often shared with other teachers in the same school, action research has tended to become co-operative, involving many or all of the teachers in the school. Group interaction is frequently another characteristic, therefore.

A feature which makes action research a very suitable procedure for work in classrooms and schools (as well as other field settings) is its flexibility and adaptability. These qualities are revealed in the changes that may take place during its implementation and in the course of on-the-spot experimentation and innovation characterising the approach. They come out particularly strongly

Box 9.3: The Ideal Teacher for an Integrated Studies Project

> The ideal teacher for an Integrated Studies Project would be one willing to maintain his subject discipline within a team and to engage in planning integrated work through discussions with other specialist colleagues. This teacher would be an active producer of new materials, teaching methods and ideas for integrated subject work. He would keep accounts of his innovatory work, fill in the questionnaires sent him by the project team and feed his experience back to them. He would organise his work so that children would not only come to see and use the concepts within separate subject disciplines, but would learn the skills of those subjects through enquiry-based programmes.

Source: adapted from Shipman.[12]

when set against the usual background of constraints in schools — those to do with organisation, resources, timetabling, staff deployment and teachers' attitudes, for example, as well as pressures from other agencies involved and from competing interests.[11]

Action research relies chiefly on observation and behavioural data. That it is therefore empirical is another distinguishing feature of the method. This implies that over the period of a project information is collected, shared, discussed, recorded in some way, evaluated and acted upon; and that from time to time, this sequence of events forms the basis of reviews of progress. In this one respect at least it is superior to the more usual subjective, impressionistic methods we have already alluded to. Where an experimental note is introduced into a project, it is generally achieved through the use of control groups with a view to testing specific hypotheses and arriving at more generalisable knowledge.

In our earlier comparison with applied research, we said that action research took a much more relaxed view of the scientific method. We return to this point here because it is a characteristic which forms the basis of persistent criticisms of the method by its opponents. Travers,[13] for example, in reviewing a number of action research projects writes:

> The writer's evaluation of the last fifty studies which have been undertaken which compare the outcomes of one teaching methodology with another is that they have contributed almost nothing to our knowledge of the factors that influence the learning process in the classroom. Many of them do not even identify what the experimentally controlled variables are and indicate only that the study compares the outcomes of educational

practices in the community where the study originates with educational practices elsewhere.

That the method should be lacking in scientific rigour, however, is not surprising since the very factors which make it distinctively what it is — and therefore of value in certain contexts — are the antithesis of true experimental research. The points usually made are: that its objective is situational and specific (unlike the scientific method which goes beyond the solution of practical problems); its sample is restricted and unrepresentative; it has little or no control over independent variables; and its findings are not generalisable but generally restricted to the environment in which the research is carried out. While these criticisms hold in most cases, it is important that we refer again to the qualification made earlier; that as action research programmes become more extensive and use more schools, that is, become more standardised, less personalised and more 'open', some of these strictures at least will become less valid.

Occasions when Action Reseach as a Method is Appropriate

We come now to a brief consideration of the occasions when the use of action research is fitting and appropriate. The answer in short is this: that action research is appropriate whenever specific knowledge is required for a specific problem in a specific situation; or when a new approach is to be grafted on to an existing system. More than this, however, suitable mechanisms must be available for monitoring progress and for translating feedback into the on-going system. This means that, other things being equal, the action research method may be applied to any classroom or school situation where these conditions apply. We have already referred to the suitability of the approach to curriculum research and development. Let us now take this further by identifying other areas in school life where action research could be used and illustrating each area with a concrete example: (1) *teaching methods* — perhaps replacing a traditional method by a discovery method; (2) *learning strategies* — adopting an integrated approach to learning in preference to a single-subject style of teaching and learning; (3) *evaluative procedures* — improving one's methods of continuous assessment, say; (4) the realm of *attitudes and values* — possibly encouraging more positive attitudes to work, for instance, or modifying pupils' value systems with regard to some aspect of life; (5) the personal *in-service development* of teachers — improving teaching skills, developing new methods of learning, increasing powers of analysis, or heightening self-awareness, for example; (6) *management and control* — the gradual introduction of the techniques of behaviour modification; and (7) *administration* — increasing the efficiency of some aspect of the administrative side of school life.

Of course, it would be naive of us simply to select a problem area *in vacuo*, so to speak. We have also to consider the context in which the project is to be undertaken. More specifically this means bearing in mind factors that will directly affect the outcomes. One of these concerns the teachers themselves and the extent to which they are favourably disposed towards the project, particularly when they are part of a collectivity working with outside agencies for, as we shall see in our final section, this very factor on its own can be a source of intense friction. It is important, therefore, that the teachers taking part in the project are truly involved, that they know what the objectives are, what these imply, and that they are adequately motivated — or at least sufficiently open-minded for motivation to be induced. Another important factor concerns the organisational aspect of the school so that there is a reasonable amount of congruence between the setting and the programme to be initiated. This can be achieved without too much discord when a programme is internally organised by the school itself. When outside parties are involved, however, who themselves are working concurrently in other schools, difficulties may arise over such

Box 9.4: Metaphors Reflecting Teachers' Perceptions of a Curriculum Project

1.	*The exchange of gifts:*	The project as reciprocal obligation.
2.	*The other drummer:*	The project as unselected affinity.
3.	*Troubled waters:*	The project as agitation or distress.
4.	*The gift of grace:*	The project as salvation.
5.	*New props for identity:*	The project as theatre.
6.	*Free sample:*	The project as commercialism.
7.	*Ground bait:*	The project as exploitation.
8.	*Taking issue:*	The project as management consultancy.
9.	*Cargo cult:*	The project as overwhelming technology.

Source: Shipman.[12]

matters as implementing a new style of teaching, for example, or use of project materials, and so on. One further factor concerns resources: are there enough sufficiently competent researchers at hand? And has the school got reasonable access to college and university libraries to consult appropriate professional and research journals should this need arise? Some or all of these factors need to be reviewed as part of the planning stage of an action research programme.

Again we refer the reader to Nixon,[9] especially Part Two which examines, *inter alia,* the problems of school-based research, working with colleagues, and assembling a team.

Some Issues

We have already seen that the participants in a change situation may be either a teacher, a group of teachers working internally, or else teachers and researchers working on a collaborative basis. It is this latter category, where action research brings together two professional bodies each with its own objectives and values, that we shall consider further at this point because of its inherent problematic nature. Both parties share the same interest in an educational problem, yet their respective orientations to it differ. It has been observed,[1] for instance, that research values *precision, control, replication* and attempts to generalise from specific events. Teaching, on the other hand, is concerned with *action,* with *doing things,* and translates generalisations into specific acts. The incompatibility between action and research in these respects, therefore, can be a source of problems. Marris and Rein,[14] for example, on reviewing the relationship between the two in a number of American community action programmes concluded that the principles of *action* and *experienced research* are so different and so often mutually exclusive that attempts to link them into a single process are likely to produce internal conflict and the subordination of one element to another. They express it thus:

> Research requires a clear and constant purpose, which both defines and precedes the choice of means; that the means be exactly and consistently followed; and that no revision takes place until the sequence of steps is completed. Action is tentative, non-commital and adaptive. It concentrates upon the next

step, breaking the sequence into discrete, manageable decisions. It casts events in a fundamentally different perspective, evolving the future out of present opportunities, where research perceives the present in the context of the final outcomes. Research cannot interpret the present until it knows the answers to its ultimate questions. Action cannot foresee what questions to ask until it has interpreted the present. Action attempts to comprehend all the factors relevant to an immediate problem whose nature continually changes as events proceed, where research abstracts one or two factors for attention, and holds to a constant definition of the problem until the experiment is concluded.

Those who are not quite as pessimistic about the viability of the action/reseach coupling would question whether the characterisation of *action* and *research* as put forward by Marris and Rein necessarily holds in all contexts. They would advocate a more flexible approach to the relationship. Some researchers,[1] for instance, suggest that projects could vary along a number of dimensions such as the degree of control exercised by the action and research components, the amount of knowledge about the means of achieving the desired outcomes, and the level of co-operation between action and research. Such a classification could be linked to different kinds of action research (see p. 209) and suggest what combinations of action and research were most appropriate for particular conditions. In short, what seems to be needed is a clear and unambiguous statement of the project's objectives such that all participants understand them and their implications; and a careful analysis of the context(s) in which the programme is to be mounted to determine the precise, but flexible, relationship between the two components. This would help to ensure that the positive contributions of both are maximised and that the constraints of each on the other are kept to a minimum.

Finally, Winter[15] draws attention to the problem of *interpreting* data in action research. He writes:

> The action research/case study tradition does have a methodology for the *creation* of data, but not (as yet) for the interpretation of data. We are shown how the descriptive journal, the observer's field notes, and the open-ended interview are utilized to create accounts of events which will *confront* the practitioner's current pragmatic assumptions and definitions; we are

shown the potential value of this process (in terms of increasing teachers' sensitivity) and the problem it poses for individual and collective professional equilibrium. What we are *not* shown is *how* the teacher can or should handle the data thus collected.

The problem for Winter is how to carry out an interpretive analysis of *restricted* data, that is, data which can make no claim to be generally representative. In other words, the problem of *validity* cannot be side-stepped by arguing that the contexts are unique. For further discussion of this issue, we refer you to Winter's paper.

Procedures

We now trace the possible stages and procedures that may be followed in an action research programme, or from which a suitable selection may be made. As we have already seen, projects may vary along a number of dimensions — whether they are to be conducted by teachers only, or by teachers in collaboration with researchers, whether small or large samples of schools are involved, whether they tackle specific problems or more diffuse ones, for example. Given the particular set of circumstances, an appropriate model may be selected to guide procedures, one that will be tailor-made to meet the needs of the change situation in question. As we are here concerned with a review of procedures in general terms, however, and not with a specific instance, we offer a basic, flexible framework by way of illustration: it will need to be interpreted or adjusted in the light of the particular undertaking.

The *first stage* will involve the identification, evaluation and formulation of the problem perceived as critical in an everyday teaching situation. 'Problem' should be interpreted loosely here so that it could refer to the need to introduce innovation into some aspect of a school's established programme. The *second stage* involves preliminary discussion and negotiations among the interested parties — teachers, researchers, advisers, sponsors, possibly — which may culminate in a draft proposal. This may include a statement of the questions to be answered (e.g. Under what conditions can curriculum change be best effected? What are the limiting factors in bringing about effective curriculum change? What strong points of action research can be employed to bring about curriculum change?). The researchers in their capacity as consultants (or sometimes as programme initiators) may draw upon their expertise to bring the problem more into focus, possibly determining causal factors or recommending alternative lines of approach to established ones. This is often the crucial stage for the venture as it is at this point that the seeds of success or failure are planted, for unless the objectives, purposes and assumptions are made perfectly clear to all concerned, and unless the role of key concepts is stressed (e.g. feedback), the enterprise can easily miscarry. The *third stage* may in some circumstances involve a review of the research literature to find out what can be learned from comparable studies, their objectives, procedures and problems encountered. The *fourth stage* may involve a modification or redefinition of the initial statement of the problem at stage one. It may now emerge in the form of a testable hypothesis; or as a set of guiding objectives. In Box 9.1 we give an example of an aim and accompanying premisses which were used in this connection in the Humanities Curriculum Project. Sometimes change agents deliberately decide against the use of objectives on the grounds that they have a constraining effect on the process itself. It is also at this stage that assumptions underlying the project are made explicit (e.g. in order to effect curriculum changes, the attitudes, values, skills and objectives of the teachers involved must be changed). The *fifth stage* may be concerned with the selection of research procedures — sampling, administration, choice of materials, methods of teaching and learning, allocation of resources and tasks, deployment of staff and so on.

The *sixth stage* will be concerned with the choice of the evaluation procedures to be used and will need to take into consideration that evaluation in this context will be continuous. Box 9.5 provides a set of evaluation objectives from the Humanities Project by way of example. The *seventh stage* embraces the implementation of the project itself (over varying periods of time). It will include the conditions and methods of data collection (e.g. bi-weekly meetings, the keeping of records, interim reports, final reports, the submission of self-evaluation and group-evaluation reports, etc.); the monitoring of tasks and the transmission of feedback to the research team; and the classification and analysis of data. The *eighth and final stage* will involve the interpretation of the data; inferences to be drawn; and overall evaluation of the project.[16] Discussions on the findings will take place in the light of previously agreed evaluative criteria. Errors, mistakes and problems will be

Box 9.5: The Objectives of the Evaluation Unit in the Humanities Curriculum Project

1.	To ascertain the effects of the Project, document the circumstances in which they occur, and present this information in a form which will help educational decision-makers to evaluate the likely consequences of adopting the programme.
2.	To describe the present situation and operations of the schools we study so that decision-makers can understand more fully what it is they are trying to change.
3.	To describe the work of the project team in terms which will help the sponsors and planners of such a venture to weigh the value of this form of investment, and to determine more precisely the framework of support, guidance and control which are appropriate.
4.	To make a contribution to evaluation theory by articulating our problems clearly, recording our experiences, and perhaps most importantly, by publicising our errors.
5.	To contribute to the understanding of the problems of curriculum innovation generally.

Source: Butcher and Pont.[7]

considered. A general summing up may follow this in which the outcomes of the project are reviewed, recommendations made, and arrangements for dissemination of results to interested parties decided.

As we stressed, this is a basic framework: much activity of an incidental and possibly *ad hoc* nature will take place in and around it. This may comprise discussions among teachers, researchers and pupils; regular meetings among teachers or schools to discuss progress and problems, and to exchange information; possibly regional conferences; and related activities, all enhanced by the range of current hardware — tapes, video-recordings and transcripts.

Conclusion: Examples of Action Research in School Contexts

As the majority of action research projects in education are, or have been, concerned with the curriculum, we draw on four of these to illustrate briefly what has been undertaken in this area. Using the typology of McCormick and James,[17] we consider two studies under the heading *Evaluation by Outsiders*, and two under the heading *Evaluation by Insiders*. The former comprise the Humanities Curriculum Project[10] and the Keele Integrated Studies Project.[12]

The first of these, the Humanities Curriculum Project, was set up in 1967 under the joint sponsorship of the Schools Council and the Nuffield Foundation. Its aim and premises we have listed in Box 9.1. The overall task of the project was to discover a teaching strategy which would implement these premises in the classroom, to report this strategy, and to support teachers who wished to develop it with training and if necessary with materials.

The problems and difficulties in mounting this project appear to have stemmed in the main from mistaken or incongruent attitudes and expectations on the part of the teachers in the experimental schools. Thus, their initial outlook tended to be coloured by earlier, more traditional approaches to the curriculum based on single-subject specialisms with the emphasis on improving teaching methods in these fields. They failed to appreciate that the venture had a social science basis and that they would need to adopt a suitably detached stance in keeping with its experimental nature. Having this kind of basis, the project was seen by the researchers as a means of testing hypotheses; many of the teachers, however, in awe of the presumed authority of the Schools Council, its sponsors, felt that they themselves were on trial. As a result, some of the experimental feedback was distorted. Misunderstandings with respect to the researchers' time perspective was another source of difficulty. The research team was concerned with long-term development; yet they were often perceived as attempting an instant and easy solution to problems. Finally, the teachers in the experimental schools tended to harbour feelings that the project would in some way help to solve problems of discipline and control. As it was, 'It made them more acute [and] opened them up instead of containing them'.[10]

The second example of the use of action research is that of the Keele Integrated Studies Project initiated in 1969. Notwithstanding the success of the project and the value of the accrued experience in implementing it, we here again restrict ourselves to some of the more problematic aspects. Difficulties arose once more from the way the project was perceived or misperceived by the teachers in the experimental schools, as well as from the ambiguous relationship they had with it (we refer you to Box 9.4 which lists the metaphors selected by one of the parties involved to describe the teachers' perceptions of the project). We will, however, focus our remarks on the problem of communication between teachers and researchers which seemed to persist throughout the undertaking.

Efforts on the part of the research team to inform the schools at the outset of the project's objectives by means of meetings, conferences and circulars met with sustained complaints from the teachers about jargon and the lack of specific advice. The latter at this stage were indifferent to the researchers' attempts to explain the principles of integration and theories of curriculum development. This bears out the point we made earlier about rival characterisations of teaching and research. Subsequently, however, after having experienced the practical difficulties of implementing integrated studies, the teachers reversed their complaint, demanding explanation and theoretical reasoning for what they were doing. The discrepancy between what they requested and what they were prepared to do resulted in a lasting tension. As Shipman[12] points out, they wanted 'both academic rigour and easy-bake recipes from the same source'.

A further serious problem, yet another aspect of the communication gap, arose from the low priority given by the teachers to feedback. To this may be added their general reluctance to seek advice. In spite of the provision made by the researchers, only two out of the thirty-eight schools involved provided regular feedback to the research team. As Shipman again observes, this omission may be traced to the fact that the definitions of the project team and of the teachers were at different levels: 'The teachers were involved with their own problems and defined the project out of their own experience in their own classrooms. As a consequence the basic principles behind the project were usually misunderstood and often unconsidered.'

We see from all this that what is involved is group process and that this is not easy to handle. Favourable conditions for action research include the following: a willingness on the part of the teachers to admit limitations and to make themselves familiar with the basic techniques of research; the provision of opportunities to invent; the encouragement of new ideas; the provision of time for experimentation; a mutual trust of those involved; and a knowledge on the part of the participants of the fundamentals of group processes. Additionally, it must be realised that many minds working on the same problem will increase the number of ways of looking at it. There will be more suggested solutions.

Finally, we illustrate the concept of *Evaluation by Insiders* by studies described by King[18] and McCormick and James.[17] King described the work of the school-based research action group in

Box 9.6: Research Action Group in English

> The group believes:
>
> 1. Teachers work best when they identify their own problems in their own way and at their own pace;
> 2. Teachers often become more effective (and as a result the pupils often have a better deal) when they have a regular chance (through systematic talking and writing) to reflect and exchange views on what they think is happening in their own classrooms;
> 3. Working in open partnership with other observers is often more useful for teachers than having academic findings handed down from on high;
> 4. A direct and vulnerable style of enquiry often makes more sense to other busy teachers than a style that has 'an aura of infallibility';
> 5. Educational research needs to be re-defined as a continuing conversation between classroom practice and relevant theory, where both elements can reinforce and change each other at the point of classroom perception.

Source: King.[18]

English formed in 1980 to investigate what is meant by progress and development in talking, reading and writing in the English classroom from 11 to 19. Members of the group came from middle and secondary schools in the Midlands and Yorkshire. The group's *raison d'être* is expressed in Box 9.6.

Three strands were identified in the group's enquiries: (1) the need to produce a more coherent, long-term approach through a developmental framework to the teaching of English, as opposed to the randomness of approach that characterised the work of at least one English department in the study. The model selected identified four different but linked phases of development from 11 to 19 and explored how children learn and grow through talking, reading and writing. (2) Teachers, working in groups to examine each of the suggested phases of the model, questioned the framework in the light of different schools' intentions and the local evidence of the children's work. (3) An action research method of investigation was used. A three-way observation exchange was set up where teachers record their own detailed interpretations of classroom experience, pupils keep their own diaries or comment on tape, and outside observers in the classroom record their own impressions. Through cross-checking the three different representations, the group pointed out for themselves any significant mismatches between accounts. This study is ongoing and information is available from the Loughborough English Teaching Centre (see King[18]).

The second of our two *Evaluation by Insiders* studies, quoted in McCormick and James,[17] is that of Quinton Kynaston School and nicely illustrates the flexibility of action-based research in the way the participants deviate from the original model. The school is an 11–18 mixed comprehensive in North London. Since 1976 a number of working groups have met to consider ways of promoting effective learning across the curriculum. Their work is co-ordinated and reviewed by a Support for Learning Group (SLG). In the first stage the SLG would identify and publish the criteria to guide classroom observations. These were intended to cover areas such as language use and the acquisition of study skills. The second stage concerned chiefly observation. This was to include lesson observation; analysis of teaching materials; departmental policy documents; discussion with course planning teams; monitoring learning outcomes; and involvement with INSET activities. The third stage of the project involved reporting and discussion at the end of the observation period. In addition to the production of reports the research would also be expected to collect and disseminate examples of good practice.

And what was the outcome? McCormick and James explain:

In actuality this particular research project got no further than stage one. It became clear to the teachers that many of the objectives of the research model ... could be achieved by building up skills of co-observation and self-evaluation within and between teachers. Further, self-evaluation was found to be most profitably focused in departments and on those structures which brought departments together to develop and evaluate whole-school policies. The idea of classroom observation encouraged some teachers to observe each other, and one group, for example, began some research on girls' talk.

The picture in September 1982 revealed the fruits of such work. Departments were making effective use of their review reports in identifying priorities for course planning. The SLG had chosen the theme of 'girls and schooling' as one of its priorities for the next academic year. Quinton Kynaston has therefore chosen to continue to build self-evaluation into the organisation of the school and the fabric of all lessons before it invites one person to reflect on what has to be a whole-school activity.

In conclusion it might be added that in a representative sample of action research studies conducted in the United States, it was found[6] that the teachers taking part were generally enthusiastic. They seemed to feel that the staff worked more as a unit than before the research, that staff members were drawn closer together with the knowledge that they shared problems and goals, and that respect for individuals, both teachers and pupils, had increased.

References

1. Halsey, A.H. (ed.), *Educational Priority: Volume 1: E.P.A. Problems and Policies* (HMSO, London, 1972).
2. National Educational Association of the United States: Association for Supervision and Curriculum Development, *Learning about Learning from Action Research* (Washington, DC, 1959).
3. Stenhouse, L., 'What is action research?' (C.A.R.E., University of East Anglia, Norwich (mimeograph) 1979).
4. Corey, S.M., *Action Research to Improve School Practices* (Bureau of Publications, Teachers College, Columbia University, New York, 1953).
5. See, for example: Brown, R.K., 'Research and consultancy in industrial enterprises: a review of the contribution of the Tavistock Institute of Human Relations to the development of Industrial Sociology', *Sociology*, 1, 1 (1967) 33–60.
6. Hodgkinson, H.L., 'Action research — a critique', *J. Educ. Sociol.*, 31, 4 (1957) 137–53.
7. Butcher, H.J. and Pont, H.B. (eds), *Educational Research in Britain 3* (University of London Press, London, 1973).
8. Hill, J.E. and Kerber, A., *Models, Methods, and Analytical Procedures in Educational Research* (Wayne State University Press, Detroit, 1967).
9. Nixon, J. (ed.), *A Teacher's Guide to Action Research* (Grant McIntyre, London, 1981).
10. Stenhouse, L. 'The Humanities Curriculum Project', in Butcher and Pont.[7] For a recent evaluation of the Humanities Curriculum Project see: Brown, A., 'The Practice of Educational Research: Contrasting Case Studies,' unpublished D.Phil. dissertation, The New University of Ulster, Coleraine, 1984.
11. See also Nixon, op. cit.
12. Shipman, M.D., *Inside a Curriculum Project* (Methuen, London, 1974).
13. Travers, R.M.W., Extract quoted in Halsey (ed.)[1]
14. Marris, P. and Rein, M. *Dilemmas of Social Reform: Poverty and Community Action in the United States* (Routledge and Kegan Paul, London, 1967).
15. Winter, R., ' "Dilemma Analysis": A contribution to methodology for action research', *Cambridge Journal of Education*, 12, 3 (1982) 161–74.
16. We refer the reader again to Winter[15] in this connection.
17. McCormick, R. and James, M., *Curriculum Evaluation in Schools* (Croom Helm, Beckenham, 1983).
18. King, P. (ed.), *Working with Third Years*. A report of the Research Action Group in English, 1983. (The Loughborough English Teaching Centre, Department of Education, Loughborough University, and School of Education, Nottingham University, 1983).

10 ACCOUNTS

Introduction

Although each of us sees the world from our own point of view, we have a way of speaking about our experiences which we share with those around us. Explaining our behaviour towards one another can be thought of as accounting for our actions in order to make them intelligible and justifiable to our fellowmen. Thus, saying 'I'm terribly sorry, I didn't mean to bump into you', is a simple case of the explication of social meaning, for by locating the bump outside any planned sequence and neutralising it by making it intelligible in such a way that it is not warrantable, it ceases to be offensive in that situation.[1]

Accounting for actions in those larger slices of life called social episodes is the central concern of a new participatory psychology which focuses upon an actor's intentions, his beliefs about what sorts of behaviour will enable him to reach his goals, and his awareness of the rules that govern those behaviours. Studies carried out within this new framework have been termed *ethogenic*, an adjective which expresses a view of the human being *as a person*, that is, a plan-making, self-monitoring agent, aware of goals and deliberately considering the best ways to achieve them.[2] Ethogenic studies represent a new approach to the study of social behaviour and their methods stand in bold contrast to those commonly employed in much of the educational research which we describe in Chapter 8. Before discussing the elicitation and analysis of accounts we need to outline the ethogenic approach in more detail. This we do by reference to the work of one of its foremost British exponents.

The Ethogenic Approach

Harré[3] identifies five main principles in the ethogenic approach:

1. An explicit distinction is drawn between *synchronic analysis*, that is, the analysis of social practices and institutions as they

exist at any one time, and *diachronic analysis,* the study of the stages and the processes by which social practices and institutions are created and abandoned, change and are changed. Neither type of analysis can be expected to lead directly to the discovery of universal social psychological principles or laws.

2.   In social interaction, it is assumed that action takes place through endowing intersubjective entities with meaning; the ethogenic approach therefore concentrates upon the *meaning system,* that is, the whole sequence by which a social act is achieved in an episode. Consider, for example, the action of a kiss in the particular episodes of (a) leaving a friend's house; (b) the passing-out parade at St Cyr; and (c) the meeting in the garden of Gethsemane.

3.   The ethogenic approach is concerned with speech which accompanies action. That speech is intended to make the action intelligible and justifiable in occurring at the time and the place it did in the whole sequence of unfolding and co-ordinated action. Such speech is *accounting.* In so far as accounts are socially meaningful, it is possible to derive *accounts of accounts.*

4.   The ethogenic approach is founded upon the belief that a human being tends to be the kind of person his language, his traditions, his tacit and explicit knowledge tell him he is.

5.   The skills that are employed in ethogenic studies therefore make use of common-sense understandings of the social world. As such the activities of the poet and the playwright offer the ethogenic researcher a better model than those of the physical scientist.

Characteristics of Accounts and Episodes

The discussion of accounts and episodes that now follows develops some of the ideas contained in the principles of the ethogenic approach outlined above.

We have already noted that accounts must be seen within the context of social episodes. The idea of an episode is a fairly general one. The concept itself may be defined as any coherent fragment of social life. Being a natural division of life, an episode will often have a recognisable beginning and end, and the sequence of actions that constitute it will have some meaning for the participants.

Episodes may thus vary in duration and reflect innumerable aspects of life. A pupil entering primary school at seven and leaving at eleven would be an extended episode. A two-minute television interview with a political celebrity would be another. And, as we shall shortly illustrate, prospective house buyers recounting their experiences of negotiating a purchase, yet another. The contents of an episode which interest the ethogenic researcher include not ony the perceived behaviour such as gesture and speech, but also the thoughts, the feelings and the intentions of those taking part. And the 'speech' that accounts for those thoughts, feelings and intentions must be conceived of in the widest connotation of the word. Thus, accounts may be personal records of the events we experience in our day-to-day lives, our conversations with neighbours, our letters to friends, our entries in diaries. Accounts serve to explain our past, present and future-oriented actions.

Providing that accounts are authentic, it is argued, there is no reason why they should not be used as scientific tools in explaining people's actions. Just how accounts can be authenticated will become clear in the following example of how an account may be elicited and analysed (see p. 267 for a discussion of triangulation methods in analysing accounts). The study is to do with an experience familiar to many readers — the processes involved in buying a house.[4]

Procedures in Eliciting, Analysing and Authenticating Accounts: an Example

From the outset of this research project, prime importance was placed upon the authority of each informant to account for his own actions. This meant that leading questions and excessive guidance were avoided by the research team although they established the format of the interview in pilot work before the main research endeavour. Care was taken to select informants who were representative of various house buyer needs (newly-weds, large families, divorcees, etc.) and of a range of house styles and prices. The researchers were concerned with the degree to which respondents were actually involved in the house purchase, the recency of the experience, their reasons for participating in the study, and their articulateness and competence in providing information.

Box 10.1: Accounts of a Social Episode: House Purchase

Mrs Y: 'Agents put us in touch with three people who were interested. Couple X seemed to be the absolutely perfect customer. They gave us the offer we wanted, bought some brand new carpets over and above the asking price. Some problems followed and things were delayed.

'I don't think the X's were quite aware of the urgency. We got the impression from the agents that they were cash buyers. But it turned out they weren't and it was a bit naughty to give us this impression.

'We didn't get on so well with Mr X and Mrs X was a bit of a tough cookie. My husband had words with her and he got a bit ruffled.'

Mrs X: 'It started off a very amicable relationship. We came over here and agreed to buy carpets and curtains. But the whole situation deteriorated which made the whole thing unpleasant. Mr Y would call every night sometimes he would call twice and harangue and harangue. They seemed to think we were cash buyers, the agents having told them so. So I said we are cash buyers only in the sense that we don't have anything to sell.

'It all became more and more abusive, finally I got so upset that I refused any more calls and anything that had to be said should go via a solicitor. Every time the 'phone goes I would just cringe.'

Source: adapted from Brown and Sime.[4]

These early stages of the research, involving selection and collection activities, serve as checks on the authenticity of the accounts provided by those from whom it was possible to obtain adequate information. Further ways of establishing authenticity involved: (1) checking with respondents through a process of negotiation during the account-gathering stage about their perceptions of the events they described; (2) using secondary evidence such as expert corroboration from solicitors and estate agents, that is, comparing objective and subjective realities; and (3) comparing the separate accounts of other participants in the same event, that is, looking at various subjective realities. We illustrate this latter aspect in Box 10.1.

Once accounts had been gathered from informants, the researchers' task was to transform them into working documents which could be coded and analysed. Checks on the authenticity of the accounts were again incorporated at this state of the research as well as standard checks on the intercoder reliability of those engaged in the transformation of the materials. Depending on the nature of the research problem and the objectives of the enquiry, the analyses that then followed could either be qualitative or quantitative. The final stage in the research was the production of an *account of the accounts*. Here, the researchers made explicit the

Box 10.2: Account Gathering

	Research strategy	Control procedure
1.	INFORMANTS	
	Definition of episode and role groups representing domain of interest	rationale for choice of episode and role groups
	Identification of exemplars	degree of involvement of potential informants
	Selection of individual informants	contact with individuals to establish motive for participation, competence and performance
2.	ACCOUNT GATHERING SITUATION	
	Establishing venue	contextual effects of venue
	Recording the account	appropriateness and accuracy in documenting account
	Controlling relevance of account	accounts agenda
	Authenticating account	negotiation and internal consistency
	Establishing role of interviewer and interviewee	degree of direction
	Post account authentication	corroboration
3.	TRANSFORMATION OF ACCOUNTS	
	Provision of working documents	transcription reliability; coder reliability
	Data reduction techniques	appropriateness of statistical and content analyses
4.	RESEARCHERS' ACCOUNTS	
	Account of the account — summary, overview, interpretation	description of research operations, explanatory scheme and theoretical background

Source: Brown and Sime.[5]

controls that they had applied in eliciting accounts from informants and in the transformation process itself. Having satisfied the demands of authenticity in respect of their own account, the final product was then ready to be evaluated. Only when accounts were subjected to these periodic stringent checks for authenticity were they considered as scientific data. The account-gathering method proposed by Brown and Sime is summarised in Box 10.2.

Problems of eliciting, analysing and authenticating accounts are further illustrated in the following outlines of two educational studies. The first is concerned with valuing among older boys and girls; the second is to do with teachers' judgements about their own competence as classroom practitioners.

Qualitative Analysis of Accounts of Social Episodes: Further Examples

In a study of adolescent values, Kitwood[6] developed an *experience-sampling method*, that is, a qualitative technique for gathering and analysing accounts based upon tape-recorded interviews that were themselves prompted by the 15 situations listed in Box 10.3.

Because the experience-sampling method avoids interrogation, the material which emerges is less organised than that obtained from a tightly structured interview. Successful handling of individual accounts therefore requires the researcher to know the interview content extremely well and to work toward the gradual emergence of tentative interpretive schemata which he then modifies, confirms or falsifies as the research continues. Kitwood identifies eight methods for dealing with the tape-recorded accounts. Methods 1–4 are fairly close to the approach adopted in handling questionnaires; and methods 5–8 are more in tune with the ethogenic principles that we identified earlier.

Method 1: The Total Pattern of Choice

The frequency of choice of various items permits some surface generalisations about the participants, taken as a group. The most revealing analyses may be those of the least and most popular items.

Method 2: Similarities and Differences

Using the same technique as in Method 1, it is possible to investigate similarities and differences within the total sample of accounts according to some characteristic(s) of the participants such as age, sex, level of educational attainment, etc.

Method 3: Grouping Items Together

It may be convenient for some purposes to fuse together categories that cover similar subject matter. For example, items 1, 5 and 14 in Box 10.3 relate to conflict; items 4, 7 and 15, to personal growth and change.

Method 4: Categorisation of Content

The content of a particular item is inspected for the total sample and an attempt is then made to develop some categories into which

Box 10.3: Experience Sampling Method

Below are listed 15 types of situation which most people have been in at some time. Try to think of something that has happened in your life in the last year or so, or perhaps something that keeps on happening, which fits into each of the descriptions. Then choose the ten of them which deal with the things that seem to you to be most important, which cover your main interests and concerns, and the different parts of your life. When we meet we will talk together about the situations you have chosen. Try beforehand to remember as clearly as you can what happened, what you and others did, and how you yourself felt and thought. Be as definite as you can. If you like, write a few notes to help you keep the situation in mind.

1. When there was a misunderstanding between you and someone else (or several others) ...
2. When you got on really well with people ...
3. When you had to make an important decision ...
4. When you discovered something new about yourself ...
5. When you felt angry, annoyed or resentful ...
6. When you did what was expected of you ...
7. When your life changed direction in some way ...
8. When you felt you had done something well ...
9. When you were right on your own, with hardly anyone taking your side ...
10. When you 'got away with it', or were not found out ...
11. When you made a serious mistake ...
12. When you felt afterwards that you had done right ...
13. When you were disappointed with yourself ...
14. When you had a serious clash or disagreement with another person ...
15. When you began to take seriously something that had not mattered much to you before ...

Source: adapted from Kitwood.[6]

all the material will fit. The analysis is most effective when two or more researchers work in collaboration, each initially proposing a category system independently and then exchanging views to negotiate a final category system.

Method 5: Tracing a Theme

This type of analysis transcends the rather artificial boundaries which the items themselves imply. It aims to collect as much data as possible relevant to a particular topic regardless of where it occurs in the interview material. The method is exacting because it requires very detailed knowledge of content and may entail going through taped interviews several times. Data so collected may be further analysed along the lines suggested in Method 4 above.

Method 6: The Study of Omissions

The researcher may well have expectations about the kind of issues likely to occur in the interviews. When some of these are absent, that fact may be highly significant. The absence of an anticipated topic should be explored to discover the correct explanation of its omission.

Method 7: Reconstruction of a Social Life-world

This method can be applied to the accounts of a number of people who have part of their lives in common, for example, a group of friends who go around together. The aim is to attempt some kind of reconstruction of the world which the participants share in analysing the fragmentary material obtained in an interview. The researcher seeks to understand the dominant modes or orienting to reality, the conceptions of purpose and the limits to what is perceived.

Method 8: Generating and Testing Hypotheses

New hypotheses may occur to the researcher during the analysis of the tape-recordings. It is possible to do more than simply advance these as a result of tentative impressions; one can loosely apply the hypothetico-deductive method to the data. This involves putting the hypothesis forward as clearly as possible, working out what the verifiable inferences from it would logically be, and testing these against the account data. Where these data are too fragmentary, the researcher may then consider what kind of evidence and method of obtaining it would be necessary for a more thorough hypothesis testing. Subsequent sets of interviews forming part of the same piece of research might then be used to obtain relevant data.

The experience-sampling method used by Kitwood led him to identify three key second-order concepts by which to explore the nature of adolescent values. The first he called *confict in personal relationships*, having found a general theme of interpersonal conflict running strongly through the interviews. The second, he identified as *decision-making* on the evidence of a deep concern and realism among the adolescents interviewed about what might lie ahead of them. The third he termed *standing alone*, a major preoccupation among his subjects and a second-order concept of

Box 10.4: 'Competence' in the Comprehensive Classroom

Competence is regarded as a shared method for interpreting events; teacher competence appears to owe more to control in the classroom than to the inculcation of knowledge *per se*.

Competent teachers are expected to achieve control without the aid of others and are considered responsible for the control of their own classrooms.

Classroom teaching, however, rarely becomes observable to colleagues. To assess the control of others therefore, teachers have to rely on publicly available indicators which transcend the isolation of setting, principally, *noise*. Control, then, is a socially organised phenomenon which is inferred rather than observed.

Source: Denscombe.[7]

some complexity which was further broken down into five subcategories for more detailed analysis.

In the light of the weaknesses in account gathering and analysis to which we refer on p. 249 ff., Kitwood's suggestions of safeguards are worth mentioning. First he calls for *cross-checking* between researchers as a precaution against consistent but unrecognised bias in the interviews themselves. Second he recommends *member tests*, that is, taking hypotheses and unresolved problems back to the participants themselves or to persons in similar situations to them for their comments. Only in this way can the researcher be sure that he understands the participants' *own* grounds for action. Since there is always the possibility that an obliging participant will readily confirm the researcher's own speculations, every effort should be made to convey to the participant that one wants to know the truth as he or she sees it, and that one is as glad to be proved wrong as right.

Denscombe's[7] study of teaching as a practical activity approached the problem of authentication from a similar direction to that proposed by Kitwood. Denscombe's tape-recorded interviews with some 67 comprehensive school teachers *followed* a series of observations of the teachers' classroom activities. He used his observations as checks on the validity of the taped accounts. More importantly however, he provided opportunities for his participants to explain why a lesson had taken a particular course and why pupils had reacted in a particular way. In a word, teachers had a chance to *justify* their actions to the researcher.

As a further precaution against social desirability responses,

Box 10.5: Network Analysis: Pupils' Views of their Teachers

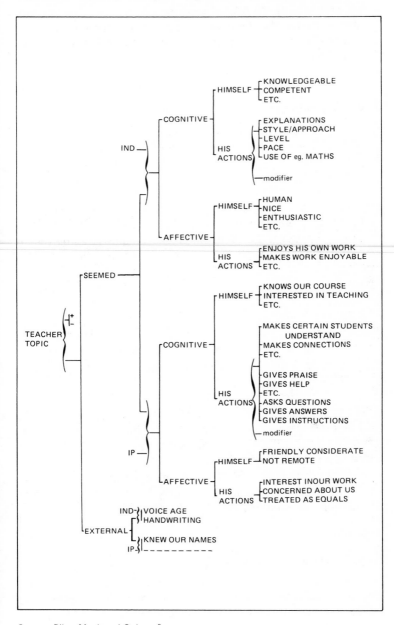

Source: Bliss, Monk and Ogborn.[8]

Denscombe adopted a trainee identity, that is, as one seeking advice and needing the help of experienced teachers. That identity greatly facilitated the normalising of the researcher's presence in classrooms both from the point of view of teachers and of pupils. Some of Denscombe's findings are reported in Box 10.4.

Network Analyses of Qualitative Data

Another technique that has been successfully employed in the analysis of qualitative data is described by its originators as *systematic network analysis.*[8]

Essentially, network analysis involves the development of an elaborate system of categories by way of classifying qualitative data and preserving the essential complexity and subtlety of the materials under investigation. A notational technique is employed to generate network-like structures that show the interdependencies of the categories as they are developed. An example from the work of Bliss and her associates[8] is set out in Box 10.5 to illustrate the network analysis technique. It is concerned with the classification of children's stories about their teachers. Notice how the very first distinction that the researchers introduce has to do with the difference between things that *seemed* to the pupil to be the case and things that *could be observed* and, in principle, objectively agreed upon. This was found necessary because some of the statements about teachers referred to their age, colour of hair, etc., while others were more a matter of the children's personal judgements such as their views on a teacher's enthusiasm or competence. A second major classificatory system that the researchers then introduced had to do with the fact that a teacher could seem different when he was on his own (IND = individual) or when he was dealing with a number of pupils (IP = interpersonal). The rest of the teacher network shown in Box 10.5 is self-explanatory.

What Makes a Good Network?

Bliss *et al.* point out that there cannot be one overall account of criteria for judging the merits of a particular network. They do, however, attempt to identify a number of factors that ought to feature in any discussion of the standards by which a network might fairly be judged as adequate.

First, any system of description needs to be *valid* and *reliable*, *valid* in the sense that it is appropriate in kind and, within that kind, sufficiently complete and faithful, *reliable* in the sense that there exists an acceptable level of agreement between people as to how to use the network system to describe data.

Second, there are properties that a network description should possess such as *clarity, completeness,* and *self-consistency.* These relate to a further criterion of network utility, the *sufficiency of detail* contained in a particular network. A third property that a network should possess is termed *learnability.* Communicating the terms of the analysis to others, say the authors, is of central importance. It follows therefore that much hinges on whether networks are relatively easy or hard to teach to others. A fourth aspect of network acceptability has to do with its *testability.* Bliss *et al.* identify two forms of testability, the first having to do with testing a network as a 'theory' against data, the second with testing data against a 'theory' or expectation via a network.

Finally, the terms *expressiveness* and *persuasiveness* refer to qualities of language used in developing the network structure. And here, the authors proffer the following advice. 'Helpful as the choice of an expressive coding mood or neat use of indentation or brackets may be, *the code actually says no more than the network distinguishes*' (our italics).

To conclude, network analysis would seem to have a useful role to play in educational research by providing a technique for dealing with the bulk and the complexity of the accounts that are typically generated in qualitative studies.

Quantitative Analysis of Judgemental Ratings of Social Episodes

A major problem in the investigation of that natural unit of social behaviour, the *social episode,* has been the ambiguity that surrounds the concept itself and the lack of an acceptable taxonomy by which to classify an interaction sequence on the basis of empirically quantifiable characteristics.[9] In this section we describe a number of quantitative approaches to the study of social episodes in educational settings.

Box 10.6: Students' Perceptions of Social Episodes

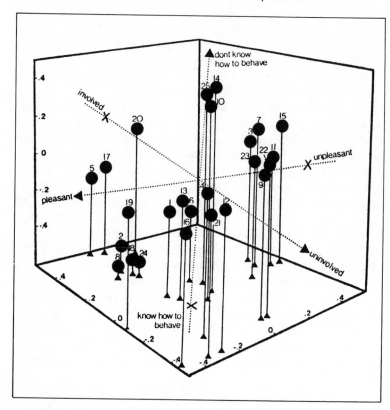

Episodes

{ 14 Meeting new people at a sherry party in college
  25 Play chess
  10 Getting acquainted with a new person during dinner at hall.

{ 2   Having a drink with some friends in a pub
  18 Going to see a play at the theatre with friends
  24 Watching TV with some friends
  8   Going to the pictures with some friends

Source: adapted from Forgas.[9]

Examples of Studies Using Factor Analysis and Linkage Analysis

The use of factor analysis and linkage analysis in studies of children's judgements of educational situations is illustrated in the work of Magnusson[10] and Ekehammar and Magnusson.[11] In the latter study, pupils were required to rate descriptions of various educational episodes on a scale of perceived similarity ranging from *0 = not at all similar to 4 = identical.* Twenty different situations were presented two at a time in the same randomised order for all subjects. For example, 'listening to a lecture but do not understand a thing' would be judged against 'sitting at home writing an essay'. Product moment correlation coefficients between pairs of similarity matrices calculated for all subjects varied between 0.57 and 0.79, with a median value of 0.71. No individual matrix deviated markedly from any of the others. A factor analysis of the total correlation matrix showed that the descriptions of situations had very clear structures for the children involved. Moreover, judgements of perceived similarity between situations had a considerable degree of consistency over time. Ekehammar and Magnusson compared their dimensional analysis with a categorical approach to the data using elementary linkage (McQuitty[12]). They reported that this latter approach gave a result which was entirely in agreement with the result of the dimensional analysis. Five categories of situations were obtained with the same situations distributed in categories in the same way as they were distributed in factors in the dimensional analysis.

Examples of Studies using Multidimensional Scaling and Cluster Analysis

Forgas[9] studied housewives' and students' perceptions of typical social episodes in their lives, the episodes having been elicited from the respective groups by means of a diary technique. Subjects were required to supply two adjectives to describe each of the social episodes they had recorded as having occurred during the previous 24 hours. From a pool of some 146 adjectives thus generated, 10 (together with their antonyms) were selected on the basis of their salience, their diversity of usage and their independence of one another. Two more scales from speculative taxonomies were added to give 12 undimensional scales purporting to describe the underlying episode structures. These scales were used in the second part of the study to rate 25 social episodes in each group, the episodes being chosen as follows: an *index of relatedness* was computed on the basis of the number of times a pair of episodes was placed in the same category by respective housewife and student judges. Data were aggregated over the total number of subjects in each of the two groups. The 25 'top' social episodes in each group were retained. Forgas's analysis is based upon the ratings of 26 housewives and 25 students of their respective 25 episodes on each of the 12 undimensional scales. Box 10.6 shows a three-dimensional configuration of 25 social episodes rated by the student group on three of the scales. For illustrative purposes some of the social episodes numbered in Box 10.6 are identified by specific content.

In another study, Forgas[13] examined the social environment of a university department consisting of tutors, students and secretarial staff all of whom had interacted both inside and outside the department for at least six months prior to the research and thought of themselves as an intensive and cohesive social unit. Forgas's interest was in the relationship between two aspects of the social environment of the department — the perceived structure of the group and the perceptions that were held of specific social episodes. Participants were required to rate the similarity between each possible pairing of group members on a scale ranging from (1) extremely similar to (9) extremely dissimilar. An individual differences multidimensional scaling procedure (INDSCAL) produced an optimal three-dimensional configuration of group structure accounting for 68 per cent of the variance, group members being differentiated along the dimensions of *sociability, creativity* and *competence.*

A semi-structured procedure requiring participants to list typical and characteristic interaction situations was used to identify a number of social episodes. These in turn were validated by participant observation of the ongoing activities of the department. The most commonly occurring social episodes (those mentioned by nine or more members) served as the stimuli in the second stage of the study. Bi-polar scales similar to those reported by Forgas[9] above and elicited in like manner were used to obtain group members' judgements of social episodes.

An interesting finding reported by Forgas was that formal status differences exercised no significant effect upon the perception of the group by its members, the absence of differences being attributed to the strength of the department's cohesiveness and intimacy. In Forgas's analysis of the group's perceptions of social episodes, the INDSCAL scaling procedure produced an optimal four-dimensional solution accounting for 62 per cent of the variance, group members perceiving social episodes in terms of *anxiety, involvement, evaluation* and *socio-emotional versus task orientation.*

Box 10.7 illustrates how an average group member would see the characteristics of various social episodes in terms of the dimensions by which the group commonly judged them.

Finally we outline a classificatory system that has been developed to process materials elicited in a rather structured form of account gathering.

Peevers and Secord's[14] study of developmental changes in children's use of descriptive concepts of persons illustrates the application of quantitative techniques to the analysis of one form of account.

In individual interviews, children of varying ages were asked to describe three friends and one person whom they disliked, all four persons being of the same sex as the interviewee. Interviews were tape-recorded and transcribed. A person concept coding system was developed, the categories of which are illustrated in Box 10.8. Each person-description was divided into items, each item consisting of one discrete piece of information. Each item was then coded on each of four major dimensions. Detailed coding procedures are set out in Peevers and Secord.[14]

Tests of interjudge agreement on descriptiveness, personal involvement and evaluative consistency in which two judges worked independently on the interview transcripts of 21 boys and girls aged between 5 and 16 years resulted in interjudge agreement on those three dimensions of 87 per cent, 79 per cent and 97 per cent respectively.

Peevers and Secord also obtained evidence of the degree to which the participants themselves were consistent from one session to another in their use of concepts to describe other persons. Children were re-interviewed between one week and one month after the first session on the pretext of problems with the original recordings. Indices of test-retest-reliability were computed for each of the major coding dimensions. Separate correlation coefficients (eta) were obtained for younger and older children in respect of their descriptive concepts of liked and disliked peers. Reliability coefficients are as set out on p. 246. Secord and Peevers[15] conclude that their approach offers the possibility of an exciting line of

Box 10.7: Perception of Social Episodes

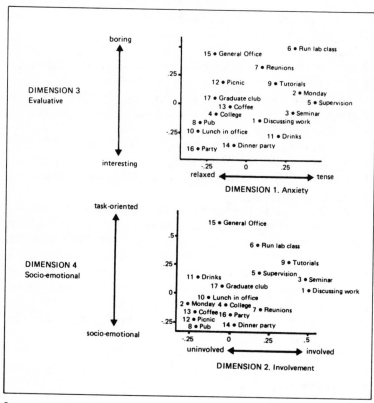

Source: adapted from Forgas.[13]

enquiry into the depth of insight that an individual has into the personality of his acquaintances. Their 'free commentary' method is a modification of the more structured interview, requiring the interviewer to probe for explanations of why a person behaves the way he does or why a person is the kind of person he is. Peevers and Secord found that older children in their sample readily volunteered this sort of information. Harré[16] observes that this approach could also be extended to elicit commentary upon children's friends and enemies and the ritual actions associated with the creation and maintenance of these categories.

Box 10.8: Person Concept Coding System

Dimension	Levels of descriptiveness
DESCRIPTIVENESS	1. *Undifferentiating* ... (person not differentiated from his environment) 2. *Simple differentiating* ... (person differentiated in simple global terms) 3. *Differentiating* ... (person differentiated in specific characteristics) 4. *Dispositional* ... (person differentiated in terms of traits)
PERSONAL INVOLVEMENT	*Degrees of involvement* 1. *Egocentric* ... (other person described in self-oriented terms) 2. *Mutual* ... (other person described in terms of his relationship to perceiver) 3. *Other oriented* ... (no personal involvement expressed by perceiver)
EVALUATIVE CONSISTENCY	*Amount of consistency* 1. *Consistent* ... (nothing favourable about 'disliked', nothing unfavourable about 'liked') 2. *Inconsistent* ... (some mixture of favourableness and unfavourableness)
DEPTH	*Levels of depth* *Level 1* (includes all undifferentiated and simple differentiated descriptions) *Level 2* (includes differentiated and some dispositional descriptions) *Level 3* (includes explanation-type differentiated and dispositional descriptions)

Source: adapted from Peevers and Secord.[14]

Dimension	Liked peers		Disliked peers	
	Younger subjects	Older subjects	Younger subjects	Older subjects
Descriptiveness	0.83	0.91	0.80	0.84
Personal involvement	0.76	0.80	0.84	0.77
Depth	0.65	0.71	0.65	0.75
Evaluative consistency	0.69	0.92	0.76	0.69

Account Gathering in Educational Research: Two Examples

The 'free commentary' method that Secord and Peevers recommend as a way of probing for explanations of people's behaviour lies at the very heart of the ethnographer's skills. In the two very different examples of ethnographic research that now follow, what is common to both is the attempt of the researchers to get below the surface data and to search for the deeper, hidden patterns that are only revealed when attention is directed to the *ways that group members interpret the flow of events in their lives.*

Heath's[17] study of misunderstandings existing between black children and their white teachers in classrooms in the south of the United States brought to light teachers' assumptions that pupils would respond to language routines and the uses of language in building knowledge and skills just as other children (including their own) did. Specifically, she sought to understand why these particular children did *not* respond just as others did. Her research involved eliciting explanations from both the children's parents and teachers. 'We don't talk to our children like you folks do,' the parents observed when questioned about their children's behaviour. Those children, it seemed to Heath, were not regarded as information givers or as appropriate conversational partners for adults. That is not to say that the children were excluded from language participation. They did, in fact, participate in a language that Heath describes as rich in styles, speakers and topics. Rather, it seemed to the researcher that the teachers' characteristic mode of questioning was 'to pull attributes of things out of context, particularly out of the context of books and name them — queens, elves, police, red apples'. The parents did *not* ask these kinds of questions of their children, and the children themselves had their

Box 10.9: 'Ain't nobody can talk about things being about theirselves'

The above comment by a nine-year-old boy was directed to his teacher when she persisted in interrogating him about the story he had just completed in his reading group.

TEACHER: What is the story about?
CHILDREN: (silence)
TEACHER: Uh ... Let's see ... Who is it the story talks about?
CHILDREN: (silence)
TEACHER: Who is the main character? ... Um ... What kind of story is it?
CHILD: Ain't nobody can talk about things being about theirselves.

The boy was saying There's no way anybody can talk (and ask) about things being about themselves.

Source: adapted from Spindler.[18]

own ways of deflecting such questions, as the example in Box 10.9 well illustrates.

Heath elicited both parents' and teachers' accounts of the children's behaviour and their apparent communication 'problems' (see Box 10.10). Her account of accounts arose out of periods of participation and observation in classrooms and in some of the teachers' homes. In particular, she focused upon the ways in which 'the children learned to use language to satisfy their needs, ask questions, transmit information, and convince those around them that they were competent communicators'. This involved her in a much wider and more intensive study of the total fabric of life in Trackton, the southern community in which the research was located.

> Over five years... I was able to collect data across a wide range of situations and to follow some children longitudinally as they acquired communicative competence in Trackton. Likewise, at various periods during these years, I observed Trackton adults in public service encounters and on their jobs... The context of language use, including setting, topic, and participants (both those directly involved in the talk and those who only listened) determined in large part how community members, teachers, public service personnel, and fellow workers judged the communicative competence of Trackton residents.

Box 10.10: Parents and Teachers: Divergent Viewpoints on Children's Communicative Competence

---

Parents

The teachers won't listen. My kid, he too scared to talk, 'cause nobody play by the rules he know. At home, I can't shut 'im up.

Miss Davis, she complain 'bout Ned not answerin' back. He say she asks dumb questions she already know 'bout.

Teachers

They don't seem to be able to answer even the simplest questions.

I would almost think some of them have a hearing problem; it is as though they don't hear me ask a question. I get blank stares to my questions. Yet when I am making statements or telling stories which interest them, they always seem to hear me.

The simplest questions are the ones they can't answer in the classroom; yet on the playground, they can explain a rule for a ballgame or describe a particular kind of bait with no problem. Therefore, I know they can't be as dumb as they seem in my class.

I sometimes feel that when I look at them and ask a question I'm staring at a wall I can't break through. There's something there; yet in spite of all the questions I ask, I'm never sure I've gotten through to what's inside that wall.

Source: adapted from Spindler.[18]

A second example of the use of accounts in educational research is given in Dobbert's[19] analysis of a school carnival in which careful and systematic examination of archival and written materials led to the discovery of information that was not envisioned when the study began; information, incidentally, that led to new insights about the relationships existing between three neighbourhoods supposedly working together for the success of the event.

What purported to be a co-operative venture between the three distinctly different social class neighbourhoods turned out to be a bureaucratically organised, middle-class dominated event monopolised by an influential self-recruiting clique of prominent male citizens. Some of Dobbert's insights are reported in Box 10.11.

Box 10.11: An Ethnographic Account of a School Carnival

During the first year of the study, it became apparent that my original perception of the event as a cooperative school endeavour was not completely substantiated by the data being collected. The particular procedures and questions asked in an event analysis uncovered a second, neighbourhood-based, aspect of the carnival of which I had not been aware. It also became evident that the two aspects of the school carnival were in some ways antithetical and existed as the result of the operations of the school Carnival-Coordinating Committee. I then turned my attention from the actual carnival to a study of the committee itself and how its actions in putting the carnival together resulted from the more local customs and beliefs of the neighbourhood that surrounded the school and from which all the committee members came ...

The result of the way the committee operated was the establishment of a bureaucratic structure in which the committee made all of the major decisions regarding the carnival. It also selected the next level of workers at the carnival, the chairpersons of individual events. The chairpersons were then responsible for finding helpers. Since the selection of chairpersons was similar to the selection of committee members — by personal contact — the committee determined to a large extent the composition of the group that actually worked at the carnival. So, although carnival attendance from all three neighbourhoods was high, an analysis of the working patterns revealed that there were very few chairpersons or helpers from any neighbourhood other than the one in which the committee members lived. In two years, with an average of 35 activities, all but two or three were chaired by people from the first neighbourhood. In fact, one activity run by people from the second neighbourhood was never even listed on the activity sheet, although it had been in existence for several years prior. Further analysis showed that there were sex-based distinctions as well. The Coordinating Committee was predominantly male; so were its recruited activity chairpersons.

Source: adapted from Dobbert.[19]

Problems in Gathering and Analysing Accounts

The importance of the meaning of events and actions to those who are involved is now generally recognised in social research. The implications of the ethogenic stance in terms of actual research techniques, however, remain problematic. Menzel[20] discusses a number of ambiguities and shortcomings in the ethogenic approach arising out of the mutiplicity of meanings that may be held for the same behaviour. Most behaviour, Menzel observes, can be assigned meanings and more than one of these may very well be valid simultaneously. It is fallacious therefore, Menzel argues, to insist upon determining *the* meaning of an act. Nor can it be said that the task of interpreting an act is done when one has identified one meaning of it, or the one meaning that the researcher is pleased to designate as the true one.

A second problem that Menzel raises is to do with actors' meanings as sources of bias. How central a place, he asks, ought to be given to actors' meanings in formulating explanations of events? Should the researcher exclusively and invariably be guided by these considerations? To do so would be to ignore a whole range of potential explanations which few researchers would wish to see excluded from consideration.

These are far-reaching, difficult issues though by no means intractable. What solutions does Menzel propose?

First we must specify 'to whom' when asking what acts and situations mean. Second, researchers must make choices and take responsibility in the assignment of meanings to acts; moreover, problem formulations must respect the meaning of the act to us, the researchers. And third, explanations should respect the meanings of acts to the actors themselves but need not invariably be centred around these meanings.

Menzel's plea is for the usefulness of an outside observer's account of a social episode alongside the explanations that participants themselves may give of that event. A similar argument is

Box 10.12: Justification of Objective Systematic Observation in Classroom Settings

> ... When Smith looks at Jones and says, 'Jones, why does the blue substance spread through the liquid?' (probably with a particular kind of voice inflection), and then silently looks at Jones (probably with a particular kind of facial expression), the observer can unambiguously categorize the event as 'Smith asks Jones a question seeking an explanation of diffusion in a liquid.' Now Smith might describe the event as 'giving Jones a chance to show he knows something', and Jones might describe the event as 'Smith trying to get at me'; but if either of them denied the validity of the observer's description, they would be simply wrong, because the observer would be describing at least part of what the behaviour which occurred means in English in Britain. No assumptions are made here about the effectiveness of classroom communication; but the assumption is made that ... communication is dependent on the system of conventional meanings available within the wider culture. More fundamentally, this interpretation implies that the systematic observer is concerned with an objective reality (or, if one prefers, a shared intersubjective reality) of classroom events. This is not to suggest that the subjective meanings of events to participants are not important, but only that these are not accessible to the observer and that *there is an objective reality to classroom activity which does not depend on these meanings* [our emphasis].

Source: McAleese and Hamilton.[21]

implicit in McIntyre and McLeod's[21] justification of objective, systematic observation in classroom settings. Their case is set out in Box 10.12.

Strengths of the Ethogenic Approach

The advantages of the ethogenic approach to the educational researcher lie in the distinctive insights that are made available to him through the analysis of accounts of social episodes. The benefits to be derived from the exploration of accounts are best seen by contrasting[22] the ethogenic approach with a more traditional educational technique such as the survey which we discussed in Chapter 4.

There is a good deal of truth in the assertion of the ethogenically-oriented researcher that approaches which employ survey techniques such as the questionnaire take for granted the very things that should be treated as problematic in an educational study. Too often, the phenomena that ought to be the focus of attention are taken as given, that is, they are treated as the starting point of the research rather than becoming the centre of the researcher's interest and effort to discover how the phenomena arose or came to be important in the first place. Numerous educational studies, for example, have identified the incidence and the duration of disciplinary infractions in school; only very recently, however, has the *meaning* of classroom disorder, as opposed to its frequency and type, been subjected to intensive investigation.[23] Unlike the survey, which is a cross-sectional technique that takes its data at a single point in time, the ethogenic study employs an ongoing observational approach that focuses upon *processes* rather than *products.* Thus it is the process of becoming deviant in school which would capture the attention of the ethogenic researcher rather than the frequency and type of misbehaviour among k types of ability in children located in n kinds of school.

References

1. Harré, R., 'The ethogenic approach: theory and practice' in L. Berkowitz (ed.), *Advances in Experimental Social Psychology*, vol. 10 (Academic Press, New York, 1977).

2. Harré, R., 'Some remarks on "rule" as a scientific concept', in T. Mischel (ed.), *On Understanding Persons* (Basil Blackwell, Oxford, 1974).
3. Harré, R., 'Accounts, actions and meanings — the practice of participatory psychology', in M. Brenner, P. Marsh and M. Brenner (eds), *The Social Context of Method* (Croom Helm, London, 1978).
4. Brown, J. and Sime, J.D. 'Accounts as general methodology', paper presented to the British Psychological Society Conference (University of Exeter, 1977).
5. Brown, J. and Sime, J.D. 'A methodology of accounts', in M. Brenner (ed.). *Social Method and Social Life* (Academic Press, London, 1981).
6. Kitwood, T.M., 'Values in adolescent life: towards a critical description', unpublished PhD dissertation, School of Research in Education (University of Bradford, 1977).
7. Denscombe, M., 'The social organization of teaching: a study of teaching as a practical activity in two London comprehensive schools', unpublished PhD dissertation (University of Leicester, 1977).
8. Bliss, J., Monk, M. and Ogborn, J. *Qualitative Data Analysis for Educational Research* (Croom Helm, London, 1983).
9. Forgas, J.P., 'The perception of social episodes: categoric and dimensional representations in two different social milieux', *J. Pers. & Soc. Psycho.*, 34, 2(1976) 199–209.
10. Magnusson, D., 'An analysis of situational dimensions', *Perceptual and Motor Skills*, 32 (1971) 851–67.
11. Ekehammar, B. and Magnusson, D., 'A method to study stressful situations', *J. Pers. & Soc. Psychol.*, 27, 2(1973) 176–9.
12. McQuitty, L.L., 'Elementary linkage analysis for isolating orthogonal and oblique types and relevancies', *Educ. & Psychol. Meas.*, 17(1957) 207–29.
13. Forgas, J.P., 'Social episodes and social structure in an academic setting: the social environment of an intact group', *J. Exp. Soc. Psychol.*, 14 (1978) 434–48.
     For a fuller account of Forgas' work on the study of social episodes see;
     Forgas, J.P., *Social Episodes: The Study of Interaction Routines* (Academic Press, London, 1981).
14. Peevers, B.H. and Secord, P.F., 'Developmental changes in attribution of descriptive concepts to persons', *J. Pers. & Soc. Psychol.*, 27, 1(1973) 120–8.
15. Secord, P.F. and Peevers, B.H., 'The development and attribution of person concepts', in T. Mischel (ed.), *On Understanding Persons* (Basil Blackwell, Oxford, 1974).
16. Harré, R., 'Friendship as an accomplishment', in S. Duck (ed.), *Theory and Practice in Interpersonal Attraction* (Academic Press, London, 1977).
17. Heath, S.B., 'Questioning at home and at school: a comparative study', in G. Spindler (ed.), *Doing the Ethnography of Schooling* (Holt, Rinehart and Winston, New York, 1982). Two interesting ethnographic studies of children in classrooms and playgrounds appear in the Routledge and Kegan Paul series, 'Social Worlds of Childhood': Davies, B., *Life in the Classroom and Playground: The Accounts of Primary School Children* (Routledge and Kegan Paul, London, 1982), and: Sluckin, A., *Growing up in the Playground: The Social Development of Children* (Routledge and Kegan Paul, London, 1981).
18. Spindler, G. (ed.), *Doing the Ethnography of Schooling* (Holt, Rinehart and Winston, New York, 1982).
19. Dobbert, M.L., *Ethnographic Research: Theory and Application for Modern Schools and Societies* (Praeger, New York, 1982).
20. Menzel, H., 'Meaning — who needs it?', in M. Brenner, P. Marsh and M. Brenner (eds), *The Social Context of Method* (Croom Helm, London, 1978).

For a recent discussion of the problem see: Gilbert G.N., 'Accounts and those accounts called actions', in G.N. Gilbert and P. Abell, *Accounts and Action* (Gower, Aldershot, 1983).

21. McIntyre, D. and MacLeod, G., 'The characteristics and uses of systematic classroom observation', in R. McAleese and D. Hamilton (eds), *Understanding Classroom Life* (NFER, Windsor, 1978) 102–31.
22. The discussion at this point draws on that in K.D. Bailey, *Methods of Social Research* (Collier-Macmillan, London, 1978) 261.
23. See, for example: Hargreaves, D.H., Hester, S.K. and Mellor, F.J., *Deviance in Classrooms* (Routledge and Kegan Paul, London, 1975); Marsh, P., Rosser, E. and Harré, R., *The Rules of Disorder* (Routledge and Kegan Paul, London, 1978).

11 TRIANGULATION

Introduction

Triangulation may be defined as the use of two or more methods of data collection in the study of some aspect of human behaviour. It is a technique of research to which many subscribe in principle, but which only a minority use in practice. The use of multiple methods, or the multimethod approach as it is sometimes called, contrasts with the ubiquitous but generally more vulnerable single-method approach that characterises so much of research in the social sciences. In its original and literal sense, triangulation is a technique of physical measurement: maritime navigators, military strategists and surveyors, for example, use (or used to use) several locational markers in their endeavours to pinpoint a single spot or objective. By analogy, triangular techniques in the social sciences attempt to map out, or explain more fully, the richness and complexity of human behaviour by studying it from more than one standpoint and, in so doing, by making use of both quantitative and qualitative data.

The advantages of the multimethod approach in social research are manifold and we examine two of them. First, whereas the single observation in fields such as medicine, chemistry and physics normally yields sufficient and unambiguous information on selected phenomena, it provides only a limited view of the complexity of human behaviour and of situations in which human beings interact. It has been observed that as research methods act as filters through which the environment is selectively experienced, they are never atheoretical or neutral in representing the world of experience.[1] Exclusive reliance on one method, therefore, may bias or distort the researcher's picture of the particular slice of reality he is investigating. He needs to be confident that the data generated are not simply artefacts of one specific method of collection.[2] And this confidence can only be achieved as far as normative research is concerned when different methods of data collection yield substantially the same results. (Where triangulation is used in interpretive research to investigate different actors' viewpoints, the same method, e.g. accounts, will naturally produce different sets of data.) Further, the more the methods contrast with each other, the greater the researcher's confidence. If, for example, the outcomes of a questionnaire survey correspond to those of an observational study of the same phenomena, the more the researcher will be confident about the findings. Or, more extreme, where the results of a rigorous experimental investigation are replicated in, say, a role-playing exercise, the researcher will experience even greater assurance. If findings are artefacts of method, then the use of contrasting methods considerably reduces the chances that any consistent findings are attributable to similarities of method.[2]

We come now to a second advantage: some theorists have been sharply critical of the limited use to which existing methods of enquiry in the social sciences have been put. One writer[1], for example, comments, 'Much research has employed particular methods or techniques out of methodological parochialism or ethnocentrism. Methodologists often push particular pet methods either because those are the only ones they have familiarity with, or because they believe their method is superior to all others.' The use of triangular techniques, it is argued, will help to overcome the problem of 'method-boundedness', as it has been termed. One of the earliest scientists to predict such a condition was Boring[3], who wrote:

> as long as a new construct has only the single operational defini-
> tion that it received at birth, it is just a construct. When it gets
> two alternative operational definitions, it is beginning to be
> validated. When the defining operations, because of proven
> correlations, are many, then it becomes reified.

The following typify the kinds of current problems that critics point to:[4] attitude scales are often selected for their convenience and accessibility rather than for their psychological criteria; many studies are culture-bound, that is, they are limited to one country; the vast majority are also time-bound, that is, they are limited to one point in time and do not take into consideration the fact of social change; sociological studies, which by definition imply a macro level of analysis, make excessive use of individuals; and rarely are studies replicated. Criticisms of this sort can be met by taking a more extended view of triangulation which we will consider shortly.

The principle of triangulation is illustrated at its most simple in

Box 11.1: A Teacher's Attitude to His Role

The scale below measures the extent to which a teacher interprets his role in either 'educational' or 'academic' terms. In using different 'locational markers', it gives a more representative picture of the respondent's orientation to his role and in so doing illustrates the principle of triangulation in simple form.

1. A teacher should teach informally most of the time.
2. A teacher should be emotionally involved with his pupils.
3. A teacher should use many and varied materials.
4. He should regard scholarly attitudes to be of primary importance for his pupils.
5. He should develop most of the work done in class from the children's own interests.
6. A teacher should get to know children as individuals.
7. A teacher should use corporal punishment.
8. A teacher should look out for children with serious personal problems.
9. A teacher should maintain discipline at all times.
10. A teacher should get his chief satisfaction from interest in his subject or from administrative work in the school, rather than from classroom teaching.

Source: constructed by David Marsland.

a typical attitude scale. If you examine the example in Box 11.1, you will find ten items making up an attitude scale measuring a teacher's view of his role. One item, or 'locational marker', by itself will tell us very little about a teacher's attitude in this respect. But ten such related items, or 'locational markers', will give a much fuller picture. Imagine now a detailed study of a class of pupils in a secondary school which involves teachers' ratings of pupils, school records, psychometric data, sociometric data, case studies, questionnaires and observation. Add to this the findings of investigations of similar classes in ten other secondary schools and we then have an illustration of the principle of triangulation at a more complex level.

In its use of multiple methods, triangulation may utilise either normative or interpretive techniques; or it may draw on methods from both these approaches and use them in combination.

Types of Triangulation and Their Characteristics

We have just seen how triangulation is characterised by a multi-method approach to a problem in contrast to a single-method approach. Denzin[4] has, however, extended this view of triangulation to take in several other types as well as the multimethod kind which he terms 'methodological triangulation'. These he designates *time triangulation, space triangulation, combined levels of triangulation, theoretical triangulation, investigator triangulation* and — as already noted — *methodological triangulation.* The use of these several types of triangulation goes some way to meet the kinds of methodological criticisms we have already referred to. We now briefly identify the characteristics of each type and refer you to Box 11.2 for a summary of their purpose.

The vast majority of studies in the social sciences are conducted at one point only in time, thereby ignoring the effects of social change and process. *Time triangulation* goes some way to rectifying these omissions by making use of cross-sectional and longitudinal approaches. Cross-sectional studies collect data concerned with time-related processes from different groups at one point in time; longitudinal studies collect data from the same group at different points in the time sequence. The use of panel studies and trend studies may also be mentioned in this connection. The former compare the *same* measurements for the *same* individuals in a sample at several *different* points in time; and the latter examine selected processes continually over time. The weaknesses

Box 11.2: The Principal Types of Triangulation Used in Research

1.	*Time triangulation*: this type attempts to take into consideration the factors of change and process by utilising cross-sectional and longitudinal designs.
2.	*Space triangulation*: this type attempts to overcome the parochialism of studies conducted in the same country or within the same subculture by making use of cross-cultural techniques.
3.	*Combined levels of triangulation*: this type uses more than one level of analysis from the three principal levels used in the social sciences, namely, the individual level, the interactive level (groups), and the level of collectivities (organisational, cultural or societal).
4.	*Theoretical triangulation*: this type draws upon alternative or competing theories in preference to utilising one viewpoint only.
5.	*Investigator triangulation*: this type engages more than one observer.
6.	*Methodological triangulation*: this type uses either (a) the same method on different occasions, or (b) different methods on the same object of study.

Source: based on Denzin's[4] typology.

of each of these methods can be strengthened by using a combined approach to a given problem (see p. 70).

Space triangulation attempts to overcome the limitations of studies conducted within one culture or subculture. As one writer[1] says, 'Not only are the behavioural sciences culture-bound, they are sub-culture-bound. Yet many such scholarly works are written as if basic principles have been discovered which would hold true as tendencies in any society, anywhere, anytime.' Cross-cultural studies may involve the testing of theories among different people, as in recent cross-cultural studies in Piagetian and Freudian psychology; or they may measure differences between populations by using several different measuring instruments. Levine[5] describes how he used this strategy of convergent validation in his comparative studies:

> I have studied differences of achievement motivation among three Nigerian ethnic groups by the analysis of dream reports, written expressions of values, and public opinion survey data. The convergence of findings from the diverse set of data (and samples) strengthens my conviction ... that the differences among the groups are not artifacts produced by measuring instruments.

Social scientists are concerned in their research with the individual, the group and society. These reflect the *three levels of analysis* adopted by researchers in their work. Those who are critical of much present-day research argue that some of it uses the wrong level of analysis — individual when it should be societal, for instance — or limits itself to one level only when a more meaningful picture would emerge by using more than one level. Smith[1] extends this analysis and identifies seven possible levels: the aggregative or individual level and six levels that are more global in that 'they characterize the collective as a whole, and do not derive from an accumulation of individual characteristics'.

The six include: (1) group analysis (the interaction patterns of individuals and groups); (2) organisational units of analysis (units which have qualities not possessed by the individuals making them up); (3) institutional analysis (relationships within and across the legal, political, economic and familial institutions of society; (4) ecological analysis (concerned with spatial explanation); (5) cultural analysis (concerned with the norms, values, practices, traditions and ideologies of a culture); and (6) societal analysis (concerned with gross factors such as urbanisation, industrialisation, education, wealth, etc.).

Where possible, studies combining *several* levels of analysis are to be preferred.

Researchers are sometimes taken to task for their rigid adherence to one particular theory or theoretical orientation to the exclusion of competing theories. Thus, advocates of Piaget's developmental theory of cognition rarely take into consideration Freud's psychoanalytic theory of development in their work; and Gestaltists work without reference to S–R theorists. Few published works, as Smith [1] points out, even go as far as to discuss alternative theories after a study in the light of methods used, much less consider alternatives prior to the research. As he recommends, 'The investigator should be more active in designing his research so that competing theories can be tested. Research which tests competing theories will normally call for a wider range of research techniques than has historically been the case; this virtually assures more confidence in the data analysis since it is more oriented towards the testing of rival hypotheses.'

Investigator triangulation refers to the use of more than one observer (or participant) in a research setting. Observers and participants working on their own each have their own observational styles and this is reflected in the resulting data. The careful use of two or more observers or participants independently, therefore, can lead to more valid and reliable data. Smith comments:

> Perhaps the greatest use of investigator triangulation centres around validity rather than reliability checks. More to the point, investigators with differing perspectives or paradigmatic biases may be used to check out the extent of divergence in the data each collects. Under such conditions if data divergence is minimal then one may feel more confident in the data's validity. On the other hand, if their data is significantly different, then one has an idea as to possible sources of biased measurement which should be futher investigated.

We have already considered methodological triangulation in our introduction. Denzin identifies two categories in his typology: *within methods* triangulation and *between methods* triangulation. Triangulation *within methods* concerns the *replication* of a study as a check on reliability and theory confirmation.[1] Triangulation *between methods*, as we have seen, involves the use of more than one method in the pursuit of a given objective. As a check on validity, the *between methods* approach embraces the notion of convergence between independent measures of the same objective as has been defined by Campbell and Fiske.[6]

Occasions When Triangulation is Particularly Appropriate

Having outlined the principle of triangulation and described the types and their characteristics, we now consider the occasions when the technique is particularly appropriate and in so doing will be mainly concerned with the field of education. So complex and involved is the teaching-learning process in the context of the school that the single-method approach yields only limited and sometimes misleading data. Yet, ironically, this is the method that figures most in educational research. It is only comparatively recently that the utility of the multiple-method approach has come to be appreciated. Of the six categories of triangulation in Denzin's typology, something like four have been used in education. These are: time triangulation with its longitudinal and cross-sectional studies; space triangulation as on the occasions when a number of schools in an area or across the country are investigated in some way [7]; investigator triangulation as when a team of inspectors visits and reports on a school or sample of schools; [8] and methodological triangulation. Of these four, methodological triangulation is the one used most frequently and the one that possibly has the most to offer. All four approaches, however, present practical and financial obstacles to researchers and sponsors.

The following are instances of where the multiple-method approach in educational settings is appropriate:

1. Triangular techniques are suitable when a more holistic view of *educational outcomes* is sought. Isaac and Michael,[9] for example, quote a study by Cronbach which investigated the effects of praise and blame on the outcomes of reading instruction. No significant differences were found among the various groups on the criterion of *gain in reading*. It was suggested that had a second criterion been used, such as *attitudes towards reading*, a significant treatment difference might have been found. The authors

Box 11.3: A Multimethod Approach to the Study of Two
Top-junior Classes: one taught formally; the other, informally

Objective: To investigate the practices, interactions, climates and outcomes of
a formal and informal classroom in two junior schools over the period of
one term.

Methods:
1. Measures of achievement in reading, written language and maths.
2. Analysis and classification of children's written and practical work.
3. Classroom observation.
4. Examination of records.
5. Tests of attitudes of children to school and school work.
6. Tests of attitudes of teachers to respective teaching methods.
7. Interviews with samples of children.
8. Interviews with teachers.

comment, 'Most research of this kind looks at an achievement or
skill outcome rather than the development of attitudes. The failure
of people to choose to read following their formal education, or to
choose mathematics in their higher education, given the skill
development to do both, strongly suggests that a counter-current
of *negative attitudes* to avoid these experiences lies hidden under-
neath.'

2. Triangulation has special relevance where a *complex phenomenon* requires elucidation. Imagine a comparative study of a
formal and an informal classroom. Because of the contrasting
philosophies, objectives and practices in the two classes, a single-
method approach — say a measure of achievement in basic skills —
would provide data of very limited value in that it would in no way
reflect the more subtle, intangible features and the non-academic
factors distinguishing the two classrooms. The adoption of the
multimethod approach would give a very different picture. Box
11.3 gives some suggested methods for tackling this kind of problem. The combination of academic criteria (achievement tests,
record cards, assessment of class work) and non-academic factors
(attitudes of children and teachers, relationships, interview data
and observation by a researcher) will generate a fuller and more
realistic view of the respective classes and thus enable the investigators to talk about them on a comparative basis.

3. Triangulation is also appropriate when *different methods of
teaching* are to be evaluated. Isaac and Michael also quote a study

by Brownell comparing four methods of teaching subtraction. He found only small differences both on a *skill criterion* and on a *retention criterion* but clearly superior results favouring one method over all others when he measured transfer to a new process. Had he limited himself to a skill or retention criterion only, this valuable transfer criterion would have remained undisclosed.

4. Multiple methods are suitable where a *controversial aspect of education* needs to be evaluated more fully. The issue of comprehensive schools, for example, has been hotly debated since their inception; yet even at this point there has been little serious research investigating these institutions as totalities. It is not sufficient to judge these schools solely on the grounds of academic achievement with 'league tables' based on O- and A-level results, important as these are. A much more rounded portrayal of these institutions is required and here is a clear case for the advocacy of multiple methods. These could measure and investigate factors such as academic achievement, teaching methods, practical skills, cultural interests, social skills, interpersonal relationships, community spirit and so on. Validity could then be greatly increased by researching a large sample of schools (space triangulation) for, say, once a year over a period of five years (time triangulation).

5. Triangulation is useful when an established approach yields a limited and frequently distorted picture. We are reminded here of the traditional dichotomies — normative v. interpretive, nomothetic v. idiographic, statistical v. clinical. The first of each pairing is associated with groups and more objective scientific data; the second, with individuals and subjective data. Again, by using, or drawing from, each of these usually mutually exclusive categories, contrasting perspectives are disclosed.

6. And finally, triangulation can be a useful technique where a researcher is engaged in *case study*, a particular example of the 'complex phenomena' we mentioned under point 2 above. In this connection, Adelman *et al.*[10] write:

> The advantages of a paricular technique for collecting witnesses' accounts of an event — *triangulation* — should be stressed. This is at the heart of the intention of the case study worker to respond to the multiplicity of perspectives present in a social situation. All accounts are considered in part to be expressive of the social position of each informant. Case study

needs to represent, and represent fairly, these differing and sometimes conflicting viewpoints.

Some Issues and Problems

The chief problem confronting the researcher using triangulation is that of *validity*. This is particularly the case where researchers use only qualitative techniques as, for example, in ethnographic research to collect data on a particular or single event. McCormick and James[11] write,

> there is no absolute guarantee that a number of data sources that purport to provide evidence concerning the same construct in fact do so ... In view of the apparently subjective nature of much qualitative interpretation, validation is achieved when others, particularly the subjects of the research, recognise its authenticity. One way of doing this is for the researcher to write out his/her analysis for the subjects of the research in terms that they will understand, and then record their reactions to it. This is known as *respondent validation.*

Having given primacy to his/her consideration of validity, the researcher is then confronted with three broad questions when contemplating a multimethod approach to a problem: Which methods are to be selected? How are they to be combined? And how are the data to be used?

As far as the first question is concerned — which methods are to be selected — we take it as axiomatic that any one method can be efficient, less efficient or inefficient depending on the kind of information desired and the context of the research. Where a researcher seeks information from which his inferences can be generalised to wider populations, methods yielding statistical data will be most efficient. Where he looks for information representing a personal or phenomenological perspective, or process rather than product, accounts or interviews will meet his need more successfully. If he wants to integrate objective and subjective perspectives, he will use contrasting methods. The first task, therefore, will be to decide *what kinds* of information the researcher wants and, further, what he is to do with it. Perhaps he might want to raise educational standards, introduce correctives, make modifications,

Box 11.4: Kinds of Information Sought and Methods for Obtaining Them

Kinds of information	Methods used	1 Achievement tests	2 Personality tests	3 Attitude tests	4 Sociometric tests	5 Participant observation	6 Interviewing	7 Accounts	8 Teachers' assessments
1 Academic skills		xx					x		xx
2 Personality characteristics			xx			x	x		xx
3 Social skills				x	xx	xx	x		xx
4 Social relationships				x		xx	x		xx
5 Individual pupil viewpoint				xx			x	xx	
6 Classroom climate						xx			x

xx = most efficient means,
x = supportive means.

or merely acquire a fuller understanding of some situation. The next stage is to decide the most appropriate methods (or sources) for providing this information. To make all this more comprehensible, we have given a hypothetical example in Box 11.4. Imagine a researcher wanting to compare a formal and an informal classroom in two junior schools with particular reference to academic and non-academic factors, children's personality characteristics, social behaviour and classroom climates. The left-hand vertical column itemises the *kinds* of information he wants from each classroom — knowledge of the class's academic skills, children's personality characteristics and so on. The top horizontal row identifies the total number of methods (or sources) in respect of the information sought. Broadly speaking, the first four methods itemised yield quantifiable data (1–4); and the remaining four, non-quantifiable data (5–8). The system of double and single crosses illustrates the methods most efficient and the methods most supportive of these respectively so that, for example, the perspective of the individual pupil will best be expressed through an attitude questionnaire, a taped account of his view of classroom life, and an interview. So to return to our original question, the researcher will combine those methods (or sources) that will, in complementing each other, build up as full a picture of the areas he is investigating as time and facilities permit. You will notice that the combined methods approach may break down the traditional barriers between the normative and the interpretive approaches, the idiographic and the nomothetic, and the statistical and clinical.

No simple directive can be given for the question, how are the methods to be combined, for the answer will depend to a great extent on the objectives of the study, the particular situation, and the relative *weightings* which the researcher considers desirable to assign to the methods providing him with data. To take the issue of weightings further, in some schools, for example, teachers' assessments of pupil achievement (Box 11.4, column 8) will serve merely as glosses on formal examinations of academic achievement. In others, by contrast, teachers' opinions may play a much more decisive part in such assessments. These are the kinds of factors affecting a researcher's weightings. The crucial factor when it comes to integrating or contrasting the data and drawing inferences from them is the researcher's own judgement.

The third question, how are the data to be used, will depend on the researcher's original objectives in undertaking the study, his choice of methods and the kinds of data he accumulates. He will attempt, for instance, to impose some kind of meaning on *normative* or *quantifiable* data, possibly in line with a favoured theory or hypothesis. With *interpretive* or *qualitative* data, however, he will endeavour to draw meanings or explanations from the data themselves or, where appropriate, negotiate meanings with the subjects who are their source. Two kinds of problems face him here: (1) those stemming from inconsistencies between quantified measures because of weaknesses in available measuring instruments; and (2) differences between quantifiable and qualitative data, or between different sets of qualitative data. The first calls for more refined and valid instrumentation; the second, an imaginative leap. The lurking danger in the case of the second problem is that of presenting discrepant sets of data in the form of a collage. Naturally enough, it is not to be expected that complete consensus among data can or should be achieved. Indeed, the very burden of the interpretive approach is that different actors in a situation will have different meanings and that each meaning is equally valid. What is required, however, is that some attempt be made to relate incongruent sets of data in some way or other. Accounting for differences would be one way; using them as a basis for further hypotheses, another.

Procedures

We now outline a possible sequence of procedures for implementing a multimethod approach to a chosen problem. The first stage is to select an area of interest and then to formulate a specific *research problem* or a *set of research objectives* within this general framework so as to reduce the scope of the project to manageable proportions. The second stage will be concerned with the more practical aspects of the research — choosing a school or setting, administrative or organisational factors, financial requirements and procedural problems. The third stage will involve decisions concerning the extent and range of information required so as to meet the research objectives or to solve the problems stated. The aim here will be to provide a balanced framework within which to operate. The fourth stage will be concerned with the choice of methods or sources necessary to provide the information desired. This will involve listing the possibilities and setting them against the kinds of information required so as to get a total picture of which ones will be efficient, which supportive and which unsuitable. It is at this point that the researcher will need to decide the extent to which he will seek quantifiable and/or non-quantifiable data, or use individual and/or group responses, for example. This stage will also be a suitable point in the sequence of procedures to consider the respective weightings that are to be given to the chosen methods. The fifth stage will involve implementing the research, and this will include collecting and analysing the data. The sixth and final stage will be the point where the data are interpreted and inferences drawn.

Examples of the Use of Triangular Techniques in Educational Research

In conclusion, we refer to two instances of the use of triangulation in educational research. The first is a literal application of the technique at its simplest; and the second, an excellent example of the multiple method approach.

In the first example, triangulation was used as part of the Ford Teaching Project, one of the purposes of which was to make explicit from the teachers' and pupils' viewpoints the problems inherent in attempting enquiry/discovery methods of learning. The method was applied to episodes of classroom interaction between pupils and teachers. The procedure was to collect and analyse viewpoints on the episodes from three participants — the teachers, the pupils and the participant observer. As Walker and MacDonald[12] have explained in this connection:

> The process of gathering accounts from three distinct standpoints has an epistemological justification. Each point of the triangle stands in a unique epistemological position with respect to access to relevant data about a teaching situation. The teacher is in the best position to gain access via introspection to his own intentions and aims in the situation. The students are in the best position to explain how the teacher's actions influence the way they respond to the situation. The participant-observer is in the best position to collect data about the observable features of the interaction between teachers and pupils. By comparing his own account with accounts from the other two

Box 11.5: Extract from the Researcher's Interview with Pupils

Pupil	But he wouldn't ask you what you think your conclusions were, he'll put his own conclusion up on the board, and you have to write it. He says do you agree, not always but he don't want to rub it off so you just say yes to keep him quiet.
Observer	You say yes to keep him quiet?
Pupil	Keep him happy ...
Observer	There was a time when he said he was making a guess and he asked you if you agreed whether it was a reasonable guess. I don't know if you remember that?
Pupils	Yes.
Observer	And one person said yes and everybody else kept quiet. Now what I want to know is whether the person who said yes really did agree with him or just said yes because they thought he wanted to them to say yes, and why everybody else kept quiet?
Pupil	Well he would have liked us to say yes, really, 'cause I mean you could see it.
Pupil	If you'd said no you waste time arguing wouldn't you.
Pupil	Yeh, if you ever say no he'll stand there and just keep on and on.
Pupil	He'll keep on till you come to his way of thinking.
Pupil	So it's best to say yes to start with.
Observer	So even if you did disagree when he said 'Do you all agree?' you wouldn't.
Pupil	If you said no he'd keep on to you until you said yes.
Pupil	If you said no he's going to say why not.
Pupil	And if you argued with him he'd come round to the same point where you left off.
Pupil	Back to his way of thinking.

Source: quoted, along with other extracts, in Walker and MacDonald.[12]

standpoints a person at one point of the triangle has an opportunity to test and perhaps revise it on the basis of more sufficient data.

The procedure consisted of three stages: (1) recording the original activity or episode; (2) playing back the recordings to the teachers and pupils in turn and eliciting their comments and explanations of what took place. To these interviews were added the observer's interpretation for further comment and discussion; and (3) eliciting teachers' views on playbacks of the pupils' accounts. The researchers themselves[13] say:

As the project attempted to encourage teachers to monitor their own actions, the choice of triangulation seemed appropriate. The teachers or pupils may intend an action (including talk) to have a particular meaning, but how the recipient interprets the action is another matter. In spite of miscommunication, the classroom inhabitants have a remarkable ability to 'remedy' or 'fill-in' the action so that it makes sense to them. Through recording lessons, selecting portions and playing them back to pupils with questions like 'what did you understand the teacher to mean?', and playing these back to the teacher, a simple but powerful technique was put into operation.

One of the outcomes of the study was that the triangulation data convinced the teacher that in spite of his professed aspirations to implement enquiry/discovery methods his teaching was in fact formal/structured/directed and that behaviours like 'Do you all agree with that?' deliberately fostered his pupils' dependence on his authority position.[12] As Walker explains, 'Having clarified and tested the theory implicit in his practice in this way he later dramatically switched to an unstructured/open-ended approach which he hoped would protect the self-directed learning of his pupils. His conscious switch to a new teaching approach reflected the development of a new theory, the applicability of which would require further self-monitoring.' Box 11.5 contains a short extract from a researcher's interview with pupils. For further extracts, we refer you to the reference cited.

It can be seen from this brief review that triangulation enables the teacher to make some assessment of his ability to self-monitor his teaching situation and was a significant way of constructing classroom realities.

Our second example is drawn from the research project into mixed ability teaching conducted by a research team from the National Foundation of Educational Research.[14]

It is the second phase of the project that is utilising the multi-method approach. Being a detailed study of some of the major issues in mixed ability teaching,[14] it is concerned with: (1) organisation, preparation and in-service training for mixed ability teaching; (2) classroom methods and organisation; (3) the more able pupil — an examination of methods adopted to help him achieve in accordance with his capabilities; (4) the less able pupil — a study of strategies used to cater for his needs in a mixed ability class; (5) the implications of mixed ability teaching for methods of assessment; and (6) subject differences — the objectives and approaches employed by teachers in two subject areas (English and modern languages) where teachers' attitudes are known to differ, are being examined with a view to identifying factors associated with the ease or difficulty with which a subject can effectively be taught to mixed ability classes.

While a triangular approach is being used towards the project as a whole, units of investigation within the main project are also being subjected to a multimethod approach. For instance, one first-year class has been selected for detailed study in each school and three kinds of evidence are being sought: these arise from (1) the written material produced in class, (2) the observation of classes during group work, and (3) discussions with the teachers of the selected classes. For further details of this undertaking and of the instruments and schedules used, we refer you to the Foundation's report on the project.[14]

References

1. Smith, H.W., *Strategies of Social Research: The Methodological Imagination* (Prentice-Hall, London, 1975).
2. Lin, Nan, *Foundations of Social Research* (McGraw-Hill, New York, 1976).
3. Boring, E.G., 'The role of theory in experimental psychology', *Amer. J. Psychol.*, 66 (1953) 169–84.
4. Denzin, N.K., *The Research Act in Sociology: A Theoretical Introduction to Sociological Method* (The Butterworth Group, London, 1970).
5. Levine, R.A., 'Towards a psychology of populations: the cross-cultural study of personality', *Human Development* 3 (1966) 30–46.
6. Campbell, D.T., and Fiske, D., 'Convergent and discriminant validation by the multi-trait multimethod matrix', *Psychol. Bull.*, 56 (1959) 81–105.
7. For example: Bennett, N., *Teaching Styles and Pupil Progress* (Open Books, London, 1975).
8. For example: Department of Education and Science, *Primary Education in England* (HMSO, London, 1978).
9. Isaac, S. and Michael, W.B., *Handbook in Research and Evaluation* (R.R. Knapp, California, 1971).
10. Adelman, C., Jenkins, D. and Kemmis, S., 'Rethinking case study: Notes from the Second Cambridge Conference', in H. Simons, (ed.), *Towards a Science of the Singular* (Centre for Applied Research in Education, University of East Anglia, 1980).
11. McCormick, R. and James, M., *Curriculum Evaluation in Schools* (Croom Helm, Beckenham, 1983).
12. Walker, R. and MacDonald, B., *Curriculum Innovation at School Level*, (E 203, Units 27 and 28) (The Open University Press, Bletchley, 1976).
13. Adelman, C. and Walker, R. 'Developing pictures for other frames: action research and case study', in G. Chanan and S. Delamont (eds), *Frontiers of Classroom Research* (NFER, Windsor, 1975).
14. Reid, M., Clunies-Ross, L., Goacher, B. and Vile, C., *Mixed Ability Teaching: Problems and Possibilities* (NFER-Nelson, Windsor, 1981).

12 ROLE-PLAYING

Introduction

Much current discussion of role-playing occurs within the context of a protracted and continuing debate over the use of deception in experimental social psychology. Inevitably therefore, the following account of role-playing as a research tool involves some detailed comment on the 'deception' versus 'honesty' controversy. But role-playing has a much longer history of use in the social sciences than as a substitute for deceit. It has been employed for decades in assessing personality, in business training and in psychotherapy.[1] In this latter connection, role-playing was introduced to the United States as a therapeutic procedure by Moreno in the 1930s. His group therapy sessions were called 'psychodrama', and in various forms they spread to the group dynamics movement which was developing in America in the 1950s. Current interest in encounter sessions and sensitivity training can be traced back to the impact of the originator of studies in role-taking and role-enactment, J.L. Moreno.

The focus of the present chapter is on the use of role-playing as a technique of educational research. Role-playing is defined as participation in simulated social situations that are intended to throw light upon the role/rule contexts governing 'real' life social episodes. The present discussion aims to extend some of the ideas set out in Chapter 10 which dealt with account gathering and analysis. We begin by itemising a number of role-playing methods that have been reported in the literature.

Various role-play methods have been identified by Hamilton[2] and differentiated in terms of a *passive-active* distinction. Thus, an individual may role-play merely by reading a description of a social episode and filling in a questionnaire about it; on the other hand, a person may role-play by being required to improvise a characterisation and perform it in front of an audience. This *passive-active* continuum, Hamilton notes, glosses over three important analytical distinctions.

First, the individual may be asked simply to imagine a situation or actually to perform it. Hamilton terms this an *imaginary-*

Box 12.1: Dimensions of Role-play Methods

FORM		CONTENT
Set:	imaginary v. performed	*Person:* self v. another
Action:	scripted v. improvised	*Role:* subject role v. another role
Dependent variables:	verbal v. behavioural	*Context:* scenario other actors audience

Source: adapted from Hamilton.[2]

performed situation. Second, in connection with performed role-play, he distinguishes between structured and unstructured activities, the difference depending upon whether the individual is restricted by the experimenter to present forms or lines. This Hamilton calls a *scripted-improvised* distinction. And third, the participant's activities may be verbal responses, usually of the paper and pencil variety, or behavioural, involving something much more akin to acting. This distinction is termed *verbal-behavioural*. Turning next to the content of role-play, Hamilton distinguishes between relatively involving or uninvolving contents, that is, where a subject is required to act or to imagine *himself* in a situation or, alternatively, to react as he believes *another* person would in those circumstances, the basic issue here being what *person* the subject is supposed to portray. Furthermore, in connection with the role in which the person is placed, Hamilton differentiates between studies that assign the individual to the role of laboratory subject and those that place him in any other role. Finally, the content of the role-play is seen to include the *context* of the acted or the imagined performance, that is, the elaborateness of the scenario, the involvement of other actors, and the presence or absence of an audience. The various dimensions of role-play methods identified by Hamilton are set out in Box 12.1.

To illustrate the extremes of the range in the role-playing methods identified in Box 12.1 we have selected two studies, the first of which is *passive, imaginary* and *verbal,* typical of the way in which role-playing is often introduced to pupils; the second is *active, performed* and *behavioural,* involving an elaborate scenario

Box 12.2: Developing Empathising Skills

1.	How do you think the individual(s) is (are) feeling?
2.	Why do you think this is? (Encourage students to be specific about observations from which they infer emotions. Distinguish between observations and inferences.)
3.	Might the person(s) be feeling a different emotion than the one you inferred? Give an example.
4.	Have you ever felt this way? Why?
5.	What do you think might happen next to this person?
6.	If you inferred an unpleasant emotion, what possible action might the person(s) take in order to feel better?

Source: Rogers and Atwood.[3]

Box 12.3: The Stanford Prison Experiment

The study was conducted in the summer of 1971 in a mock prison constructed in the basement of the psychology building at Stanford University. The subjects were selected from a pool of 75 respondents to a newspaper advertisement asking for paid volunteers to participate in a psychological study of prison life. On a random basis half of the subjects were assigned to the role of guard and half to the role of prisoner. Prior to the experiment subjects were asked to sign a form, agreeing to play either the prisoner or the guard role for a maximum of two weeks. Those assigned to the prisoner role should expect to be under surveillance, to be harassed, but not to be physically abused. In return, subjects would be adequately fed, clothed and housed and would receive 15 dollars per day for the duration of the experiment.

The outcome of the study was quite dramatic. In less than two days after the initiation of the experiment, violence and rebellion broke out. The prisoners ripped off their clothing and their identification numbers and barricaded themselves inside the cells while shouting and cursing at the guards. The guards, in turn, began to harass, humiliate and intimidate the prisoners. They used sophisticated psychological techniques to break the solidarity among the inmates and to create a sense of distrust among them. In less than 36 hours one of the prisoners showed severe symptoms of emotional disturbance, uncontrollable crying and screaming and was released. On the third day, a rumour developed about a mass escape plot. The guards increased their harassment, intimidation and brutality toward the prisoners. On the fourth day, two prisoners showed symptoms of severe emotional disturbance and were released. On the fifth day, the prisoners showed symptoms of individual and group disintegration. They had become mostly passive and docile, suffering from an acute loss of contact with reality. The guards on the other hand, had kept up their harassment, some behaving sadistically. Because of the unexpectedly intense reactions generated by the mock prison experience, the experimenters terminated the study at the end of the sixth day.

Source: adapted from Banuazizi and Movahedi.[5]

and the participation of numerous other actors.

In a lesson designed to develop empathising skills,[3] a number of magazine pictures were selected. The pictures included easily observed clues that served as the basis for inferring an emotion or a situation. Some pictures showed only the face of an individual, others depicted one or more persons in a particular social setting. The pictures exhibited a variety of emotions such as anger, fear, compassion, anxiety and joy. Pupils were asked to look carefully at a particular picture and then to respond to questions that included or were similar to those in Box 12.2.

The second example of a role-playing study is the well-known Stanford Prison experiment carried out by Zimbardo and his associates,[4] a brief overview of which is given in Box 12.3.

Enthusiasts of role-playing as a research methodology cite experiments such as the Stanford Prison study to support their claim that where realism and spontaneity can be introduced into role-play, then such experimental conditions do, in fact, simulate both symbolically and phenomenologically, the real-life analogues that they purport to represent. Advocates of role-play would concur with the conclusions of Zimbardo and his associates that the simulated prison developed into a psychologically compelling prison environment[4] and they, too, would infer that the dramatic differences in the behaviour of prisoners and guards arose out of their location in different positions within the institutional structure of the prison and the social psychological conditions that prevailed there rather than from personality differences between the two groups of subjects.[5]

On the other hand, the passive, imaginary role-play required of subjects taking part in the lesson cited in the first example has been the focus of much of the criticism levelled at role-playing as a research technique. Ginsburg[1] summarises the argument against role-playing as a device for generating scientific knowledge:

1. Role-playing is unreal with respect to the variables under study in that the subject reports what he *would do*,* and that is taken as though he did do it.
2. The behaviour displayed is not spontaneous even in the more active forms of role-playing.

*However, this is not what advocates of role-play as an alternative to deception generally mean by role-play. See Hamilton[2] and Forward, Canter and Kirsch[6] for a fuller discussion.

3. The verbal reports in role-playing are very susceptible to arte-factual influence such as social desirability.
4. Role-playing procedures are not sensitive to complex inter-actions whereas deception designs are.

In general, Ginsburg[1] concludes, critics of role-playing view science as involving the discovery of natural truths and they contend that role-playing simply cannot substitute for deception — a sad but unavoidable state of affairs.

Role-playing Versus Deception: the Argument

As we shall shortly see, those who support role-playing as a legitimate scientific technique for systematic research into human social behaviour reject such criticisms by offering role-playing alternatives to deception studies of phenomena such as destructive obedience to authority and to conventional research in, for example, the area of attitude formation and change.

The objections to the current widespread use of deception in experimental research are articulated as follows:

1. Lying, cheating and deceiving contradict the norms that we typically try to apply in our everyday social interactions. The use of deception in the study of interpersonal relations is equally reprehensible. In a word, deception is unethical.
2. The use of deception is epistemologically unsound because it rests upon the acceptance of a less than adequate model of the subject *as a person*. Deception studies generally try to exclude the human capacities of the subject for choice and self-presentation. They tend therefore to focus upon 'incidental' social behaviour, that is, behaviours that are *outside* of the subject's field of choice, intention and self-presentation that typically constitute the main focus of social activity among human actors.[6]
3. The use of deception is methodologically unsound. Deception research depends upon a continuing supply of subjects who are naive to the intentions of the researchers. But word soon gets round and potential subjects come to expect that they will be deceived. It is a fair guess that most subjects are suspicious

and distrustful of psychological research despite the best intentions of deception researchers.

Finally, advocates of role-playing methods deplore the common practice of comparing the outcomes of role-playing replications against the standard of their deception study equivalents as a means of evaluating the relative validity of the two methods. The results of role-playing and deception, it is argued,[6] are not directly comparable since role-playing introduces a far wider range of human behaviour into experiments. If comparisons are to be made, then role-playing results should provide the yardstick against which deception study data are measured and not the other way round as is generally the case. We invite readers to follow this last piece of advice and to judge the well-known experiments of Milgram[7] on destructive obedience to authority against their role-playing replications by Mixon.[8, 9]

Role-playing Versus Deception: the Evidence

Milgram's Obedience-to-authority Experiments

In a series of studies from 1963 to 1974, Milgram carried out numerous variations on a basic obedience experiment which involved individuals acting, one at a time, as 'teachers' of another subject (who was, in reality, a confederate of the experimenter). Teachers were required to administer electric shocks of increasing severity every time the learner failed to make a correct response to

Box 12.4: Obedience to Authority: an Explanation

Milgram believes that an orientation to obedience to authority essentially follows from the hierarchical organisation of all sorts of social systems. Social hierarchy, he argues, is a form of organisation that has repeatedly evolved in animal species because it promotes the survival of the species. For human beings, too, various forms of social hierarchy have survival value. When the individual operates in a hierarchy, he cedes control to superior persons who co-ordinate the system. Since system coherence must be the most important consideration in a hierarchy, the individual in the hierarchy must be able to operate in what Milgram calls the *agentic mode*. 'The person entering into an authority system', Milgram explains, 'no longer views himself as acting out of his own purposes but rather comes to see himself as an agent for executing the wishes of another person.' Milgram's experiments on obedience are said to reveal some of the factors that trigger the agentic frame of mind.

Source: adapted from Brown and Herrnstein.[10]

a verbal learning task. Over the years, Milgram involved over 1,000 subjects in the experiment — subjects, incidentally, who were drawn from all walks of life rather than from undergraduate psychology classes. Summarising his findings, Milgram [7] reported that typically some 67 per cent of his teachers delivered the maximum electric shock to the learner despite the fact that such a degree of severity was clearly labelled as highly dangerous to the physical well-being of the person on the receiving end.

Milgram's explanation of destructive obedience to authority is summarised in Box 12.4.

Mixon's Role-playing Replications of the Milgram Experiment

Mixon's starting point was a disaffection for the deceit that played such an important part in generating emotional stress in Milgram's subjects, and a desire to explore alternative approaches to the study of destructive obedience to authority. Since Milgram's dependent variable was a rule-governed action, Mixon[8] reasoned, the rule-governed behaviour of Milgram's subjects could have been uniform or predictable. But it was not. Why, then, did some of Milgram's subjects obey and some defy the experimenter's instructions? The situation, Mixon notes, seemed perfectly clear to most commentators; the command to administer an electric shock appeared to be obviously immoral and all subjects *should* therefore have disobeyed the experimenter. If defiance was so obviously called for when looking at the experiment from the outside, why, asks Mixon, was it not obvious to those taking part on the inside? Mixon found a complete script of Milgram's experiment and proceeded to transform it[8] into an active role-playing exercise.

Box 12.5: Milgram's Experiment: an Alternative Explanation

> The 'all-or-none' method utilised continuous interaction and feedback from participants in the role-playing replication. Mixon succeeded in constructing several versions of the Milgram 'script' and produced the full range of possible obedience responses ranging from 0 per cent to 100 per cent. By exploring and specifying the particular meanings attributed to variations in the role/rule context of 'legitimate authority in experiments', and by being able to produce and observe the whole range of possible obedience responses, Mixon was better able to claim that he had an adequate conceptualisation and description of obedience in this particular social context.

Source: adapted from Forward, Canter and Kirsch.[6]

One of the first things I did was to take the role of the naive subject in order to look at the scene through his eyes. Later I took the roles of both experimenter and victim and repeated the scene over and over again using a different person each time in the role of naive subject. The repetition allowed me to become thoroughly familiar with each detail of the scene and by changing actors I was able to question many people about what was going on.

Mixon's role-playing replication of the Milgram experiment involved an exploratory method that he calls the 'all-or-none' technique, an account of which is given in Box 12.5.

But let Mixon[8] speak for himself:

Previous interpretations [of the Milgram data] have rested on the assumption that obedient subjects helplessly performed an obviously immoral act. From the outside the situation seemed clear. It was otherwise to the actors. The actors in my role playing version could not understand why the experimenter behaved as if feedback from the 'victim' was unimportant. The feedback suggested that something serious had occurred, that something had gone badly wrong with the experiment. The experimenter behaved as if nothing serious had or could happen. The experimenter in effect contradicted the evidence that otherwise seemed so clearly to suggest that the 'victim' was in serious trouble ... Using the 'all-or-none' method I found that when it became perfectly clear that the experimenter believed the 'victim' was being seriously harmed all actors indicated defiance to experimental commands. Briefly summarised, the 'all-or-none' analysis suggests that people will obey seemingly inhumane experimental commands so long as there is no good reason to think experimental safeguards have broken down; people will defy seemingly inhumane experimental commands when it becomes clear that safeguards have broken down — when consequences may indeed be what they appear to be. *When the experimental situation is confusing and mystifying as in Milgram's study, some people will obey and some will defy experimental commands* [our emphasis].

We leave readers to compare Mixon's explanations with Milgram's account set out in Box 12.4.

In summary, sophisticated role-playing methods such as those used by Mixon offer exciting possibilities to the educational researcher. They avoid the disadvantages of deception designs yet are able to incorporate many of the standard features of experiments such as constructing experimental conditions across factors of interest (in the Mixon studies for example, using scripts that vary the states of given role/rule contexts), randomly assigning actors to conditions as a way of randomising out individual differences, using repeated-measures designs, and standardising scripts and procedures to allow for replication of studies.[6]

Despite what has just been said about the possibilities of incorporating experimental features into role-playing research, empirical studies have more commonly employed role-playing methodologies in exploratory rather than experimental settings. Harré and Secord[11] distinguish between *exploration* and *experiment* as follows.

Whereas the experiment is employed to test the authenticity of what is known, exploration serves quite a different purpose:[11] 'In exploratory studies, a scientist has no very clear idea of what will happen, and aims to find out. He has a feeling for the direction in which to go ... but no clear expectations of what to expect. He is not confirming or refuting hypotheses.' Increasingly, exploratory (as opposed to experimental) research into human social behaviour is turning to role-playing methodologies. The reason is plain enough. Where the primary objective of such research is the identification and elucidation of the role/rule frameworks governing social interaction, *informed* rather than *deceived* subjects are essential if the necessary data on how they genuinely think and feel are to be made available to the researcher. Contrast the position of the fully participating, informed subject in such research with that of the deceived subject under the more usual experimental conditions. Argyris's[12] experimenter speaks to his subject thus:

I want to design the environment in such a way that when you enter it, I will have done my best to have induced you to behave as I predicted you would. However, I must be certain that if you behaved in the way I predicted you would, it was because you wanted to, because it made sense to you to do so, because the choice was genuinely yours. In order to maximise this possibility, I must design the entire experiment rigorously and keep all of the key elements of the design secret from you until you have finished participating in it. Also I cannot permit or encourage you to learn (ahead of time or during the experiment) anything about the experiment. I cannot encourage you to confront it, or to alter it. The only learning that I permit is learning that remains within the purposes of the experiment.

It can be argued that many of the more pressing social problems that society faces today arise out of our current ignorance of the role/rule frameworks governing human interactions in diverse social settings. If this is the case, then role-playing techniques could offer the possibility of a greater insight into the natural episodes of human behaviour that they seek to elucidate than the burgeoning amount of experimental data already at hand. The danger may lie in too much being expected of role-playing as a key to such knowledge. Ginsburg[1] offers a timely warning. Role-playing, he urges, should be seen as a complement to conventional experiments, survey research and field observations. That is, it is an important addition to our investigative armamentarium, *not* a replacement.

Role-playing in Educational Settings

Role-playing, gaming and machine or computer simulation are three strands of development in simulation studies that have only recently found their way into British classrooms.[13] Their discovery and introduction into primary and secondary schools in the late 1960s is somewhat surprising in view of the unqualified support that distinguished educational theorists from Plato onwards have accorded to the value of play and games in education.[14]

The distinction between these three types of simulation — role-playing, games and machines/computers — is by no means clear-cut; for example, simulation games often contain role-playing activities and may be designed with computer back-up services to expedite their procedures.[13]

In this section we focus particularly upon role-playing aspects of simulation, beginning with some brief observations on the purposes of role-playing in classroom settings and some practical suggestions directed towards the less experienced practitioners of role-playing methods.

The Uses of Role-playing

Van Ments[15] classifies the uses of role-playing as:

(1) *Developing sensitivity and awareness.* The definitions of positions such as mother, teacher, policeman and priest, for example, explicitly or implicitly incorporate various role characteristics which often lead to the stereotyping of position occupants. Role-playing provides a means of exploring such stereotypes and developing a deeper understanding of the point of view and feelings of someone who finds himself in a particular role.

(2) *Experiencing the pressures which create roles.* Role-playing provides study material for group members on the ways in which roles are created in, for example, a committee. It enables subjects to explore the interactions of formal structure and individual personalities in role taking.

(3) *Testing out for oneself possible modes of behaviour.* In effect, this is *rehearsal*; trying out in one's mind in advance of some new situation that one has to face. Role-playing can be used for a wide variety of situations where the subject, for one reason or another, needs to learn to cope with the rituals and conventions of social intercourse and to practise them so that they can be repeated under stress.

(4) *Simulating a situation for others (and possibly oneself) to learn from.* Here, the role-player provides materials for others to use and work upon. In the simplest situation, there is just one role-player acting out a specific role. In more complex situations such as the Stanford Prison study discussed in Box 12.3, role-playing is used to provide an environment structured on the interaction of numerous role incumbents. Van Ments'[16] suggestions for running role-play sessions are set out in Box 12.6. They are particularly appropriate to teachers intent upon using role play in classroom settings.

Setting Objectives

Van Ments' first observation is that teachers must begin by asking themselves what exactly their intentions are in teaching by means of role-play. Is it, for example, to teach facts, or concepts, or skills, or awareness, or sensitivity? Depending on the specific nature of the teacher's objective, role-play can be fitted into the timetable in several ways. Van Ments identifies the following:

Box 12.6: A Flow Chart for Using Role-play

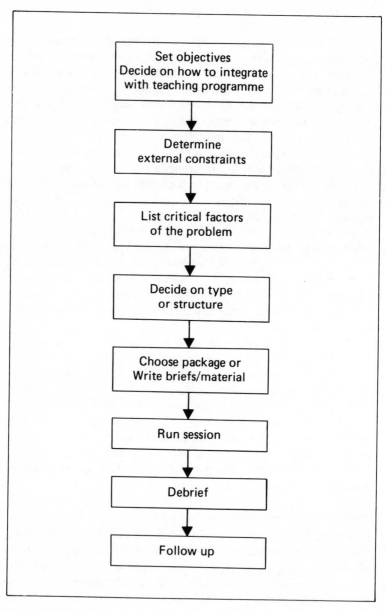

Source: Van Ments.[16]

(i)   as an introduction to the subject;
(ii) as a means of supplementing or following on from a point that is being explored;
(iii) as the focal point of a course or a unit of work;
(iv) as a break from the routine of the classroom or the workshop;
(v)   as a way of summarising or integrating diverse subject matter;
(vi) as a way of reviewing or revising a topic;
(vii) as a means of assessing work.

Determining External Constraints

Role-play can be extremely time consuming. It's vital therefore that from the outset, teachers should be aware of factors that may inhibit or even preclude the running of a role-play. Van Ments identifies the following:

(i)   suitable room or space (size, layout, furniture, etc.);
(ii) sufficient time for warm up, running the actual role-play and debriefing;
(iii) availability of assistance to help run the session.

Critical Factors

The teacher, Van Ments advises, must look at the critical issues involved in the problem area encompassed by the role-play and decide who has the power to influence those issues as well as who is affected by the decisions to be taken. By way of example, Box 12.7 identifies some of the principal protagonists in a role-play session to do with young people smoking.

Choosing or Writing the Role-play

The choice lies with teachers either to buy or borrow a ready-made role-play or to write their own. In practice, Van Ments observes, most role-plays are written for specific needs and with the intention of fitting into a particular course programme. Existing role-plays can, of course, be adapted by teachers to their own particular circumstances and needs. On balance it's probably better to write the role-play in order to ensure that the background is familiar to the intended participants and they can see its relevance to the specific problem that concerns them.

Box 12.7: Critical Factors in a Role-play: Smoking and Young People

Roles involved:	young people, parents, teachers, doctors, youth leaders, shopkeeper, cigarette manufacturer.
Critical issues:	responsibility for health, cost of illness, freedom of action, taxation revenue, advertising, effects on others.
Key communication channels:	advertisements, school contacts, family, friends.

Source: adapted from Van Ments.[16]

Running the Role-play

The counsel of perfection, Van Ments reminds us, is always to pilot test the role-play material that one is going to use, preferably with a similar audience. In reality, pilot testing can be as time consuming as the play itself and may therefore be totally impracticable given timetable pressures. But however difficult the circumstances, *any* form of piloting, says Van Ments, is better than none at all, even if it is simply a matter of talking procedures through with one or two colleagues.

Once the materials are prepared, then the role-play follows its own sequence: (i) introduction, (ii) warm up, (iii) running, and (iv) ending. One final word of caution. It's particularly important to time the ending of the role-play in such a way as to fit into the whole programme. One method of ensuring this is to write the mechanism for ending into the role-play itself. Thus:

> You must have reached agreement on all five points before 11.30 a.m. when you have to attend a meeting of the board of directors.

Debriefing

Debriefing is more than simply checking that the right lesson has been learnt and feeding this information back to the teacher. Rather, Van Ments reminds us, it is a *two-way* process during which the consequences of actions arising in the role-play can be analysed and conclusions drawn. It is that point in the role-play sequence when mistakes and misunderstandings can be rectified. Most important of all, it is from well-conducted debriefing sessions that the teacher can draw out the implications of what the pupils have been experiencing and can then plan the continuation of their learning about the topic at hand.

Follow-up

To conclude, Van Ments notes the importance of the follow-up session in the teacher's planning of the ways in which the role-play exercise will lead naturally into the next learning activity. Thus, when the role-play session has attempted to teach a skill or rehearse a novel situation, then it may be logical to repeat it until the requisite degree of competence has been reached. Conversely, if the purpose of the exercise has been to raise questions, then a follow-up session should be arranged to answer them. 'Whatever the objectives of using role play', Van Ments advises, 'one must always consider the connection between it and the next learning activity.' Above all else, avoid leaving the role-play activity in a vacuum.

Strengths and Weaknesses of Role-playing and Other Simulation Exercises

Taylor and Walford[13] identify two prominent themes in their discussion of some of the possible advantages and disadvantages in the use of classroom simulation exercises. They are, first, the claimed enhancement of pupil motivation and second, the role of simulation in the provision of relevant learning materials. The motivational advantages of simulation are said to include (1) a heightened interest and excitement in learning; (2) a sustained level of freshness and novelty arising out of the dynamic nature of simulation tasks; (3) a transformation in the traditional pupil-teacher subordinate-superordinate relationship; and (4) the fact that simulation is a universal behavioural mode. As to the learning gains arising out of the use of simulation, the authors identify (1) the learning that is afforded at diverse levels (cognitive, social and emotional); (2) the decision-making experiences that participants acquire as well; (3) an increased role awareness; (4) the ability of simulation to provide a vehicle for free interdisciplinary communication; and (5) the success with which the concrete approach afforded by simulation exercises bridges the gap between 'school-work' and 'the real world'.

What reservations are there in connection with simulation

exercises? Taylor and Walford identify the following: (1) simulations, however interesting and attractive, are time-demanding activities and ought therefore to justify fully the restricted time-tabling allotted to competing educational approaches; (2) many simulation exercises are in the form of game kits and these can be quite expensive; and (3) simulation materials may pose problems of logistics, operation and general acceptance as legitimate educational techniques particularly by parent associations.

Our discussion of the strengths and weaknesses of role-playing has focused upon its application in pupil groups. To illustrate Taylor and Walford's point that simulation is a universal behavioural mode, the detailed example of a role-playing exercise that now follows is to do with adults in higher education.

Role-playing in an Educational Setting: an Example

Ferguson's[17] Toreside Comprehensive School is a simulation game for teachers in training that has been run successfully with PGCE students at Liverpool University School of Education. Its objectives are to encourage student teachers to think about the relationships between their subject disciplines in a social setting that is typical of many secondary school senior common rooms. The simulation is structured on realism and conflict.

The game involves four distinct phases:

Phase 1: Volunteer subjects are assigned to subject departments in the imaginary Toreside Comprehensive School (hereinafter TCS). They are required to act out the roles of teachers in the actual subjects they themselves will eventually teach. They must devise and learn their own scripts. One person in each department is designated Head of Department.

Phase 2: TCS staff under the direction of the Headmaster (played by the University tutor) take part in a staffroom discussion the object of which is to reinforce their roles and establish their identities in the minds of other role-players.

Phase 3: The Headmaster injects a crisis in the staffroom discussion, forcing participants to justify their positions as subject specialists and to explore the overlap and interrelationships with other subjects. This is done within the atmosphere charged with those irrational elements that characterise the real situation.

Phase 4: The simulation game is terminated and participants are asked to discuss the exercise in which they have taken part.

Organising the Simulation Game

During the first briefing (Phase 1), Ferguson's instructions to his volunteers offer guidance by means of a role-proforma specifying personal and biographical details and requesting role-players to think out in advance of the actual game their role attitudes to potentially emotive issues such as corporal punishment, long hair, school uniforms and discipline in general. Each role-player also receives an information pack giving details of TCS — its pupil intake, system of organisation, timetabling, etc. At this first briefing, the purpose of the game is made clear to the participants but no mention is made of the crisis. The whole simulation exercise is to be recorded on TV and the reasons for this are explained.

At the second briefing (Phase 2), participants meet for the first time in the staffroom duly set out for the headmaster-led discussion. The locations of other rooms to be used during the simulation are identified and a detailed timetable of events for the rest of the simulation programme is handed out. The purpose of the third briefing (still Phase 2) is to reinforce the roles of participants. Each Head of Department is required to give a short resumé of his department to be followed by a short question period. This session gives participants opportunties to incorporate details from the role-proforma and information kit into their role portrayals.

Phase 3 constitutes the actual game in which the headmaster's policy announcement induces conflict into a situation in which some degree of tension may already be present following the role-play in Phase 2. The conflict arises out of the headmaster's declared intention to introduce a scheme to break down subject boundaries in the first three years of the secondary school time-table. Staff are required to work out among themselves a basis for co-operation in implementing the head's wishes. Full details of his policy statement including financial implications for departments are provided in written form to all participants who then divide up, initially, into subject departments, to produce a departmental policy in relation to the crisis. At a second staff meeting, the headmaster asks for a progress report from each department and the negotiations and interdepartmental discussions become general knowledge. Later in the simulation game, at a final staff meeting, the difficulties and issues involved in integrating the school curriculum again became public knowledge and the arguments put forward bear a very close resemblance to what would probably be heard in a real school staffroom. The final staff meeting is the arena for negotiation and compromise among the role actors, including the headmaster.

The final session (Phase 4) is the debriefing period during which discussions of the exercise as a whole are held and participants are asked to complete a questionnaire about the simulation game and their reactions to it.

Ferguson reports on the comments of some of the student teachers with whom he has participated in the TCS simulation game. The great majority voted the experience as 'extremely interesting' on a Likert-type scale. The exercise was also found to be enjoyable by most of those taking part. Individual comments included the following:

> It gave me a chance to meet and learn some of the problems of other departments.
> It highlighted some interesting points in personal relationships.
> It brought some aspects of the lectures [in the Certificate of Education course] into perspective.
> It knitted a large part of our Education course together.

Evaluating Role-playing and Other Simulation Exercises

Because the use of simulation methods in classroom settings is growing, there is increasing need to evaluate claims concerning the advantages and effectiveness of these newer approaches against more traditional methods. Yet here lies a major problem. To date, as Megarry[14] observes, a high proportion of evaluation efforts has been directed towards the *comparative experiment* involving empirical comparisons between simulation-type exercises and more traditional teaching techniques in terms of specified learning pay-offs. One objection[14] to this approach to evaluation has been detailed earlier in the present chapter (p. 274) but is worth reiterating here:

> the limitations [of the classical, experimental method] as applied

to evaluating classroom simulation and games are obvious: not only are the inputs multiple, complex, and only partly known, but the outputs are disputed, difficult to isolate, detect or measure and the interaction among participants is considerable. Interaction forms, in some views, a major part of what simulation and gaming is about; it is *not* merely a source of 'noise' or experimental error.

What alternatives are there to the traditional type of evaluative effort? Megarry lists the following promising approaches to simulation evaluation: (1) using narrative reports; (2) using checklists gathered from students' recollections of outstanding positive and negative learning experiences; (3) encouraging players to relate ideas and concepts learned in games to other areas of their lives; and (4) using the instructional interview, a form of tutorial carried out earlier with an individual learner or a small group in which materials and methods are tested by an instructor who is versed not only in the use of the materials, but also in the ways in which pupils learn. (See also Percival's[18] discussion of observational and self-reporting techniques.)

Notice how each of the above evaluative techniques is primarily concerned with the *process* rather than the *product* of simulation.

By way of summary, simulation methods provide a means of alleviating a number of problems inherent in laboratory experiments. At the same time, they permit the retention of some of their virtues. Simulations, notes Palys,[19] share with the laboratory experiment the characteristic that the experimenter has complete manipulative control over every aspect of the situation. At the same time, the subjects' humanity is left intact in that they are given a realistic situation in which to act in whatever way they think appropriate. The inclusion of the time dimension is another important contribution of the simulation, allowing as it does the subject to take an active role in interacting with the environment, and the experimenter the opportunity of observing a social system in action with its feedback loops, multidirectional causal connections and so forth. Finally, Palys observes, the high involvement normally associated with participation in simulations shows that the self-consciousness usually associated with the laboratory experiment is more easily dissipated.

References

1. Ginsburg, G.P., 'Role playing and role performance in social psychological research', in M. Brenner, P. Marsh and M. Brenner (eds), *The Social Context of Method* (Croom Helm, London, 1978).
2. Hamilton, V.L., 'Role play and deception: a re-examination of the controversy', *Journal for the Theory of Social Behaviour*, 6 (1976) 233–50.
3. Rogers, V.M. and Atwood, R.K., 'Can we put ourselves in their place', *Yearbook of the National Council for Social Studies*, 44 (1974) 80–111.
4. Haney, C., Banks, C. and Zimbardo, P., 'Interpersonal dynamics in a simulated prison', *International Journal of Criminology and Penology*, 1 (1973) 69–97.
5. Banuazizi, A. and Movahedi, A., 'Interpersonal dynamics in a simulated prison: a methodological analysis', *American Psychologist*, 30 (1975) 152–60.
6. Forward, J., Canter, R. and Kirsch, N., 'Role-enactment and deception methodologies', *American Psychologist*, 35 (1976) 595–604.
7. Milgram, S., *Obedience to Authority* (Harper and Row, New York, 1974).
8. Mixon, D., 'If you won't deceive, what can you do?', in N. Armistead (ed.), *Reconstructing Social Psychology* (Penguin Books, London, 1974).
9. Mixon, D., 'Instead of deception', *Journal for the Theory of Social Behaviour*, 2 (1972) 146–77.
10. Brown, R. and Herrnstein, R.J., *Psychology* (Methuen, London, 1975).
11. Harré, R. and Secord, P.F., *The Explanation of Social Behaviour* (Basil Blackwell, Oxford, 1972).
12. Argyris, C., 'Dangers in applying results from experimental social psychology', *American Psychologist*, 30 (1975) 469–85.
13. Taylor, J.L. and Walford, R., *Simulation in the Classroom* (Penguin Books, London, 1972).
14. Megarry, J., 'Retrospect and prospect', in R. McAleese (ed.), *Perspectives on Academic Gaming and Simulation 3: Training and Professional Education* (Kogan Page, London, 1978).
15. van Ments, M., 'Role playing: playing a part or a mirror to meaning?' *Sagset Journal*, 8, 3 (1978) 83–92.
16. van Ments, M. *The Effective Use of Role-Play: A Handbook for Teachers and Trainers* (Croom Helm, London, 1983).
17. Ferguson, S., 'Toreside Comprehensive School: a simulation game for teachers in training', in J. Megarry (ed.), *Aspects of Simulation and Gaming* (Kogan Page, London, 1977).
18. Percival, F., 'Evaluation procedures for simulating gaming exercises', in R. McAleese (ed.), *Perspectives on Academic Gaming and Simulation 3: Training and Professional Education* (Kogan Page, London, 1978).
19. Palys, T.S., 'Simulation methods and social psychology', *Journal for the Theory of Social Behaviour*, 8 (1978) 341–68.

13 THE INTERVIEW

Introduction

Although the interview as a research technique is normally considered as one of a range of survey methods in social research, we treat it separately here chiefly to give us additional room to address ourselves more effectively to the details involved. The purposes of the interview in the wider context of life are many and varied. It may thus be used as a means of evaluating or assessing a person in some respect; for selecting or promoting an employee; for effecting therapeutic change, as in the psychiatric interview; for testing or developing hypotheses; for gathering data, as in surveys or experimental situations; or for sampling respondents' opinions, as in doorstep interviews. Although in each of these situations the respective roles of the interviewer and interviewee may vary and the motives for taking part may differ, a common denominator is the transaction that takes place between seeking information on the part of one and supplying information on the part of the other. As our interests lie primarily in reviewing research methods and techniques, we will subsequently limit ourselves to the use of the interview as a specific *research* tool. Interviews in this sense range from the *formal interview* in which set questions are asked and the answers recorded on a standardised schedule; through *less formal* interviews in which the interviewer is free to modify the sequence of questions, change and wording, explain them or add to them; to the *completely informal interview* where the interviewer may have a number of key issues which he raises in conversational style instead of having a set questionnaire. Beyond this point is located the *non-directive interview* in which the interviewer takes on a subordinate role.

The research interview has been defined[1] as 'a two-person conversation initiated by the interviewer for the specific purpose of obtaining research-relevant information, and focused by him on content specified by research objectives of systematic description, prediction, or explanation'. It is an unusual method in that it involves the gathering of data through direct verbal interaction between individuals. In this sense it differs from the *questionnaire*

Box 13.1: Summary of Relative Merits of Interviewing Versus Questionnaire

Consideration	Interview	Questionnaire
1. Personal need to collect data	Requires interviewers	Requires a clerk
2. Major expense	Payment to interviewers	Postage and printing
3. Opportunites for response-keying (personalisation)	Extensive	Limited
4. Opportunites for asking	Extensive	Limited
5. Opportunities for probing	Possible	Difficult
6. Relative magnitude of data reduction	Great (because of coding)	Mainly limited to rostering
7. Typically, the number of respondents who can be reached	Limited	Extensive
8. Rate of return	Good	Poor
9. Sources of error	Interviewer, instrument, coding, sample	Limited to instrument and sample
10. Overall reliability	Quite limited	Fair
11. Emphasis on writing skill	Limited	Extensive

Source: Tuckman.[3]

where the respondent is required to record in some way his responses to set questions. By way of interest, we illustrate the relative merits of the interview and the questionnaire in Box 13.1. It has been pointed out[2] that the direct interaction of the interview is the source of both its advantages and disadvantages as a research technique. One advantage, for example, is that it allows for greater depth than is the case with other methods of data collection. A disadvantage, on the other hand, is that it is prone to subjectivity and bias on the part of the interviewer.

As a distinctive research technique, the interview may serve three purposes. First, it may be used as the principal means of gathering information having direct bearing on the research objectives. As Tuckman[3] describes it, 'By providing access to what is "inside a person's head", [it] makes it possible to measure what a person knows (knowledge or information), what a person likes or dislikes (values and preferences), and what a person thinks (attitudes and beliefs).' Second, it may be used to test hypotheses or to suggest new ones; or as an explanatory device to help identify variables and relationships. And third, the interview may be used in conjunction with other methods in a research undertaking. In this connection, Kerlinger[4] suggests that it might be used to follow up unexpected results, for example, or to validate other methods, or to go deeper into the motivations of respondents and their reasons for responding as they do.

There are four kinds of interview that may be used specifically as research tools: *the structured interview; the unstructured interview; the non-directive interview;* and *the focused interview.* The structured interview is one in which the content and procedures are organised in advance. This means that the sequence and wording of the questions are determined by means of a schedule and the interviewer is left little freedom to make modifications. Where some leeway is granted him, it too is specified in advance. It is therefore characterised by being a *closed* situation. In contrast to it in this respect, the unstructured interview is an *open* situation, having greater flexibility and freedom. As Kerlinger notes, although the research purposes govern the questions asked, their content, sequence and wording are entirely in the hands of the interviewer. This does not mean, however, that the unstructured interview is a more casual affair, for in its own way it also has to be carefully planned.

The non-directive interview as a research technique derives from the therapeutic or psychiatric interview. The principal features of it are the minimal direction or control exhibited by the interviewer and the freedom the respondent has to express his subjective feelings as fully and as spontaneously as he chooses or is able. As Moser and Kalton[5] put it,

> The informant is encouraged to talk about the subject under investigation (usually himself) and the course of the interview is mainly guided by him. There are no set questions, and usually no predetermined framework for recorded answers. The interviewer confines himself to elucidating doubtful points, to rephrasing the respondent's answers and to probing generally. It is an approach especially to be recommended when complex attitudes are involved and when one's knowledge of them is still in a vague and unstructured form.

The need to introduce rather more interviewer control into the non-directive situation led to the development of the focused interview. The distinctive feature of this type is that it focuses on a respondent's subjective responses to a known situation in which he has been involved and which has been analysed by the interviewer prior to the interview. He is thereby able to use the data from the interview to substantiate or reject previously formulated hypotheses. As Merton and Kendall[6] explain, 'In the usual depth interview, one can urge informants to reminisce on their experiences. In the focused interview, however, the interviewer can, when expedient, play a more active role: he can introduce more explicit verbal cues to the stimulus pattern or even *represent* it. In either case this usually activates a concrete report of responses by informants.'

We shall be examining both the non-directive interview and the focused interview in more detail later in the chapter.

Conceptions of the Interview

In his examination of views of the interview held by those who write theoretically about it and those who actually use it as a research tool, Kitwood[7] lucidly contrasts three conceptions of it. The first conception is that of a potential means of *pure information transfer*. He explains that

> if the interviewer does his job well (establishes rapport, asks questions in an acceptable manner, etc.), and if the respondent is sincere and well-motivated, accurate data may be obtained. Of course all kinds of bias are liable to creep in, but with skill these can largely be eliminated. In its fullest expression, this view accords closely with that of the psychometricians, who apparently believe that there is a relatively permanent, consistent, 'core' to the personality, about which a person will give information under certain conditions. Such features as lying, or the tendency to give a socially desirable response, are to be eliminated where possible.

This conception of the interview appears to be widely held.

A second conception of the interview is that of *a transaction which inevitably has bias, which is to be recognised and controlled.*

According to this viewpoint, Kitwood explains that 'each participant in an interview will define the situation in a particular way. This fact can be best handled by building controls into the research design, for example by having a range of interviewers with different biases.' The interview is best understood in terms of a theory of motivation which recognises a range of non-rational factors governing human behaviour, like emotions, unconscious needs and interpersonal influences. Kitwood points out that both these views of the interview regard the inherent features of interpersonal transactions as if they were 'potential obstacles to sound research, and therefore to be removed, controlled, or at least harnessed in some way'.

The third conception of the interview sees it as *an encounter necessarily sharing many of the features of everyday life.* Kitwood suggests that what is required, according to this view, is not a technique for dealing with bias, but a theory of everyday life that takes account of the relevant features of interviews. These may include role-playing, stereotyping, perception and understanding. One of the strongest advocates of this viewpoint is Cicourel[8] who lists five of the unavoidable features of the interview situation that would normally be regarded as problems. Briefly, these state that[7]:

1. There are many factors which inevitably differ from one interview to another, such as mutual trust, social distance and the interviewer's control.
2. The respondent may well feel uneasy and adopt avoidance tactics if the questioning is too deep.
3. Both interviewer and respondent are bound to hold back part of what it is in their power to state.
4. Many of the meanings which are clear to one will be relatively opaque to the other, even when the intention is genuine communication.
5. It is impossible, just as in everyday life, to bring every aspect of the encounter within rational control.

The message that proponents of this view would express is that no matter how hard an interviewer may try to be systematic and objective, the constraints of everyday life will be a part of whatever interpersonal transactions he initiates. Kitwood concludes, 'The solution is to have as explicit a theory as possible to take the various factors into account. For those who hold this view, there are not good interviews and bad in the conventional sense. There are simply social encounters; goodness and badness are predicates applicable, rather, to the theories within which the phenomena are explained.'

Some Features of the Research Interview

We turn our attention now to the *structured interview* since this is one of the most frequently used methods of eliciting information in social and educational research. From here onwards, we shall comply with convention and refer to it as the *research interview*. After reviewing the types of schedule items used, we shall examine question format and the kinds of answers, or response modes, that may be elicited.

Three kinds of items are used in the construction of schedules used in research interviews:[4] *fixed-alternative items; open-ended items*; and *scale items*.

The fixed-alternative items allow the respondent to choose from two or more alternatives. The most frequently used is the dichotomous item which offers two alternatives only: *yes-no* or *agree-disagree*, for instance. Sometimes a third alternative such as *undecided* or *don't know* is also offered.

> *Example:*
> Do you feel it is against the interests of a school
> to have to make public its examination results?
>
> Yes . . . .
> No . . . .
> Don't know . . . .

Kerlinger[4] has identified the chief advantages and disadvantages of fixed-alternative items. They have, for example, the advantage of achieving greater uniformity of measurement and therefore greater reliability; of making the respondents answer in a manner fitting the response category; and of being more easily coded. Disadvantages include their superficiality; the possibility of irritating respondents who find none of the alternatives suitable; and the possibility of forcing responses that are inappropriate, either because the alternative chosen conceals ignorance on the part of the respondent or because he may choose an alternative that does not accurately represent the true facts. These weaknesses can be overcome, however, if the items are written with care, mixed with open-ended ones, and used in conjunction with probes on the part of the interviewer.

Open-ended items have been succinctly defined by Kerlinger as 'those that supply a frame of reference for respondents' answers, but put a minimum of restraint on the answers and their expression'. Other than the subject of the question, which is determined by the nature of the problem under investigation, there are no other restrictions on either the content or the manner of the interviewee's reply.

Example:
What kind of television programmes do you most prefer to watch?

....

....

Open-ended questions have a number of advantages: they are flexible; they allow the interviewer to probe so that he may go into more depth if he chooses, or clear up any misunderstandings; they enable the interviewer to test the limits of the respondent's knowledge; they encourage co-operation and help establish rapport; and they allow the interviewer to make a truer assessment of what the respondent really believes. Open-ended situations can also result in unexpected or unanticipated answers which may suggest hitherto unthought-of relationships or hypotheses.

A particular kind of open-ended question is *the funnel*. This starts with a broad question or statement and then narrows down to more specific ones. Kerlinger quotes an example from the study by Sears, Maccoby and Levin:[9]

All babies cry, of course. Some mothers feel that if you pick up a baby every time it cries, you will spoil it. Others think you should never let a baby cry for very long. How do you feel about this? What did you do about it? How about the middle of the night?

The *scale* is a set of verbal items to each of which the interviewee responds by indicating degrees of agreement or disagreement. The individual's response is thus located on a scale of fixed-alternatives. The use of this technique along with open-ended questions is a comparatively recent development and means that scale scores can be checked against data elicited by the open-ended questions.

Example:
Attendance at school after the age of 14 should be voluntary:

Strongly agree   Agree   Undecided   Disagree
Strongly disagree

It is possible to use one of a number of scales in this context: attitude scales, rank-order scales, rating scales, and so on. We touch upon this subject again subseqently.

We now look at the kinds of questions and modes of response associated with interviewing. First, the matter of question format: how is a question to be phrased or organised? One commentator[3] has listed four such formats that an interviewer may draw upon. Questions may, for example, take a *direct* or *indirect* form. Thus an interviewer could ask a teacher whether he likes teaching: this would be a direct question. Or else he could adopt an indirect approach by asking for the respondent's views on education in general and the ways schools function. From the answers proffered, the interviewer could make inferences about the teacher's opinions concerning his own job. Tuckman suggests that by making the purpose of questions less obvious, the indirect approach is more likely to produce frank and open responses.

There are also those kinds of questions which deal with either a *general or specific* issue. To ask a child what he thought of the teaching methods of the staff as a whole would be a *general* or *non-specific* question. To ask him what he thought of his teacher as a teacher would be a specific question. We have already made reference to that sequence of questions designated the funnel in which the movement is from the general and non-specific to the more specific. Tuckman comments, 'Specific questions, like direct ones, may cause a respondent to become cautious or guarded and give less-than-honest answers. Non-specific questions may lead circuitously to the desired information but with less alarm by the respondents.'

A further distinction is that between questions inviting *factual* answers and those inviting *opinions.* To ask a person what political party he supports would be a factual question. To ask him what he thinks of the current government's foreign policy would be an opinion question. Both fact and opinion questions can yield less than the truth, however: the former do not always produce factual answers; nor do the latter necessarily elicit honest opinions. In both instances, inaccuracy and bias may be minimised by careful structuring of the questions.

We may also note that an interviewee may be presented with either a *question* or a *statement*. In the case of the latter he will be asked for his response to it in one form or another. We illustrate the difference thus:

Do you think homework should be compulsory for all children between 11 and 16? ....

And:

Homework should be compulsory for all children between 11 and 16.

Agree   Disagree   Don't know

If there are varied ways of *asking* questions, it follows there will be several ways in which they may be answered. It is to the different *response modes* that we now turn. In all, Tuckman lists seven such modes:

The first of these is the *unstructured response*. This allows the respondent to give his answer in whatever way he chooses. A *structured response*, by contrast, would limit him in some way. Thus:

Why did you not go to university?

And:

Can you give me two reasons for not going to university?

Although the interviewer has little control over the unstructured response, it does insure that the respondent has the freedom to give his own answer as fully as he chooses rather than being constrained in some way by the nature of the question. The chief disadvantage of the unstructured response concerns the matter of quantification. Data yielded in the unstructured response is more difficult to code and quantify than data in the structured response.

A *fill-in response* mode requires the respondent to supply rather than choose a response, though the response is often limited to a word or phrase. Consider the following examples:

What is your present occupation? ....

How long have you lived at your present address? ....

The difference between the fill-in response and the unstructured response is one of degree.

A *tabular response* is similar to a fill-in response though more structured. It may demand words, figures or phrases. For example:

University	Subject	Degree	Dates	
			From	To

It is thus a convenient and short-hand way of recording complex information.

A *scaled response* is one structured by means of a series of gradations. The respondent is required to record his response to a given statement by selecting from a number of alternatives. Thus:

What are your chances of reaching a top managerial position within the next five years?

Excellent   Good   Fair   Poor   Very poor

Tuckman draws our attention to the fact that, unlike an unstructured response which has to be coded to be useful as data, a scaled response is collected in the form of usable and analysable data.

A *ranking response* is one in which a respondent is required to rank-order a series of words, phrases or statements according to a particular criterion. Here is an example:

Rank order the following persons in terms of their usefulness to you as sources of advice and guidance on problems you have encountered in the classroom. Use numbers 1 through 5 with 1 representing the person most useful: education tutor, subject tutor, class teacher, headteacher, other student.

Ranked data can be analysed by adding up the rank of each response across the respondents, thus resulting in an overall rank order of alternatives.

A *checklist response* requires that the respondent selects one of the alternatives presented to him. In that they do not represent points on a continuum, they are nominal categories. For example:

I get most satisfaction in college from:

   the social life
   studying on my own
   attending lectures
   college societies
   giving a paper at a seminar

This kind of response tends to yield less information than the other kinds considered.

Finally, the *categorical response* mode is similar to the checklist but simpler in that it offers respondents only two possibilities. For example:

Material progress results in greater
happiness for people   True   False

Or:

In the event of another war, would you
be prepared to fight for your country?   Yes   No

Summing the numbers of respondents with the same responses yields a nominal measure.

Some Problems Surrounding the Use of the Interview in Research

A number of problems appear to attend the use of the interview as a research technique. One of these is that of invalidity, at least as far as the first two conceptions of the interview that we spoke of earlier are concerned. Studies reported by Cannell and Kahn,[1] for instance, in which the interview was used seemed to indicate that this was a persistent problem. In one such study,[10] subjects interviewed on the existence and state of their bank accounts often presented a misleading picture: fewer accounts were reported than actually existed and the amounts declared frequently differed from bank records, often in the direction of understating assets. The reviewers suggest that inferences about validity are made too often on the basis of *face validity*, that is, whether the questions asked look as if they are measuring what they claim to measure. The cause of invalidity, they argue, is *bias* which they define as 'a systematic or persistent tendency to make errors in the same direction, that is, to overstate or understate the "true value" of an attribute'. The problem, it seems, is not limited to a narrow range of data but is widespread. One way of validating interview measures is to compare the interview measure with another measure that has already been shown to be valid. This kind of comparison is known as *convergent validity*. If the two measures agree, it can be assumed that the validity of the interview is comparable with the proven validity of the other measure.

Perhaps the most practical way of achieving greater validity is to minimise the amount of bias as much as possible. The sources of bias are the characteristics of the interviewer, the characteristics of the respondent, and the substantive content of the questions. More particularly, these will include: the attitudes and opinions of the interviewer; a tendency for the interviewer to see the respondent in his own image; a tendency for the interviewer to seek answers that support his preconceived notions; misperceptions on the part of the interviewer of what the respondent is saying; and misunderstandings on the part of the respondent of what is being asked. Studies have also shown that colour, religion, social class and age can in certain contexts be potent sources of bias. Various writers have suggested the following as means of reducing bias: careful formulation of questions so that the meaning is crystal clear; thorough training procedures so that an interviewer is more aware of the possible problems; probability sampling of respondents; and sometimes by matching interviewer characteristics with those of the sample being interviewed.

In his critique of the interview as a research tool, Kitwood[7] draws attention to the conflict it generates between the traditional concepts of reliability and validity. Where increased reliability of the interview is brought about by greater control of its elements, this is achieved, he argues, at the cost of reduced validity. He explains,

> In proportion to the extent to which 'reliability' is enhanced by rationalization, 'validity' would decrease. For the main purpose of using an interview in research is that it is believed that in an interpersonal encounter people are more likely to disclose aspects of themselves, their thoughts, their feelings and values, than they would in a less human situation. At least for some purposes, it is necessary to generate a kind of conversation in which the 'respondent' feels at ease. In other words, the distinctively human element in the interview is necessary to its 'validity'. The more the interviewer becomes rational, calculating, and detached, the less likely the interview is to be perceived as a friendly transaction, and the more calculated the response also is likely to be.

Where either of the first two conceptions of the interview outlined earlier is held, Kitwood suggests that a solution to the problem of reliability and validity might lie in the direction of a 'judicious compromise'; with the third conception, however, reliability and validity become 'redundant notions', for 'every interpersonal situation may be said to be valid, as such, whether or not it conforms to expectation, whether or not it involves a high degree of communication, and whether or not the participants emerge exhilarated or depressed.'

A cluster of problems surround the person being interviewed. Tuckman,[3] for example, has observed that when formulating his questions an interviewer has to consider the extent to which a question might influence the respondent to show himself in a good light; or the extent to which a question might influence the respondent to be unduly helpful by attempting to anticipate what the interviewer wants to hear; or the extent to which a question might be asking for information about a respondent that he is not certain or likely to know himself. Further, interviewing procedures are based on the assumption that the person interviewed has insight into the cause of his behaviour. It has now come to be realised that insight of this kind is rarely achieved and that when it is, it is after long and difficult effort, usually in the context of repeated clinical interviews.

As the interview has some things in common with the self-administered questionnaire, it is frequently compared with it. Each has advantages over the other in certain respects. The advantages of the questionnaire, for instance, are: it tends to be more reliable; because it is anonymous, it encourages greater honesty; it is more economical than the interview in terms of time and money; and there is the possibility that it may be mailed. Its disadvantages, on the other hand, are: there is often too low a percentage of returns; the interviewer is able to answer questions concerning both the purpose of the interview and any misunderstandings experienced by the interviewee, for it sometimes happens in the case of the latter that the same questions have different meanings for different people; if only closed items are used, the questionnaire will be subject to the weaknesses already discussed; if only open items are used, respondents may be unwilling to write their answers for one reason or another; questionnaires present problems to people of limited literacy; and an interview can be conducted at an appropriate speed whereas questionnaires are often filled in hurriedly.

One of the problems that has to be considered when open-ended questions are used in the interview is that of developing a satisfactory method of recording replies. One way is to summarise responses in the course of the interview. This has the disadvantage of breaking the continuity of the interview and may result in bias because the interviewer may unconsciously emphasise responses that agree with his expectations and fail to note those that do not. It is sometimes possible to summarise an individual's responses at the end of the interview. Although this preserves the continuity of the interview, it is likely to induce greater bias because the delay may lead to the interviewer forgetting some of the details. It is these forgotten details that are most likely to be the ones that disagree with his own expectations.

Procedures

As a guide for those using the interview as a research technique perhaps for the first time, we outline a possible sequence of stages for such an undertaking.

The preliminary stage of an interview study will be the point where the purpose of the research is decided. It may begin by out-lining the theoretical basis of the study, its broad aims, its practical value and the reasons why the interview approach was chosen. There may then follow the translation of the general goals of the research into more detailed and specific objectives. This is the most important step, for only careful formulation of objectives at this point will eventually produce the right kind of data necessary for satisfactory answers to the research problem.

This stage having been accomplished, there follows the prepara-tion of the interview schedule itself. This involves translating the research objectives into the questions that will make up the main body of the schedule. This needs to be done in such a way that the questions adequately reflect what it is the researcher is trying to find out. It is quite usual to begin this task by writing down the variables to be dealt with in the study. As one commentator[3] says, 'The first step in constructing interview questions is to *specify your variables by name.* Your variables are what you are trying to measure. They tell you where to begin.'

Before the actual interview items are prepared, it is desirable to give some thought to the *question format* and the *response mode.* The choice of *question format*, for instance, depends on a consi-deration of one or more of the following factors: the objectives of the interview; the nature of the subject matter; whether the inter-viewer is dealing in facts, opinions or attitudes; whether specificity or depth is sought; the respondent's level of education; the kind of information he can be expected to have; whether or not his thought needs to be structured; some assessment of his motiva-tional level; the extent of the interviewer's own insight into the respondent's situation; and the kind of relationship the interviewer can expect to develop with the respondent. Having given prior thought to these matters, the researcher is in a position to decide whether to use open and/or closed questions, direct and/or in-direct questions, specific and/or non-specific questions, and so on.

As a general rule, the kind of information sought and the means of its acquisition will determine the choice of *response mode.* Data analysis, then, ought properly to be considered alongside the choice of response mode so that the interviewer can be confident that the data will serve his purposes and analysis of them can be duly prepared. Box 13.2 summarises the relationship between response mode and type of data.

Once the variables to be measured or studied have been identified, questions can be constructed so as to reflect them. If, for example, one of the variables was to be a new social education project that had recently been attempted with 15-year-olds in a comprehensive school, one obvious question would be: *How do you think the project has affected the pupils?* Or, less directly, *Do you think the children have been given too much or too little responsibility?* It is important to bear in mind that more than one question format and more than one response mode may be employed when building up a schedule. The final mixture will depend on the kinds of factors mentioned earlier — the objectives of the research, and so on.

Where an interview schedule is to be used as part of a field survey in which a number of trained interviewers are to be used, it will of course be necessary to include in it appropriate instructions for both interviewer and interviewees.

Setting up and conducting the interview will make up the next stage in the procedure. Where the interviewer is initiating the research himself, he will clearly select his own respondents; where he is engaged by another agent, then he will probably be given a list of people to contact.

Tuckman[3] has succinctly reviewed the procedures to adopt at the interview itself. He writes,

At the meeting, the interviewer should brief the respondent as to the nature or purpose of the interview (being as candid as possible without biasing responses) and attempt to make the respondent feel at ease. He should explain the manner in which he will be recording responses, and if he plans to tape record, he should get the respondent's assent. At all times, an interviewer must remember that he is a data collection instrument and try not to let his own biases, opinions, or curiosity affect his behaviour. It is important that the interviewer should not deviate from his format and interview schedule although many schedules will permit some flexibility in choice of questions. The respondent should be kept from rambling away from the essence of a question, but not at the sacrifice of courtesy.

Once data from the interview have been collected, the next stage involves coding and scoring them. Coding has been defined by Kerlinger[4] as the translation of question responses and respondent information to specific categories for the purpose of analysis.

Box 13.2: The Selection of Response Mode

Response mode	Type of data	Chief advantages	Chief disadvantages
Fill-in	Nominal	Less biasing; greater response flexibility	More difficult to score
Scaled	Interval	Easy to score	Time consuming; can be biasing
Ranking	Ordinal	Easy to score; forces discrimination	Difficult to complete
Checklist or categorical	Nominal (may be interval when totalled)	Easy to score; easy to respond	Provides less data and fewer options

Source: Tuckman.[3]

As we have seen, many questions are precoded, that is, each response can be immediately and directly converted into a score in an objective way. Rating scales and checklists are examples of precoded questions.

Perhaps the biggest problem concerns the coding and scoring of open-ended questions. Two solutions are possible here. Even though a response is open-ended, the interviewer may precode his interview schedule so that while an interviewee is responding freely, the interviewer is assigning the content of his responses, or parts of it, to predetermined coding categories. Classifications of this kind may be developed during pilot studies. Here is an example:

Q.   What is it that you like least about your job?
A.   Mostly the way the place is run — and the long hours; and the prospects aren't too good.

        Coding: colleagues   ....
                  organisation ....X..........
                  the work   ....
                  conditions   ....X...........
                  other   future prospects

Alternatively, data may be postcoded. Having recorded the interviewee's response, either by summarising it during or after the interview itself, or verbatim by tape recorder, the researcher may subject it to content analysis and submit it to one of the available scoring procedures — scaling, scoring, rank scoring, response counting, etc.

Finally, the data are analysed and interpreted in the light of the research objectives.

The Non-directive Interview and the Focused Interview

Originating from psychiatric and therapeutic fields with which it is most readily associated, the *non-directive interview* is characterised by a situation in which the respondent is responsible for initiating and directing the course of the encounter and for the attitudes he expresses in it (in contrast to the *structured* or *research interview* we have already considered, where the dominating role assumed by the interviewer results in, to use Kitwood's phrase, an asymmetry of commitment). It has been shown to be a particularly valuable technique because it gets at the deeper attitudes and perceptions of the person being interviewed in such a way as to leave them free from interviewer bias. We shall examine briefly the characteristics of the therapeutic interview and then consider its usefulness as a research tool in the social and educational sciences.

The non-directive interview as it is currently understood grew out of the pioneering work of Freud and subsequent modifications to his approach by later analysts. His basic discovery was that if one can arrange a special set of conditions and have his patient talk about his difficulties in a certain way, behaviour changes of many kinds can be accomplished.[11] The technique developed was used to elicit highly personal data from patients in such a way as to increase their self-awareness and improve their skills in self-analysis. By these means they became better able to help themselves. As Madge[12] observes, it is these techniques which have greatly influenced contemporary interviewing techniques, especially those of a more penetrating and less quantitative kind.

The present-day therapeutic interview has its most persuasive advocate in Carl Rogers who has on different occasions testified to its efficacy. Basing his analysis on his own clinical studies, he has identified a sequence of characteristic stages in the therapeutic process, beginning with the client's decision to seek help.[13] He is met by a counsellor who is friendly and receptive, but not didactic.

The next stage is signalled when the client begins to give vent to hostile, critical and destructive feelings, which the counsellor accepts, recognises and clarifies. Subsequently, and *invariably*, these antagonistic impulses are used up and give way to the first expressions of positive feeling. The counsellor likewise accepts these until suddenly and spontaneously 'insight and self-understanding come bubbling through'. With insight comes the realisation of possible courses of action and also the power to make decisions. It is in translating these into practical terms that the client frees himself from dependence on the counsellor.

Rogers[14] subsequently identified a number of qualities in the interviewer which he deemed essential: that he bases his work on attitudes of acceptance and permissiveness; that he respects the client's responsibility for his own situation; that he permits the client to explain his problem in his own way; and that he does nothing that would in any way arouse the client's defences.

Such then are the principal characteristics of the non-directive interview technique in a therapeutic setting. But what of its usefulness as a purely *research* technique in societal and educational contexts? There are a number of features of the therapeutic interview which are peculiar to it and may well be inappropriate in other settings: for example, as we have seen, the interview is initiated by the respondent; his motivation is to obtain relief from a particular symptom; the interviewer is primarily a source of help, not a procurer of information; the actual interview is part of the therapeutic experience; the purpose of the interview is to change the behaviour and inner life of the person and its success is defined in these terms; and there is no restriction on the topics discussed.

A researcher has a different order of priorities, however, and what appear as advantages in a therapeutic context may be decided limitations when the technique is used for research purposes, even though he may be sympathetic to the spirit of the non-directive interview. As Madge explains, increasingly there are those 'who wish to retain the good qualities of the non-directive technique and at the same time are keen to evolve a method that is economical and precise enough to leave a residue of results rather than merely a posse of cured souls'.

One attempt to meet this need is to be found in a programme reported by Merton and Kendall[6] in which the *focused interview* was developed. While seeking to follow closely the principle of non-direction, the method did introduce rather more interviewer control in the kinds of questions used and sought also to limit the discussion to certain parts of the respondent's experience.

The focused interview differs from other types of research interview in certain respects. These have been identified by the authors as follows:

1. The persons interviewed are known to have been involved in a *particular situation*: they may, for example, have watched a TV programme; or seen a film; or read a book or article; or have been a participant in a social situation.

2. By means of the techniques of content analysis, elements in the situation which the researcher deems significant have previously been analysed by him. He has thus arrived at a set of hypotheses relating to the meaning and effects of the specified elements.

3. Using his analysis as a basis, the investigator constructs an *interview guide.* This identifies the major areas of enquiry and the hypotheses which determine the relevant data to be obtained in the interview.

4. The actual interview is focused on the *subjective experiences* of the persons who have been exposed to the situation. Their responses enable the researcher: (a) to test the validity of his hypotheses; and (b) to ascertain unanticipated responses to the situation, thus giving rise to further hypotheses.

From this it can be seen that the distinctive feature of the focused interview is *the prior analysis by the researcher of the situation in which subjects have been involved.*

The advantages of this procedure have been cogently explained by Merton and Kendall:[6]

Fore-knowledge of the situation obviously reduces the task confronting the investigator, since the interview need not be devoted to discovering the objective nature of the situation. Equipped in advance with a content analysis, the interviewer can readily distinguish the objective facts of the case from the subjective definitions of the situation. He thus becomes alert to the entire field of 'selective response'. When the interviewer, through his familiarity with the objective situation, is able to recognize symbolic or functional silences, 'distortions', avoidances, or blockings, he is the more prepared to explore their implications.

In the quest for what the authors term 'significant data', the interviewer must develop the ability to evaluate continuously the interview while it is in progress. To this end, they established a set of criteria by which productive and unproductive interview material can be distinguished. Briefly, these are: (1) *non-direction*: interviewer guidance should be minimal; (2) *specificity*: respondents' definitions of the situation should find full and specific expression; (3) *range*: the interview should maximise the range of evocative stimuli and responses reported by the subject; and (4) *depth and personal context*: the interview should bring out the effective and value-laden implications of the subjects' responses, to determine whether the experience had central or peripheral significance. It should elicit the relevant personal context, the idiosyncratic associations, beliefs and ideas.

We conclude this section with part of a transcript from the Newsons' longitudinal study of child-rearing practices.[15] It illustrates the skills involved in focused interviewing; notice particularly the subtle ways in which the interviewer (I) is able to get beneath the rather conventional initial response of the mother (M) to Question 147.

Extract from a Focused Interview

Notes		Transcript
	147	Is there any special interest which you and Oliver share — something that the two of you follow together — would you say?
nothing yet	M	Mmmm ... I don't *think* so.
	148	Is there anything which he and his Daddy are both specially interested in?
may be pause to think — but definite negative	M	(pause) ... *No*.
	149	No special thing ... would you say he's closer now to you or to his Daddy?
	M	He ... is ... closer ....?
deliberately defuses by addition	149	Would you say Oliver is closer to you, or to his Daddy? ... or is it about equal?
	M	About equal ... might be a shade towards me.
	150	Does your husband like doing things with him?

Extract from a Focused Interview (continued)

ALERT quiet, but words quick and definite	M	(sigh) ... Mmmm ... not really — no.
WAIT — nothing comes — probe probe is a challenge, retreat expected	I	(pause) .... How do you mean?
M retreats	M	Well — I suppose he *does* like doing things with him, but opportunity doesn't often present itself.
I accepts retreat	I	I see — yes ... yes ...
	M	He's ... he's ... well, he's home tonight, but some nights he's not home till 7 or 8, so he just sees them go to bed, really, and get up in the morning.
accepts, but probes from another angle, forcing issue	I	... yes, ... and does he give Oliver a lot of attention when he *is* there — would you say, um, about average, or more or less than most fathers?
M enabled to advance again voice rises	M	Well, I sometimes think he could give *more* ... um ... he could perhaps take them *off* more — the boys — and *play* with them more; if the boys play games, they play games with me! (... yes ...) — this is what I *find*, you know? (I see yes ... yes ...) 'Cause he's always ... *out*, or *busy*, (... yes ...) or doing something (... yes ...)
semi-retreat		I suppose it's circumstances not deliberate ...
I accepts retreat	I	You're, sort of, more available ...
M advances	M	Yes ... yes. If we go to the cricket match — *he's playing* cricket — *I* play with the boys!
unbiased re-statement (giving time)	I	(laughter in which M joins) ... And the boys sort of *feel* really that you're more available — that, er, you're the person they play with, I suppose?
M advances, voice rising	M	Yes! Now Oliver asks *me* to take him swimming — he doesn't ask his Daddy!

(Interview continues, but this is now recognised as a sensitive area and may be returned to if opportunity arises.)

Source: adapted from Shipman.[15]

Conclusion: Examples of the Use of Interviewing in Research

Many examples of interview studies and the use of interview techniques are to be found throughout the literature of social and educational research, the range varying from the comprehensiveness

Box 13.3: Reasons for Subject Choice

Linda:	I didn't want to do commerce.
Int:	Why have you chosen it then?
Linda:	Because my mother said so.
Int:	Why did she say that?
Linda:	Because she wants me to work in an office.
Int:	And what do you want to do?
Linda:	Be a hairdresser.
Int:	If it were left to you what to do, what would you have chosen?
Linda:	I haven't thought about it.
Int:	Will you be allowed to do commerce, do you think?
Linda:	I hope I'm knocked out.
Int:	What form will you go in?
Linda:	I'd go in 4L straight away.

Source: adapted from Woods.[16]

Box 13.4: Sample Questions Used in an Ethnographic Study in an Australian State High School

1.	If you don't understand Mr ... (teacher) what do you do?
2.	When lessons get boring what do you do?
3.	When people start to muck around what do you do?
4.	Have you ever informed on any one for any reason?
5.	How do you feel about others informing on people?
6.	In what ways have you helped teachers?
	How did other pupils feel about it?
7.	What pupils often help teachers?
	How do they help them?
8.	Do you talk to teachers after class?
	What do you talk to them about?

Source: adapted from MacPherson.[17]

and sophistication of national polls at one extreme to small-scale investigations into educational issues at the other. We conclude this chapter with brief references to two educational studies. We choose them for their dependence on interview techniques and also their accessibility.

In his ethnographic study of a secondary school, Woods[16] uses interview techniques as part of his overall strategy of participant observation to describe and analyse the principal areas of experience and methods of adapting to school life for both pupils and teachers. Numerous extracts of interview material are given throughout the text. One such example is given in Box 13.3.

Another ethnographic study, this time by MacPherson[17] working in an Australian school, directs its attention on pupils' accounts of relations and activities with classmates. The principal method of research was interviews with pupils, details of which are provided by the researcher in the appendix. We give a sample of his questions in Box 13.4.

References

1. Cannell, C.F. and Kahn, R.L., 'Interviewing', in G. Lindzey and E. Aronson (eds), *The Handbook of Social Psychology*, vol. 2, *Research Methods* (Addison-Wesley, New York, 1968).
2. Borg. W.R., *Educational Research: An Introduction* (Longman, London, 1963).
3. Tuckman, B.W., *Conducting Educational Research* (Harcourt Brace Jovanovich, New York, 1972).
4. Kerlinger, F.N., *Foundations of Behavioural Research* (Holt, Rinehart and Winston, New York, 1970).
5. Moser, C.A. and Kalton, G., *Survey Methods in Social Investigation* (Heinemann Educational Books, London, 1977. For a recent account of the use of questioning in interviews and surveys see: Hargie, O., Saunders, C. and Dickson, D., *Social Skills in Interpersonal Communication* (Croom Helm, London, 1981).
6. Merton, R.K. and Kendall, P.L., 'The focused interview', *Amer J. Sociol,* 51 (1946) 541–57.
7. Kitwood, T.M. 'Values in adolescent life: towards a critical description', unpublished PhD dissertation, School of Research in Education (University of Bradford, 1977).
8. Cicourel, A.V., *Method and Measurement in Sociology* (The Free Press, New York, 1964).
9. Sears, R., Maccoby, E. and Levin, H., *Patterns of Child Rearing* (Harper and Row, New York, 1957).
10. Lansing, J.B., Ginsberg, G.P. and Braaten, K., *An Investigation of Response Error* (Bureau of Economic and Business Research, University of Illinois, 1961). Reported in Cannell and Kahn.[1]
11. Ford, D.H. and Urban, H.B., *Systems of Psychotherapy: a Comparative Study* (John Wiley and Sons, New York, 1963).
12. Madge, J., *The Tools of Social Science* (Longman, London, 1965).
13. Rogers, C.R., *Counselling and Psychotherapy* (Houghton Mifflin, Boston, 1942).
14. Rogers, C.R., 'The non-directive method as a technique for social research', *Amer. J. Sociol.,* 50 (1945) 279–83.
15. Newson, J. and Newson, E., 'Parental roles and social contexts', in M.D. Shipman (ed.), *The Organization and Impact of Social Research* (Routledge and Kegan Paul, London, 1976) 22–48.
16. Woods, P., *The Divided School* (Routledge and Kegan Paul, London, 1979).
17. MacPherson, J., *The Feral Classroom* (Routledge and Kegan Paul, Melbourne, 1983).

14 PERSONAL CONSTRUCTS

Introduction

One of the most interesting theories of personality to have emerged this century and one that has had an increasing impact on educational research is *personal construct theory*. Personal constructs are the basic units of analysis in a complete and formally stated theory of personality proposed by George Kelly in a book entitled *The Psychology of Personal Constructs* (1955). Because Kelly's own experiences were so intimately related to the development of his imaginative theory, we begin with some observations on Kelly, the man.

Kelly began his career as a school psychologist dealing with problem children referred to him by teachers. As his experiences widened, instead of merely corroborating a teacher's complaint about a pupil, Kelly tried to understand the complaint in the way the teacher construed it. This change of perspective constituted a significant reformulation of the problem. In practical terms, it resulted in an analysis of the teacher making the complaint as well as the problem pupil. By viewing the problem from a wider perspective Kelly was able to envisage a wider range of solutions.

The insights George Kelly gained from his clinical work led him to the view that there is no objective, absolute truth and that events are only meaningful in relation to the ways that are construed by the individual. Kelly's primary focus is upon the way an individual perceives his environment, the way he interprets what he perceives in terms of his existing mental structure, and the way in which, as a consequence, he behaves towards it. In *The Psychology of Personal Constructs*, Kelly proposes a view of man actively engaged in making sense of and extending his experience of the world. Personal constructs are the dimensions that man uses to conceptualise aspects of his day-to-day world. The constructs that man creates are used by him to forecast events and rehearse situations before their actual occurrence. Man, according to Kelly, takes on the role of scientist seeking to predict and control the course of events in which he is caught up. For Kelly,[1] the ultimate explanation of human behaviour 'lies in scanning man's undertakings, the questions he asks, the lines of inquiry he initiates and the strategies he employs ...' Kelly's ideas have a good deal in common with current educational thought and practice. Education, in Kelly's view, is necessarily experimental. Its ultimate goal is individual fulfilment and the maximising of individual potential. In emphasising the need of each individual to question and explore, construct theory implies a view of education that capitalises upon the child's natural motivation to engage in spontaneous learning activities. It follows that the teacher's task is to facilitate the child's ongoing exploration of the world rather than impose adult perspectives upon him. Kelly's ideas have much in common with those to be found in Rousseau's *Emile*.

The central tenets of Kelly's theory are set out in terms of a fundamental postulate and a number of corollaries. It is not proposed here to undertake a detailed discussion of Kelly's theoretical propositions. Good commentaries are available in Bannister[2] and Ryle.[3] Instead, we look at the method suggested by Kelly of eliciting constructs and assessing the mathematical relationships between them, that is, repertory grid technique.

Characteristics of the Method

Kelly proposes that each person has access to a limited number of *constructs* by means of which he evaluates the phenomena that constitute his world. These phenomena — people, events, objects, ideas, institutions and so on — are known as *elements*. He further suggests that the constructs that each of us employ may be thought of as bipolar, that is, capable of being defined in terms of polar adjectives (good — bad) or polar phrases (makes me feel happy — makes me feel sad).

A number of different forms of repertory grid technique have been developed since Kelly's first formulation. All have the two essential characteristics in common that we have already identified, that is, *constructs* — the dimensions used by a person in conceptualising aspects of his world; and *elements* — the stimulus objects that the person evaluates in terms of the constructs he employs. In Box 14.1, we illustrate the empirical technique suggested by Kelly for eliciting constructs and identifying their relationship with elements in the form of a repertory grid.

Since Kelly's original account of what he called 'The Role

Construct Repertory Grid Test', several variations of repertory grid have been developed and used in different areas of research. It is the flexibility and adaptability of repertory grid technique that has made it such an attractive tool to researchers in psychiatric, counselling, and more recently, educational settings. We now review a number of developments in the form and the use of the technique.

'Elicited' versus 'Provided' Constructs

A central assumption of this 'standard' form of repertory grid is that it enables the researcher to elicit constructs that subjects customarily use in interpreting and predicting the behaviour of

Box 14.1: Eliciting Constructs and Constructing a Repertory Grid

A person is asked to name a number of people who are significant to him. These might be, for example, mother, father, wife, friend, employer, priest. These constitute the *elements* in the repertory grid.

The subject is then asked to arrange the elements into groups of threes in such a manner that two are similar in some way but at the same time different from the third. The ways in which the elements may be alike or different are the *constructs*, generally expressed in bi-polar form (quiet — talkative; mean — generous; warm — cold). The way in which two of the elements are similar is called the *similarity pole* of the construct; and the way in which two of the elements are different from the third, the *contrast pole* of the construct.

A grid can now be constructed by asking the subject to place each element at either the *similarity* or the *contrast* pole of each construct. Let x = one pole of the construct, and blank = the other. The result can be set out as follows:

CONSTRUCTS   *ELEMENTS*

	A	B	C	D	E	F
1. quiet — talkative	x	x	x			x
2. mean — generous	x			x	x	
3. warm — cold		x			x	

It is now possible to derive different kinds of information from the grid. By studying each *row*, for example, we can get some idea of how a person defines each construct in terms of significant people in his life. From each *column*, we have a personality profile of each of the significant people in terms of the constructs selected by the subjects. More sophisticated treatments of grid data are discussed in examples presented in the text.

Source: adapted from Kelly.[1]

those people who are important in their lives. Kelly's method of eliciting personal constructs required the subject to complete a number of cards, 'each showing the name of a person in [his] life'. Similarly, in identifying elements, the subject was asked, 'Is there an important way in which two of [the elements] — any two — differ from the third?' This insistence upon important persons and important ways that they are alike or differ, where both constructs and elements are nominated by the subjects themselves, is central to Personal Construct Theory. Kelly gives it precise expression in his Individuality Corollary — 'Persons differ from each other in their construction of events.'

Several forms of repertory grid technique now in common use represent a significant departure from Kelly's individuality corollary in that they *provide* constructs to subjects rather than *elicit* constructs from them.

One justification for the use of provided constructs is implicit in Ryle's[3] commentary on the individuality corollary: 'Kelly paid rather little attention to developmental and social processes', Ryle observes, '... his own concern was with the personal and not the social.' Ryle believes that the individuality corollary would be strengthened by the additional statement that 'persons *resemble* each other in their construction of events'.

Can the practice of providing constructs to subjects be reconciled with the individuality corollary assumptions? A review[4] of a substantial body of research suggests a qualified 'yes' (but see Fransella and Bannister[8] on elicited versus supplied constructs as a 'grid-generated' problem).

[While] it seems clear in the light of research that individuals prefer to use their own elicited constructs rather than provided dimensions to describe themselves and others ... the results of several studies suggest that normal subjects, at least, exhibit approximately the same degree of differentiation in using carefully selected supplied lists of adjectives as when they employ their own elicited personal constructs.

Bannister and Mair[5] support the use of supplied constructs in experiments where hypotheses have been formulated and in those involving group comparisons. The use of elicited constructs alongside supplied ones can serve as a useful check on the meaningfulness of those that are provided, substantially lower intercorrelations between elicited and supplied constructs suggesting, perhaps, the lack of relevance of those provided by the researcher. The danger with supplied constructs, Bannister and Mair argue, is that the researcher may assume that the polar adjectives or phrases he provides are the verbal equivalents of the psychological dimensions in which he is interested.

Allotting Elements to Constructs

When a subject is allowed to classify as many or as few elements at the similarity or the contrast pole, the result is often a very lopsided construct with consequent dangers of distortion in the estimation of construct relationships. Bannister[5] suggests two methods for dealing with this problem which we illustrate in Box 14.2. The first, the *split-half form*, requires the subject to place half the elements at the similarity pole of each construct by instructing him to decide which element *most markedly* shows the characteristics specified by each of the constructs. Those elements that are left are allocated to the contrast pole. As Bannister observes, this technique may result in the discarding of constructs (for example, male — female) which cannot be summarily allocated. A second method, the *rank order form*, as its name suggests requires the subject to rank the elements from the one which most markedly exhibits the particular characteristic (shown by the similarity pole description) to the one which least exhibits it. As the second example in Box 14.2 shows, a rank order correlation coefficient can be used to estimate the extent to which there is similarity in the allotment of elements on any two constructs. Following Bannister, a construct *relationship* score can be calculated by squaring the correlation coefficient and multiplying by 100. (Because correlations are not linearly related they cannot be used as scores.) The construct relationship score gives an estimate of the percentage variance that the two constructs share in common in terms of the rankings on the two grids.

A third method of allotting elements is the *rating form*. Here, the subject is required to judge each element on a 7-point or a 5-point scale, for example, absolutely beautiful (7) to absolutely ugly (1). Commenting on the advantages of the rating form, Bannister[5] notes that it offers the subject greater latitude in distinguishing between elements than that provided for in the original form

Box 14.2: Allotting Elements to Constructs: Three Methods

Example 1: Split-half form

Elements

1	2	3	4	5	6	7	8	9	10
x		x	x		x		x		
	x	x		x		x			x
		x	x		x			x	x

Constructs

1. fast–slow
2. late–early
3. dangerous–safe

Since the subject is forced to allocate half of the elements to one pole, the chance expectancy of matchings occurring on 10 elements when two constructs are compared is 5. Deviation scores can be computed from chance level. Thus 5 matchings = 0; in constructs 1 and 2, matchings = −3; in constructs 1 and 3, matchings = +1; and in constructs 2 and 3, matchings = −1. The probability of particular matching scores being obtained can be had by reference to statistical tables.

Example 2: Rank-order form

Elements

1	2	3	4	5	6	7	8	9	10
10	1	2	5	8	7	3	4	9	6
9	4	10	1	6	8	5	2	3	7
7	9	5	6	10	2	1	4	8	3

Constructs

1. fast–slow
2. late–early
3. dangerous–safe

Spearman's rho (r_s)

Constructs 1 and 2 = .15
Constructs 1 and 3 = .24
Constructs 2 and 3 = −.16

Relationship scores

$(0.15)^2 \times 100 = +23$
$(0.24)^2 \times 100 = +58$
$(-0.16)^2 \times 100 = -26$

Example 3: Rating form

Elements

1	2	3	4	5	6	7	8	9	10
4	4	2	1	4	3	5	1	5	2
1	1	3	5	1	3	2	2	5	5
5	1	3	2	2	1	4	5	1	2

Constructs

1. fast
2. late
3. dangerous

A 5-point rating scale is shown in which, in this example, single poles of the constructs are rated as follows:

Not at all like		Average		Very much like
1	2	3	4	5

Bannister and Mair[5] suggest several methods for calculating relationships between constructs from the rating form (pp. 63–5). For a detailed discussion of measures of construct relationships, see Fransella and Bannister[8] (pp. 60–72).

Source: adapted from Bannister and Mair.[5]

proposed by Kelly. At the same time the degree of differentiation asked of the subject may not be as great as that demanded in the ranking method. As with the rank order method, the rating form approach also allows the use of most correlation techniques. The rating form is the third example we illustrate in Box 14.2.

Laddering

The technique known as laddering arises out of Hinkle's[6] important revision of the theory of personal constructs and the method employed in his research. Hinkle's concern was for the location of any construct within an individual's construct system, arguing that a construct has differential *implications* within a given hierarchical context. He went on to develop an Implication Grid or Impgrid in which the subject is required to compare each of his constructs with every other to see which implies the other. The question *why?* is asked over and over again to identify the position of any construct in an individual's hierarchical construct system. In Box 14.3, we illustrate Hinkle's laddering technique with an example from educational research reported by Fransella.[7]

Grid Administration and Analysis

The example of grid administration and analysis outlined below employs the split-half method of allocating elements to constructs and a form of *anchor analysis* devised by Bannister. We assume that 16 elements and 15 constructs have already been elicited by means of a technique such as the one illustrated in Box 14.1.

Procedures in Grid Administration

Draw up a grid measuring 16 (elements) by 15 (constructs) as in Figure 14.1 below, writing along the top the names of the elements, but first inserting the additional element, *self.* Alongside the rows write in the construct poles.

You now have a grid in which each intersection or cell is defined by a particular column (element) and a particular row (construct). The administration takes the form of allocating every

Box 14.3: Laddering

Constructs	Elements teachers							
	A	B	C	D	E	F	G	H
masculine	2	1	5	4	3	6	8	7
serious	6	2	1	3	8	4	5	7
good teacher								
authoritarian								
sexy								
old								
gets on with others								
lonely								
like me in character								
like I hope to become								

A matrix of rankings for a repertory grid with teachers as elements

You may decide to stop when you have elicited seven or eight constructs from the teacher elements. But you could go on to 'ladder' two or three of them. This process of laddering is in effect asking yourself (or someone else) to abstract from one conceptual level to another. You could ladder from *man–woman*, but it might be easier to start off with *serious–light-hearted*. Ask yourself which you would prefer to be — *serious or light-hearted*. You might reply *light-hearted*. Now pose the question 'why'. Why would you rather be a *light-hearted* person than a *serious* person? Perhaps the answer would be that *light-hearted* people *get on better with others* than do *serious* people. Ask yourself 'why' again. Why do you want to be the sort of person who gets on better with others? Perhaps it transpires that you think that people who do not get on well with others are *lonely*. In this way you elicit more constructs but ones that stand on the shoulders of those previously elicited. Whatever constructs you have obtained can be put into the grid.

Source: adapted from Fransella.[7]

element on every construct. If, for example, your first construct is 'kind–cruel', allocate each element in turn on that dimension, putting a cross in the appropriate box if you consider that person (element) kind, or leaving it blank if you consider that person cruel. Make sure that half of the elements are designated kind and half cruel.

Proceed in this way for each construct in turn, *always* placing a *cross* where the construct pole to the *left* of the grid applies, and leaving it blank if the construct pole to the *right* is applicable.

Every element must be allocated in this way, and *half* of the elements must always be allocated to the left-hand pole.

Procedures in Grid Analysis

The grid may be regarded as a reflection of conceptual structure in which constructs are linked by virtue of their being applied to the same persons (elements). This linkage is measured by a process of matching construct rows.

To estimate the linkage between constructs 1 and 2 in Figure 14.1, for example, count the number of matches between corresponding boxes in each row. A match is counted where the same element has been designated with a cross (*or* a blank) on both constructs. So, for constructs 1 and 2 in Figure 14.1, we count 6 such matches. By chance we would expect 8 (out of 16) matches, and we may subtract this from the observed value to arrive at an estimate of such deviation from chance.

Constructs	Match	Difference score
1–2	6	$6 - 8 = -2$

By matching construct 1 against all remaining constructs (3 ... 15), we get a score for each comparison. Beginning then with construct 2, and comparing this with every other construct (3 ... 15), and so on, every construct on the grid is matched with every other one and a difference score for each obtained. This is recorded in matrix form, with the reflected half of the table also filled in (see difference score for constructs 1–2 in Figure 14.2). The *sign* of the difference score is retained. It indicates the direction of the linkage. A positive sign shows that the constructs are positively associated, a negative sign that they are negatively associated.

Now add up (without noting sign) the sum of the difference scores for each column (construct) in the matrix. The construct with the largest difference score is the one which, statistically, accounts for the greatest amount of variance in the grid. Note this down. Now look in the body of the matrix for that construct which has the largest non-significant association with the one which you have just noted (in the case of a 16-element grid as in Figure 14.1,

Figure 14.1: Elements

Construct	Self 1	2	3	4	5	6	7	8	9	10	11	12	13	14	15	Construct
KIND	x	x		x		x	x			x	x	x			x	CRUEL
CONFIDENT	x		x			x			x		x		x			UNSURE

Figure 14.2: Difference Score for Constructs

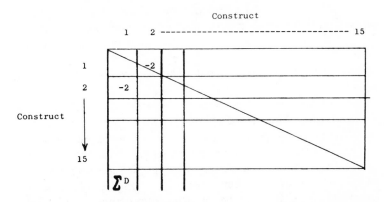

this will be a difference score of ±3 or less). This second construct can be regarded as a dimension which is orthogonal to the first, and together they may form the axes for mapping the person's psychological space.

If we imagine the construct with the highest difference score to be 'kind–cruel' and the highest non-significant associated

Figure 14.3: Grid Matrix

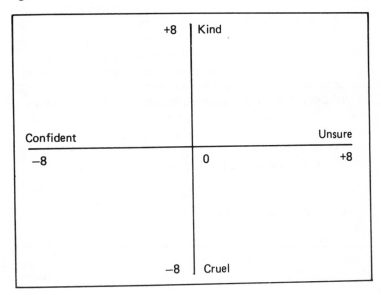

construct to be 'confident–unsure', then every other construct in the grid may be plotted with reference to these two axes. The co-ordinates for the map are provided by the difference scores relating to the matching of each construct with the two used to form the axes of the graph. In this way a pictorial representation of the individual's *personal construct space* can be obtained, and inferences made from the spatial relationships between plotted constructs.

By rotating the original grid 90° and carrying out the same matching procedure on the columns (figures), a similar map may be obtained for the people (figures) included in the grid.

Grid matrices can be subjected to analyses of varying degrees of complexity. We have illustrated one of the simplest ways of calculating relationships between constructs in Figure 14.2. For the statistically minded researcher, a variety of programs exist in GAP, the Grid Analysis Package developed by Slater and described by Chetwynd.[9] GAP programs analyse the single grid, pairs of grids and grids in groups. Grids may be aligned either by construct, by element or both. A fuller discussion of metric factor analysis is given in Fransella and Bannister[8] (pp. 73-81), and Pope and Keen[28] (pp. 77-91).

Non-metric methods of grid analysis make no assumptions about the linearity of relationships between the variables and the factors. Moreover, where the researcher is primarily interested in the relationships between elements, multidimensional scaling may prove a more useful approach to the data than principal components analysis (see the educational example on p. 330).

The choice of one method rather than another must ultimately rest both upon what is statistically correct and what is psychologically desirable. The danger in the use of advanced computer programs, as Fransella and Bannister point out, is being caught up in the numbers game. Their plea is that grid users should have at least an intuitive grasp of the processes being so competently executed by their computers!

Strengths of Repertory Grid Technique

It is in the application of interpretive perspectives in classroom research, where the investigator seeks to understand the meaning of events to those participating, that repertory grid technique offers exciting possibilities. It is particularly able to provide the researcher with an abundance and a richness of interpretable material. Repertory grid technique is, of course, especially suitable for the exploration of relationships between an individual's personal constructs. It is equally adaptable to the problem of identifying changes in individuals that occur as a result of some educational experience as the studies of Ryle and Breen[10] and Lifshitz[11] show in the case of social work students undergoing professional training. In modified formats (the *dyad,*, and the *double dyad*) repertory grid has employed *relationships between people* as elements rather than people themselves and demonstrated the increased sensitivity of this type of grid in identifying problems of adjustment between married partners (Ryle and Breen[12]) and the concerns of students attending psychiatric clinics (Ryle and Lunghi[13]). Finally, repertory grid technique can be employed in studying the changing nature of construing and the patterning of relationships between constructs in groups of children from relatively young ages as the work of Salmon[14] and Applebee[15] has shown.

Difficulties in the Use of Repertory Grid Technique

Fransella and Bannister[8] point to a number of difficulties in the development and use of grid technique, the most important of which is, perhaps, the widening gulf between technical advances in grid forms and analyses and the theoretical basis from which these are derived. There is, it seems, a rapidly expanding grid industry. Small wonder, then, as Fransella and Bannister wryly observe, that studies such as a one-off analysis of the attitudes of a group of people to asparagus, which bear little or no relation to personal construct theory, are on the increase.

A second difficulty relates to the question of bi-polarity in those forms of the grid in which customarily only one pole of the construct is used. Researchers may make unwarranted inferences about constructs' polar opposites. Yorke's illustration of the possibility of the researcher obtaining 'bent' constructs suggests the usefulness of the *opposite method* (Epting *et al.*[16]) in ensuring the bi-polarity of elicited constructs.

A third caution is urged with respect to the elicitation and laddering of constructs. Laddering, note Fransella and Bannister, is an art, not a science. Great care must be taken not to *impose* constructs. Above all, the researcher must learn to *listen* to his subject(s).

A number of practical problems commonly experienced in rating grids are identified by Yorke.[17] these are:

1. Variable perception of elements of low personal relevance;
2. Varying the context in which the elements are perceived during the administration of the grid;
3. Halo effect intruding into the ratings where the subject sees the grid matrix building up;
4. Accidental reversal of the rating scale (mentally switching from 5 = high to 1 = high, perhaps because 'five points' and 'first' are both ways of describing high quality). This can happen both within and between constructs, and is particularly likely where a negative or implicity negative property is ascribed to the *pair* during triadic elicitation.
5. Failure to follow the rules of the rating procedure. For example, where the pair has had to be rated at the high end of a five-point scale triads have been found *in a single grid* rated as 5, 4, 4; 1, 1, 2; 1, 2, 4 which must call into question the constructs and their relationship with the elements.

Finally, growing sophistication in computer-based analyses of repertory grid forms leads inevitably to a growing language of concepts by which to describe the complexity of what can be found within matrices. It would be ironic, would it not, ask Fransella and Bannister, if repertory grid technique were to become absorbed into the traditions of psychological testing and employed in terms of the assumptions which underpin such testing. From measures to traits is but a short step, they warn.

Some Examples of the Use of Repertory Grid in Educational Research

What attributes of pupil achievement do teachers *actually* assess as opposed to those they are *supposed* to assess? This intriguing question formed the basis of a repertory grid study by Wood and Napthali.[18] Twelve bi-polar constructs were elicited from each of

16 secondary school teachers in a London comprehensive school. The eight constructs which constituted the core of each teacher's judgemental repertoire were identified by requiring teachers to rank order their twelve constructs according to the criterion, 'If you were taking over a new class, which pieces of information about pupils contained in these constructs would you find the most useful?' Factor analysis of 23 correlation matrices showed that the highest correlations were between cognitive constructs. The thrust of Wood and Napthali's analysis was to discover whether some common framework existed that underpinned the construing of all 16 teachers with respect to pupil achievement. By further classifying the factors identified in the teachers' grids the researchers showed that on over 90 per cent of the occasions on which cognitive constructs were used to rate pupils a factor loading of $\geqslant 0.7$ was achieved. From the results of the study, it seems that teachers differentiated between pupils on the basis of all or some of the following derived constructs: (a) the overall ability of the pupil; (b) the ability of the pupil in the particular subject; (c) the involvement of the pupil in the learning situation; (d) the interest displayed by the pupil in the subject; (e) the quality and the tidiness of the work presented; and (f) the behaviour of the pupil.

The Wood and Napthali study was only concerned with teachers of mathematics and geography. It remains to be seen whether their results would hold across a wider range of subject specialisms. What other variables condition teachers' construing (do less experienced teachers use constructs such as *behaviour, discipline, quietness* more often than their experienced colleagues?) is yet to be systematically researched.

Another study of secondary school teachers used their construing of particular pupils as a means of understanding the differential treatment accorded to individual children by the teachers in the course of their day-to-day classroom work. Nash[19] used repertory grid to elicit a number of constructs commonly held by three secondary school teachers about a pupil called Alec. All agreed that Alec was *very bright, very lively, sociable* and *given to misbehave when bored.* Nash observed 36 lessons and made extensive field notes on the frequency and the quality of the interaction between Alec and his teachers. He was able to demonstrate a close association between the teachers' construing of Alec as a pupil, their behaviour towards him, and his behaviour towards them. Nash's summary is insightful:

The point about Alec is that his sheer ability and obvious enthusiasm when his interest was sparked were sufficient to weight his teachers' perceptions heavily in his favour. They are not unaware of his tendency to disrupt things when he feels bored but there are signs that they don't blame him for it. My assessment of Alec's situation suggests that he knows that he is bright, knows that his teachers know he is bright. We can assume that his teachers have a parallel degree of knowledge and meta-knowledge. Alec's awareness of his teachers' knowledge and meta-knowledge enables him to negotiate successfully with them the behavioural concomitants of his identity as 'bright'. For example, when he asks his science teacher if he can write up the account of an experiment the class have just performed in his own words, rather than copy from the board, it is certain that he knows that the teacher will allow him to do this. And she does. But it is clear from her reply that she is making an exception for Alec. 'Most people', she says, 'had better stick pretty closely to what's on the board.' Alec is here transacting with the teacher an important aspect of his self-identity. The teacher implicitly recognizes his own evaluation of himself as 'bright'. In a similar way, Alec manages to transact with most of his teachers licence to pursue his own activities (often potentially disruptive) when he has finished his work.

A study by Ravenette[20] illustrates the ease with which techniques of linkage analysis[21] can be applied to grid data. Box 14.4 shows the constructs elicited from the pupil, the strength of the relationships between the constructs, and their groupings into two distinct clusters.

By contrast, Duckworth and Entwistle[22] developed a repertory grid to explore the attitudes of some 600 grammar school pupils towards their school subjects. Identifying appropriate constructs was ensured by preliminary interviews with pupils and by screening elicited constructs in a pilot grid with about 120 boys and girls. In the final form of the grid, the elements listed were school subjects. Analysis of responses involved computing matching scores for elements on each construct in the manner we have illustrated on p. 323. Each construct was summed over the various elements to produce matrices of matching scores for each pupil. Summary matrices were then constructed for each subsample of pupils. From these summary matrices Kappa (K) coefficients were calculated for

Box 14.4: Hierarchical Linkage Analysis Applied to Grid Data

CORRELATION MATRIX TO SHOW CONSTRUCT RELATIONSHIPS

Constructs Most likely that/least likely that		1	2	3	4	5	6	7	8
1. You would be pleased with yourself	1.								
2. Teachers would think that you are different from other children in class	2.	0.95							
3. Other children would be pleased with you	3.	0.90	0.90						
4. Parents would think you are different from other children in the class	4.	0.60	0.64	0.55					
5. Parents would be pleased with you	5.	0.31	0.33	0.38	0.48				
6. Other children would think you were different from them	6.	0.60	0.57	0.62	0.93	0.62			
7. Teachers would be pleased with you	7.	0.90	0.88	0.93	0.64	0.64	0.74		
8. You would feel different from other children in the class	8.	0.31	0.26	0.31	0.79	0.76	0.90	0.55	

Hierarchical linkage analysis for constructs.

Source: adapted from Ravenette.[20]

the total sample. K is interpreted as the proportion of agreement over and above that expected by chance and is given by the formula:

$$K = \frac{\text{Proportion of observed agreements} - \text{proportion of expected agreements}}{1 - \text{proportion of expected agreements}}$$

Duckworth and Entwistle went on to factor analyse their matrices of K coefficients to identify the structuring of pupils' construing about school subjects. Their report of the rank ordering of school subjects by sex, interest, degree of difficulty and perceived freedom and social benefit offers useful insights into the reasons behind subject choice in the sixth form.

Recent Applications of Repertory Grid to Teaching and Learning

The 'Perception of Trouble in School' Technique

Harré and Rosser's[23] account of ethogenically-oriented research into the rules governing disorderly behaviour among secondary school leavers parallels both the spirit and the approach of an extension of repertory grid described by Ravenette.[24]

Ravenette's interest is in children's perception of troubles in school. His approach is to offer the participant eight pictures of ordinary situations in school that are purposely drawn with some ambiguity as to detail but otherwise are straightforward. The individual is then invited, by a series of questions, to isolate and describe the child who might be troubled or upset. 'What do you think is happening?', he is asked, and similarly, 'Who might be troubled and why?', 'How did this come about?', etc.

Ravenette goes on to describe a method of 'shaking out' the personal attributes' implications for the participant which shows how that individual actually perceives various school situations, how he understands some of the interactions occurring there, how willingly he identifies himself with these situations, and the extent of his grasp of various ways of coping with them. Ravenette then uses an implications grid procedure to reduce to manageable proportions the wealth of ideas generated by the 'perception of troubles in school' technique.

'Impoverishing' Repertory Grid Data

In a study of student teachers' perceptions of the teaching practice situation, Osborne[25] employed 13 × 13 matrices to elicit elements (significant role incumbents) whose names remained secret from the researcher. Randomised triads were then identified and used to obtain constructs. Cluster analysis of the data provided a hier-archical picture of each student's grouping of constructs. Following a method devised by Smith and Leach,[26] she then quantified the hierarchical structure by impoverishing each subject's construct system, all constructs interrelating above the 0.05 level of signifi-cance being collapsed into one construct.

Osborne demonstrated the utility of her repertory grid data in illuminating case study reports of individual students compiled by teaching practice supervisors and headteachers over three teaching practice sessions.

Grid Technique and Audio/Video Lesson Recording

Parsons, Graham and Honess[27] show how grid technique and audio/video recordings of teachers' work in classrooms can be used to make explicit the 'implicit models' that teachers have of how children learn.

Fourteen children were randomly selected and, on the basis of individual photographs, triadic comparisons were made to elicit constructs concerning one teacher's ideas about the similarities and differences in the manner in which these children learned. In addi-tion, extensive observations of the teacher's classroom behaviour were undertaken under naturalistic conditions and verbatim recordings (audio and video) were made for future review and discussion between the teacher and the researchers at the end of each recording session. The authors stress that the whole study was carried out in a spirit of mutual enquiry, the researchers and the teacher joining together in using the analysis of the repertory grid as a source of counter or confirmatory accounts in the gradual identification of her implicit view of children's learning.

What very soon became evident in these ongoing complemen-tary analyses was the clear distinction that Mrs C. (the teacher)

Box 14.5: Mrs C's Model of the Manner in which Children Learn

DRAWN LARGELY FROM
QUANTITATIVE ANALYSIS

DRAWN LARGELY FROM
THEMATIC ANALYSIS

High achievers

Retain concepts
Are intelligent
Comprehend easily
Appear able to order
    thoughts in written
    work
Independent learners
Good memories
Prefer discovery
Can concretise alone
Cope better with
    uncertainty
More able to transfer
    concepts
More able to follow logical
    progression

Tend to thrive on
    competition
Less anxious if wrong[x]
Less easily satisfied
Less likely to misbehave
Weaker emotional
    attachment if
    motivated
Less likely to suffer
    functional fixity
More likely to question*
High work rate[x]

All learning needs
to be meaningful
(New material must be related
to old)

Average achievers

Coping with uncertainty
    depends on the
    problem
Same rate learning
    important[x] for all
Discovery learning not
    helpful[x]

All pupils to be
taught as
individuals

Low achievers

Do not retain concepts
Less intelligent
Comprehend less easily
Less able to order
    thoughts in written
    work
Dependent learners
Poor memories
Prefer instruction
Need help to concretise
Cope less well with
    uncertainty
Less able to transfer
    concepts
Less able to follow logical
    progression

Tend not to worry
    about competition
More anxious if wrong[x]
More easily satisfied
More likely to misbehave
Stronger emotional
    attachment if
    motivated
More likely to suffer
    functional fixity
Less likely to question[x]
Less likely to be
    encouraged by
    success
Low work rate[x]

[x]Central themes for Mrs C.

Source: Parsons, Graham and Honess.[27]

held for *high* and *low achievers.* The analysis of the children in class as shown in the video tapes revealed that not only did high and low achievers sit in separate groups but the teacher's whole approach to these two groupings differed:

> With high achievers, Mrs C would often adopt a 'working with' approach, i.e. verbalising what children had done, with their help. When confronted with low achievers, Mrs C would more often ask 'why' they had tackled problems in a certain manner, and wait for an answer.

The final picture of Mrs C's model of children as learners is shown in Box 14.5. The researchers point to the usefulness of their approach as a starting point for working with teachers on in-service education programmes.

Focused Grids, Non-verbal Grids, Exchange Grids and Sociogrids

A number of recent developments have been reported in the use of computer programs in repertory grid research.[28] We briefly identify these as follows:

(a) Focusing a grid assists in the interpretation of raw grid data. Each element is compared with every other element and the ordering of elements in the grid is changed so that those most alike are clustered most closely together. A similar rearrangement is made in respect of each construct.

(b) Physical objects can be used as elements and grid elicitation is then carried out in non-verbal terms. Thomas claims that this approach enhances the exploration of sensory and perceptual experiences.

(c) Exchange grids are procedures developed to enhance the quality of conversational exchanges. Basically, one person's construing provides the format for an empty grid which is offered to another person for completion. The empty grid consists of the first person's verbal descriptions from which his ratings have been deleted. The second person is then invited to test his comprehending of the first person's point of view by filling in the grid as he believes the other has already completed it. Various computer programs (PAIRS, CORES and DIFFERENCE) are available to assist analysis of the processes of negotiation elicited in exchange grids.

(d) In the PAIRS analysis, all constructs in one grid are

compared with all constructs in the other grid and a measure of commonality in construing is determined. PAIRS analysis leads on to SOCIOGRIDS in which the pattern of relationships between the grids of one group can be identified. In turn, SOCIOGRIDS can provide a mode grid for the whole group or a number of mode grids identifying cliques. Socionets which reveal the pattern of shared construing can also be derived.

With these brief examples, the reader will catch something of the flavour of what can be achieved using the various manifestations of repertory grid techniques in the field of educational research.

References

1. Kelly, G.A., *Clinical Psychology and Personality: the Selected Papers of George Kelly*, edited by B.A. Maher (Wiley, New York, 1969).
2. Bannister, D. (ed.), *Perspectives in Personal Construct Theory* (Academic Press, London, 1970).
3. Ryle, A., *Frames and Cages: The Repertory Grid Approach to Human Understanding* (Sussex University Press, Brighton, 1975).
4. Adams-Webber, J.R., 'Elicited versus provided constructs in repertory grid technique: a review', *Brit. J. Med. Psychol.*, 43 (1970) 349–54.
5. Bannister, D. and Mair, J.M.M., *The Evaluation of Personal Constructs* (Academic Press, London, 1968).
6. Hinkle, D.N., 'The change of personal constructs from the viewpoint of a theory of implications', unpublished PhD thesis (Ohio State University, 1965).
7. Fransella, F., *Need to Change?* (Methuen, London, 1975).
8. Fransella, F. and Bannister, D., *A Manual for Repertory Grid Technique* (Academic Press, London, 1977).
9. Chetwynd, S.J., 'Outline of the analyses available with G.A.P., the Grid Analysis Package' (St. George's Hospital, London, SW17, 1974).
10. Ryle, A. and Breen, D., 'Change in the course of social work training: a repertory grid study', *Brit. J. Med. Psychol.*, 47 (1974) 139–47.
11. Lifshitz, M., 'Quality professionals: does training make a difference? A personal construct theory study of the issue', *Brit. J. Soc. Clin. Psychol.*, 13 (1974) 183–9.
12. Ryle, A. and Breen, D., 'A comparison of adjusted and maladjusted couples using the double dyad grid', *Brit. J. Med. Psychol.*, 45 (1972) 375–82.
13. Ryle, A. and Lunghi, M., 'The dyad grid: a modification of repertory grid technique', *British Journal of Psychiatry*, 117 (1970) 323–7.
14. Salmon, P., 'Differential conforming of the developmental process', *Brit. J. Soc. Clin. Psychol.*, 8 (1969) 22–31.
15. Applebee, A.N. 'The development of children's responses to repertory grids', *Brit. J. Soc. Clin. Psychol.*, 15 (1976) 101–2.
16. Epting, F.R., Suchman, D.I. and Nickeson, K.J., 'An evaluation of elicitation procedures for personal constructs', *Brit. J. Psychol.*, 62 (1971) 513–17.
17. Yorke, D.M., 'Repertory grids in educational research: some methodological

considerations', *Brit. Educ. Res. Journ.*, 4,2 (1978) 63–74.

18. Wood, R. and Napthali, W.A., 'Assessment in the classroom: What do teachers look for?', *Educational Studies*, 1,3 (1975) 151–61.

19. Nash R., *Classrooms Observed* (Routledge and Kegan Paul, London, 1973).

20. Ravenette, A.T., 'Grid techniques for children', *Journal of Child Psychology and Psychiatry*, 16 (1975) 79–83.

21. McQuitty, L.L., 'Single and multiple hierarchical classification by reciprocal pairs and rank order types', *Educational and Psychological Measurement*, 26 (1966) 253–65.

22. Duckworth, D. and Entwistle, N.J., 'Attitudes to school subjects: a repertory grid technique', *Brit. J. Educ. Psychol.*, 44, 1 (1974) 76–83.

23. Harré, R. and Rosser, E., 'The rules of disorder', *The Times Educational Supplement*, 25 July 1975.

24. Ravenette, A.T., 'Psychological investigation of children and young people', in D. Bannister (ed.), *New Perspectives in Personal Construct Theory* (Academic Press, London, 1977).

25. Osborne, J.I., 'College of education students' perceptions of the teaching situation', unpublished MEd dissertation (University of Liverpool, 1977).

26. Smith, S. and Leach, C., 'A hierarchical measure of cognitive complexity', *Brit. J. Psychol.*, 63, 4 (1972) 561–8.

27. Parsons, J.M., Graham, N. and Honess, T., 'A teacher's implicit model of how children learn', *Brit. Educat. Res. Journal*, 9, 1 (1983) 91–101.

28. Thomas, L.F., 'A personal construct approach to learning in education, training and therapy', in F. Fransella (ed.), *Personal Construct Psychology* (Academic Press, London, 1978). See also: Pope, M.L. and Keen, T.R., *Personal Construct Psychology and Education* (Academic Press, London, 1981), especially chapters 8 and 9. Shaw, M.L.G., (ed.) *Recent Advances in Personal Construct Technology* (Academic Press, London, 1981).

15 MULTIDIMENSIONAL MEASUREMENT

Introduction

However limited our knowledge of astronomy, most of us have learned to pick out certain clusterings of stars from the infinity of those that crowd the Northern skies and to name them as the familiar Plough, Orion, and the Great Bear. Few of us would identify constellations in the Southern Hemisphere that are instantly recognisable by our Australian friends. But we don't happen to live 'down under'.

Our predilection for reducing the complexity of elements that constitute our lives to a more simple order doesn't stop at star gazing. In numerous ways, each and every one of us attempts to discern patterns or shapes in seemingly unconnected events in order to better grasp their significance for us in the conduct of our daily lives. The educational researcher is no exception.

As research into a particular aspect of human activity progresses, the variables being explored frequently turn out to be more complex than was first realised. Investigation into the relationship between teaching styles and pupil achievement is a case in point. Global distinctions between behaviour identified as progressive or traditional, informal or formal, are vague and woolly and have led inevitably to research findings that are at worst inconsistent, at best, inconclusive. In reality, epithets such as informal or formal in the context of teaching and learning relate to *multidimensional concepts*, that is, concepts made up of a number of variables. *Multidimensional scaling*, on the other hand, is a way of analysing judgements of similarity between such variables in order that the dimensionality of those judgements can be assessed.[1] As regards research into teaching styles and pupil achievement, it has been suggested that multidimensional typologies of teacher behaviour should be developed. Such typologies, it is believed, would enable the researcher to group together similarities in teachers' judgements about specific aspects of their classroom organisation and management, and their ways of motivating, assessing and instructing pupils.

Techniques for grouping such judgements are many and various.

What they all have in common is that they are methods for 'determining the number and nature of the underlying variables among a large number of measures', a definition which Kerlinger[2] uses to describe one of the best-known grouping techniques, *factor analysis*. We begin the chapter by illustrating a number of methods of grouping or clustering variables ranging from *elementary linkage analysis* which can be undertaken by hand, to *factor analysis* which is best left to the computer. We then outline one way of analysing data cast into multidimensional tables.

Elementary Linkage Analysis: an Example

Seven constructs were elicited from an infant school teacher who was invited to discuss the ways in which she saw the children in her class (see Chapter 14, 'Personal constructs'). She identified favourable and unfavourable constructs as follows: *intelligent (+), sociable (+), verbally-good (+), well-behaved (+), aggressive (−), noisy (−) and clumsy (−)*.

Four boys and six girls were then selected at random from the class register and the teacher was asked to place each child in rank order under each of the seven constructs, using rank position 1 to indicate the child most like the particular construct, and rank position 10, the child least like the particular construct. The teacher's rank ordering is set out in Box 15.1. Notice that on three constructs, the rankings have been reversed in order to maintain the consistency of favourable = 1, unfavourable = 10.

Elementary linkage analysis (McQuitty[4]) is one way of exploring the relationship between the teacher's personal constructs, that is, of assessing the dimensionality of the judgements that she makes about her pupils. It seeks to identify and define the clusterings of certain variables within a set of variables. Like factor analysis which we shortly illustrate, elementary linkage analysis searches for interrelated groups of correlation coefficients. The objective of the search is to identify *types*. By *type*, McQuitty refers to 'a category of people or other objects (personal constructs in our example) such that the members are internally self-contained in being like one another'. Box 15.2 sets out the intercorrelations between the seven personal construct ratings shown in Box 15.1 (Spearman's rho is the method of correlation used in the present example).

Box 15.1: Rank Ordering of Ten Children on Seven Constructs

		INTELLIGENT				SOCIABLE
(favourable)	1	Heather	(favourable)		1	Caroline
	2	Richard			2	Richard
	3	Caroline			3	Sharon
	4	Tim			4	Jane
	5	Patrick			5	Tim
	6	Sharon			6	Janice
	7	Janice			7	Heather
	8	Jane			8	Patrick
	9	Alex			9	Karen
(unfavourable)	10	Karen	(unfavourable)		10	Alex

		AGGRESSIVE				NOISY
(unfavourable)	10	Alex	(unfavourable)		10	Alex
	9	Patrick			9	Patrick
	8	Tim			8	Karen
	7	Karen			7	Tim
	6	Richard			6	Caroline
	5	Caroline			5	Richard
	4	Heather			4	Heather
	3	Jane			3	Janice
	2	Sharon			2	Sharon
(favourable)	1	Janice	(favourable)		1	Jane

		VERBALLY-GOOD				CLUMSY
(favourable)	1	Richard	(unfavourable)		10	Alex
	2	Caroline			9	Patrick
	3	Heather			8	Karen
	4	Janice			7	Tim
	5	Patrick			6	Richard
	6	Tim			5	Sharon
	7	Alex			4	Jane
	8	Sharon			3	Janice
	9	Jane			2	Caroline
(unfavourable)	10	Karen	(favourable)		1	Heather

		WELL-BEHAVED
(favourable)	1	Janice
	2	Jane
	3	Sharon
	4	Caroline
	5	Heather
	6	Richard
	7	Tim
	8	Karen
	9	Patrick
(unfavourable)	10	Alex

Source: Cohen.[3]

Steps in Elementary Linkage Analysis

1. In Box 15.2, underline the strongest, that is the highest correlation coefficient in each *column* of the matrix. Ignore negative signs.
2. Identify the highest correlation coefficient in the *entire matrix*. The two variables having this correlation constitute the first two of Cluster 1.
3. Now identify all those variables which are most like the variables in Cluster 1. To do this, *read along the rows* of the variables which emerged in Step 2, selecting any of the coefficients which are underlined in the rows. In Box 15.3 we diagram the ways in which these new cluster members are related to the original pair which initially constituted Cluster 1.
4. Now identify any variables which are most like the variables elicited in Step 3. Repeat this procedure until no further variables are identified.
5. Excluding all those variables which belong within Cluster 1, repeat Steps 2 to 4 until all the variables have been accounted for.

Box 15.2: Intercorrelations Between Seven Personal Constructs

		(1)	(2)	(3)	(4)	(5)	(6)	(7)
Intelligent	(1)		53	−10	−16	83	−52	13
Sociable	(2)	53		−50	−59	44	−56	61
Agressive	(3)	−10	−50		91	−07	79	−96
Noisy	(4)	−16	−59	91		−01	73	−93
Verbally-good	(5)	83	44	−07	−01		−43	12
Clumsy	(6)	−52	−56	79	73	−43		−81
Well-behaved	(7)	13	61	−96	−93	12	−81	

(decimal points omitted)

Source: Cohen.[3]

Box 15.3: The Structuring of Relationships Among the Seven Personal Constructs

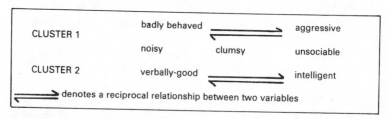

Source: Cohen.[3]

Cluster Analysis*: an Example

Elementary linkage analysis is one method of grouping or clustering together correlation coefficients which show similarities among a set of variables. We now illustrate another method of clustering which was used by Bennett[5] in his study of teaching styles and pupil progress. His starting point was a disaffection for global descriptions such as progressive and traditional as applied to teaching styles in junior school classrooms. A more adequate theoretical and experimental conceptualisation of the elements constituting teaching styles was attempted through the construction of a questionnaire containing 28 statements illustrating six major areas of teacher classroom behaviour: (1) classroom management and contol; (2) teacher control and sanctions; (3) curriculum content and planning; (4) instructional strategies; (5) motivational techniques; and (6) assessment procedures.

Bennett constructed a typology of teaching styles from the responses of 468 top junior school class teachers to the questionnaire. His cluster analysis of their responses involved calculating coefficients of similarity between subjects across all the variables that constituted the final version of the questionnaire. This technique involves specifying the number of clusters of subjects to which the researcher wishes the data to be reduced. Examination of the central profiles of all solutions from 22 to 3 clusters showed that at the 12-level cluster solutions, between-cluster differences

*For a fuller discussion of clustering methods, see B.S. Everitt, *Cluster Analysis* (Heinemann Educational Books, London 1974).

were maximised in relation to within-cluster error.[5] An essential prerequisite to the clustering technique employed in this study was the use of factor analysis (see p. 345) to ensure that the variables were relatively independent of one another and that groups of variables were not overweighted in the analysis. Principal Components analysis followed by varimax rotation reduced the 28 variables in Bennett's original questionnaire to the 19 shown in Box 15.4. For purposes of exposition, Bennett ordered the types of teaching style shown in Box 15.4 from the most progressive cluster (type 1) to the most traditional cluster (type 12), noting, however, that whilst the extreme types could be described in these terms, the remaining types all contained elements of both progressive and traditional teaching styles. The figures in heavy typeface show percentage response levels that were considered significantly different from the total population distribution.

Bennett described the twelve types of teacher styles as follows.

Type 1: These teachers favour integration of subject matter, and, unlike most other groups, allow pupil choice of work, whether undertaken individually or in groups. Most allow pupils choice of seating. Less than half curb movement and talk. Assessment in all its forms, tests, grading and homework appears to be discouraged. Intrinsic motivation is favoured.

Type 2: These teachers also prefer integration of subject matter. Teacher control appears to be low, but less pupil choice of work is offered. However, most allow pupils choice of seating, and only one-third curb movement and talk. Few test or grade work.

Type 3: The main teaching mode of this group is class teaching and group work. Integration of subject matter is preferred, associated with taking pupils out of school. They appear to be strict, most curbing movement and talk, and offenders are smacked. The amount of testing is average, but the amount of grading and homework is below average.

Type 4: These teachers prefer separate subject teaching but a high proportion allow pupil choice of work both in group and individual work. None seat their pupils by ability. They test and grade more than average.

Type 5: A mixture of separate subject and integrated subject teaching is characteristic of this group. The main teaching mode is pupils working in groups of their own choice on tasks set by the teacher. Teacher talk is lower than average. Control is high with regard to movement but not to talk. Most give tests every week

Box 15.4: Central Profiles (percentage occurrence) at 12-cluster Levels

Item		Type 1	2	3	4	5	6	7	8	9	10	11	12
1.	Pupils have choice in where to sit	63	66	17	46	50	18	7	17	3	7	77	00
2.	Pupils allocated to seating by ability	14	16	25	0	12	45	20	7	81	58	3	50
3.	Pupils not allowed freedom of movement in the classroom	49	38	83	76	100	84	87	100	86	97	97	100
4.	Teacher expects pupils to be quiet	31	34	92	61	23	55	56	90	81	74	90	100
5.	Pupils taken out of school regularly as normal teaching activity	51	50	83	49	81	45	17	47	31	19	26	42
6.	Pupils given homework regularly	9	22	8	27	65	3	13	43	36	29	21	56
7.	*Teaching emphasis*												
8.	(i) Above average teacher talks to whole class	29	16	79	58	30	74	83	73	33	94	85	70
	(ii) Above average pupils working on groups on teacher tasks	46	13	83	12	77	92	3	3	22	68	10	8
9.	(iii) Above average pupils working in groups of own choice	89	3	29	94	19	32	13	3	0	23	0	0
10.	(iv) Above average pupils working individually on teacher tasks	9	97	0	3	42	0	73	83	100	0	72	92
11.	(v) Above average pupils working individually on work of own choice	94	9	42	85	42	18	57	57	8	3	8	28
12.	Pupils' work marked and graded	3	3	13	15	31	16	33	33	8	32	31	97
13.	Stars given to pupils who produce best work	9	31	38	55	8	18	17	73	17	87	69	75
14.	Arithmetic tests given at least once a week	9	9	71	88	100	8	10	70	50	94	56	81
15.	Spelling tests given at least once a week	23	19	67	94	92	18	7	73	92	94	87	92
16.	Teacher smacks for persistent disruptive behaviour	34	34	96	24	31	45	80	93	42	68	64	58
17.	Teacher sends pupil out of room for persistent disruptive behaviour	11	25	13	6	8	3	7	10	25	0	33	11
18.	Allocation of teaching time												
19.	(i) Above average separate subject teaching	20	31	4	82	81	95	100	47	81	100	100	92
	(ii) Above average integrated subject teaching	97	91	100	24	65	8	10	93	14	7	0	0
	N in cluster	35	32	24	33	26	38	30	30	36	31	39	36

and many give homework regularly. Stars are rarely used, and pupils are taken out of school regularly.

Type 6: These teachers prefer to teach subjects separately with emphasis on groups working on teacher-specified tasks. The amount of individual work is small. These teachers appear to be fairly low on control, and are below average on assessment and the use of extrinsic motivation.

Type 7: This group is separate subject oriented, with a high level of class teaching together with individual work. Teacher control appears to be tight, few allow movement or choice of seating, and offenders are smacked. Assessment, however, is low.

Type 8: This group of teachers has very similar characteristics to those in type 3, the difference being that these prefer to organise the work on an individual rather than group basis. Freedom of movement is restricted, and most expect pupils to be quiet.

Type 9: These teachers favour separate subject teaching, the predominant teaching mode being individuals working on tasks set by the teacher. Teacher control appears to be high; most curb movement and talk, and seat by ability. Pupil choice is minimal. Regular spelling tests are given, but few mark or grade work or use stars.

Type 10: All these teachers favour separate subject teaching. The teaching mode favoured is teacher talk to whole class, and pupils working in groups determined by the teacher, on tasks set by the teacher. Most curb movement and talk, and over two-thirds smack for disruptive behaviour. There is regular testing and most give stars for good work.

Type 11: All members of this group stress separate subject teaching by way of class teaching and individual work. Pupil choice of work is minimal, although most teachers allow choice of seating. Movement and talk are curbed, and offenders smacked.

Type 12: This is an extreme group in a number of respects. None favour an integrated approach. Subjects are taught separately by class teaching and individual work. None allow pupils' choice of seating, and every teacher curbs movement and talk. These teachers are above average on all assessment procedures, and extrinsic motivation predominates.

Bennett's typology of teacher styles and his analysis of pupil performance based on the typology has aroused considerable debate. Readers may care to follow up critical comments[6] on the cluster analysis procedures we have outlined here.

Factor Analysis: an Example

Factor analysis, we said earlier, is a way of determining the nature of underlying variables among a large number of measures. It is particularly appropriate in exploratory research where the investigator aims to impose an 'orderly simplification'[7] upon a number of interrelated measures. We illustrate the use of factor analysis in a study of the expectations of headteachers and their deputies for the role of the primary school deputy head. The exploratory nature of the enquiry is shown in the strategy adopted by Coulson, the researcher.[8]

First, a search was undertaken to identify relevant issues from previous leadership studies. Once located, the issues provided the focus for interviews with headteachers, deputy heads, teachers and advisory staff. Second, arising out of the interviews, a tentative role definition instrument was constructed consisting of 114 statements describing a range of activities in the day-to-day work of a deputy head. Third, a small pilot sample of heads and deputy heads was given the task of winnowing out irrelevant items and rephrasing pertinent statements so that they were simple and unambiguous. The preliminary pilot work reduced the original group of statements to 40. These appeared to have some underlying structure, suggesting to Coulson six principal areas of concern for deputy heads which he identified as (a) interpersonal relations among teachers; (b) instrumental or task emphasis; (c) administrative control and procedural standardisation; (d) collegiality; (e) mediation and consultation; and (f) school leadership — subordination to the head. Later in the study, Coulson was able to check his *a priori* grouping of role statements against the structure which he derived by means of factor analysis. As Child[7] observes,

> In most instances, the factor analysis is preceded by a hunch as to the factors which might emerge. In fact, it would be difficult to conceive of a manageable analysis which started in an empty-headed fashion. In selecting test material in the first place it must have occurred to the experimenter that the tests have something in common or that some are markedly different. Even the 'let's see what happens' approach is pretty sure to have a hunch at the back of it somewhere. It is this testing and the generation of hypotheses which forms the principal concern of most factor analysts.

Finally, the 40-item role definition instrument (Box 15.5) was completed by 232 headteachers and 246 deputy heads using a five-point scale to indicate the direction and the intensity of their agreement/disagreement with the items contained therein.

The correlation matrix composed of the intercorrelations of the 40 role items was then factor analysed. The technical details of factor analysis are beyond the scope of this section. Briefly, however, the procedures followed by Coulson involved a method called Principal Components by means of which ten factors or groupings were extracted. These were rotated to produce a more meaningful interpretation of the underlying structure than that provided by the Principal Components method. (Readable accounts of factor analysis may be found in Kerlinger[2] and Child.[7])

Box 15.6 shows the ten factors that were identified, together with what are called their *factor loadings*. These are like correlation coefficients, ranging from − 1.00 to + 1.00, and are interpreted similarly.[2] This is to say, they indicate the correlations between the role items shown in Box 15.6 and the factors. Looking at Factor 1, it can be seen that item 3 loads more highly than any of the other five items that go to make up the first factor. The footnote at the bottom of Box 15.6 to the effect that loadings less than ±0.3 are omitted refers to the criterion adopted when interpreting the significance of factor loadings. Because factor loadings are interpreted like correlation coefficients, Coulson would have been in order to have accepted loadings of about 0.12 as significant at $p < 0.01$ with a sample size of over 400. His adoption of ±0.3 was arbitrary though his decision shows commendable caution.

Having extracted factors, the researcher's next task was to interpret them and give them names. This part of the work can be relatively straightforward or extremely difficult. For example, the loadings on four of the six items (items 3,7,14 and 25) that constitute Factor I suggest a concern for the standardisation and routinisation of school procedures. The factor was appropriately named *Bureaucratic Organisation.* Notice how this interpretation squares with the hunch the researcher had about his data prior to factor analysis.

Factors VII and X, however, are obscure. Take Factor VII, for example. Start with the highest loading (item 23, loading 0.75) as the primary focus for its interpretation. The next highest loading (item 24, loading 0.71) is of no help in clarifying any underlying structure to the factor suggested by item 23. The addition of item

Box 15.5: The Deputy Head Role Definition Instrument

Item no.	Abbreviated form of item
1	Look out for personal welfare of individual teachers ....
2	Persuade teachers to try new methods ....
3	Put welfare of staff above that of individual teachers ....
4	Discourage 'outlandish' classroom methods ....
5	Help staff with personal teaching problems ....
6	Ensure recognition for jobs well done ....
7	Apply general school rules policy ....
8	Encourage equity between young and old teachers ....
9	Co-ordinate departments or year groups ....
10	Be friendly and accessible to all ....
11	Supervise and evaluate teachers' work ....
12	Secure teachers' approval on school matters ....
13	Allow individuality in teaching methods ....
14	Ask teachers to follow standard routines ....
15	Keep teachers informed about policy and changes ....
16	Inform teachers of expected standards ....
17	Put teachers' suggestions into operation ....
18	Keep informed of staff opinions on school issues ....
19	Reprimand teachers who don't conform to agreed procedures ......
20	Encourage teachers to work up to capacity ....
21	Be a good organiser of staff duties and schedules ....
22	Put over own ideas about teaching and organisation ....
23	Attend to welfare of children throughout school ....
24	Make own attitudes clear to staff ....
25	Emphasise the meeting of deadlines ....
26	Expect head to seek his agreement before proposing changes ......
27	Relay teachers' suggestion to the head ....
28	Have complete responsibility for some aspects of school life ....
29	Allow loyalty to head to precede loyalty to staff ....
30	Relay head's decisions and instructions to staff ....
31	Question head's decisions if these considered unwise ....
32	Have duties separate from those of the head ....
33	Expect head to make final decisions in all school matters ....
34	Have his own class ....
35	Act as a 'go-between' for head and teachers ....
36	Be a good classroom teacher ....
37	Have had varied teaching experience in other schools ....
38	Regard the post as a preparation for headship ....
39	Have his own room other than a classroom ....
40	Put head's point of view when staff are critical of policies ....

Source: Coulson.[8]

Box 15.6: Deputy Head Role Definition Instrument Loadings on Ten Promax Factors

Item no.	A priori group	Factors									
		I	II	III	IV	V	VI	VII	VIII	IX	X
1	A				−31			30			
2	B		55				32				
3	C	70									
4	B		65								
5	A			34							
6	D					31					
7	C	50						−35			
8	D						65				
9	D		45				39				
10	A			75							
11	B		73								
12	D						49				45
13	D	−48					36				
14	C	46									
15	A					34					
16	B		61								
17	D										64
18	A			55				32			
19	C		71								
20	B		39					43			
21	C			59						−38	
22	B				36			75			
23	F							71			
24	D										
25	C	43									68
26	E										
27	E					68					
28	F									30	
29	F	56									
30	E					65					
31	F									−61	
32	C	48									68
33	F								−73		
34	F										
35	E					80	−32				
36	B				60						
37	F				68						
38	F				61				76		
39	F										
40	E					44					
% variance accounted for		5.1	8.1	4.6	4.9	5.8	4.1	5.1	3.8	3.5	3.8

Decimal points omitted   Loadings less than ± 0.3 omitted.

Source: Coulson.[8]

20 (loading 0.45) serves only to make the task of interpretation even more difficult. With the introduction of the negatively loaded item 7 (−0.35), confusion is total!

Because the ten factors extracted in the analysis shown in Box 15.7 (called the *first order* analysis) are correlated, the correlations between them can be treated as a correlation matrix and subjected to what is termed *second order* factor extraction. In effect, what this process does is to search for further underlying structures that may more parsimoniously describe the relationships between the factors identified in the first order analysis. Box 15.8 identifies four second order factors extracted by second order factor analysis.

By now the reader may well be asking where all this is leading to. Recall that the purpose of factor analysis and of other grouping or clustering techniques is to determine the 'nature and the number of the underlying variables among a large number of measures'.[2] As a result of the factor analysis, Coulson was able to describe the nature of the deputy head's role with a greater degree of parsimony and refinement than in his initial Role Definition Instrument set out in Box 15.5. Moreover, the first order factor analysis brought out aspects of the deputy's role that the researcher's *a priori* classification failed to make explicit. Look at Factor IV in Box 15.6, for example. Its high loadings on items 36, 37 and 38, together with the negatively loaded item 1, suggests a *career orientation* factor — an important element in the deputy head's role not specified in the *a priori* classification. In reducing

Box 15.7: Matrix of Correlations Among Ten First Order Factors

	I	II	III	IV	V	VI	VII	VIII	IX	X
I	—									
II	−16	—								
III	09	−30	—							
IV	−22	14	03	—						
V	32	−17	21	−13	—					
VI	02	01	01	03	−13	—				
VII	30	−21	13	−14	34	−24	—			
VIII	02	05	−25	−07	−03	−09	18	—		
IX	−10	14	02	13	−15	01	−18	−17	—	
X	01	04	10	−01	−02	−02	16	13	02	—

Decimal points omitted.

Source: Coulson.[8]

Box 15.8: Item Loadings on Second Order Factors

Item	Factors			
	I	II	III	IV
1		45		
2			31	
3				
4	32	33		
5		44	36	
6	30		44	
7	33			
8			46	
9			37	
10		33		
12			38	40
13			41	
14		45		−31
15			51	
16		44		
17				48
18		35	36	
19				
20		45		
21			55	
22	61			
23				
24	38		42	
25	52			
26				61
27			33	
28	55			
29	37			
30		30		
31	41			
36	30			
37	30			
37	37			
38	39			
39	32			30
40	31			
% Variance accounted for	16.6	15.6	13.7	11.4

Decimal points omitted   Loadings less than ±0.3 omitted

Source: Coulson.[8]

the data even further, the second order factor analysis illuminated the expressive leadership dimension of the deputy head's role with greater clarity.

Coulson interprets the second order factor loadings as follows:

Second Order Factor I: Quasi Headship

This associates a strong dimension of independent, 'head-like' career items ('Have own ideas which he should want to put over'; 'Regard post as preparation for headship') with alignment with and support of the head ('Loyalty to head to take precedence over loyalty to teachers'; 'Put head's point of view when teachers critical'). This appears to represent a joint leadership view of the deputy head partnership and is identified as *quasi headship.*

Second Order Factor II: Facilitation

This is loaded by items relating to administrative clarity and routine ('Be a good organiser and administrator'; 'Ask that teachers follow standard routines') and considerate interpersonal relations between the deputy and teachers ('Know staff well enough to help with personal problems'; 'Encourage pleasant atmosphere'). Communication is predominantly downward and the factor seems to be concerned with the deputy head's part in keeping the school running smoothly and at the same time encouraging and helping the teachers to give of their best efforts (perhaps two sides of the same thing). The factor represents the deputy head as a considerate foreman and is tentatively identified as a *facilitation* dimension.

Second Order Factor III: Expressive Leadership

This gathers together the collegial items and the acts on behalf of teachers ('Keep teachers informed'; 'Encourage an equal voice to young and old'; 'Let teachers work in the way they think best') and is identified as *expressive leadership.*

Second Order Factor IV: Professionalism

Significant positive loadings on instrumental items in which the opinions of teachers or the deputy head are taken into account before changes are made ('Expect that head will seek agreement before proposing changes'; 'Put teachers' suggestions into operation'), and a significant negative loading on 'ask that teachers follow standard routines' suggest that this factor may have to do with professional *versus* bureaucratic forms of organisation. It is tentatively called *professionalism.*

Multidimensional Tables

Methods of analysing data cast into 2 × 2 contingency tables by means of the chi square test are generally well covered in research methods books. Increasingly however, educational data are classified in multiple rather than two-dimensional formats. Everitt[9] provides a useful account of methods for analysing multidimensional tables and has shown, incidentally, the erroneous conclusions that can result from the practice of analysing multidimensional data by summing over variables to reduce them to two-dimensional formats. In this section (p. 360) we too illustrate the misleading conclusions that can arise when the researcher employs bivariate rather than multivariate analysis. The outline that follows draws closely on a recent exposition by Whiteley.[10]

Multidimensional Data: Some Words on Notation

The hypothetical data in Box 15.9 refer to a survey of voting behaviour in a sample of men and women in Britain.

Box 15.9: Sex, Voting Preference and Social Class: a Three-way Classification Table

	Middle-class		Working-class	
	Conservative	Labour	Conservative	Labour
Men	80	30	40	130
Women	100	20	40	110

Source: adapted from Whiteley.[10]

In Box 15.9:

the row variable (sex) is represented by i;
the column variable (voting preference) is represented by j;
the layer variable (social class) is represented by k.

The number in any one cell in Box 15.9 can be represented by the symbol n_{ijk} that is to say, the score in row category i, column category j, and layer category k, where i = 1 (men), 2 (women); j = 1 (Conservative), 2 (Labour); k = 1 (middle-class), 2 (working-class). It follows therefore that the numbers in Box 15.9 can also be represented as in Box 15.10.

Box 15.10: Sex, Voting Preference and Social Class: a Three-way Notational Classification

	Middle-class		Working-class	
	Conservative	Labour	Conservative	Labour
Men	n_{111}	n_{121}	n_{112}	n_{122}
Women	n_{211}	n_{221}	n_{212}	n_{222}

Thus,

$$n_{121} = 30 \text{ (Men, Labour, Middle-class)}$$

and

$$n_{212} = 40 \text{ (Women, Conservative, Working-class)}$$

Three types of marginals can be obtained from Box 15.10 by:

(1) *Summing over two variables to give the marginal totals for the third*
Thus:

n_{++k} = summing over sex and voting preference to give *social class,* for example:

$$n_{111} + n_{121} + n_{211} + n_{221} = 230 \text{ Middle-class}$$

$$n_{112} + n_{122} + n_{212} + n_{222} = 320 \text{ Working-class}$$

and n_{+j+} = summing over sex and social class to give *voting preference* and n_{i++} = summing over voting preference and social class to give *sex.*

(2) *Summing over one variable to give the marginal totals for the second and third variables*
Thus:

$$n_{+11} = 180 \text{ (Middle-class Conservative)}$$

$$n_{+21} = 50 \text{ (Middle-class Labour)}$$

$n_{+12} = 80$ (Working-class Conservative)

$n_{+22} = 240$ (Working-class Labour)

(3) *Summing over all three variables to give the grand total*
Thus:

$$n_{+++} = 550 = N$$

Using the Chi Square Test in a Three-way Classification Table

Whiteley shows how easy it is to extend the 2×2 chi square test to the three-way case. The probability that an individual taken from the sample at random in Box 15.9 will be a woman is:

$$p_{2++} = \frac{n_{2++}}{n_{+++}} = \frac{270}{550} = 0.49$$

and the probability that a respondent's voting preference will be *Labour* is:

$$p_{+2+} = \frac{n_{+2+}}{n_{+++}} = \frac{290}{550} = 0.53$$

and the probability that a respondent will be *working-class* is:

$$p_{++2} = \frac{n_{++2}}{n_{+++}} = \frac{320}{550} = 0.58$$

To determine the *expected probability* of an individual being a *woman, Labour supporter* and *working-class* we assume that these variables are statistically independent (that is to say, there is no relationship between them) and simply apply the multiplication rule of probability theory:

$$p_{222} = (p_{2++}) (p_{+2+}) (p_{++2}) = (0.49) (0.53) (0.58) = 0.15$$

This can be expressed in terms of the expected frequency in cell n_{222} as:

$$N (p_{2++}) (p_{+2+}) (p_{++2}) = 550 (0.49) (0.53) (0.58) = 82.8$$

Similarly, the expected frequency in cell n_{112} is:

$$N(p_{1++}) (p_{+1+}) (p_{++2}) \text{ where :}$$

$$p_{1++} = \frac{n_{1++}}{n_{+++}} = \frac{280}{550} = 0.51$$

and

$$p_{+1+} = \frac{n_{+1+}}{n_{+++}} = \frac{260}{550} = 0.47$$

and

$$p_{++2} = \frac{n_{++2}}{n_{+++}} = \frac{320}{550} = 0.58$$

Thus $N (p_{1++}) (p_{+1+}) (p_{++2}) = 550 (0.51) (0.47) (0.58) = 77.0$

Box 15.11 gives the expected frequencies for the data shown in Box 15.9.

Box 15.11: Expected Frequencies in Sex, Voting Preference and Social Class

	Middle-class		Working-class	
	Conservative	Labour	Conservative	Labour
Men	55.4	61.7	77.0	85.9
Women	53.4	59.5	74.3	82.8

Source: adapted from Whiteley.[10]

With the *observed* frequencies and the *expected* frequencies to hand, chi square is calculated in the usual way:

$$\chi^2 = \sum \frac{(O - E)^2}{E} = 159.41$$

Degrees of Freedom

As Whiteley observes, degrees of freedom in a three-way contingency table is more complex than in a 2×2 classification. Essentially, however, degrees of freedom refer to the freedom with which the researcher is able to assign values to the cells, given fixed marginal totals. This can be computed by first determining the degrees of freedom for the marginals.

Each of the variables in our example (sex, voting preference, and social class) contains two categories. It follows therefore that we have $(2-1)$ degrees of freedom for each of them, given that the marginal for each variable is fixed. Since the grand total of all the marginals (i.e. the sample size) is also fixed, it follows that one more degree of freedom is also lost. We subtract these fixed numbers from the total number of cells in our contingency table. In general therefore:

degrees of freedom (d.f.) = the number of cells in the table − 1
(for N) − the number of cells fixed
by the hypothesis being tested.

Thus, where r = rows, c = columns and l = layers:

$$
\begin{aligned}
\text{d.f.} &= \text{rcl}\,(r-1) - (c-1) - (l-1) - 1 \\
&= \text{rcl} - r - c - l + 2
\end{aligned}
$$

that is to say d.f. = rcl − r − c − l + 2 when we are testing the hypothesis of the *mutual independence of the three variables.*

In our example:

$$
\text{d.f.} = (2)\,(2)\,(2) - 2 - 2 - 2 + 2 = 4
$$

From chi square tables we see that the critical value of χ^2 with 4 degrees of freedom is 9.49 at p = 0.05. Our obtained value greatly exceeds that number. We reject the null hypothesis and conclude that sex, voting preference, and social class are significantly inter-related.

Having rejected the null hypothesis with respect to the *mutual independence* of the three variables, the researcher's task now is to identify which variables cause the null hypothesis to be rejected. We cannot simply assume that because our chi square test has given a significant result, it therefore follows that there are significant associations between all three variables. It may be the case, for example, that an association exists between two of the variables whilst the third is completely independent. What we need now is a test of *partial independence*. Whiteley shows the following three such possible tests in respect of the data in Box 15.9.

First, that sex is independent of social class and voting preference

(1) $p_{ijk} = (p_i)(p_{jk})$

Second, that voting preference is independent of sex and social class

(2) $p_{ijk} = (p_j)(p_{ik})$

And third, that social class is independent of sex and voting preference

(3) $p_{ijk} = (p_k)(p_{ij})$

The following example shows how to construct the expected frequencies for the first hypothesis. We can determine the probability of an individual being, say, *woman, Labour,* and *working-class,* assuming hypothesis (1), as follows:

$$p_{222} = (p_{2++})(p_{+22}) = \frac{(n_{2++})}{(N)}\frac{(n_{+22})}{(N)}$$

$$p_{222} = \frac{(270)}{(550)}\frac{(240)}{(550)} = 0.214$$

$$E_{222} = N(p_{2++})(p_{+22}) = 550\frac{(270)}{(550)}\frac{(240)}{(550)} = \underline{117.8}$$

That is to say, assuming that sex is independent of social class and voting preference, the expected number of female, working class Labour supporters is 117.8.

When we calculate the expected frequencies for each of the cells in our contingency table in respect of our first hypothesis (p_{ijk}) = $(p_i)(p_{jk})$, we obtain the results shown in Box 15.12.

$$\chi^2 = \sum\frac{(O-E)^2}{E} = \underline{5.71}$$

Box 15.12: Expected Frequencies Assuming that Sex is Independent of Social Class and Voting Preference

	Middle-class		Working-class	
	Conservative	Labour	Conservative	Labour
Men	91.6	25.5	40.7	122.2
Women	88.4	24.5	39.3	117.8

Source: adapted from Whiteley.[10]

Degrees of freedom is given by:

$$d.f. = rcl - (cl - 1) - (r - 1) - 1$$
$$= rcl-cl-r+1=8-4-2+1 = 3$$

Whiteley observes:

> Note that we are assuming c and l are interrelated so that once, say, p_{+11} is calculated, then p_{+12}, p_{+21} and p_{+22} are determined, so we have only 1 degree of freedom; that is to say, we lose (cl−1) degrees of freedom in calculating that relationship.

From chi square tables we see that the critical value of χ^2 with 3 degrees of freedom is 7.81 at $p = 0.05$. Our obtained value is less than this. We therefore accept the null hypothesis and conclude *that there is no relationship between sex on the one hand and voting preference and social class on the other.*

Suppose now that instead of casting our data into a three-way classification as shown in Box 15.9, we had simply used a 2 × 2 contingency table and that we had sought to test the null hypothesis that there is no relationship between *sex and voting preference.* The data are shown in Box 15.13.

Box 15.13: Sex and Voting Preference: a Two-way Classification Table

	Conservative	Labour
Men	120	160
Women	140	130

Source: adapted from Whiteley.[10]

When we compute chi square for the above data our obtained value is $\chi^2 = 4.48$. Degrees of freedom are given by $(r-1)$ $(c-1) = (2-1)$ $(2-1) = 1$.

From chi square tables we see that the critical value of χ^2 with 1 degree of freedom is 3.84 at $p = 0.05$. Our obtained value exceeds this. We reject the null hypothesis and conclude that sex is significantly associated with voting preference.

But how can we explain the differing conclusions that we have arrived at in respect of the data in Boxes 15.9 and 15.13?

These examples illustrate an important and general point, Whiteley observes. In the *bivariate* analysis (Box 15.13) we concluded that there was a significant relationship between sex and voting preference. In the *multivariate* analysis (Box 15.9) that relationship was found to be non-significant when we controlled for social class.

The lesson is plain; use a multivariate approach to the analysis of contingency tables wherever the data allow.

References

1. Bennett, S. and Bowers, D., *An Introduction to Multivariate Techniques for Social and Behavioural Sciences* (Macmillan, London, 1977).
2. Kerlinger, F.N., *Foundations of Behavioural Research* (Holt, Rinehart and Winston, New York, 1970).
3. Cohen, L., *Educational Research in Classrooms and Schools: A Manual of Materials and Methods* (Harper and Row, London, 1977).
4. McQuitty, L.L., 'Elementary linkage analysis for isolating orthogonal and oblique types and typal relevancies', *Educational and Psychological Measurement*, 17 (1957) 207–29.
5. Bennett, N., *Teaching Styles and Pupil Progress* (Open Books, London, 1976); Bennett, N. and Jordan, J., 'A typology of teaching styles in primary schools', *Brit. J. Educ. Psychol.*, 45 (1975) 20–8.
6. Gray, J. and Satterly, D., 'A chapter of errors: teaching styles and pupil progress in retrospect', *Educational Research*, 19 (1976) 45–56.
7. Child, D., *The Essentials of Factor Analysis* (Holt, Rinehart and Winston, 1970).
8. Coulson, A.A., 'The attitudes of primary school heads and deputy heads to deputy headship', *Brit. J. Educ. Psychol.*, 46 (1976) 244–52.
9. Everitt, B.S., *The Analysis of Contingency Tables* (Chapman and Hall, London, 1977).
10. Whiteley, P., 'The analysis of contingency tables', in D. McKay, N. Schofield and P. Whiteley (eds), *Data Analysis and the Social Sciences* (Frances Pinter, London, 1983).

BIBLIOGRAPHY

Action, H.B., 'Positivism', in J.O. Urmson (ed.), *The Concise Encyclopedia of Western Philosophy* (Hutchinson, London, 1975).

Adams, R.S. and Biddle, B.J., *Realities of Teaching: Explorations with Videotape* (Holt, Rinehart and Winston, New York, 1970).

Adams-Webber, J.R., 'Elicited versus provided constructs in repertory grid technique: a review', *Brit. J. Med. Psychol.*, 43 (1970) 349–54.

Adelman, C. and Walker, R., 'Developing pictures for other frames: action research and case study', in G. Chanan and S. Delamont (eds), *Frontiers of Classroom Research*, (NFER, Windsor, 1975).

Adelman, C., Jenkins, D. and Kemmis, S., 'Rethinking case study: notes from the Second Cambridge Conference, in H. Simons (ed.), *Towards a Science of the Singular* (Centre for Applied Research in Education, University of East Anglia, 1980).

Applebee, A.M., 'The development of children's responses to repertory grids', *Brit. J. Soc. Clin. Psychol.*, 15 (1976) 101–2.

Argyle, M., 'Discussion chapter: an appraisal of the new approach to the study of social behaviour', in M. Brenner, P. Marsh and M. Brenner (eds), *The Social Context of Method* (Croom Helm, London, 1978).

Argyris, C., 'Dangers of applying results from experimental social psychology', *American Psychologist*, 30 (1975) 469–85.

Armistead, N. (ed.), *Reconstructing Social Psychology* (Penguin Books, London, 1974).

Aronson, E., *The Social Animal* (Freeman, San Francisco, 1976).

Ary, D., Jacobs, L.C. and Razavieh, A., *Introduction to Research in Education* (Holt, Rinehart and Winston, New York, 1972).

Backstrom, C.H. and Hursh, G.D., *Survey Research* (Northwestern University Press, Evanston, 1963).

Bailey, K.D., *Methods of Social Research* (Collier-Macmillan, London, 1978).

Ball, S.J., *Beachside Comprehensive: A Case Study of Secondary Schooling* (Cambridge University Press, Cambridge, 1981).

Bannister, D. (ed.), *Perspectives in Personal Construct Theory* (Academic Press, London, 1970).

Bannister, D. (ed.), *New Perspectives in Personal Construct Theory* (Academic Press, London, 1977).

Bannister, D. and Mair, J.M.M., *The Evaluation of Personal Constructs* (Academic Press, London, 1968).

Banuazizi, A. and Movahedi, S., 'Interpersonal dynamics in a simulated prison: a methodological analysis', *American Psychologist*, 30 (1975) 152–60.

Barr Greenfield, T., 'Theory about organizations: a new perspective and its implications for schools, in M.G. Hughes (ed.), *Administering Education : International Challenge* (Athlone Press, London, 1975).

Barratt, P.E.H., *Bases of Psychological Methods* (John Wiley and Sons, Australasia Pty Ltd, Queensland, Australia, 1971).

Beard, R., Cohen, L. and Verma, G., *The Bradford Book Flood Experiment* (School of Research in Education, University of Bradford, 1978).

Beck, R.N., *Handbook in Social Philosophy* (Macmillan, New York, 1979).

Bennett, N., *Teaching Styles and Pupil Progress* (Open Books, London, 1975).

Bennett, N. and Jordan, J., 'A typology of teaching styles in primary schools', *Brit. J. Educ. Psychol.*, 45 (1975) 20–8.

Bennett, S. and Bowers, D., *An Introduction to Multivariate Techniques for Social and Behavioural Sciences* (Macmillan, London, 1977).

Berkowitz, L. (ed.), *Advances in Experimental Social Psychology*, vol. 10 (Academic Press, New York, 1977).

Bernstein, B., 'Sociology and the sociology of education: a brief account', in J. Rex (ed.), *Approaches to Sociology: an Introduction to Major Trends in British Sociology* (Routledge and Kegan Paul, London, 1974).

Best J.W., *Research in Education* (Prentice-Hall, Englewood Cliffs, New Jersey, 1970).

Bliss, J., Monk, M. and Ogborn, J., *Qualitative Data Analysis For Educational Research* (Croom Helm, London, 1983).

Bloor, M., 'On the analysis of observational data: a discussion of the worth and uses of induction techniques and respondent validation', *Sociology*, 12, 3 (1978) 545–52.

Borg, W.R., *Applying Educational Research: A Practical Guide For Teachers* (Longman, New York, 1981), 218–19.

Borg, W.R., *Educational Research: An Introduction* (Longman, London, 1963).

Boring, E.G., 'The role of theory in experimental psychology', *Amer. J. Psychol.*, 66 (1953) 169–84.

Borkowsky, F.T., 'The relationship of work quality in undergraduate music curricula to effectiveness in instrumental music teaching in the public schools', *J. Exp. Educ.*, 39 (1970) 14–19.

Bracht, G.H. and Glass, G.V., 'The external validity of experiments', *Amer. Educ. Res. Journ.*, 4, 5 (1968) 437–74.

Bradburn, N.M. and Berlew, D.E., *Economic Development and Cultural Change* (University of Chicago Press, Chicago, 1961).

Brenner, M., Marsh, P. and Brenner, M. (eds), *The Social Context of Method* (Croom Helm, London, 1978).

Brown, A., 'The practice of educational research: Contrasting case studies', unpublished D.Phil. dissertation, The New University of Ulster, Coleraine, 1984.

Brown, J. and Sime, J.D., 'Accounts as a general methodology'. Paper presented to the British Psychological Society Conference, Exeter University, 1977.

Brown, J. and Sime, J.D., 'A methodology of accounts', in M. Brenner (ed.), *Social Method and Social Life* (Academic Press, London, 1981).

Brown, R.K., 'Research and consultancy in industrial enterprises: a review of the contribution of the Tavistock Institute of Human Relations to the development of Industrial Sociology', *Sociology*, 1, 1 (1967) 33–60.

Brown, R. and Herrnstein, P.J., *Psychology* (Methuen, London, 1975).

Buhler, C. and Allen, M., *Introduction to Humanistic Psychology* (Brooks/Cole, Monterey, California, 1972).

Burgess, R.G., *Experiencing Comprehensive Education* (Methuen, London, 1983).

Burrell, G. and Morgan, G., *Sociological Paradigms and Organisational Analysis* (Heinemann Educational Books, London, 1979).

Butcher, H.J. and Pont, H.B. (eds), *Educational Research in Britain 3* (University of London Press, London, 1973).

Caldwell, O. and Courtis, S., *Then and Now in Education* (Harcourt, New York, 1925).

Campbell, D.T. and Fiske, D., 'Convergent and discriminant validation by the multi-trait multimethod matrix', *Psychol. Bull.*, 56 (1959) 81–105.

Campbell, D.T. and Stanley J.C., 'Experimental and quasi-experimental designs for research on teaching', in N.L. Gage (ed.), *Handbook of Research on Teaching* (Rand McNally, Chicago, 1963).

Cannell, C.F. and Kahn, R.L., 'Interviewing', in G. Lindzey and E. Aronson (eds), *The Handbook of Social Psychology*, vol. 2, *Research Methods* (Addison Wesley, New York, 1968).

Cantor, L.M. and Matthews, G.F., *Loughborough: From College to University. A History of Higher Education at Loughborough 1909–1966* (Loughborough University of Technology, Loughborough, 1977).

Central Advisory Council for Education, *Children and their Primary Schools* (HMSO, London, 1967).

Chanan, G. and Delamont, S. (eds), *Frontiers of Classroom Research* (NFER, Windsor, 1975).

Chapin, F.S., *Experimental Designs in Sociological Research* (Harper and Row, New York, 1947).

Chetwynd, S.J., 'Outline of the analyses available with G.A.P., the Grid Analysis Package' (St. George's Hospital, London, SW17, 1974).

Child, D., *The Essentials of Factor Analysis* (Holt, Rinehart and Winston, London, 1970).

Christie, T. and Oliver, R.A.C., 'Academic performance at age 18+ as related to school organization', *Research in Education*, 2 (Nov. 1969) 13–31.

Cicourel, A.V., *Method and Measurement in Sociology* (The Free Press, New York, 1964).

Cohen, L., *Educational Research in Classrooms and Schools, a Manual of Materials and Methods* (Harper and Row, London 1977).

Cohen, L. and Child, D., 'Some sociological and psychological factors in university failure', *Durham Research Review*, 22 (1969) 365–72.

Cohen, L. and Holliday, M., *Statistics for Education and Physical Education* (Harper and Row, London, 1979).

Cohen, L. and Holliday, M., *Statistics for Social Scientists: An Introductory Text with Computer Programs in BASIC* (Harper and Row, London, 1982).

Cohen, L. and Manion, L., *Perspectives on Classrooms and Schools* (Holt-Saunders, Eastbourne, 1981).

Collins, L., *The Use of Models in the Social Sciences* (Tavistock Publications, London, 1976).

Corey, S.M., *Action Research to Improve School Practices* (Bureau of Publications, Teachers College, Columbia University, New York, 1953).

Coulson, A.A., 'The attitudes of primary school heads and deputy heads to deputy headship', *Brit. J. Educ. Psychol.*, 46 (1976) 244–52.

Cox, T., 'Children's adjustment to school over six years', *Journal of Child Psychology and Psychiatry*, 19 (1978) 363–72.

Cox, T., 'A follow-up study of reading attainment in a sample of eleven year old disadvantaged children', *Educational Studies*, 5, 1 (1979) 53–60.

Cox, T., 'Disadvantaged fifteen year olds: initial findings from a longitudinal study', *Educational Studies*, 8, 1 (1982) 1–13.

Crook, Z. and Simon, B., 'Private schools in Leicester and the County 1780–1840' in B. Simon (ed.), *Education in Leicestershire 1540–1940* (Leicester University Press, Leicester, 1968).

Cuff, E.C. and Payne, G.C.F. (eds), *Perspectives in Sociology* (George Allen and Unwin, London, 1979).

Curtis, B. and Mays, W. (eds), *Phenomenology and Education* (Methuen, London, 1978).

Dahrendorf, R., *Class and Class Conflict in Industrial Society* (Routledge and Kegan Paul, 1959).

Davidson, J., *Outdoor Recreation Surveys: The Design and Use of Questionnaires for Site Surveys* (Countryside Commission, London, 1970).

Davie, R., 'The longitudinal approach', *Trends in Education*, 28 (1972) 8–13.

Davies, B., *Life in the Classroom and Playground: The Accounts of Primary School Children* (Routledge and Kegan Paul, London, 1982).

Delamont, S., *Interaction in the Classroom* (Methuen, London, 1976).

Denscombe, M., 'The social organization of teaching: a study of teaching as a practical activity in two London comprehensive schools', unpublished Ph.D. dissertation, University of Leicester, 1977.

Denzin, N.K., *The Research Act in Sociology: A Theoretical Introduction to Sociological Methods* (The Butterworth Group, London, 1970).

Department of Education and Science, *A Study of School Buildings* (HMSO, London, 1977).

Department of Education and Science, *Primary Education in England* (HMSO, London, 1978).

Diesing, P., *Patterns of Discovery in the Social Sciences* (Aldine, Chicago, 1971).

Dietz, S.M., 'An analysis of programming DRL schedules in educational settings', *Behaviour Research and Therapy*, 15 (1977) 103–11.

Dixon, K., *Sociological Theory: Pretence and Possibility* (Routledge and Kegan Paul, London, 1973).

Dobbert, M.L., *Ethnographic Research: Theory and Application For Modern Schools and Societies* (Praeger, New York, 1982).

Douglas, J.D., *Understanding Everyday Life* (Routledge and Kegan Paul, London, 1973).

Douglas, J.W.B., 'The use and abuse of national cohorts', in M.D. Shipman, *The Organization and Impact of Social Research* (Routledge and Kegan Paul, London, 1976).

Douglas, J.W.B. and Blomfield, J.M., *Children Under Five* (Allen and Unwin, London, 1958).

Douglas, J.W.B. and Blomfield, J.M., *Maternity in Great Britain* (Oxford University Press, London, 1948).

Douglas, J.W.B., Ross, J.M. and Simpson, H.R., *All Our Future* (P. Davies, London, 1968).

Duck, S. (ed.), *Theory and Practice in Interpersonal Attraction* (Academic Press, London, 1977).

Duckworth, D. and Entwistle, N.J., 'Attitudes to school subjects: a repertory grid technique', *Brit. J. Educ. Psychol.*, 44, 1 (1974) 76–83.

Duncan Mitchell, G., *A Dictionary of Sociology* (Routledge and Kegan Paul,

London, 1968).

Ekehammar, B. and Magnusson, D., 'A method to study stressful situations', *Journal of Personality and Social Psychology*, 27, 2 (1973) 176–9.

English, H.B. and English, A.C., *A Comprehensive Dictionary of Psychological and Psychoanalytic Terms* (Longman, London, 1958).

Epting, F.R., Suchman, D.I. and Nickeson, K.J., 'An evaluation of elicitation procedures for personal constructs', *Brit. J. Psychol.*, 62 (1971) 513–17.

Eron, L.D., Huesman, L.R., Lefkowitz, M.M. and Walder, L.E., 'Does television violence cause aggression?', *Amer. Psychol.* (April 1972) 253–62.

Evans, K.M., *Planning Small Scale Research* (NFER, Windsor, 1978).

Everett, M., 'The Scottish Comprehensive School: its function and the roles of its teachers with special reference to the opinions of the pupils and student teachers'. Unpublished Ph.D. dissertation, School of Education, University of Durham, 1984.

Everitt, B.S., *Cluster Analysis* (Heinemann Educational Books, London, 1974).

Everitt, B.S., *The Analysis of Contingency Tables* (Chapman and Hall, London, 1977).

Ferguson, S., 'Toreside Comprehensive School: a simulation game for teachers in training', in J. Megarry (ed.), *Aspects of Simulation and Gaming* (Kogan Page, London, 1977).

Filstead, W.J. (ed.), *Qualitative Methodology: Firsthand Involvement with the Social World* (Markham Pub. Co., Chicago, 1970).

Floud, R., *An Introduction to Quantitative Methods for Historians*, 2nd edn, (Methuen, London, 1979).

Fogelman, K. (ed.), *Growing Up in Great Britain: Papers From the National Child Development Study* (London, Macmillan, 1983).

Ford, D.H. and Urban, H.B., *Systems of Psychotherapy: A Comparative Study* (John Wiley and Sons, New York, 1963).

Forgas, J.P., *Social Episodes: The Study of Interaction Routines* (Academic Press, London, 1981).

Forgas, J.P., 'The perception of social episodes: categoric and dimensional representations in two different social milieu', *Journal of Personality and Social Psychology*, 34, 2 (1976) 199–209.

Forgas, J.P., 'Social episodes and social structure in an academic setting: the social environment of an intact group', *Journal of Experimental Social Psychology*, 14 (1978) 434–48.

Forward, J., Canter, R. and Kirsch, N., 'Role-enactment and deception methodologies', *American Psychologist*, 35 (1976) 595–604.

Fox, D.J., *The Research Process in Education* (Holt, Rinehart and Winston, New York, 1969).

Fransella, F., *Need to Change?* (Methuen, London, 1975).

Fransella, F. (ed.) *Personal Construct Psychology* (Academic Press, London, 1978).

Fransella, F. and Bannister, D., *A Manual for Repertory Grid Technique* (Academic Press, London, 1977).

Gage, N.L. (ed.), *Handbook of Research on Teaching* (Rand McNally, Chicago, 1963).

Galloway, D., 'A study of pupils suspended from schools', *Brit. J. Educ. Psychol.*, 52 (1982) 205–212.

Gardiner, P., *The Nature of Historical Explanation* (Oxford University Press,

Oxford, 1961, reprinted 1978).

Garfinkel, H., *Studies in Ethnomethodology* (Prentice-Hall, Englewood Cliffs, N.J., 1968).

Gelwick, R., *The Way to Discovery: an Introduction to the Thought of Michael Polanyi* (Oxford University Press, New York, 1977).

Giddens, A. (ed.), *Positivism and Sociology* (Heinemann Educational Books, London, 1975).

Giddens, A., *New Rules of Sociological Method: a Positive Critique of Interpretive Sociologies* (Hutchinson, London, 1976).

Gilbert, G.N., 'Accounts and those accounts called actions', in G.N. Gilbert and P. Abell, *Accounts and Action* (Gower, Aldershot, 1983).

Ginsburg, G.P., 'Role playing and role performance in social psychological research' in M. Brenner, P. Marsh and M. Brenner (eds), *The Social Context of Method* (Croom Helm, London, 1978).

Glaser, B.G. and Strauss, A.L., *The Discovery of Grounded Theory* (Aldine, Chicago, 1967).

Good, C.V., *Introduction to Educational Research* (Appleton-Century-Crofts, New York, 1963).

Gottschalk, L., *Understanding History* (Alfred A. Knopf, New York, 1951).

Gray, J., McPherson, A.F. and Raffe, D., *Reconstructions of Secondary Education: Theory, Myth and Practice Since The War* (Routledge and Kegan Paul, London, 1983).

Gray, J. and Satterly, D., 'A chapter of errors: teaching styles and pupil progress in retrospect', *Educational Research*, 19 (1976) 45–56.

Guilford, J.P. and Fruchter, B., *Fundamental Statistics in Psychology and Education* (McGraw-Hill, New York, 1973).

Halsey, A.H. (ed.), *Educational Priority: Volume 1: E.P.A. Problems and Policies* (HMSO, London, 1972).

Hamilton, V.L., 'Role play and deception: a re-examination of the controversy', *Journal for the Theory of Social Behaviour*, 6 (1976) 233–50.

Hampden-Turner, C., *Radical Man* (Schenkman, Cambridge, Mass., 1970).

Haney, C., Banks, C. and Zimbardo, P., 'Interpersonal dynamics in a simulated prison', *International Journal of Criminology and Penology*, 1 (1973) 69–97.

Hargie, O., Saunders, C. and Dickson, D., *Social Skills in Interpersonal Communication* (Croom Helm, London, 1981).

Hargreaves, D.H., *Social Relations in a Secondary School* (Routledge and Kegan Paul, London, 1967).

Hargreaves, D.H., Hester, S.K. and Mellor, F.J., *Deviance in Classrooms* (Routledge and Kegan Paul, London 1975).

Harré, R., 'Some remarks on "rule" as a scientific concept', in T. Mischel (ed.), *On Understanding Persons* (Basil Blackwell, Oxford, 1974).

Harré, R., 'The constructive role of models', in Collins, L. (ed.), *The Use of Models in the Social Sciences* (Tavistock Publications, London, 1976).

Harré, R., 'The ethogenic approach: theory and practice', in L. Berkowitz (ed.), *Advances in Experimental Social Psychology*, vol. 10 (Academic Press, New York, 1971).

Harré, R., 'Friendship as an accomplishment', in S. Duck (ed.), *Theory and Practice in Interpersonal Attraction* (Academic Press, London, 1977).

Harré, R., 'Accounts, actions and meanings — the practice of participatory psychology', in M. Brenner, P. Marsh and M. Brenner (eds), *The Social Context of Method* (Croom Helm, London, 1978).

Harré, R. and Rosser, E., 'The rules of disorder', *The Times Educational Supplement*, 25 July 1975.

Harré, R. and Secord, P.F., *The Explanation of Social Behaviour* (Basil Blackwell, Oxford, 1972).

Harvey, T.J. and Cooper, C.J., 'An investigation into some possible factors affecting children's understanding of the concept of an electric circuit in the age range 8–11 years old', *Educational Studies*, 4, 2 (1978) 149–55.

Heath, S.B., 'Questioning at home and at school: a comparative study', in G. Spindler (ed.), *Doing the Ethnography of Schooling* (Holt, Rinehart and Winston, New York, 1982).

Heather, N., *Radical Perspectives in Psychology* (Methuen, London, 1976).

Herbert, D.J.and Holmes, A.F., 'Graduate record examinations aptitude test scores as a predictor of graduate grade point average', *Educational and Psychological Measurement*, 39 (1979) 415–19.

Hill, J.E. and Kerbert, A., *Models, Methods, and Analytical Procedures in Educational Research* (Wayne State University Press, Detroit, 1967).

Hinkle, D.N., 'The change of personal constructs from the viewpoint of a theory of implications', unpublished Ph.D. thesis, Ohio State University, 1965.

Hockett, H.C., *The Critical Method in Historical Research and Writing* (Macmillan, London 1955).

Hodgkinson, H.L., 'Action research — a critique', *J. Educ. Sociol.*, 31, 4 (1957) 137–53.

Hoinville, G. and Jowell, R., *Survey Research Practice* (Heinemann Educational Books, London, 1978).

Holbrook, D., *Education, Nihilism and Survival* (Darton, Longman and Todd, London, 1977).

Holsti, O.R., 'Content analysis', in G. Lindzey and E. Aronson, *The Handbook of Social Psychology*, vol. 2, *Research Methods* (Addison-Wesley, Reading, Mass., 1968).

Hughes, J.A., *Sociological Analysis : Methods of Discovery* (Nelson and Sons, Sunbury-on-Thames, 1978).

Hughes, M.G. (ed.), *Administering Education : International Challenge* (Athlone Press, London, 1975).

Ingham, J., *Books and Reading Development* (Heinemann Educational Books, London, 1981).

Ions, E., *Against Behaviouralism : a Critique of Behavioural Science* (Basil Blackwell, Oxford, 1977).

Isaac, S. and MacDonald, B., *Curriculum Innovation at School Level*, E203, Units 27 and 28 (The Open University Press, Bletchley, 1976).

Isaac, S. and Michael, W.B., *Handbook in Research and Evaluation* (R.R. Knapp, California, 1971).

Jackson, D. and Marsden, D., *Education and the Working Class* (Routledge and Kegan Paul, 1962).

Jelinek, M.M., 'Multiracial education 3. Pupils' attitudes to the multiracial school', *Educational Research*, 19, 2 (1977) 129–41.

Jelinek, M.M. and Brittan, E.M., 'Multiracial education 1, Inter-ethnic friendship patterns', *Educational Research*, 18, 1 (1975) 44–53.

Kaplan, A., *The Conduct of Inquiry* (Intertext Books, Aylesbury, 1973).

Kazdin, A.E., *Single Case Research Designs* (Oxford University Press, New York, 1982).

Kelly, G.A., *Clinical Psychology and Personality: the Selected Papers of George Kelly*, edited by B.A. Maher (John Wiley and Sons, New York, 1969).

Kerlinger, F.N., *Foundations of Behavioural Research* (Holt, Rinehart and Winston, New York, 1970).

Kierkegaard, S., *Concluding Unscientific Postscript* (Princeton University Press, Princeton, 1974).

King, P. (ed.), *Working with Third Years*, Report of the Research Action Group in English, 1983 (Department of Education, Loughborough University and School of Education, Nottingham University, 1983).

King, R., *All Things Bright and Beautiful?* (John Wiley, Chichester, 1979).

Kitwood, T.M., 'Values in adolescent life: towards a critical description', unpublished Ph.D. dissertation, School of research in Education, University of Bradford, 1977.

Lacey, C., *Hightown Grammar* (Manchester University Press, Manchester, 1970).

Lambert, R., Bullock, R. and Millham, S., *The Chance of a Lifetime?* (Weidenfeld and Nicolson, London, 1975).

Lambert, R., Millham, S. and Bullock, R., *A Manual to the Sociology of the School* (Weidenfeld and Nicolson, London, 1970).

Lansing, J.B., Ginsberg, G.P. and Braaten, K., *An Investigation of Response Error* (Bureau of Economic and Business Research, University of Illinois, 1961).

Levine, R.A., 'Towards a psychology of populations: the cross-cultural study of personality', *Human Development*, 3 (1966) 30–46.

Levine, R.H., 'Why the ethogenic method and the dramaturgical perspective are incompatible', *Journal of the Theory of Social Behaviour*, 7, 2 (1977) 237–47.

Lifshitz, M., 'Quality professionals: does training make a difference? A personal construct theory study of the issue', *Brit. J. Soc. Clin. Psychol.*, 13 (1974) 183–9.

Lin, Nan, *Foundations of Social Research* (McGraw-Hill, New York, 1976).

Lindzey, G. and Aronson, E., *The Handbook of Social Psychology*, vol. 2, *Research Methods* (Addison-Wesley, New York, 1968).

Lofland, J., *Analysing Social Settings* (Wadsworth Pub. Co., Belmont, Calif., 1971).

McAleese, R. (ed.), *Perspectives on Academic Gaming and Simulation 3: Training and Professional Education* (Kogan Page, London, 1978).

McAleese, R. and Hamilton, D., *Understanding Classroom Life* (NFER, Windsor, 1978).

McClelland, D.C., Atkinson, J.W., Clark, R.A. and Lowell, E.L., *The Achievement Motive* (Appleton-Century-Crofts, New York, 1953).

McCormick, R. and James, M., *Curriculum Evaluation in Schools* (Croom Helm, Beckenham, 1983).

McIntyre, D. and MacLeod, G., 'The characteristics and uses of systematic observation', in R. McAleese and D. Hamilton (eds), *Understanding Classroom Life* (NFER, Windsor, 1978) 102–131.

MacPherson, J., *The Feral Classroom* (Routledge and Kegan Paul, Melbourne, 1983).

McQuitty, L.L., 'Elementary linkage analysis for isolating orthogonal and oblique types and typal relevancies', *Educational and Psychological Measurement*, 17 (1957) 207–9.

McQuitty, L.L., 'Single and multiple hierarchical classification by reciprocal pairs and rank order types', *Educational and Psychological Measurement*, 26 (1966) 253–65.

Madge, J., *The Origin of Scientific Sociology* (Tavistock Publications, London, 1963).

Madge, J., *The Tools of Social Science* (Longmans, London, 1965).

Magnusson, D., 'An analysis of situational dimensions', *Perceptual and Motor Skills*, 32 (1971) 851–67.

Marris, P. and Rein, M., *Dilemmas of Social Reform: Poverty and Community Action in the United States* (Routledge and Kegan Paul, London, 1967).

Marsh, P., Rosser, E. and Harré, R., *The Rules of Disorder* (Routledge and Kegan Paul, London, 1978).

Maslow, A.H., *Motivation and Personality* (Harper and Row, New York, 1954).

Mead, G.H., *Mind, Self and Society*, ed. Charles Morris (University of Chicago Press, Chicago, 1934).

Medawar, P.B., *The Hope of Progress* (Methuen, London, 1972).

Medawar, P.B., *Advice to a young Scientist* (Pan Books, London, 1981).

Megarry, J. (ed.), *Aspects of Simulation and Gaming* (Kogan Page, London, 1977).

Megarry, J., 'Retrospect and prospect', in R. McAleese (ed.), *Perspectives on Academic Gaming and Simulation 3: Training and Professional Education* (Kogan Page, London, 1978).

Menzel, H., 'Meaning — who needs it?', in M. Brenner, P. Marsh and M. Brenner (eds), *The Social Context of Method* (Croom Helm, London, 1978).

Merton, R.K. and Kendall, P.L., 'The focused interview', *Amer. J. Sociol.*, 51 (1946) 541–57.

Milgram, S., *Obedience to Authority* (Harper and Row, New York, 1974).

Mischel, T. (ed.), *On Understanding Persons* (Basil Blackwell, Oxford, 1974).

Mixon, D., 'Instead of deception', *Journal for the Theory of Social Behaviour*, 2 (1972) 146–77.

Mixon, D., 'If you won't deceive, what can you do?', in N. Armistead (ed.), *Reconstructing Social Psychology* (Penguin Books, London, 1974).

Moser, C.A. and Kalton, G., *Survey Methods in Social Investigation* (Heinemann Educational Books, London, 1977).

Mouly, G.J., *Educational Research: the Art and Science of Investigation* (Allyn and Bacon, Boston, 1978).

Nash, R., *Classrooms Observed* (Routledge and Kegan Paul, London, 1973).

National Educational Association of the United States: Association for Supervision and Curriculum Development, *Learning about Learning from Action Research*, Washington, D.C., 1959.

Newson, J. and Newson, E., *Infant Care in an Urban Community* (Allen and Unwin, London, 1963).

Newson, J. and Newson, E., *Four Years Old in an Urban Community* (Allen and Unwin, London, 1968).

Newson, J. and Newson, E., *Seven Years Old in an Urban Environment* (Allen and Unwin, London, 1976).

Newson, J. and Newson, E., 'Parental roles and social contexts,' in M.D. Shipman (ed.), *The Organisation and Impact of Social Research* (Routledge and Kegan Paul, London, 1976) 22–48.

Newson, J. and Newson, E., *Perspectives on School at Seven Years Old* (Allen and

Unwin, London, 1977).

Nixon, J. (ed.), *A Teacher's Guide to Action Research* (Grant McIntyre, London, 1981).

Osborne, J.I., 'College of Education students' perceptions of the teaching situation', unpublished M.Ed. dissertation, University of Liverpool, 1977.

Palmer, M., 'An experimental study of the use of archive materials in the secondary school history curriculum', unpublished Ph.D. dissertation, University of Leicester, 1976.

Palys, T.S., 'Simulation methods and social psychology', *Journal for the Theory of Social Behaviour*, 8 (1978) 341–68.

Parker, H.J., *View from the Boys* (David and Charles, Newton Abbott, 1974).

Parsons, J.M., Graham, N. and Honess, T., 'A teacher's implicit model of how children learn', *British Educational Research Journal*, 9, 1 (1983) 91–101.

Parsons, T., *The Social System* (Free Press, New York, 1951).

Patrick, J., *A Glasgow Gang Observed* (Eyre Methuen, London, 1973).

Peevers, B.H. and Secord, P.F., 'Developmental changes in attribution of descriptive concepts of persons', *Journal of Personality and Social Psychology*, 27, 1 (1973) 120–8.

Percival, F., 'Evaluation procedures for simulation gaming exercises', in R. McAleese (ed.), *Perspectives on Academic Gaming and Simulation 3: Training and Professional Education* (Kogan Page, London, 1978).

Pilliner, A., *Experiment in Educational Research, (E341. Block 5)* (The Open University Press, Bletchley, 1973).

Platt, J., 'Evidence and proof in documentary research. 1. Some specific problems of documentary research; and 2. Some shared problems of documentary research', *Sociol. Review*, 29, 1 (1981) 31–52, 53–66.

Plummer, K., *Documents of Life: An Introduction to the Problems and Literature of a Humanistic Method* (George Allen and Unwin, London, 1983).

Pope, M.L. and Keen, T.R., *Personal Construct Psychology and Education* (Academic Press, London, 1981).

Ravenette, A.T., 'Psychological investigation of children and young people', in D. Bannister (ed.), *New Perspectives in Personal Construct Theory* (Academic Press, London, 1977).

Ravenette, A.T., 'Grid techniques for children', *Journal of Child Psychology and Psychiatry*, 16 (1975) 79–83.

Reid, M., Clunies-Ross, L., Goacher, B. and Vile, C., *Mixed Ability Teaching: Problems and Possibilities* (NFER-Nelson, Windsor, 1981).

Review Article, 'Why can't children do proportion sums?', *Education*, 18 May (1984) 403.

Rex, J. (ed.), *Approaches to Sociology: an Introduction to Major Trends in British Sociology* (Routledge and Kegan Paul, London, 1974).

Riley, M.W., *Sociological Research I: A Case Approach* (Harcourt, Brace and World, New York, 1963).

Rogers, C.R., *Counselling and Psychotherapy* (Houghton Mifflin, Boston, 1942).

Rogers, C.R., 'The non-directive method as a technique for social research', *Amer. J. Sociol.*, 50 (1945) 279–83.

Rogers, C.R., *Freedom to Learn* (Merrill Pub. Co., Columbus, Ohio, 1969).

Rogers, C.R. and Stevens, B., *Person to Person: The Problems of Being Human* (Souvenir Press, London, 1967).

Rogers, V.M. and Atwood, R.K., 'Can we put ourselves in their place?', *Yearbook of the National Council for Social Studies*, 44 (1974) 80–111.

Rosen, C. and Rosen, H., *The Language of Primary School Children* (Penguin, London, 1973).

Roszak, R., *The Making of a Counter Culture* (Faber and Faber, London, 1970).

Rutter, M., Maughan, B., Mortimore, P. and Ouston, J., *Fifteen Thousand Hours* (Open Books, London, 1979).

Ryle, A., *Frames and Cages: The Repertory Grid Approach to Human Understanding* (Sussex University Press, Brighton, 1975).

Ryle, A. and Breen, D. 'A comparison of adjusted and maladjusted couples using the double dyad grid', *Brit. J. Med. Psychol.*, 45 (1972) 375–82.

Ryle, A. and Breen, D., 'Change in the course of social work training: a repertory grid study', *Brit. J. Med. Psychol.*, 47 (1974) 139–47.

Ryle, A. and Lunghi, M., 'The dyad grid: a modification of repertory grid technique', *British Journal of Psychiatry*, 117 (1970) 323–7.

Salmon, P., 'Differential conforming of the developmental process', *Brit. J. Soc. Clin. Psychol.*, 8 (1969) 22–31.

Sarnoff, I. *et al.*, 'A cross-cultural study of anxiety among American and English school children', *J. Educ. Psychol.*, 49 (1958) 129–36.

Schutz, A., *Collected Papers* (Nijhoff, The Hague, 1962).

Sears, R., Maccoby, E. and Levin, H., *Patterns of Child Rearing* (Harper and Row, New York, 1957).

Secord, P.F. and Peevers, B.H., 'The development and attribution of person concepts', in T. Mischel (ed.), *On Understanding Persons* (Basil Blackwell, Oxford, 1974).

Selltiz, C., Wrightsman, L.S. and Cook, S.W., *Research Methods in Social Relations* (Holt, Rinehart and Winston, New York, 1976).

Sharp, R. and Green, A. (assisted by Lewis, J.), *Education and Social Control: A Study in Progressive Primary Education* (Routledge and Kegan Paul, London, 1975).

Shaw, M.L.G. (ed.), *Recent Advances in Personal Construct Technology*, (Academic Press, London, 1981).

Shields, R.W., *A Cure of Delinquents* (Heinemann Educational Books, London, 1962).

Shipman, M.D., *The Limitations of Social Research* (Longman, London, 1972).

Shipman, M.D., *Inside a Curriculum Project* (Methuen, London, 1974).

Shipman, M.D. (ed.), *The Organization and Impact of Social Research* (Routledge and Kegan Paul, London, 1976).

Simon, N. (ed.), *Education in Leicestershire 1540–1940* (Leicester University Press, 1968).

Simon, J.L., *Basic Research Methods in Social Sciences* (Random House, New York, 1978).

Simons, H. (ed.), *Towards a Science of the Singular* (Centre for Applied Research in Education, University of East Anglia, 1980). C.A.R.E. Occasional Publications No. 10.

Sluckin, A., *Growing Up in the Playground: The Social Development of Children* (Routledge and Kegan Paul, London, 1981).

Smith, H.W., *Strategies of Social Research: The Methodological Imagination* (Prentice-Hall, London, 1975).

Smith, S. and Leach, C., 'A hierarchical measure of cognitive complexity', *Brit. J.*

Psychol., 63, 4 (1972) 561–8.

Social and Community Planning Research, *Questionnaire Design Manual No. 5* (London, 16 Duncan Terrace, N1 8BZ, 1972).

Social Science Research Council, *Research in Economic and Social History* (Heinemann, London, 1971).

Solomon, R.L., 'An extension of control group design', *Psychol. Bull.*, 46 (1949) 137–50.

Spindler, G. (ed.), *Doing the Ethnography of Schooling* (Holt, Rinehart and Winston, New York, 1982).

Stenhouse, L., 'The Humanities Curriculum Project', in H.J. Butcher and H.B. Pont (eds), *Educational Research in Britain 3* (University of London Press, London, 1973).

Stenhouse, L., 'What is action-research?' (Norwich C.A.R.E., University of East Anglia, Norwich (mimeograph), 1979).

Sutherland, G., 'The study of the history of education', *History*, vol. LIV, no. 180, Feb. 1969.

Taylor, J.L. and Walford, R., *Simulation in the Classroom* (Penguin Books, London, 1972).

Thomas, L.F., 'A personal construct approach to learning in education, training and therapy', in F. Fransella (ed.), *Personal Construct Psychology* (Academic Press, London, 1978).

Thomas, W.I. and Znaniecki, F., *The Polish Peasant in Europe and America* (University of Chicago Press, Chicago, 1918).

Travers, R.M.W., *An Introduction to Educational Research* (Collier-Macmillan, London, 1969).

Travers, R.M.W., Extract quoted in Halsey, A.H. (ed.), *Educational Priority: Volume I: E.P.A. Problems and Policies* (HMSO, London, 1972).

Tuckman, B.W., *Conducting Educational Research* (Harcourt Brace Jovanovich, New York, 1972).

Urmson, J.O. (ed.), *The Concise Encyclopedia of Western Philosophy* (Hutchinson, London, 1975).

van Ments, M., *The Effective Use of Role-Play: a Handbook for Teachers and Trainers* (Croom Helm, London, 1983).

van Ments, M., 'Role playing: playing a part or a mirror to meaning?', *Sagset Journal*, 8, 3 (1978) 83–92.

Vasta, R., *Studying Children: An Introduction to Research Methods* (W.H. Freeman, San Francisco, 1979).

Verma, G. and Bagley, C. (eds), *Race, Education and Equality* (Macmillan, London, 1979).

Verma, G.K. and Beard, R.M., *What is Educational Research?* (Gower, Aldershot, 1981).

Walker, R., 'Making sense and losing meaning: Problems of selection in doing Case Study', in Simons, H. (ed.), *Towards a Science of the Singular* (Centre for Applied Research in Education, University of East Anglia, 1980).

Walker, R. and MacDonald, B., *Curriculum Innovation at School Level*, E. 203 Units 27 and 28 (The Open University Press, Bletchley, 1976).

Warnock, M., *Existentialism* (Oxford University Press, London, 1970).

Weber, M., *Essays in Sociology* (Routledge and Kegan Paul, London, 1948).

Weber, M., *The Theory of Social and Economic Organization* (Free Press, Glencoe, 1964).

Whitley, P., 'The analysis of contingency tables', in D. McKay, N. Schofield and P. Whitley (eds), *Data Analysis and the Social Sciences* (Frances Pinter, London, 1983).

Willis, P.E., *Learning to Labour* (Saxon House, London, 1977).

Winter, R., '"Dilemma Analysis": A contribution to methodology for action research', *Cambridge Journal of Education*, 12, 3 (1982) 161–74.

Wolcott, H.F., *The Man in the Principal's Office* (Holt, Rinehart and Winston, New York, 1973).

Wood, R. and Napthali, W.A., 'Assessment in the classroom: What do teachers look for?', *Educational Studies*, 1, 3, (1975) 151–61.

Woods, P., *The Divided School* (Routledge and Kegan Paul, London, 1979).

Yorke, D.M. 'Repertory grids in educational research: Some methodological considerations', *Brit. Educ. Res. Journ.*, 4, 2 (1978) 63–74.

Young, J., *The Drugtakers* (Paladin, London, 1971).

Young, M.F.D. (ed.), *Knowledge and Control: New Directions for the Sociology of Education* (Collier-Macmillan, London, 1971).

INDEX

accidental sampling 100
account gathering 232, 246-8
accounts 228-53
    account gathering 232, 246-8
    accounts of accounts 229, 231-2
    characteristics 229-30
    cluster analysis 241-4
    episodes, characteristics of 229-30
    ethogenic approach 228-9
        diachronic analysis 229
        principles of 228-9
        synchronic analysis 228-9
    explained 228
    factor analysis 241
    hypotheses, use of 235
    linkage analysis 241
    multidimensional scaling 241-4
    network analysis 239-40
    problems of 249-51
    procedures 230-2
        analysis 230-2, 233-8, 239-44
        authentication 230-2
        elicitation 230-2
    qualitative analysis of accounts
        233-5
        experience-sampling method
            233
        network analysis of 238-9
    quantitative analysis of ratings of
        239-44
        cluster analysis 241-4
        episodes 239
        factor analysis 241
        linkage analysis 241
        multidimensional scaling 241-4
    social episodes 239, 240
    strengths of 251
    systematic network analysis 238-9
accounts of accounts 229, 231-2,
    267-8
action 39
action research 208-27
    action and *research* contrasted
        208, 213, 218-19
    action research and the scientific
        method 209, 211, 215-16
    applied research and 209

    characteristics of 208, 213-16
    criticisms of 215-16
    definition 208
    early history 210-11
    empirical nature of 215
    examples of:
        by outsiders 222-4
        by insiders 224-7
    functional knowledge and 209
    issues surrounding 218-20
    kinds of 209-10
    occasions for use 216-18
    origins 210
    procedures 220-2
    research, characteristics of 218-19
    school and classroom use 211-12
    scope 208-9
    situations for 210
    stages in 208
    teacher-researcher conflict 223-4
    teacher's role in 223-6
    teaching, characteristics of 218
aggression and television 166-9
alternatives to positivistic social
    science 27-38
    anthropomorphic model of man
        29
    criticisms of 36-8
    ethnomethodology 31, 33-4, 36
    ethogenic method 29-30
    humanistic psychology 28
    phenomenology 31-3, 36
    'science of persons' 29
    social episodes 29
    social psychology 29-31
    sociology 31-6
    symbolic interactionism 31, 34-6
analysis of multidimensional data 353
anthropomorphic model of man 29,
    36-8
anti-positivist movement 7-8, 27-8
applied research 209
Aristotle 3, 4
assumptions of science 13-17
attitude scale 256
audio/visual recording in grid
    technique 333-5

374

authenticity in historical research 56-7

authoritative knowing 1-2, 3, 4

Bacon, F. 3-4
behaviour 39, 40-2
Bennett, N. 342-5
Bernstein, B. 37-8
bias:
  in historical research 58, 59
  in interviewing 302
Bible, the 1
bi-polar adjectives 316, 328-9
book flood studies 188-202

Case studies 120-48
  advantages of 146
  definition 120
  examples of 127-47
  external validity 125-6
  internal validity 125-6
  non-participant observation 122-3
  observation 122-4
    cover, use of 122-3
    non-participant observation 122-3
    participant observation 122-3, 124-6
    recording observations 126-7
    setting of observation 122
    style of observation 122
    videotape, use of 140
  participant observation 124-6
    advantages of 124-5
    criticisms of 125
    reasons for 124-6
    search for exceptions 138, 139
    tape recorder, use of 130
    validity of 125-6
  popularity of 122
  purpose 122
  settings for 123-4
  typology 120, 121, 122-3
categorical response 301
causal research 171-2
causal-comparative research 171, 172-3
'cause-to-effect' studies 179, 180
central limit theorem 102
checklist response 301
cluster analysis 241-4, 342-4
cluster sampling 99
coding of data in interview 306-8
cohort studies 69, 70-4

combined levels of triangulation 257, 258-9
compromise designs 192-3
computer use 113
computers and simulation 280
Comte, A. 10, 12
conceptions of social reality 6-10
  epistemological assumptions 7
  human nature, assumptions of 7-8
  methodology 8-9
  ontological assumptions 6-7
  qualitative approach to 9
  quantitative approach to 8-9
concepts 17-19
consciousness 31-3
construct *see* concept
constructs, personal 316, 317-19
content analysis 61-5, 310
continuous variables 150-1
control 187-8, 188-93 *passim*
control effect 71
control in *ex post facto* research 174, 181-3
convenience sampling 100
convergent validity 302
co-relational studies 171-2
correlation *see* correlational research
correlational research 149-69
  advantages 156, 160-1
  characteristics 156-9
  compared with experimental research 160
  correlation 149-56, 161-4
    and association 149-51
    causal relations 156
    continuous variables 150-1
    cross correlations 167-9
    definition 156
    direction of correlation coefficient 152-3
    discrete variable 152
    guidelines for interpreting 163-4
    Guttman's lambda 150
    interpreting the correlation coefficient 161-4
    Kendall's tau 151
    Kruskal's gamma 150
    magnitude of the correlation coefficient 152, 153, 158
    measure of association 149, 150
    multiple correlation 153-4
    negative correlation 152-3

nominal scale 151-2
ordinal scale 151
partial correlation 153, 155, 157
Pearson's product moment coefficient of correlation 150, 152
positive correlation 152
purpose of 155
ratio scale 151
regression 153-5
relationship, meaning of 152-6 *passim*
scatter diagram 153, 154
Somer's *d* 150
squaring the correlation coefficient 162
statistical significance of correlation coefficient 162, 165-6
strength of correlation coefficient 161
true dichotomies 151
definition 155-6
disadvantages 161
examples of 164-9
occasions when appropriate 159-60
prediction studies 156, 157-60 *passim,* 163-4
purpose of 152-6 *passim,* 156-9 *passim*
Criswell Index of Self-Preference 79
criterion group studies 171, 172-3
criticisms of interpretive perspectives 36-8
criticisms of positivism 24-7
cross correlations 167-9
cross-sectional studies 68, 69, 70, 73-4
curriculum 41

data, coding of in interview 306-8
data collection in historical research 54-6
data-gathering techniques *see* surveys
data-processing *see* surveys
data reduction 113
debriefing in role-playing 284
deception in role-playing 275-6, 276-80
deduction 3, 4-5
degress of freedom 356-60
dependent variables 187

descriptive research 68
designs in experimental education 188-93
determinism 7-8, 13
developmental research 68-92
cohort studies 69, 70-4
control effect 71
cross-sectional studies 68, 69, 70, 73-4
definition 68-9
descriptive research 68
compared with experimental research 68
definition 68
types of 68-9
examples of 74-92
cohort studies 74-9
cohort/cross-sectional designs 85-8
cross-sectional 79-85
trend of prediction study 88-92
follow-up studies 69
in education 68-9
interviewing 77
longitudinal studies 68, 69, 70-1
measurement effect 71
National Census 70
panel studies 69
prediction studies 68, 90-2
prospective studies 69
retrospective studies 69
sample mortality 71, 76
sampling 75-6, 86
strategies in 74-92
terminology of 69-70, 72
trend studies 68, 69, 70, 90-2
diachronic analysis 229
dimensional sampling 100
direct questions 298
discrete variables 152
distribution of sample means 102
documentary research 56
Douglas, J.W.B. 74-7

'effect-to-cause' studies 179, 180
elements, in personal construct theory 316
elicitation of accounts 230-2
elicited constructs in personal construct theory 317-18
empathy studies 272-4
empiricism 3, 4, 13-14
enquiry *see* inquiry, nature of

episodes 229-30
ethnomethodology 31, 33-4, 36
ethogenic method and research 29-30, 228-9
evaluation in historical research 57-9, 61
exchange grids 335-6
existential phenomenology 32
experience 1-3, 5, 14
experience-sampling method 233
experimental education 188-93
experimental research and *ex post facto* research 171, 173, 174
experiments, quasi-experiments and single-case research 187-207
  compromise designs 192-3
  control 187-8, 188-93 *passim*
  definitions 187, 204
  dependent variables 187
  designs in experimental education 188-93
  differences between experimental and quasi-experimental designs 187
  examples of 199-206
    pre-experimental designs 199-201
    quasi-experimental designs 201-2
    single-case design 205-6
    true experimental design 202-4
  independent variables 187
  interaction effect 192
  pre-experimental design 188-90
  procedures in 197-99
  quasi-experimental design 192-3
  randomisation 190, 191
  single-case research 204-6
  symbols used in 188
  true experimental designs 190-2
  validity in experiments 194-7
  variables 187, 197
exploration and experiment 279
ex post facto research 170-86
  advantages 177
  causal-comparative research 171, 172-3
  causal research 171-2
  'cause-to-effect' studies 179-180
  characteristics of 173-5
  control and *ex post facto* research 174, 175, 181-3
  co-relational studies 171-2
  criterion group studies 171, 172-3
  definition 170-1, 173
  designing an *ex post facto* study 178-80
  disadvantages 177-8
  'effect-to-cause' studies 179, 180
  examples of *ex post facto* research 171-2, 176-7, 183-6
  experimental research and 171, 173, 174
  in education 175
  large-scale *ex post facto* study 176
  occasions for *ex post facto* research 175-7
  post hoc fallacy 174
  procedures in *ex post facto* research 180-3
  retrospective nature of 170
  reverse causality 174-5, 178, 183
  small-scale *ex post facto* studies 176-7
  uses 185-6
external criticism in historical research 57
external validity 125-6, 194, 196-7

face validity 302
factor analysis 241, 345-53
factor loadings 347
factual questions 298-9
fill-in response 300
first order factors 350
fixed alternative items 296-7
flow chart techniques 104, 112
focused grids 335-6
focused interview 293, 294, 309-11, 311-12
follow-up studies 69
Ford Teaching Project 267-9
formal interview 291
friendship patterns 79, 81
functional knowledge 209
funnel, the 297

Galileo 12
games 280
Garfinkel, H. 33-4
generality 14
general questions 298
grid technique 316, 321-36
Guttman's lambda 150

halo effect 328
Harré, R. 228-9
Harré, R. and Secord, P.F. 279

Hawthorne effect 196
historical criticism 57
historical evidence 57
historical research 47-66
    authenticity 56, 57
    bias, source of 58-9
        checklist 58
    caution on choice of subject 51,
        51-4
    content analysis and 61-5
    contrasted with other techniques
        51, 54, 56
    data collection for 54-6
    definition 48
    documentary research 56
    education and 47-8, 53-4
        objectives of study 49-50
        purposes of 49
        role of historical research in
            53-4
        status of 49
        types of 49
    evaluation 57-9, 61
    examples of 53, 63-5, 65-6
    external criticism 57
    historical criticism 57
    historical evidence 57
    hypotheses, use of 52
    identifying and choosing a topic
        51-2
    internal criticism 57-8
    justification for inclusion 47
    primary sources of data 55
    process of synthesis 59
    quantitative methods and 60-5
    research report, problems of 59-
        60
    review of literature 56
    scientific method contrasted 47
    secondary sources of data 55-6
    skills developed in study of 50
    stages in 48, 51
    values of 48-9
history of role playing 271
human behaviour 6-10
    idiographic approach to 9
    nomothetic approach to 8-9
humanistic psychology 28
Humanities Curriculum Project 211,
    213
Husserl, E. 32
hypotheses 4-5, 19-20, 22-3, 170-7
    passim
    and *ex post facto* research 170,

        173, 174, 176-7
    criteria 19
    definition 19
    functions of 19
    historical research and 52
    reasons for importance of 19-20
    relationships as a source of 159

idiographic approach to human
    behaviour 9, 28
independent variable 187
indexicality 33-4
indirect questions 298
individuality corollary 318
induction 3, 4-5
inductive-deductive reasoning 3, 4
informal interview 291
inquiry, nature of 1-44 *passim*
    alternatives to positivistic social
        science 27-31
    assumptions of science 13-17
    conceptions of social reality 6-10
    criticism of newer perspectives
        36-8
    criticisms of positivism and
        scientific method 24-7
    ethnomethodology 31, 33-4, 36
    methodology 8-9, 42-3
    phenomenology 31-3, 36
    positivism 10-13
    research 1, 4-6, 9-10, 43-4
    search for truth 1-6
    scientific method 20-3
    symbolic interactionism 31, 34-6,
        36-8
    terminology, problems of 38-42
    tools of science 17-20
Integrated Studies Project 223-4
interaction effect 192
internal criticism in historical research
    57-8
internal validity 125-6, 194-5, 197
interpretation of factors in factor
    analysis 350, 352-3
interpretive paradigm 38-42 *passim*
interview, the 291-314
    coding of data 306-8
    compared with questionnaire
        291-2, 304
    conceptions of 294-6
    critique of 302-3
    definition 291
    examples:
        educational research 312-14

focused interview 311-12
features of research interview
  296-304
focused interview 293, 294,
  309-11
formal interview 291
informal interview 291
kinds of 291-3
merits of 291-2
non-directive interview 291, 293,
  308-9
problems of research interview
  301-4
procedures 304-8
purposes of 292-3
questionnaires and the interview
  291-2, 304
questions 298-301
  direct 298
  factual 298-9
  general 298
  indirect 298
  opinion 298-9
  specific 298
reliability 302-4
research interview 296-304
  features 296-304
  fixed alternative items 296-7
  funnel, the 297
  items used 296
  modes of response 298,
    299-301
  open-ended items 296-7
  problems of 301-4
  question format 296-301
  scale 297-8
responses 298-301
  categorical 301
  checklist 301
  fill-in 300
  ranking 300
  scaled 300
  structured 299
  tabular 300
  unstructured 299
structured interview 293, 296
unstructure interview 293
validity of 301-3
interviewing 77
investigator triangulation 257, 259
items used in research interview 296

Kelly, G. 315-17
Kendall's tau 151

Kierkegaard, S. 24-5
Kruskal's gamma 150

laboratory experiments and role-play
  289
laddering 321
linkage analysis 241, 339-42
Lloyd Morgan 14
logical positivism 12
longitudinal studies 68, 69, 70-1

Mead, G.H. 34-5
measurement effect 71
methodological triangulation 254-5,
  257, 259-60
methodology 8-9, 42-3
Milgram and role-playing 276-7
mixed ability teaching 269-70
Mixon and role-playing 277-9
models 17
Moreno, J.L. 271
multidimensional concepts 338
multidimensional data 353
multidimensional measurement 338-
  60
  analysing multidimensional data
    353
  Bennett, N. 342
  cluster analysis 342-4
  degrees of freedom 356-60
  factor analysis 346-53
    example 346
    factor loadings 347
    first order factors 350
    interpretation of factors 350,
      352-3
    second order factors 350
  linkage analysis 339-42
    example of 339
    steps in its use 341
  multidimensional concepts 338
  multidimensional data 353
  multidimensional scaling 338
  multidimensional tables
    notation 353-6
multidimensional scaling 241-4, 338
multidimensional tables 353
multimethod approach to research
  254-5
multiple correlation 153-4
multiple realities 33
multiracial education 79

National Census 70

National Foundation of Educational Research (NFER) Project on Mixed Ability Teaching 269-70
nature of science 13-17
    assumptions of 13-14
    concepts 17-19
    determinism 13
    empiricism 13-14
    functions of science 15
    generality 14
    hypothesis 19-20
    model 17
    nature of science 14-15
    parsimony 14
    provisional nature of 17
    theory 15-17
    tools of 17-20
negative correlation 152-3
network analysis 239-40
new sociology of education 41
Newsom, J. and E. 85-8
nominal scale 151-2
nomothetic approach to human behaviour 8-9, 28
non-directive interview 291, 293, 308-9
non-participant observation 122-3
non-probability sampling 98, 100-1
non-verbal grids 335-6
normative paradigm 38-42 *passim*
notation in multidimensional measurement 353-6

objectivity 24-5
observation 122-4
Occam, William of 14
open-ended items 296-7
opinion questions 298-9
ordinal scale 151

panel studies 69
paradigms 38-42
parsimony, principles of 14
partial correlation 153, 155, 157
participant observation 124-6
Pearson's product moment coefficient of correlation 150, 152
personal constructs 315-37
    allotting elements to constructs 319-21
        rank order form 319
        rating form 319-20
        split half form 319
    characteristics of 316-17

constructs 316, 317-19
elements 316
'elicited' constructs 317-18
exchange grids 335-6
focused grids 335-6
grid technique 333-5
individuality corollary 318
Kelly, George 315-17
laddering 321
non-verbal grids 335-6
'provided' constructs 318-19
repertory grid 316, 321-36
    administration 321-3, 323-6
    analysis of 321-6
    difficulties in using 327-8
    examples of use in education 328-32, 333-6
    practical problems 332
    procedures 323-6
    recent applications in education 332-6
sociogrids 335-6
personal knowledge 1-3
phenomenology 31-3, 36
Plowden Committee 94
positive correlation 152
positivism 7-8, 10-13
postal questionnaire 108-13
post hoc fallacy 174
prediction studies 68, 90-2, 156, 157-60 *passim*, 164
pre-experimental designs 188-90
premiss 3
primary sources of data in historical research 55
probability sampling 98-9
prospective studies 68, 90-2
'provided' constructs 318-19
psychodrama 271
pupil attitudes 81, 84-5
purposive sampling 100

qualitative analysis of accounts 233-5
qualitative research 9
quantitative analysis of accounts 239-44
quantitative methods in historical research 60-5
quantitative research 8-9
quasi-experimental designs 192-3
question construction 105-7
question format in research interview 296-301
questionnaire and the interview 291-

2, 304
questionnaires 103-13
questions 298-301
quota sampling 100, 138

randomisation 190, 191
random sampling 98
ranking response 300
ratio scale 151
reasoning 1, 3-4
reflexivity 33-4
regression 153-5
reliability and the interview 302-4
repertory grid *see* personal constructs
research 1, 4-6, 9-10, 22, 43-4, 208,
    213, 218-19
research interview 296-304
research report in historical research
    59-60
researcher roles 7
respondent validation 263
response modes 298, 299-301
responses in interview/questionnaire
    construction 298-301
retrospective studies 69
reverse causality 174-5, 178, 183
review of literature in historical
    research 56
Rogers, C.R. 28
Role Construct Repertory Grid Test,
    The 316-17
role-playing 271-90
    arguments against 274-5, 286
    choosing and writing the role-play
        283-4
    compared with laboratory
        experiments 289
    computers/machines and
        simulation 280
    content of 272
    debriefing 284
    deception v. honesty debate 275-
        6, 276-80
    definition 271
    distinction between exploration
        and experiment 279
    early history 271
    empathising studies 272-4
    evaluation of 288-9
    example of in educational setting
        286-8
    further examples 272-5, 286-8
    games 280
    Harré and Secord 279

methods 271-5
    imaginary-performed 271-2
    passive-active 271
    scripted-improvised 272
    verbal-behavioural 272
Milgram's studies 276-7
Mixon's replications of Milgram's
    work 277-9
Mereno, J.L. 271
objections to use of deception
    272-6
organisation of
    debriefing 284-5
    follow-up 285
    preparation for 281-4
    running the simulation 284
psychodrama 271
role-playing in educational settings
    280, 286-8
role-playing versus deception
    275-80
Stanford Prison Experiment 273,
    274
strengths 285
uses 281
weaknesses 286
Rousseau 316

sample mortality 71, 76, 195
sample size 101
sampling 75-6, 86
sampling distribution 103
sampling error 101, 102-3
sampling frame 98
sampling, kinds of 98-101
scaled response 300
scales 297-8
scatter diagram 153, 154
Schools Council 211, 223
Schutz, A. 32, 124
science *see* nature of science
'science of persons' 29, 36-8
scientific method 20-3
secondary sources of data in historical
    research 55-6
second order factors 350
self-completion questionnaires 103-
    13
single-case research 204-6
snowball sampling 100-1, 138
social episodes 29, 239, 240
social psychology 29-31, 36-8
social reality *see* conceptions of social
    reality

sociogrids 335-6
sociology 31-6, 36-8
Somer's *d* 150
space triangulation 257, 258
specific questions 298
stage sampling 99-100
standard error of the mean 103
Stanford Prison Experiment 272, 274
statistical significance 162, 165-6
stratified sampling 86, 99, 137
structured interview 293, 296
structured response 299
subject choice in historical research
    51-4
subjectivity 24-5
surveys 94-119
    central limit theorem 102
    computer use 113
    data-gathering techniques used 94
    data processing 113-14
        coding 114
        editing 113-14
    data reduction 113
    distribution of sample means 102
    example of survey research
        115-19
    flow chart technique 104, 112
    non-probability sampling 98,
        100-1
    planning 94, 95, 96, 96-8
    Plowden Committee 94
    preliminaries to design of 96-8
        population 97
        purpose 96-7
    probability sampling 98-9
    purpose 94, 96-7
    question construction, guide to
        105-7
    questionnaires 103-13
        covering letter 110
        design 103-5
        follow-up letter 111-13
        incentives 112-13
        initial mailing 110
        postal questionnaire 107-13
        questions 105-7
        self-completion questionnaires
            103-7
    sample size 101
    sampling distribution 103
    sampling error 101, 102-3
    sampling frame 98
    sampling, kinds of 98-101
        accidental 100

        cluster 99
        convenience 100
        dimensional 100
        non-probability 98-99
        probability 98, 100-1
        purposive 100
        quota 100
        simple random 98
        snowball 100-1
        stage 99-100
        stratified 99
        systematic 99
    scope of 94
    self-completion questionnaires
        103-13
    stages in planning 94, 95, 96
    standard error of the mean 103
syllogism 3
symbolic interactionism 31, 34-6, 36-8
symbols used in experimental research
    188
synchronic analysis 228-9
synthesis in historical research,
    process of 59
systematic network analysis 238-9
systematic sampling 99

tabular response 300
tape-recorder, use of 130
Tavistock Institute of Human
    Relations 210
teacher-researcher conflict 223-4
teacher's role in action research 223-6
teaching, characteristics of compared
    with research 218
terminology, problem of in social
    science 38-42
theoretical triangulation 257, 259
theory 15-17, 40-1
    characteristics of 16
    contrasting role in normative and
        interpretive research 40-1
    definition 15-16
    provisional nature of 17
    status of 16
time triangulation 257-8
tools of science 17-20
    concepts 17-19
    hypotheses 19-20
transcendental phenomenology 32
trend studies 68, 69, 70, 90-2
triangulation 254-70
    advantages 254-5

attitude scale illustrating principle of 256
characteristics 256-60
definition 254
examples:
Ford Teaching Project 267-9
NFER Project on mixed ability teaching 269-70
issues 263-6
multimethod approach 254-5
occasions when suitable 260-3
principle of 254-5
problems 266
procedures 266-7
respondent validation 263
simple form of 255-6
types of 256-60
combined levels of triangulation 257, 258-9
investigator triangulation 257, 259
methodological triangulation 254-5, 257, 259-60
space triangulation 257, 258
theoretical triangulation 257, 259
time triangulation 257
validity and triangulation 263

weaknesses in other research methodologies 255
true dichotomies 151
true experimental designs 190-2
truth, search for 1-6
role of experience 1-3
role of reasoning 1, 3-4
role of research 1, 4-6
typification 32-3
typology of case studies 120, 121, 122-3

United States 210
unstructured interview 293
unstructured response 299

validity and triangulation 263
validity in experiments 194-7
validity of interviews 301-3
variables 187, 197
Verstehen 137
videotape, use of in research 140
voluntarism 7-8

weaknesses in research methodologies 255
William of Occam 14